THE POWER
TO PERSUADE

A Rhetoric and Reader
for Argumentative Writing

Second Edition

Sally De Witt Spurgin

Southern Methodist University

PRENTICE HALL
Englewood Cliffs, New Jersey 07632

Library of Congress Cataloging-in-Publication Data

Spurgin, Sally De Witt.
    The power to persuade: a rhetoric and reader for argumentative
writing / Sally De Witt Spurgin.—2nd ed.
      p. cm.
    Bibliography: p.
    Includes index.
    ISBN 0-13-688383-4
    ISBN 0-13-688391-5 (Instructor's Edition)
    1. English language—Rhetoric. 2. Persuasion (Rhetoric)
3. College readers. I. Title.
PE1431.S68 1989
808'.0427—dc19

Cover design: Ben Santora
Manufacturing buyer: Laura Crossland

© 1989, 1985 by Prentice-Hall, Inc.
A Division of Simon & Schuster, Inc.
Englewood Cliffs, New Jersey 07632

Printed in the United States of America

10 9 8 7 6 5 4 3 2 1

ISBN 0-13-688383-4
ISBN 0-13-688391-5
INSTRUCTOR'S EDITION

Prentice-Hall International (UK) Limited, *London*
Prentice-Hall of Australia Pty. Limited, *Sydney*
Prentice-Hall Canada Inc., *Toronto*
Prentice-Hall Hispanoamericana, S.A., *Mexico*
Prentice-Hall of India Private Limited, *New Delhi*
Prentice-Hall of Japan, Inc., *Tokyo*
Simon & Schuster Asia Pte. Ltd., *Singapore*
Editora Prentice-Hall do Brasil, Ltda., *Rio de Janeiro*

THE POWER
TO PERSUADE

For two who would rather read Dr. Seuss

Alice Ann Spurgin
(Born March 11, 1986)

and

Stephen Benjamin Spurgin
(Born November 19, 1987)

And for all the college students who just said, "Me, too!"

Contents

Preface   xv

Acknowledgments   xix

Chapter 1: Argument and Persuasion   1

The Ethics of Persuasion   2
The Need for Argument   4
RELATIONSHIPS IN ARGUMENT   6
Verbal Signals of Argument   8
Exercise 1–1   9
Assumptions   10
Limiting Arguments with Qualifiers   11
LOGIC, EMOTION, AND *ETHOS* IN ARGUMENT   12
The Logical Appeal   12
The Emotional Appeal   13
The Ethical Appeal   14
Exercises 1–2 to 1–5   16
READINGS
"What So Proudly We Hailed?" (Student Essay), Debbie Sapp   19
"Why Don't We Complain?" William F. Buckley, Jr.   22
SUGGESTIONS FOR WRITING AND FURTHER DISCUSSION   28

Chapter 2: Creating Arguments   30

THE RHETORICAL CONTEXT   31
Consider Your Purpose   32
Consider Your Audience   33

The Invented Reader   35
   Exercise 2–1   36
WORKING TOWARD A THESIS   37
  Invention Strategy: Topical Checklists   37
   Exercise 2–2   40
  Invention Strategy: Finding and Resolving Contradictions   41
   Exercise 2–3   43
  Invention Strategy: Examining Influences and Consequences   44
THE ENTHYMEME AS THESIS   46
SHAPING THE ARGUMENT   48
   Exercise 2–4   51
READINGS
  "Group Discussions Are Beneficial" (Student Draft)   53
  "Pay Equity Is Unfair to Women," Linda Chavez   55
SUGGESTIONS FOR WRITING AND FURTHER DISCUSSION   57

Chapter 3: Definition in Argument   59

HOW TO DEFINE   60
  Reportive Definitions   60
  Stipulative Definitions   61
HOW TO JUDGE DEFINITIONS   61
   Exercises 3–1 to 3–3   62
THE ROLES OF DEFINITION IN ARGUMENT   64
  Using Definition to Clarify   65
  Using Definition to Control   66
  Persuasive Definitions   67
READINGS
  "The Right Stuff," Tom Wolfe   69
  "Ars Poetica," Archibald MacLeish   74
  "On Morality," Joan Didion   76
SUGGESTIONS FOR WRITING AND FURTHER DISCUSSION   80

Chapter 4: Research and the Uses of Evidence   82

CREATIVITY IN RESEARCH   82
FINDING EVIDENCE FOR ARGUMENTS   84
  Kinds of Evidence   84
  Locating Background and Historical Evidence   88
  Locating Current Evidence   90
  Selected Database Sources   93

EVALUATING EVIDENCE   95
  Recent Evidence   96
  Primary Evidence   97
  Unbiased Evidence   98
  Representative Evidence   99
  Sufficient Evidence   100
    Exercises 4–1 to 4–3   100
USING EVIDENCE IN DOCUMENTED ESSAYS AND RESEARCH
      PAPERS   103
  Summarizing, Paraphrasing, and Quoting   103
  Incorporating Quotations   104
CITING SOURCES   109
  Avoiding Plagiarism   109
  Citations in the Humanities   111
  Citations in the Social Sciences   114
  Citations in the Natural Sciences   115
READINGS
  "Reports, Inferences, Judgments," S. I. Hayakawa   117
  "The Problem of Bias in Television News Reporting" (Student
      Essay), Mark Alsop   126
SUGGESTIONS FOR WRITING AND FURTHER
      DISCUSSION   133

Chapter 5: Revising   135

THE AIMS OF REVISION   136
MACRO-REVISION: THE DRAFT AS A WHOLE   137
  Testing for Unity and Completeness   138
    Exercises 5-1 to 5-5   146
MICRO-REVISION: PARAGRAPHS, SENTENCES, WORDS   151
  Paragraph Completeness   151
  Revising for Coherence   153
    Exercises 5–6 to 5–10   159
  Improving Clarity   162
    Exercises 5–11 to 5–16   169
READINGS
  "Conformity and Nonconformity: The Prices Paid for Each" (Student
      Draft), Kathy Taylor   173
  "Nonconformity: The Price and the Payoff" (Student Essay), Kathy
      Taylor   175
SUGGESTIONS FOR WRITING AND FURTHER
      DISCUSSION   177

Chapter 6: The Power of Style   179

WHAT IS STYLE? 179
THE ELEMENTS OF STYLE 182
   Exercises 6–1 and 6–2 182
FIGURES OF SPEECH 184
  Tropes 184
  Schemes 186
   Exercise 6–3 188
  The Power of Metaphor 190
   Exercises 6–4 and 6–5 193
REVISING FOR STYLE 194
   Exercises 6–6 to 6–8 198
READINGS
  "War and Reason," William James 201
  "Sculptures in Snow," Lewis Lapham 205
SUGGESTIONS FOR WRITING AND FURTHER
   DISCUSSION 209

Chapter 7: Inductive Reasoning   211

PATTERNS OF INDUCTIVE REASONING 211
ARGUING FROM ANALOGY 214
  Literal Analogy 214
  Metaphorical Analogy 215
  Evaluating Arguments from Analogy 216
   Exercises 7–1 and 7–2 217
ARGUING FROM CAUSE OR EFFECT 219
  The Post Hoc Fallacy 221
  Evaluating Arguments from Cause or Effect 222
   Exercise 7–3 223
ARGUING FROM EXAMPLES 224
  Evaluating Arguments from Examples 225
   Exercise 7–4 227
  Limiting Generalizations 227
   Exercise 7–5 228
READINGS
  "Is Business Bluffing Ethical?" Albert Z. Carr 230
  "Why I Want a Wife," Judy Syfers 234
  "The Trouble with Architects," Andrew Ward 237
  "How Annandale Went Out," Edwin Arlington Robinson 241

SUGGESTIONS FOR WRITING AND FURTHER
    DISCUSSION 242

Chapter 8: Deductive Reasoning 244

DEDUCTION IN FICTION AND FACT 244
INDUCTION AND DEDUCTION 246
VALIDITY, TRUTH, AND SOUNDNESS 247
DISTRIBUTION OF TERMS 248
    Exercise 8–1 253
TESTING VALIDITY: THE SYLLOGISM 254
    Exercises 8–2 and 8–3 256
FORMAL FALLACIES 258
    Exercise 8–4 261
THE LIMITATIONS OF LOGIC: TOULMIN'S CORRECTIVE 262
THE ENTHYMEME 263
    Exercises 8–5 to 8–7 265
HYPOTHETICAL AND ALTERNATIVE ARGUMENTS 267
    Exercise 8–8 270
READINGS
    "Should We Abolish the Presidency?" Barbara Tuchman 273
    "We'll Never Conquer Space," Arthur C. Clarke 279
    "The Tell-Tale Hat," Arthur Conan Doyle 286
    "The Logic Lesson, or My Cat Socrates," Eugene Ionesco 291
    "Sonnet for a Philosopher," Anonymous 294
SUGGESTIONS FOR WRITING AND FURTHER
    DISCUSSION 294

Chapter 9: Fallacies 296

WHY STUDY FALLACIES? 296
KINDS OF FALLACIES 297
ASSUMPTIONS 299
    Circular Reasoning 299
    Loaded Phrases 300
    Complex Questions 300
APPEALS 301
    Appeal to Popular Sentiments 301
    Snob Appeal 302
    Bandwagon Fallacy 302

Fallacious Appeal to Pity   303
Fallacious Appeal to Authority   304
ATTACKS   304
Personal Attack   304
Threats   305
DISTORTIONS   305
Exaggeration   306
Oversimplification   306
Trivial Objections   307
DODGES   307
Lack of Contrary Evidence   307
Shifting Burden of Proof   308
Shifting Ground   308
DETECTING FALLACIES   309
Exercises 9–1 to 9–4   310
READINGS
"The Checkers Speech," Richard M. Nixon   316
"Lies, Fallacies, and Santa Claus" (Student Essay), T. J. Stone   321
"The Language of Advertising Claims," Jeffrey Schrank   323
Advertisements for Analysis   330
"Love Is a Fallacy," Max Shulman   336
SUGGESTIONS FOR WRITING AND FURTHER
DISCUSSION   345

Chapter 10: Readings for Further Discussion   347

SMOKING
"When Smoke Gets in Your Eyes . . . Shut Them," Fran
Lebowitz   348
"A Question of Rights," Rhoda Nichter   351
VOTING
"Let's Not Get Out the Vote," Robert E. Coulson   352
"For Compulsory Voting," Alan Wertheimer   356
REPRODUCTIVE SURROGACY
"The Rationale for Surrogate Motherhood," Ethics Committee of the
American Fertility Society   358
"Surrogate Motherhood: An Ethical Dilemma," William E. May   364
CENSORSHIP
"Pornography, Obscenity, and the Case for Censorship," Irving
Kristol   369
"Defending Intellectual Freedom," Eli M. Oboler   373

AIDS TESTING
  "We Need Routine Testing for AIDS," William J. Bennett   375
  "AIDS: The Legal Epidemic," Arthur S. Leonard   378
CHRISTIANITY
  "Why I Am an Agnostic," Clarence Darrow   383
  "What Are We to Make of Jesus Christ?" C. S. Lewis   389
WOMEN'S RIGHTS
  "The Case for Equality," Caroline Bird   393
  "Paid Homemaking: An Idea in Search of a Policy," William J.
    Byron, S. J.   398
MINORITIES' RIGHTS
  "A Call for Unity," Members of the Birmingham Clergy   404
  "Letter from Birmingham Jail," Martin Luther King, Jr.   406
THE MIDDLE EAST
  "Sharing the Land and the Legacy," Rami Khouri   417
  "Maps of Revenge," Meron Benvenisti   420

Selected References   423

Index   427

Preface

No doubt my fondness for alliteration got the better of me when I titled the first edition of this book *The Power to Persuade*. I realized at the time that both *power* and *persuade* were words rather out of favor in rhetorical circles. But I liked the title then, and still do—because students do. Students want to be persuasive, and they recognize the power that goes with persuasiveness: So, they are willing to read the book. They must recognize as well the difference between persuading and convincing, and the need for ethical and logical soundness in their arguments. When they read the book, they meet with these concerns on nearly every page.

As in the first edition, this book reflects the conviction that students in expository writing classes want and need the abilities to reason logically, to express their ideas effectively in writing, and to recognize and avoid committing fallacious attempts at persuasion. They want practical communicative skills that will help them secure jobs and further their future careers.

So this is a book that still focuses on those aims by, first, integrating the study of reasoning with the study of writing. As in the first edition, coherent, logically ordered, and grammatical writing is presented as furthering not only comprehension but also persuasion. Second, the book gives attention to the writer's tools: how words and definition are used to persuade and how evidence is evaluated and used to support argument. Third, it treats the importance of style to persuasion and discusses ways in which novice writers can polish and perfect writing style. Fourth, it offers examples of persuasive writing that have been chosen for the quality of writing as well as for the quality or provocativeness of argument. Some of the reading selections are about argument, most are argumentative, and all reflect the persuasive power of language. Many succeed at their aims, and some fall short; the student of writing and reasoning can learn from both. A number of the essays are written by students—a feature students responded to favorably in the first edition. A rough draft and a final draft of one student essay are included. The last chapter of the book offers—for analysis, comparison, or rebuttal—paired readings in which two (often, but not always, opposing) viewpoints on each of several issues are argued. And fifth, the presentation of rhetorical persuasion in *The Power to Persuade* is recursive; elements of writing and reasoning are not taken up, discussed, and then dropped. Instead, each chapter builds on those that precede it. The emphasis throughout the book is on the rhetorical context of audience and purpose that determines the form, extent, and manner of presentation of arguments. And every chapter continues to focus on argumentation in its broadest sense, the sense in which any piece of writing with a thesis concept is argumentative.

Some elements of the book, however, are new or expanded. The chapters are now arranged so that the book moves from problems of writing (Chapters 1 through 6) to problems of reasoning (Chapters 7 through 9). In this way, instructors who prefer to omit formal deductive reasoning can easily do so: Syllogisms are discussed only in Chapter 8, along with a brief presentation of the Toulmin model for instructors who prefer to use it.

Chapter 1 provides, as before, an overview of argument and persuasion and the crucial distinctions between them—along with the question of ethics in persuasion. It offers a nontechnical introduction to the concerns of argument: how relationships between ideas constitute arguments; how assumptions underlie arguments; how language limits, defines, and slants arguments; and how logical, emotional, and ethical appeals imbue arguments. Chapter 2, "Creating Arguments," offers a greatly expanded treatment of invention, with specific and detailed advice on three key invention strategies, including the enthymeme as a heuristic tactic.

Once a thesis, a skeletal framework for the argument, is decided, the next two chapters offer some suggestions for fleshing out that argument. Chapter 3 focuses on the writer's tools—words—and the uses of definition in developing arguments. Chapter 4, "Research and the Uses of Argument," brings forward what was formerly near the end of the book, in recognition of the importance of evidence to support most arguments. The chapter can be omitted or postponed, however, by instructors who prefer to do so. A unique and useful feature of Chapter 4 is its arrangement of sources of evidence according to the frequency of their updating: Many subjects require current, up-to-date information. Another useful feature of the chapter is its thorough discussion of how to incorporate quoted material into a writer's own essay. Then, Chapter 5, "Revising," shows how a writer can modify and complete a draft, strengthening its persuasiveness through clear and coherent prose. Taking the concerns of Chapter 5 still further, Chapter 6, "The Power of Style," discusses the role style plays in persuasion and ways a writer can call upon metaphor and other stylistic elements to enhance an argument.

Chapters 7 and 8 take up the logical elements of inductive and deductive reasoning as means of analyzing a writer's own arguments and those of others. These chapters are little changed from the first edition beyond the addition of new exercises and a section explaining the specific differences between inductive and deductive reasoning. Chapter 9, "Fallacies," points as straight a path as possible through the tangled underbrush of reasoning gone awry. And the last chapter, with its paired "Readings for Further Discussion," may be used to conclude the course, or its readings may be taken up along with earlier chapters.

The second edition contains many new exercises, examples, and writing suggestions, and a number of new reading selections. I have tried, however, not to throw out the baby with the bath water; much of what was well received in the first edition has been retained. As before, the emphasis is on practical skills, on giving students specific selections for dealing with writing and reasoning tasks. The visual layout of the book has been improved through the increased use of checklists to make reference to those suggestions still easier.

In continuing to center on real-world skills of reasoning and writing, the aim of this book is still to assist students in refining and polishing those skills both within and beyond the context of college studies. Accordingly, its examples include, as before, both nonfiction and fiction and range from Ann Landers to Socratic dialogue, from fraternities and college football to running meetings and making sales, and from dishwashing to political crises. It applies principles of argument and persuasion that were formulated two thousand years ago to the issues and problems of two years ago—and the same principles can be applied to the issues and problems that have arisen in the past two minutes.

Writing is hard work, as any student of writing well knows. It is usually solitary work as well. I am fortunate that such was not my lot with *The Power to Persuade,* for many kind friends, students, and colleagues provided help, inspiration, and, where needed, correction and instruction as I toiled. In addition to those whose advice so helped with the first edition, I have these to thank for help with the second: Lynne Rosenfeld, my editor at Prentice Hall; Laura Cleveland of WordCrafters, Inc., the production editor; Wendy Osborne, who was much more than a proofreader, and reviewers Kathleen Carroll, University of Maryland; Delryn Fleming, Brookhaven College; George Hammerbacher, King's College; Gary Kriewald, University of California, Santa Barbara; Sonia Manuel-Dupont, Utah State University; Thomas A. Mozola, Macomb Community College; Susan B. Smith, McLennan Community College; Sharon K. Wilson, Fort Hays State University; and Edith J. Wynne, East Texas State University.

Among my colleagues at Southern Methodist University who provided examples and ideas are Virginia Oram (now of Richland College), Carolyn Channell, Tony Howard (now of Collin County College), and Theresa Enos (now of the University of Arizona). I owe a special thanks as well to "the kindness of strangers": Carol Ann Britt of the University of Texas at San Antonio and Barbara J. Biasiolli of St. Mary's University both provided invaluable assistance and considerable time to the development of Chapter 2, all on behalf of someone quite unknown to them. Along with my thanks go my apologies to one and all of these kind people for not having always taken their excellent advice.

And I will thank again my family (which has grown since last I wrote a preface) for their encouragement, help, and tolerance. Bob, Alice Ann, and Stephen Benjamin have kept me going throughout this project: I never dreamed how much fun it could be to write a book with a toddler on my knee.

Acknowledgments

The author and publisher are grateful to the following for permission to reprint their material.

Chapter 1

p. 1: Louisiana State University Press for "Language Is Sermonic" by Richard Weaver. Reprinted by permission of Louisiana State University Press.

p. 3: Alinari/Art Resource for *The School of Athens* by Raphael.

pp. 19–20: Debbie Sapp for "What So Proudly We Hailed?"

pp. 22–26: The Wallace Literary Agency, Inc., for "Why Don't We Complain?" by William F. Buckley, Jr. Reprinted by permission of The Wallace Literary Agency, Inc. Copyright 1961 by William F. Buckley, Jr. Reprinted by permission of *Esquire*, Inc., 1961.

Chapter 2

p. 30: Dorothy Van Doren for an excerpt from *Liberal Education* by Mark Van Doren. Reprinted by permission of Dorothy Van Doren. Copyright held by Dorothy G. Van Doren.

pp. 53–54: Erik Johnson for "Group Discussions Are Beneficial."

pp. 55–56: *Fortune*, Inc. for "Pay Equity Is Unfair to Women" by Linda Chavez. Reprinted by permission of *Fortune*, Inc. Copyright © 1985.

Chapter 3

pp. 65–66: Longman, Inc. for an excerpt from *Bakke, De Funis, and Minority Admissions* by Allan P. Sindeler. Copyright © 1978 by Longman, Inc. Reprinted by permission.

pp. 69–72: Farrar, Straus, Giroux for excerpts from *The Right Stuff* by Tom Wolfe, © 1979.

p. 74: Houghton Mifflin Company for "Ars Poetica" by Archibald MacLeish. Reprinted from *New and Collected Poems 1917–1976* by Archibald MacLeish. Reprinted by permission of Houghton Mifflin Company.

pp. 76–79: Farrar, Straus, Giroux for excerpts from "On Morality" by Joan Didion, © 1968.

Chapter 4

pp. 85–86: News America Syndicate for an excerpt from the Ann Landers column. Ann Landers and News America Syndicate.

pp. 114–115: Prentice Hall for excerpt from *Simon & Schuster Handbook for Writers* by Lynn Quitman Troyka. Reprinted by permission of Prentice Hall. Copyright © 1987 by Lynn Quitman Troyka.

pp. 117–122: Harcourt Brace Jovanovich, Inc. for "Reports, Inferences, Judgments" excerpted from *Language in Thought and Action*, Fourth Editions, by S. I. Hayakawa, copyright © 1978 by Harcourt Brace Jovanovich, Inc. Reprinted by permission of the publisher.

Chapter 5

p. 140: *The Atlantic Monthly* for excert from "The Trouble with Architects" by Andrew Ward. Copyright © 1977 by The Atlantic Monthly Company.

p. 141: Curtis Brown, Ltd., London for "What Are We to Make of Jesus Christ?" From *God in the Dock*. Copyright © 1970 by C. S. Lewis Pte Ltd., reproduced by permission of Curtis Brown Ltd., London.

p. 141: Harper & Row for "Letter from Birmingham Jail" by Martin Luther King, Jr. Specified abridgement of "Letter from Birmingham Jail, April 16, 1963" from *Why We Can't Wait* by Martin Luther King, Jr. Copyright © 1963 by Martin Luther King, Jr. Reprinted by permission of Harper & Row Publishers, Inc.

p. 145: *The Wall Street Journal* for excerpt from "The Death of Socrates" by Vermont Royster. Reprinted by permission of *The Wall Street Journal*, Dow Jones & Co., Inc. Copyright © 1984. All rights reserved.

Chapter 6

p. 194: *The Wall Street Journal* for excerpts from "The Purpose of Presidents." *The Wall Street Journal*, November 21, 1986. Reprinted by permission of *The Wall Street Journal*, Dow Jones & Co., Inc. Copyright © 1986. All rights reserved.

pp. 201–203: *The Atlantic Monthly* for "Remarks at the Peace Banquet" by William James. Copyright by *The Atlantic Monthly Company*.

pp. 205–208: *Harper's Magazine* for "Sculptures in Snow" by Lewis Lapham. Copyright © 1981 by *Harper's Magazine*. All rights reserved. Reprinted from the August 1981 issue by special permission.

Chapter 7

p. 217: Houghton Mifflin Company for excerpt from "How to Keep the Air Clean" by Sydney J. Harris. Reprinted from *For the Time Being* by Sydney J. Harris. Copyright © 1982 by Sydney J. Harris. Copyright © 1969, 1970, 1971, 1972 by

Publishers-Hall Syndicate. Reprinted by permission of Houghton Mifflin Company.

pp. 230–233: *Harvard Business Review* for "Is Business Bluffing Ethical?" by Albert Z. Carr (January/February 1968). Copyright © 1968 by the President and Fellows of Harvard College; all rights reserved.

pp. 234–235: *Ms. Magazine* for "Why I Want a Wife" by Judy Syfers. Reprinted by permission of the author.

pp. 237–239: *The Atlantic Monthly* for excerpt from "The Trouble with Architects" by Andrew Ward. Copyright © 1977 by The Atlantic Monthly Company.

p. 241: Scribner's for "How Annandale Went Out" by Edward Arlington Robinson. Reprinted from *Tillbury Town: Selected Poems of Edward Arlington Robinson.* © 1953 by Scribner's.

Chapter 8

pp. 273–275: Alfred A. Knopf for "Should We Abolish the Presidency?" by Barbara Tuchman. Reprinted from *Practicing History* by Barbara Tuchman. Copyright © 1981 by Alma Tuchman, Luch T. Eisenberg, and Jessica Tuchman Matthews. Reprinted by permission of Alfred A. Knopf, Inc.

pp. 279–284: Scott Meredith Literary Agency, Inc. for "We'll Never Conquer Space" by Arthur C. Clarke. Reprinted by permission of the author and the author's agents, Scott Meredith Literary Agency, Inc., 845 Third Avenue, New York, New York 10022.

pp. 291–293: Grove Press for an excerpt from Act I of *Rhinoceros* by Eugene Ionesco. Reprinted by permission of the Grove Press.

Chapter 9

pp. 321–322: T. J. Stone for "Lies, Fallacies, and Santa Claus."

pp. 323–329: *Media and Methods* for "The Language of Advertising Claims" by Jeffrey Schrank. Reprinted by permission of *Media and Methods*, America's Magazine of the Teaching Technologies.

p. 330: Lorillard, Inc. for the True cigarette advertisement.

p. 331: North by Northeast Co. for their advertisement. © 1981 by North by Northeast Co. Reprinted by permission.

p. 332: Institute of Advanced Thinking for the Instant Memory advertisement.

p. 333: Van Munching & Co. for permission to reprint the Heineken advertisement.

p. 334: Bost Enterprises, Inc., for the golf ball advertisement. © Bost Enterprises Inc. 1987.

pp. 336–344: Harold Matson Company for "Love Is a Fallacy" by Max Schulman. © 1951, © renewed 1979 by Max Schulman. Reprinted by permission of Harold Matson Company, Inc.

Chapter 10

pp. 348–350: Random House, Inc., for "When Smoke Gets in Your Eyes" by Fran Lebowitz. From *Social Studies* by Fran Lebowitz. Copyright © 1981 by Fran Lebowitz. Reprinted by permission of Random House, Inc.

p. 351: Ashley Books for "A Question of Rights" by Rhoda Nichter. Reprinted with permission of Ashley Books, Inc., Port Washington, N.Y. 11050 from *Yes, I Do Mind if You Smoke* by Rhoda Nichter.

pp. 352–355: *Harper's Magazine* for "Let's Not Get Out the Vote" by Robert E. Coulson. © 1955 by *Harper's Magazine*. All rights reserved. Reprinted from the November 1955 issue by special permission.

pp. 356–357: The New York Times Book Company, Inc., for "For Compulsory Writing" by Alan Wertheimer. Copyright © 1976 by The New York Times Book Company, Inc. Reprinted by permission.

pp. 358–363: The American Fertility Society for "The Rationale for Surrogate Motherhood." Abstracted from "Surrogate Mothers from The Ethics Committee of the American Fertility Society: Ethical Considerations of the New Reproductive Technologies." *Fertil. Steril.* (Suppl.): 62S, 1986. Reproduced with permission of the publisher, The American Fertility Society.

pp. 364–386: *Eternity* magazine for "Surrogate Motherhood: An Ethical Dilemma" by William E. May. Reprinted by permission of *Eternity* magazine. Copyright 1987, Evangelical Ministries, Inc., 1716 Spruce St., Philadelphia PA 19103.

pp. 369–372: *Reader's Digest* for "The Case for Liberal Censorship" by Irving Kristol. © 1971 by Irving Kristol. Reprinted by permission of Irving Kristol.

pp. 373–374: American Library Association for "Viewpoint" by Eli M. Oboler. Reprinted by permission of the American Library Association from *Newsletter of Intellectual Freedom* 21(1): 30 (Jan. 1972).

pp. 375–377: *The Wall Street Journal* for "We Need Routine Testing for AIDS," by William J. Bennett. *The Wall Street Journal*, May 26, 1987. Reprinted by permission of *The Wall Street Journal*, Dow Jones & Co., Inc. Copyright © 1986. All rights reserved.

p. 378: *The New York Native* for "AIDS: The Legal Epidemic" by Arthur S. Leonard. Reprinted by permission of *The New York Native*. © 1987.

pp. 383–388: The New York Times Book Company, Inc. for "Why I Am an Agnostic" by Clarence Darrow. Reprinted from *Verdicts Out of Court* by permission of The New York Times Book Company, Inc.

pp. 389–392: Curtis Brown, Ltd., London for "What Are We to Make of Jesus Christ?" From *God in the Dock*. Copyright © 1970 by C. S. Lewis Pte Ltd., reproduced by permission of Curtis Brown Ltd., London.

pp. 393–397: Caroline Bird for "The Case for Equality" from *Born Female*. Reprinted by permission of the author.

pp. 398–403: Society for the Advancement of Education for "Paid Homemaking: An Idea in Search of a Policy" by William J. Byron, S. J. Reprinted from *USA Today Magazine*, July 1984. Copyright 1984 by the Society for the Advancement of Education.

pp. 406–416: Harper & Row for "Letter from Birmingham Jail" by Martin Luther King, Jr. Specified abridgement of "Letter from Birmingham Jail, April 16, 1963" from *Why We Can't Wait* by Martin Luther King, Jr. Copyright © 1963 by Martin Luther King, Jr. Reprinted by permission of Harper & Row, Publishers, Inc.

pp. 417–419: Resource Center for Nonviolence, Santa Cruz, California, for "Sharing the Land and the Legacy" by Rami Khouri. Copyright © 1985. Reprinted by permission.

pp. 420–422: Random House, Inc. for "Maps of Revenge" by Meron Benvenisti. Reprinted by permission of Villard Books, a Division of Random House, Inc. Copyright © 1986 by Meron Benvenisti.

Instructor's Edition

p. 38: *The Dallas Times Herald* for "Driving Is Safer than Flying—Right?" and "Statistics on Air Safety Sometimes Deceiving" by Bob Drummond. Reprinted by permission of *The Dallas Times Herald*. Copyright 1987 by Bob Drummond.

THE POWER
TO PERSUADE

1

Argument
and Persuasion

... the most obvious truth about rhetoric is that its object is the
whole man. It presents its arguments first to the rational part of
man, because rhetorical discourses, if they are honestly conceived,
always have a basis in reasoning. Logical argument is the plot, as
it were, of any speech or composition that is designed to persuade.
Yet it is the very characterizing feature of rhetoric that it goes beyond this and appeals to other parts of man's constitution, especially to his nature as a pathetic being, that is, a being feeling and
suffering. A speech intended to persuade achieves little unless it
takes into account how men are reacting subjectively to their hopes
and fears and their special circumstances.

Richard M. Weaver

To many people *argument* connotes unpleasantness: quarrels and disagreement, raised voices and smashed vases. But just as *rhetoric* meant
simply "the art of persuasion" long before the word acquired connotations of political doubletalk and empty verbal flourishes, so *argument*
(as we will use the term) leads not to discord but ideally to harmony. In
the rhetorical art of persuasion, an **argument** is supposed to be a reasoned
consideration of an idea. It is through argument that we try to make
sense of what we don't understand, try to refute ideas we believe are
mistaken, try to determine appropriate policy for future actions. Rhetorical argument is—or at least, should be—the search for truth.

While *argument* as we will use the term does not mean *quarrel*, it
does imply the existence of misunderstanding or disagreement. We do
not argue about things that can be verified readily or that are true by
definition; we do not argue that 24 plus 17 equals 41, that the return of
Halley's comet was first predicted in 1682, that St. Paul is the capital of
Minnesota. People may *quarrel* about such things, of course, when their

memories of experiences differ, but such disagreements are pointless. They may be resolved simply by consulting an encyclopedia, an almanac, or any other appropriate authority. The issues of rhetorical arguments may not be resolved so easily, for there is likely to be more than one possible way of treating the question, and often more than one plausible answer. Was Kennedy responsible for initial U.S. involvement in Vietnam, or was it really Eisenhower? Can the Social Security program be saved? Should Ellen accept the job offer in Kansas City or the one in San Diego? Is there life elsewhere in the universe?

Just as the possibility for doubt or disagreement must exist to warrant argument, so the arguer must want to search for an answer or to persuade the reader or listener, although persuasion and argument are not quite the same thing. To **argue** is to make a case for a judgment or opinion, while to **persuade** is to bring about a desired response in a reader or listener. The difference is that argument is logical; persuasion, psychological. This book will consider some of the psychological elements of persuasion as well as the logical: style, fallacies, and the persuasive power of the **persona** (the image the arguer creates of himself or herself).

The Ethics of Persuasion

Because persuasion can work by fair means or foul, by fallacious and manipulative appeals as well as by logical and just appeals, we must consider the problem of ethics that persuasion raises. If we study persuasion, do we not show the unscrupulous how better to manipulate their audiences?

Even among the scrupulous, opinions regarding what is ethical and relevant in argument may differ. In *The School of Athens*, Raphael illustrates the ethical dilemma the study of persuasion creates. In the center of the painting stand Plato and Aristotle, debating; Plato points heavenward, toward the realm of ideas, while Aristotle's hand gestures outward to the world of men and women (including a number of renowned philosophers and scientists) below them. In these gestures Raphael has captured the essential difference between the two thinkers: Plato advocates the pursuit of the True in an Ideal world; Aristotle advocates the pursuit of truth in the world of human beings. Neither man, the viewer notes, seems by his stance or expression to be winning the debate. Raphael has depicted Plato and Aristotle as equally in the right.

And so they are: Unadorned truth should be sought and accepted on its merits alone, as Plato would have it; in the real world, however, persuasive skills can work even without the support of truth, as Aristotle recognizes. Even Plato acknowledges this dimension of argument in words he ascribes to Socrates in the *Phaedrus* (Jowett trans.):

Whatever my advice may be worth, I should have told him to arrive at the truth first, and then come to me. At the same time I boldly assert that mere knowledge of the truth will not give you the art of persuasion.

Knowledge of the truth does not seem "mere" to most of us, of course, but we probably agree that truth alone is all too often not sufficient to persuade. We hope that our arguments are persuasive, but we cannot guarantee it. And we hope that we are persuaded only by sound arguments, but we suspect differently. There are forms of persuasion beyond logic, as every consumer of shampoo, deodorant, or detergent, and every person ever intimidated by a large bully or a determined aunt, well knows.

We should not infer, of course, that all nonlogical appeals are without merit. People arrange to donate organs after death out of pity for those in need of livers, kidneys, or corneas. We give toys and roast turkeys to poor families at Christmas in response to perfectly valid appeals to our emotions. But we could all testify also to the abundance of persuaders who distort or abandon the truth and yet enjoy tremendous success in persuading the rest of us to do what they wish: buy their product or their swampland, vote for them, overlook their misdeeds, and otherwise behave as they want us to. These people have mastered the art of

persuasion but have failed to assimilate a system of ethics that makes the truth the basis for persuasion.

As you study argument and persuasion, you will necessarily consider ethical issues. Argument requires value judgments: Is what is argued true or false, good or bad, effective or ineffective, practical or impractical? And, if value judgments are made, a system of values must precede and inform those judgments. In later chapters you will study the ways in which fallacious arguments are developed: What is to prevent you from deliberately employing fallacious arguments yourself? If your persuasive aim is a good one, might not any means to that end be justifiable? For that matter, who is to say that deliberate fallacies, simply because they are illogical, are also unethical? You will need to consider all these ethical questions.

The Need for Argument

If all ideas have equal merit, there is no need for argument. In that case, your assertion that Puerto Rico should be made the fifty-first state and your cousin's assertion that even its status as a territory should be taken away are equally true and acceptable ideas. But, in the real world, such is fortunately not the case, for how chaotic life then would be! We care about our ideas and we want other people at least to understand them, if not to accept them. Issues come in black, white, shades of gray— and a number of other colors. Opinions on those issues are just as varied as the issues themselves and are not all of equal value or merit. We *can* assert opinions and construct arguments to back them up. And we should try to make sense, to search for truth, in doing so.

We look for the truth not only in the explicit statements of argument but also in the unspoken assumptions that the arguer makes about the audience, the subject, and the relationship of the two to each other and to the arguer. For example, consider the argument, "Taking swimming lessons is a waste of time and money; don't do it." The arguer assumes, among other things, that the hearer or reader considers time and money important (and more important than future safety on the water), that learning how to swim is not an essential skill, or that swimming can be learned without lessons. Some of these assumptions are questionable; their truth may be challenged.

All arguers also reflect in their arguments assumptions about the nature of the world and of life itself. They may have a particular religious faith or philosophy of life, for instance, that informs and colors the premises of their arguments. Such assumptions are nonlogical; their truth is taken on faith by those who hold them. We call these assumptions **a priori** (in Latin, "before the fact") **premises.** Writers need to consider their own and their readers' *a priori* beliefs in determining their line of reasoning. In attempting to persuade an agnostic that abortion is not an acceptable form of birth control, for instance, a Christian or Jew should not limit arguments to appeals to Biblical authority. Otherwise, the arguments are likely to fall on deaf ears and the discussion will be sidetracked to the one individual's *a priori* acceptance of Biblical authority and the other individual's *a priori* rejection of it.

Therefore, while the need for argument is real, some values must be shared between writer and reader, arguer and audience, if argument is to reveal truth and resolve disagreement. *A priori* beliefs are rarely fruitful subjects of argument because they are outside the realm of reason. The strained relationships between culturally or politically dissimilar nations—as seen in Lebanese and Syrian confrontations in the Middle East, American and Russian disagreement about the primacy of individual life or the primacy of the state, Chinese and Taiwanese competing claims to represent all the Chinese people—illustrate the difficulty of arguing any issue concerning which *a priori* premises differ. Even individuals living side by side may find that they have *a priori* differences: One believes that a clean house or dormitory room is a sure sign of a misspent life, while the other is just as certain that cleanliness is at least next to godliness, if not greater.

Nor are matters of personal taste profitable subjects of argument. One person may prefer the color yellow to pink, American primitive furniture to Danish modern, chocolate to butterscotch. Another person may have entirely different tastes. Neither is likely to have logical grounds for those preferences, and neither is "wrong."

This is not to say, however, that matters of personal opinion can never be argued. If *a priori* standards of value and judgment are shared, even questions of esthetics are arguable. After all, the conclusion to any argument is a statement of opinion, a judgment. But how often have you heard, "Of course, that's just my opinion"? Some people act as if the disclaimer absolves them from any need to offer reasons for their assertions, believing that all opinions have the same—little—worth. However, this viewpoint is unduly narrow, for reasoned opinions have merit, and the opinions of experts speaking in their fields have particular merit.

Appropriate subjects of argument are many, and range from the merits of a musical composition to the best plan for economic stability in a nation. We may argue our reasons for moving to Buffalo or for buying a Chevrolet instead of an import. We may argue about the past (What really happened? What was important? What factors contributed to our subject issue or event?), the present (What is the present state of our subject? What is its value? What are its proper functions?), or the future (What should we do? What will our subject be like in the future? What will be the consequences of our subject?). We may argue about the abstract, wrestling with philosophical and imaginative problems; or we may argue about the concrete—advocating, for example, building a stoplight at the corner of Maple and Thornton streets. We all have opinions regarding all kinds of subjects—about some of which we have expert knowledge, about many of which we do not—and those opinions need only to be supported by sound argument to merit a hearing.

RELATIONSHIPS IN ARGUMENT

But what constitutes sound argument? What constitutes argument of any kind? **All argument centers on the relationships between ideas or observations.** An argument is a statement of opinion or judgment offered together with other statements related to and supporting the opinion. The statement of opinion or judgment toward which the argument moves is the **conclusion;** the statements offered in support of the conclusion are called **premises.** A premise and conclusion may be combined in a single sentence, as in this example:

Aspirin should be banned because *excessive amounts of it are poisonous.*
     CONCLUSION   PREMISE

This argument includes a statement of opinion that forms the conclusion, "Aspirin should be banned," and a statement of fact offered in support of the conclusion, "Excessive amounts of [aspirin] are poisonous."

In argument both kinds of statements—premises and conclusions—are called **propositions.** A proposition is any declarative statement that can be affirmed or denied; it can express either fact or opinion. Propositions that express judgments and opinions are called **assertions.** By definition, all conclusions are assertions, and premises may or may not be. The premise in the argument above—"Excessive amounts of aspirin are poisonous"—is a statement of fact (but we will discuss in Chapter 4 some problems occasioned by the casual use of the word *fact*). In a different argument the premise might be a statement of judgment or opinion: "Aspirin should be banned because some people abuse it." The premise in this case, like the conclusion, is an assertion.

An asserted idea unrelated to supporting propositions remains an assertion only and does not constitute argument of any kind, sound or unsound. If I say, "It will rain later today," I have offered an assertion but not an argument. You may nod sagely and say, "You're probably right"; you may simply disagree with a brusque "I doubt it" or "No, it won't"; or you may disagree and also offer an argument in support of your own conclusion: "No, it won't rain. Those are high clouds, and the humidity is low. Besides, the weather forecast mentioned no chance of rain until Thursday." But even if your imagination races on to consider all the reasons why I might have offered such an assertion (perhaps, like the White Queen in Looking-Glass Land, I have resolved to believe six impossible things every morning before breakfast), my single claim, without support, is an assertion—not an argument—until I express at least one of those reasons.

An assertion is arguable if it can be supported by reasons or evidence. It is not arguable if it is simply a statement of personal taste or a verifiable report. Given that distinction, determine which of the following propositions are arguable assertions.

1. I like pistachio pudding.
2. The board of directors will meet next Thursday.
3. The situation in Jordan is not resolvable by Western intervention.
4. Margaret dislikes the color red.
5. Spiders are not insects.
6. Every college needs a career-counseling office.

Sentences 2, 4, and 5 purport to be reports, not expressions of opinion, and as such are in principle verifiable, not arguable. They are "statements of fact," even if the facts are in error. The board of directors actually may be scheduled to meet on Friday, not Thursday, but I could check with the chairperson's secretary to verify the day. Sentence 4 is tricky, because it looks like a statement of unarguable opinion. But, while Margaret's own assertion, "I dislike the color red," would be an unarguable personal opinion, the statement "Margaret dislikes the color red" is a *report* of that opinion. Sentence 5 is true by definition. Scientists long ago decided that spiders, having eight legs rather than six, require a separate category in the animal kingdom. Despite the capitulation of some dictionaries, spiders are arachnids, not true insects. The other propositions in the list are assertions; they express opinions. Still, none of the six propositions is related logically to any other proposition: They can be affirmed or denied, but that is all. None forms part of an argument.

Propositions do not become part of an argument until the observations expressed by them are related to other ideas. Suppose we say,

Harry, worthless bum though he may be, is a citizen of this country. He ought to get out of his lawn chair and go to the polls.

Here we have inferred a relationship between citizens in general, Harry in particular, and the act of voting. The proposition "All citizens should be legally obligated to vote" has become an implicit premise which, together with the stated premise that Harry is a citizen, supports a conclusion about what Harry ought to do. Together they constitute an argument.

Any proposition can become either a premise or a conclusion when we begin to relate it to other statements. Take the proposition "All citizens should be legally obligated to vote." That sentence could be a premise in a variation of the argument about Harry:

All citizens should be legally obligated to vote. Therefore, Harry should be legally obligated to vote.

And if other relationships were being examined, "All citizens should be legally obligated to vote" might appear as a conclusion:

Because voting is a right of all citizens and an important responsibility, citizens should be legally obligated to vote.

In both cases, relationships between three things are under examination: voting, citizens' rights and responsibilities, and legal obligations. These components of statements are called **classes.** A class is a group of things having a common characteristic which may be, as in the second class here—citizens' rights and responsibilities—a compound characteristic. From the relationships among the three classes we infer a conclusion. Examining relationships and inferring a conclusion about those relationships is the process of argument.

Verbal Signals of Argument

In order to fully understand and evaluate arguments, we must be able to recognize arguments readily and distinguish premises from conclusions. To do so, we rely on common sense and on transitional words and phrases that signal logical relationships. We begin with the former, looking for the main point the writer is putting forth: That assertion is usually the conclusion in the immediate argument. But arguments rarely occur in isolation. A single paragraph may contain several arguments, with the conclusions to minor arguments functioning as premises for the paragraph's main point. If an assertion seems to be the main point of an entire essay, article, or presentation, we have located the **thesis,** the controlling concept in the essay and the conclusion to its principal argument. (In the next chapter we will look closely at the concept of thesis.)

Conclusions to arguments may appear before, after, or between premises, and at times you must simply depend on the meaning to determine the conclusion and the premises. In all three arguments about voting above, the conclusion appears last, but the first argument provides no signal word to identify either premise or conclusion while the second contains the typical conclusion-signal *therefore.* The third includes a premise-signal, *because.* An argument without verbal signals to identify premises or conclusions is, fortunately, rare. When you write arguments, usually you will include such signals to make your meaning clear to your readers.

Verbal signals that conclusions follow include words and phrases such as:

therefore	consequently	accordingly
hence	as a result	in conclusion
then	thus	so

Verbal signals that premises follow include:

since	because	if

You should bear in mind three notes of caution about verbal signals of argument:

1. Signals of argument must be earned; a causal relationship must exist between two statements before a *therefore* can link them. The verbal connector does not *create* the logical connection; it calls attention to a logical connection that already exists.
2. Verbal signals are not completely interchangeable; there can be major or minor differences in meaning. *Accordingly* and *consequently,* for example, signal slightly different kinds of relationships. Be as precise as possible in the verbal signals you choose.
3. What may appear to be verbal signals of argument occasionally may be no such thing. *Because* can preface an explanation rather than an argument: "He came because I asked him." *Since* can indicate simple chronology: "We have been playing croquet ever since our friends arrived."

Verbal signals are invaluable to both writer and reader, but they must be understood accurately in the contexts in which they are used.

EXERCISE 1–1

Using your common sense about relationships between ideas and statements, locate the conclusions in the following arguments. Underline any conclusion-signals.

1. I don't care if you don't like the name. I'm serving Watergate cake for dessert because I like the pistachio pudding that goes with it. So there.
2. The board of directors will meet next Thursday, and I always find its meetings dreadfully dull. Accordingly, I will plan to be out of town that day.

3. Westerners fail to understand the Middle Eastern mindset, mores, or even the Muslim religion. They also fail to understand Middle Eastern distaste for outsiders' intervening in internal political affairs, despite protests to the contrary by some Christian Lebanese leaders. Consequently, it seems likely that the situation in Jordan is not resolvable by Western intervention.
4. I'm sure Margaret must dislike the color red. She hates all bright colors.
5. Spiders look like insects, but they have eight legs—so they can't be insects.
6. The reputation of a college is enhanced if its graduates readily find good jobs in their fields. Therefore, every college—no matter how small—needs a career-counseling office.

Assumptions

In the three arguments about voting presented earlier, one statement relating two of the three classes is implied but not stated. It is an *assumption* made by the arguer about the subject at hand. We tend to assume, rather than state, those parts of arguments that seem to us self-evident or sure to be familiar to and accepted by our audience. Often we are right to leave unstated those obvious relationships among the terms of our argument: How boring and long-winded we would seem were we always to spell out every assumption underlying and justifying our arguments. We would then have to say more than "Harry, worthless bum though he may be, is a citizen and, as such, ought to vote"; our full argument would go something like this:

All citizens ought to vote.   (implied premise)
Harry is a citizen.   (stated premise)
Therefore, Harry ought to vote.   (conclusion)

The second argument—"All citizens should be legally obligated to vote. Therefore, Harry should be legally obligated to vote"—holds an even more obvious assumption: "Harry is a citizen." The full argument could be phrased as

Voting should be a legal duty of all citizens.   (stated premise)
Harry is a citizen.   (implied premise)
Therefore, Harry should be legally obligated to vote.   (conclusion)

We hardly need to have all that spelled out in order to understand and respond to the argument.

But the third argument, which draws a conclusion identical to a premise in the argument just above, shows the importance of paying attention to the assumptions that link terms together in argument. When we say, "Because voting is a right of all citizens and an important responsibility, citizens should be legally obligated to vote," we are assuming that what is a right should also be a legal obligation. But is it fair to bury that claim as an unstated assumption? Hardly. It warrants argument itself. When we set out the full argument,

Rights of all citizens should also be their legal duties.	(implied premise)
Voting is a right of all citizens	(stated premise)
Therefore, voting should be a legal duty of all citizens.	(conclusion)

we can better examine both the truth of the implicit and explicit claims of the argument and the logical relationships among the terms of the argument. How to evaluate the truth of premises will be our concern in Chapter 4; how to evaluate the logical relationships in the argument— the ways premises are related to conclusions—will be our chief concern in Chapters 7 and 8. In the meantime, watch those assumptions, both in your own arguments and in those you read. If there is a weakness in an argument, more often than not it lies buried in what is assumed by the arguer.

Limiting Arguments with Qualifiers

The relationships among parts of an argument are also affected by the degree of certainty expressed in the premises and conclusions. We cannot push a tentative premise or a limited one to a sweeping conclusion. With that point in mind, it's easy enough to see which of the following arguments is more acceptable logically:

Utility stocks usually perform well, so you are sure to make money if you invest in Tennessee Utilities.

Utility stocks usually perform well, so you stand a fair chance of making money if you invest in Tennessee Utilities.

Both arguments use the same premise to reach their conclusions, but the second conclusion is clearly more sound than the first—and all because of the degree of certainty claimed. Adverbs and adjectives such as *usually, often, never, many, a few, some,* and the like are **qualifiers:** that is, they limit the extent of the claim a statement makes. In the arguments above, the qualifier *usually* in the premise automatically limits the degree of certainty we can claim in the conclusion; the first conclusion is too sweeping ("sure to") and the second is more appropriately qualified ("a fair chance").

Now, there is such a thing as too much caution in qualifying arguments, although that is a problem we see less often than unwarranted boldness. An arguer with strong premises should not draw a conclusion weaker than it need be just to prevent a challenge. It would be silly to argue,

Utility stocks usually perform well, so you may or may not make money if you invest in Tennessee Utilities.

How could that argument help a potential investor make a decision? Such pointless caution trivializes an argument.

A good rule of thumb as you write is to make your premises as strong as you can support—and your conclusions as qualified or sweeping (unqualified) as your premises warrant. And as you read, check to make sure arguments are appropriately and consistently qualified.

LOGIC, EMOTION, AND *ETHOS* IN ARGUMENT

By now it should be apparent that argument consists not only of what is said and how it is qualified, but also of what is implied or omitted. And arguments must offer more than dry logic formulas, for they are developed and presented not in a vacuum but among people with varying knowledge and biases. In fact, argument is at least three-dimensional and, in a sense, four-dimensional. The dimensions of argument are the **logical appeal,** the **emotional appeal,** and the **ethical appeal;** and, since argument is couched in words, its fourth dimension, on which the others depend, is the verbal—the words we choose and how we arrange them. All are essential to argument that is both persuasive and convincing.

The Logical Appeal

We often think of the logical appeal as preeminent. It concerns relationships among statements and ideas, as discussed above and, more specifically, in Chapters 7 and 8. But much of what we will be articulating and formalizing in those chapters is already part of your reasoning skills: what we unglamorously call "common sense." You already are able to ask questions such as these of arguments you read and hear:

Is there evidence? Is there enough? Is it believable?

What are the assumptions and implications? Are they fair?

Does this conclusion follow reasonably from the premises offered in support of it?

And you should ask such questions, not only of others' arguments, but also of your own as you revise and work on them. For without a sound logical foundation, the most eloquent and vivid language will not make an argument acceptable to a discerning audience.

The Emotional Appeal

The emotional appeal in argument is no less powerful than the logical. Although frequently abused, the emotional appeal is a legitimate aspect of rhetorical argument, for we want our audiences to care about the issues we address. The most effective ways for an ethical writer to achieve that end are through the use of vivid (but accurate) illustrations and examples and through a clear, graceful, and appropriately emphatic writing style. You can make sure to include specific and concrete examples and details in your arguments now. A pleasing style may come more slowly, with much writing and rewriting, much reading of well-written prose, and a heightened awareness of verbal possibilities, as Chapter 6 will demonstrate. For the moment, though, you can do wonders for your writing style simply by showing concern and courtesy for your readers: Express your ideas as simply and clearly as possible. The more complicated the ideas, the more important this point becomes.

Slanting   The particular illustrations and the specific language used in an argument involve choices that can distort unfairly even as they heighten the emotional impact of the argument. Choosing one example means omitting others, after all. And if the example a writer chooses is atypical, selected for its emotional impact only, the argument is skewed unfairly. If someone or something is described in unflattering terms when more neutral or even favorable language would have been more accurate, the argument is again skewed.

Slanting an argument through **selection** and **charged language** (as described above) may not be fair, but it is pervasive. Consider the following item from *Time* magazine, November 3, 1986:

As journalists and spectators jammed the small, steamy courtroom in Managua last week, the trial of Eugene Hasenfus began. Escorted by six guards, the jeans-clad ex-Marine glumly made his way to a seat before the People's Tribunal. For the next 80 minutes, Tribunal President Reynaldo Monterrey read the list of charges: terrorism, violation of public security, conspiracy to commit illicit acts. As Monterrey droned on, it became clear that more was at stake than the fate of Hasenfus, who was captured ferrying weapons to U.S.-backed *contra* rebels after Sandinista troops shot down an American Fairchild C-123K cargo plane over Nicaragua three weeks ago. The prosecution would attempt to try the U.S. Government itself for "*Yanqui* interventions" dating from the 1850s. Complained former U.S. Attorney General Griffin Bell, a member of Hasenfus' defense team: "He is an absolute pawn."

> While Hasenfus squirmed in the limelight, Washington prepared to resume direct aid to the *contras* after the expiration of a two-year congressional ban.

How would you characterize the defendant in this trial if this news article were your only source of information? What details here appear to be factual and fair? What choices of words and details contribute to slanting? What seems to be the main argumentative point (for this is clearly more than a bare-bones recitation of facts)?

From the same week's issue of *Newsweek,* we find a rather different characterization of the same man and the same trial:

> When Eugene Hasenfus sat in the dock of a Sandinista court last week and began telling all, he didn't look much like Rambo. The Sandinistas' first American prisoner in five years of war is facing up to 30 years in jail, and he seems scared and confused. On trial in Managua, the sad-faced, unemployed ironworker appeared more like a tragic portrait of "plausible deniability," than the picture of a gung-ho warrior. During an interview with NEWSWEEK in prison, his eyes twice brimmed with tears, and he worried about his three children back in Marinette, Wis. His wife, Sally, flew down for the trial, but the Sandinistas gave her less time with him than the press got. Hasenfus had assumed he was working for the CIA, he said, but he doesn't expect any help from the administration. "As far as my government saying anything, it's forgotten," he said. "Whoever I was working for out there, they just say, 'Sorry about that, Gene.' "
>
> Hasenfus's capture helped to expose a multimillion-dollar private-aid network set up in 1984 to send military supplies to the contras after Congress outlawed U.S. involvement.

What's the main argumentative point here, and where do selection and charged language contribute to a different "slant" on the issue than you noted in the *Time* article?

As readers of arguments, we would do well to be alert for such subtle emotional manipulation masquerading as reporting. As writers, we would do well to avoid slanting as much as possible, for readers who recognize it will be offended and lose faith in our arguments altogether.

The Ethical Appeal

It is of the utmost importance that our readers have faith in our arguments—that they trust us and what we say. That is the third dimension of argument: the ethical appeal. The logical and emotional elements of argument both contribute to and are dependent upon the force of the arguer's reputation and qualities such as fair-mindedness and common sense (or the lack of them) that are reflected in the argument itself. Aristotle considered the ethical appeal the single most crucial element of any argument. In his day, if a speaker was known to be a person of intelligence and integrity, his audience was likely to be receptive to his arguments. If, on the other hand, they distrusted him, they were unlikely to accept even his most eloquently expressed and rational assertions.

The same remains true today when speakers or writers are well known to their audience or readers, and are either admired or disliked intensely by them. In such circumstances the reputation speaks before the voice does. The byline persuades or dissuades before the words are read. Today, of course, because any given writer and reader are often less well known to each other than were speakers and listeners in Aristotle's time, a reader's preconception of a writer is seldom responsible for the success or failure of a written message. But even if a reader encounters a writer for the first time on the printed page, the ethical appeal remains an important factor in persuasion. The writer must, through words alone, convince the reader to accept the offered evidence and examples as honest and fair. Only in the act of reading does a reader gain a sense of a writer's personality, style, and trustworthiness. So a writer must create an appropriate image of herself or himself as well as an appropriate case for a particular thesis, for the latter is not likely to meet with approval if the former does not.

Sometimes the entire purpose of a paper or speech is to create or redefine the audience's sense of the writer or speaker. Political campaign speeches and press releases by celebrities' agents offer fine (and often creative!) examples of ethos-centered prose. Closer to everyday contexts, we find that letters to in-laws or pen pals, "personal statements" on college applications, letters proposing friends for membership in clubs, and autobiographical statements required of prospective parents by adoption agencies may all share as their primary purpose the creation of an appealing and trustworthy image. This image, or **persona,** is *the writer as perceived by the reader.*

Even when the primary purpose of a written message is something other than image building, the persona a writer creates through choices of words and arguments is of central importance to the persuasiveness of the prose. The ethical appeal of the persona is the sum of the writer's knowledge of the subject, apparent bias or lack of bias toward that subject, vocabulary, humor or earnestness, and degree of candor—as the reader perceives these attributes, that is.

That there may be some discrepancy between the persona created in a written message and the actual character and personality of the writer is suggested by the very word *persona*—Latin for "mask." Sometimes the writer does try to create a mask behind which to hide. However, a better metaphor for the usual relationship of writer to reader, as established by the writer's prose, might be "filter." What the effective writer seeks to do is not to seem to be an entirely different person, but rather to demonstrate such a regard for the subject and the needs of readers that what is conveyed through the message are qualities of integrity, good sense, and good will, as well as the particular features of the writer's own style and personality that prevent the writing from appearing nondescript and impersonal. That "appropriate image," then, is not a mask applied over the writer's real face—one's convictions and biases nearly always show through—but a filter that enhances what is really there, in much the same way that a camera filter reduces glare, intensifies colors, and sharpens the photographic image. The creation of an effective persona is almost incidental to the writer who has carefully considered the audience and who has sincerely concerned herself or himself with the issue at hand. Let these, then, be your aims if you would be both an effective and an ethical persuader.

EXERCISE 1–2

A. Identify each of the following as an argument or non-argument.
B. Identify the unstated assumptions, if any, in the arguments. Write them out. Are they as readily acceptable as the arguer assumes? If not, explain why not.
C. Convert the non-arguments into arguments by altering and/or adding to their content.

1. Polly can't be trusted. She cheats at Monopoly.
2. The Vikings beat Columbus to America, so they say.
3. I can't go to the concert because Thursday night is my TV night.
4. Willy: "The street is lined with cars. There's not a breath of fresh air in the neighborhood. The grass don't grow anymore, you can't raise a carrot in the back yard. They should've had a law against apartment houses."

   —Arthur Miller, *Death of a Salesman*
5. Because uneducated and even illiterate people are capable of rational thought and can make themselves understood, it is wrong to say that poor writing reflects poor thinking.
6. The 1987 nomination of Judge Robert Bork to the Supreme Court was successfully opposed by people who objected to his concept of "judicial restraint."
7. Burglar bars may be more dangerous than burglars. They often prevent people from escaping fires in their homes.
8. Dignants are wuffles, and all wuffles garbit. Therefore, dignants garbit.

9. Sometimes people call me an idealist. Well, that is the way I know I am an American. America is the only idealistic nation in the world.
—Woodrow Wilson

10. The more is given the less people will work for themselves, and the less they work the more their poverty will increase.
—Leo Tolstoy, *Help for the Starving*

11. Today, millions of people are unemployed. That, along with the present rate of rising inflation, brings me to the realization we can no longer afford a Republican in the White House.
—Letter to *Dallas Morning News* during the Ford/Carter presidential campaign of 1976

12. Thinking people cannot fail to realize that a Democratic victory would put a liberal, free-spending Congress in virtually complete control of government.
—Letter to *Dallas Morning News* during the Ford/Carter presidential campaign of 1976

13. David and Howard are playing gin rummy. After the first hand is dealt, Howard asks, "Are aces high or low?" David reasons: Either Howard has an ace or he is very crafty. But he isn't crafty at all. Therefore, Howard has an ace.
—Howard Pospesel, *Arguments: Deductive Logic Exercises*

14. Dependency, by its very nature, creates self-doubt, and self-doubt can lead all too quickly to self-hatred.
—Colette Downing, *The Cinderella Complex*

15. English majors should "minor in biology, if only because they need an understanding of organic structure as a way of understanding organic imagery."
—Ann Berthoff, *The Making of Meaning*

16. Elisha Gray and Alexander Graham Bell invented the prototype of the telephone almost simultaneously. Therefore, we should give them equal credit.

17. Australia needs a supplemental source of pure drinking water, and icebergs could be such a source. Therefore, we must find a way of transporting icebergs to Australia.

18. In the future, shuttle astronauts will wear simple overalls rather than cumbersome space suits as long as they remain inside the vehicle.
—*Technology Illustrated*, May 1983

19. All publicity is good, you say? Well, this review attacking your latest movie is publicity. So, according to your reasoning, this review is good!

20. All things worth doing are worth doing well, so washing dishes is worth doing well.

EXERCISE 1-3

Identify the premises and conclusion(s) in the following paragraph. Do you find the argument convincing? Comment.

Sex and reproduction are natural and nonproblematic for all animals except Man. Females come into heat, males are attracted to them, and the species is maintained. Nothing could be simpler. Compare that to the sexual tensions existing among human beings: the teenage girl who waits for a boy to call her, feeling shunned and unattractive; the college student who cannot concentrate on his studies and is contemplating suicide because his girlfriend has broken up with him; the pregnant unmarried career woman who does not believe in abortion but is not sure what other choice she has; the severely depressed housewife whose husband has left her for another woman; the victims of rape, the patrons of pornographic movies, the furtive adulterers, the self-hating promiscuous "sexual athletes." Sex is so simple and straightforward for animals, and so painful for the rest of us (unless we are willing to behave like animals), because we have entered the world of good and evil.
—Harold S. Kushner, *Why Bad Things Happen to Good People*

EXERCISE 1-4

Explain the differences in meaning in the following pairs of terms. Offer an example for each.

argument / persuasion   fallacy / lie   persuade / convince   premise / conclusion   ethical appeal / emotional appeal   assumption / qualification

EXERCISE 1-5

Write a paragraph in which you apply to the editor of the campus newspaper for the position of sports editor; or to the college president for the job of assistant director of fundraising for the school; or to your former rhetoric instructor for the job of grader and teaching assistant. After writing and revising the paragraph, label your conclusion and the premises supporting it, and underline words showing logical relationships and qualifications, such as *because* and *however*.

WHAT SO PROUDLY WE HAILED?

Debbie Sapp
(Student Essay)

1 God bless me, my country, and its flag: I am not a Communist, and by most people's standards I am not even a radical, but I am angry because I stand with a healthy majority of my fellow Americans who cannot sing—standing *or* seated—our national anthem. Folks, to face facts, "The Star-Spangled Banner" (hereafter referred to simply as the SSB) is a real SOB to sing. There. It's been said. I have spoken my vicious, unpatriotic piece. I do not like the national anthem, and I hold that there are plenty of reasons and a good number of alternatives that would justify a change.

2 The exact range of the SSB is nineteen half-steps. The average range of the human singing voice is from one and one-half to two octaves, or eighteen to twenty-four half steps. Those below-average people or those on the lowest end of the "average" voice range are destined never to sing allegiance to their country, at least not without risking a few close friendships. The average people who might be able to fit the SSB into their range are only so lucky when the band starts on the right note. And those few above-average people who can actually sing the anthem well, and can hit "land of the free" on the money every time, are resented by the rest of us who have to stand close to them at football games.

3 Of course, a national anthem is more than just music. The lyrics should express the deepest sympathies of the people who sing it. In the case of the SSB, these people represent an entire nation. So I ask: Does the entire nation hold a grudge against England, and does everyone wish to revel continually in the victory over our British brothers? "The rocket's red glare, the bombs bursting in air . . .!" Is this the appropriate way to begin every sporting event, or to welcome visiting foreign dignitaries (even those from England)? The song in its original form celebrates more than a battle and a flag—it resorts to downright name-calling. In the second, third, and fourth stanzas, of which many people are completely unaware, several offensive lines hold the potential to ignite an international incident, if not a whole new war between the United States and Great Britain, such as: "Their blood [that of the English] has washed out their foul footsteps' pollution." A wonderful tribute to a country that is now our staunchest ally!

4   These words are strong, to say the least; but then, this is powerful poetry. It must be powerful poetry because it is largely unin-
telligible, and most of us seem to require of our best poetry that it
be beyond our comprehension. I admit, although with embarrassment, that until the middle of my freshman year in high school I
thought one of the final lines read: "Oh, Sadists! That star-spangled
banner yet waves. . . ." And I'm afraid even to guess at the number
of Americans with no idea what a *rampart* might be, or what it
means to be spangled, with stars or anything else. Thank heaven we
are not expected to know the last three stanzas of the song; half the
country would be puzzling over the metaphoric message in "foul
footsteps' pollution."

5   Now is a crucial time. Although it is none too soon to change
our national anthem, neither is it too late. If we Americans are shrewd
and quick, the students of the year 2025 will read with a yawn this
brief note in their history texts:

On March 3, 1931, "The Star-Spangled Banner," written in 1814
by Francis Scott Key, was officially adopted as the National Anthem of the United States. Over fifty years later, after having
been deemed too difficult to sing, too esoteric in vocabulary, and
too belligerent in its attitude toward England, it was replaced by
————— .

6   The blank is yet to be filled, but the possibilities are numerous.
Perhaps "America the Beautiful" would do, despite its failure to distinguish the U.S.A. from all of South and Central America, Mexico,
and Canada; for at least "America the Beautiful" is more specific
than the vague flourish of "the land of the free and the home of the
brave." Or we might use "America" (also called "My Country, 'Tis
of Thee"), changing its melody so that it would no longer be identical
with that of "God Save the Queen." Or how about a good, rousing
George M. Cohan song like "Grand Old Flag"? If none of the existing
possibilities seems just right, then a new national spirit of patriotism
and unity could be ignited by the announcement of an anthem-writ-
ing competition. Barry Manilow, are you listening? The time has
come for all true-blue Americans (and even those in off-shades) to
sing together without embarrassment, pain, or bewilderment. Our
nation changes as it grows, with unfair or outdated laws and traditions replaced by new and better ones. Just as blacks were emanci-
pated, just as women were given the vote, so, too, must American
vocal chords be enabled to sing every note of their patriotism.

QUESTIONS AND IDEAS FOR DISCUSSION

1. (a) What main argumentative point (thesis conclusion) does this essay put forward? State it in a sentence. Then state the main supporting points (premises) in one sentence each. Do the premises provide good support for the conclusion? Comment. What, if anything, has the writer failed to consider?

    (b) Identify any verbal signals of argument that you find. Are they sufficient in number and appropriate in meaning?

2. What ideas does the writer appear to hold *a priori* about her subject?

3. What assumptions does the writer appear to have made about her readers? You are one of her readers: Were her assumptions correct in your case? If she were to revise this argument for a broader audience (all the readers of this text as well as her own rhetoric class), what would you suggest she do differently?

4. Of the three appeals—logical, emotional, and ethical—which is strongest in this essay? Why? Does that emphasis seem appropriate?

WHY DON'T WE COMPLAIN?

William F. Buckley, Jr.

1   It was the very last coach and the only empty seat on the entire train, so there was no turning back. The problem was to breathe. Outside the temperature was below freezing. Inside the railroad car, the temperature must have been about 85 degrees. I took off my overcoat, and a few minutes later my jacket, and noticed that the car was flecked with the white shirts of passengers. I soon found my hand moving to loosen my tie. From one end of the car to the other, as we rattled through Westchester County, we sweated; but we did not moan.

2   I watched the train conductor appear at the head of the car. "Tickets, all tickets, please!" In a more virile age, I thought, the passengers would seize the conductor and strap him down on a seat over the radiator to share the fate of his patrons. He shuffled down the aisle, picking up tickets, punching commutation cards. *No one addressed a word to him.* He approached my seat, and I drew a deep breath of resolution. "Conductor," I began with a considerable edge to my voice. . . . Instantly the doleful eyes of my seatmate turned tiredly from his newspaper to fix me with a resentful stare: what question could be so important as to justify my sibilant intrusion into his stupor? I was shaken by those eyes. I am incapable of making a discreet fuss, so I mumbled a question about what time were we due in Stamford (I didn't even ask whether it would be before or after dehydration could be expected to set in), got my reply, and went back to my newspaper and to wiping my brow.

3   The conductor had nonchalantly walked down the gauntlet of eighty sweating American freemen, and not one of them had asked him to explain why the passengers in that car had been consigned to suffer. There is nothing to be done when the temperature *outdoors* is 85 degrees, and indoors the air conditioner has broken down; obviously when that happens there is nothing to do, except perhaps curse the day that one was born. But when the temperature outdoors is below freezing, it takes a positive act of will on somebody's part to set the temperature *indoors* at 85. Somewhere a valve was turned too far, a furnace overstoked, a thermostat maladjusted: something that could easily be remedied by turning off the heat and allowing the great outdoors to come indoors. All this is so obvious. What is not obvious is what has happened to the American people.

4   It isn't just the commuters, whom we have come to visualize as a supine breed who have got onto the trick of suspending their sensory faculties twice a day while they submit to the creeping dissolution of the railroad industry. It isn't just they who have given up

trying to rectify irrational vexations. It is the American people everywhere.

5   A few weeks ago at a large movie theatre I turned to my wife and said, "The picture is out of focus." "Be quiet," she answered. I obeyed. But a few minutes later I raised the point again, with mounting impatience. "It will be all right in a minute," she said apprehensively. (She would rather lose her eyesight than be around when I make one of my infrequent scenes.) I waited. It was *just* out of focus—not glaringly out, but out. My vision is 20-20, and I assume that is the vision, adjusted, of most people in the movie house. So, after hectoring my wife throughout the first reel, I finally prevailed upon her to admit that it *was* off, and very annoying. We then settled down, coming to rest on the presumption that: a) someone connected with the management of the theatre must soon notice the blur and make the correction; or b) that someone seated near the rear of the house would make the complaint in behalf of those of us up front; or c) that—any minute now—the entire house would explode into catcalls and foot stamping, calling dramatic attention to the irksome distortion.

6   What happened was nothing. The movie ended, as it had begun, *just* out of focus, and as we trooped out, we stretched our faces in a variety of contortions to accustom the eye to the shock of normal focus.

7   I think it is safe to say that everybody suffered on that occasion. And I think it is safe to assume that everyone was expecting someone else to take the initiative in going back to speak to the manager. And it is probably true even that if we had supposed the movie would run right through with the blurred image, someone surely would have summoned up the purposive indignation to get up out of his seat and file his complaint.

8   But notice that no one did. And the reason no one did is because we are all increasingly anxious in America to be unobtrusive, we are reluctant to make our voices heard, hesitant about claiming our rights; we are afraid that our cause is unjust, or that if it is not unjust, that it is ambiguous; or if not even that, that it is too trivial to justify the horrors of a confrontation with Authority; we will sit in an oven or endure a racking headache before undertaking a head-on, I'm-here-to-tell-you complaint. That tendency to passive compliance, to a heedless endurance is something to keep one's eyes on—in sharp focus.

9   I myself can occasionally summon the courage to complain, but I cannot, as I have intimated, complain softly. My own instinct is so strong to let the thing ride, to forget about it—to expect that someone will take the matter up, when the grievance is collective, in my

behalf—that it is only when the provocation is at a very special key, whose vibrations touch simultaneously a complexus of nerves, allergies, and passions, that I catch fire and find the reserves of courage and assertiveness to speak up. When that happens, I get quite carried away. My blood gets hot, my brow wet, I become unbearably and unconscionably sarcastic and bellicose: I am girded for a total showdown.

10   Why should that be? Why could not I (or anyone else) on that railroad coach have said simply to the conductor, "Sir,"—I take that back: that sounds sarcastic—"Conductor, would you be good enough to turn down the heat? I am extremely hot. In fact, I tend to get hot every time the temperature reaches 85 degr—" Strike that last sentence. Just end it with the simple statement that you are extremely hot, and let the conductor infer the cause.

11   Every New Year's Eve I resolve to do something about the Milquetoast in me and vow to speak up, calmly, for my rights, and for the betterment of our society, on every appropriate occasion. Entering last New Year's Eve I was fortified in my resolve because that morning at breakfast I had had to ask the waitress three times for a glass of milk. She finally brought it—after I had finished my eggs, which is when I don't want it any more. I did not have the manliness to order her to take the milk back, but settled instead for a cowardly sulk, and ostentatiously refused to drink the milk—though I later paid for it—rather than state plainly to the hostess, as I should have, why I had not drunk it, and would not pay for it.

12   So by the time the New Year ushered out the Old, riding in on my morning's indignation and stimulated by the gastric juices of resolution that flow so faithfully on New Year's Eve, I rendered my vow. Henceforward I would conquer my shyness, my despicable disposition to supineness. I would speak out like a man against the unnecessary annoyances of our time.

13   Forty-eight hours later, I was standing in line at the ski-repair store in Pico Peak, Vermont. All I needed, to get on with my skiing, was the loan, for one minute, of a small screw driver, to tighten a loose binding. Behind the counter in the workshop were two men. One was industriously engaged in servicing the complicated requirements of a young lady at the head of the line, and obviously he would be tied up for quite a while. The other—"Jiggs," his workmate called him—was a middle-aged man, who sat in a chair puffing a pipe, exchanging small talk with his working partner. My pulse began its telltale acceleration. The minutes ticked on. I stared at the idle shopkeeper, hoping to shame him into action, but he was impervious to my telepathic reproof and continued his small talk with his friend,

brazenly insensitive to the nervous demands of six good men who were raring to ski.

14   Suddenly my New Year's Eve resolution struck me. It was now or never. I broke from my place in line and marched to the counter. I was going to control myself. I dug my nails into my palms. My effort was only partially successful:

15   "If you are not too busy," I said icily, "would you mind handing me a screw driver?"

16   Work stopped and everyone turned his eyes on me, and I experienced that mortification I always feel when I am the center of centripetal shafts of curiosity, resentment, perplexity.

17   But the worst was yet to come. "I am sorry, sir," said Jiggs deferentially, moving the pipe from his mouth. "I am not supposed to move. I have just had a heart attack." That was the signal for a great whirring noise that descended from heaven. We looked, stricken, out the window, and it appeared as though a cyclone has suddenly focused on the snowy courtyard between the shop and the ski lift. Suddenly a gigantic Army helicopter materialized, and hovered down to a landing. Two men jumped out of the plane carrying a stretcher, tore into the ski shop, and lifted the shopkeeper onto the stretcher. Jiggs bade his companion good-by, was whisked out the door, into the plane, up to the heavens, down—we learned—to a nearby Army hospital. I looked up manfully—into a score of maneating eyes. I put the experience down as a reversal.

18   As I write this, on an airplane, I have run out of paper and need to reach into my brief case under my legs for more. I cannot do this until my empty lunch tray is removed from my lap. I arrested the stewardess as she passed empty-handed down the aisle on the way to the kitchen to fetch the lunch trays for the passengers up forward who haven't been served yet. "Would you please take my tray?" "Just a *moment*, sir," she said, and marched on sternly. Shall I tell her that since she is headed for the kitchen *anyway*, it cannot delay the feeding of the other passengers by the two seconds necessary to stash away my empty tray? Or remind her that not fifteen minutes ago she spoke unctuously into the loudspeaker the words undoubtedly devised by the airline's highly paid public-relations counselor: "If there is anything I or Miss French can do for you to make your trip more enjoyable, *please* let us—" I have run out of paper.

19   I think the observable reluctance of the majority of Americans to assert themselves in minor matters is related to our increased sense of helplessness in an age of technology and centralized political and economic power. For generations, Americans who were too hot, or too cold, got up and did something about it. Now we call the

plumber, or the electrician, or the furnace man. The habit of looking after our own needs obviously had something to do with the assertiveness that characterized the American family familiar to readers of American literature. With the technification of life goes our direct responsibility for our material environment, and we are conditioned to adopt a position of helplessness not only as regards the broken air conditioner, but as regards the overheated train. It takes an expert to fix the former, but not the latter: yet these distinctions, as we withdrew into helplessness, tend to fade away.

20   Our notorious political apathy is a related phenomenon. Every year, whether the Republican or the Democratic Party is in office, more and more power drains away from the individual to feed vast reservoirs in far-off places; and we have less and less say about the shape of events which shape our future. From this aberration of personal power comes the sense of resignation with which we accept the political dispensations of a powerful government whose hold upon us continues to increase.

21   An editor of a national weekly news magazine told me a few years ago that as few as a dozen letters of protest against an editorial stance of his magazine was enough to convene a plenipotentiary meeting of the board of editors to review policy. "So few people complain, or make their voices heard," he explained to me, "that we assume a dozen letters represent the inarticulated views of thousands of readers." In the past ten years, he said, the volume of mail has noticeably decreased, even though the circulation of his magazine has risen.

22   When our voices are finally mute, when we have finally suppressed the natural instinct to complain, whether the vexation is trivial or grave, we shall have become automatons, incapable of feeling. When Premier Khrushchev first came to this country late in 1959 he was primed, we are informed, to experience the bitter resentment of the American people, against his tyranny, against his persecutions, against the movement which is responsible for the then great number of American deaths in Korea, for billions in taxes every year, and for life everlasting on the brink of disasters; but Khrushchev was pleasantly surprised, and reported back to the Russian people that he had been met with overwhelming cordiality (read: apathy), except, to be sure, for "a few fascists who followed me around with their wretched posters, and should be . . . horse-whipped."

23   I may be crazy, but I say there would have been lots more posters in a society where train temperatures in the dead of winter are not allowed to climb up to 85 degrees without complaint.

QUESTIONS AND IDEAS FOR DISCUSSION

1. What is Buckley's thesis? Does he state it outright? If so, quote it; if not, express it in a declarative statement.

2. Just when we have settled it that *argument* does not mean *quarrel* or *fight*, here comes William Buckley to argue that we should complain. Do *argue* and *complain* mean much the same thing to Buckley? How would he (or how does he) define both terms? Would you have defined them in the same way?

3. This essay supports its conclusions largely by examples drawn from Buckley's own everyday experiences. Can we identify with his experiences—is our response a smile of recognition? What is the effect of the one example that undermines the thesis? Does Buckley dwell on it at too great length?

4. Buckley's tone in this essay is conversational. How does the writer achieve that effect—what choices of words, phrasing, transitions, and humorous touches create it? Give examples.

SUGGESTIONS FOR WRITING AND
FURTHER DISCUSSION

1. Like the student author of "What So Proudly We Hailed?", argue for a change in an existing thing or situation. Your audience is your classmates: Show them why they should take an interest in the subject and why they should agree with your proposal regarding it. You may choose a campus tradition or residency requirement, employers' rules, the burden of income taxes on college students, or your own pet peeve. The possibilities are many.

2. Many readers might take issue with William Buckley's conclusion that we do not complain enough. Some might say that we grumble, and strike, and sue all too readily. If the latter is your contention, write an essay supporting that argument and developed with narrative examples, as Buckley's is. In working out your thesis, think about Buckley's idea that we have a "sense of helplessness in an age of technology and centralized political and economic power." Is he right? If so, do we respond to that feeling by keeping silent, or do we complain all the more?

3. Assume that a friend in another state is planning to buy a car, and, although she is knowledgeable about engines, she recognizes that she has no sense of taste and fears that she will be persuaded to buy something gaudy or ugly—a choice that she will later regret. She asks your advice. Write an essay in which you argue a set of esthetic (as opposed to mechanical) standards by which to judge automobiles, so that your friend will know what to look for.

4. In an essay entitled "How Do You Know It's Good?", art critic Marya Mannes argues that some values *are* absolute, that not everything is relative, limited to context. If you disagree with this assertion, write an essay supporting your belief that all values are relative, giving specific examples (perhaps from the fields of music, art, literature, politics, advertising, or the like) to support your case. You may find it helpful to first read "How Do You Know It's Good?", which comprises a brief chapter in Mannes's *But Will It Sell?*

5. In a book about thought and reasoning, *The Mind in the Making*, James Harvey Robinson asserts:

   Few of us take the pains to study the origin of our cherished convictions; indeed, we have a natural repugnance to so doing. We like to continue to believe what we have been accustomed to accept as true, and the resentment aroused when doubt is cast upon any of our assumptions leads us to seek every manner of excuse for clinging to them. *The result is that most of our so-called reasoning consists in finding arguments for going on believing as we already do.*

   We tend to ignore arguments and information, however telling, that conflict with our preconceptions and prejudices. As an exercise in mental agility and the clearing out of a few cobwebs, not to mention gaining the benefits of seeing things from another person's perspective for a change, write an essay that takes a view *opposite to your own* on some controversial issue (gay rights, bilingual education, abortion, the Equal Rights Amendment, fascism, the insanity defense for murder, the banning of drug abusers from professional sports, or the sale of federal park lands, for example). Treat your assumed stance on the issue seriously; try to offer a sound argument in its support.

6. After writing an essay supporting a viewpoint that in fact you oppose, write an analysis of the difficulties you encountered in the undertaking. Did you find your own position modified in any way after considering an opposite viewpoint?

7. In the same book by James Harvey Robinson quoted above, the author argues that the "good" (that is, socially acceptable or praiseworthy) and the "real" reasons for our opinions are usually quite different from each other. A person might have a whole set of "good" reasons for attending a particular college, for instance, but her real reasons might have more to do with the accessibility of beaches, the fact that her older brother went there, or the fact that her parents refused to pay tuition at any other school. Another person might be opposed to varsity athletics really out of resentment for having no athletic ability himself or herself. A third might oppose the fraternity system as much for having been cut in rush as for the cookie-cutter conformity of the Greeks. Discuss the problem for us, as students of argument and reason, of having "real" reasons that we do not recognize or will not admit. Support your argument with examples.

8. In junior high school I became a Candy Striper at a local hospital. My "good" (socially acceptable) reasons for giving up my Saturday mornings and Monday afternoons to volunteer work you could fill in yourself: to help people in need, to free the nurses from doing minor chores, and so on. My "real" reason was that I liked the uniform. But I came to like the work as well, and I stayed with it for five years through high school and another year in college. Write an essay, illustrated and supported by experiences or observations of your own, in which you demonstrate that a laughable or lamentable motive for doing something can lead to a commendable outcome all the same.

9. Find two or more news articles about an issue or event of current interest. Examine them for instances of selection and charged language. Which seems to be most fair? Which most slanted? Discuss your findings or write an essay in which you argue for your conclusions about the relative fairness of the articles. Be specific in the examples you cite and compare.

2
Creating Arguments

"Know thyself" was an oracle addressed to the individual, charging him to become a person; to know, as a matter of fact, almost everything other than himself, to know the world for what it is, for what it "honestly deeply means," and above all to substitute for the inquiry "What do I think?" the inquiry "What can be thought?" The emphasis is not upon his reason but upon reason; not upon himself but upon his kind. Obeying the oracle, he endeavors to rear within himself that third man who is present when two men speak, and who is happy when they understand each other.

Mark Van Doren

We create arguments every time someone asks us, or we ask ourselves, "Why?" or "What difference does it make?" Arguing is as natural as breathing—and nearly as common. At its best, it is an organic and even creative process, by means of which we discover causes, find solutions, decide on actions and motivations, or interpret our world. It can be a way of "knowing the world for what it is," a search for truth and understanding. At its worst, it is not creation but cloning: the mindless parroting of others' assertions and reasons.

But arguments, however organic their origin, do not grow well without attention. They tend to ramble and sprawl all over the page, or the conversation, unless staked and pruned so that reasons and evidence and the conclusions drawn from both develop in clear, logical relationship to each other. For this reason, many who think about argument consider it in architectural rather than botanical terms. We speak of "building," "constructing," or "shoring up" an argument, and even "hammering home" our points. Certainly argument lends itself to such description. With arguments we impose order; we build foundations upon which our assertions can be supported. Order does not assure a reader's understand-

30

ing, but it makes understanding more likely. Happily, the two processes, if not the two metaphors, work well together. The process of invention and that of development and revision—creation and construction—are not antithetical but complementary.

THE RHETORICAL CONTEXT

An argument begins with a question, a speculation, a reaction, an inspiration—or an assignment. While many arguments are generated spontaneously, the assigned argument is anything but spontaneous. And yet the assigned argument holds just as much potential for creative development as do the others. Your boss or your committee chairperson or your professor presents you with a problem:

"I need a report on the Wight Widget ad campaign. They're not happy with their sales profile since we took over their advertising. Emphasize the positive results if you can find any."

"We need to decide which of the local nonprofit organizations runs the most efficient operation, using donated funds wisely and well. Then we can determine who should be the beneficiary of our fund-raising efforts this year."

"Write an essay advocating or opposing a standardized syllabus and final exam for English 101."

—and you are on your own. When the problem is not one that first occurred to you, you may think initially that you have nothing to say. The whole matter may seem either too thorny (the widgets *haven't* sold), too obvious, or too dull to bother with. Or it may seem wrong-headed: If you oppose the very existence of English 101, how are you supposed to argue for or against a standardized syllabus?

But in the world at large, as well as in the academic world, many—if not most—papers are written in response to just such a request or assignment. So how do you create a convincing argument with a believable persona when even the subject is not of your own choosing? Fortunately, even the narrowest assignment usually leaves you the freedom to focus the paper as you see fit, within certain parameters. Those parameters typically include:

1. **General subject matter,** whether the first law of thermodynamics or the need for mass transit in your city.
2. **A prescribed or suggested approach to the subject,** such as opposition to or support for new zoning laws, or a favorable report to your superiors at the McClintock Company on the results of your new marketing strategy. If you cannot, in all honesty and fairness and self-interest, take the

prescribed approach (perhaps the new marketing strategy has failed abysmally), take what approach you can and express it with tact, or choose another subject if you have that option.

3. **A length requirement or guideline,** perhaps a certain number of pages in a college assignment, or "short enough to fit in the annual report" in a business assignment.

4. **An indication of a need for documented evidence** to support your thesis, and perhaps an indication of the extent of source materials required.

Such requirements give the writer an understanding of the limitations of the assignment, but not of the possibilities. However uninspiring the guidelines, you may have little choice but to come up with something. You can wait for the muse to speak, or for lightning to strike; or you can invite inspiration by more prosaic, but effective, means. Begin by considering the rhetorical context in which you will be working. Every written message is created out of a rhetorical context. It has a *purpose* (sometimes a complex one) and a potential *audience,* and communicates both *content* and a *persona* (the reader's sense of the writer). By carefully considering the first two, purpose and audience, you will discover what content your argument needs to develop and will create a believable persona.

Consider Your Purpose

You can save yourself any number of missteps and false starts if you consider your purpose before you write. After all, if your boss asks you for a summary of activity on the Wight Widget account during the past year, your purpose is to provide succinct chronological information, not an assessment of the current advertising campaign. If your committee chairperson wants a memo suggesting how to determine which nonprofit group should receive funds, your purpose is to argue for a set of standards for making that decision, not to leap ahead to a recommendation of a specific charity. And if your professor assigns a paper on the projected impact of plus/minus grading on grade point averages, your purpose is to estimate the consequences of such a policy on GPAs, not on the mental health of honors students. Sometimes you can broaden the scope of an argument; sometimes you can redirect it toward your own ends; but always, you must keep sight of your original purpose.

When a writing task is assigned, make sure you understand just what you have been asked to do. Just as important, make sure you understand what you have not been asked to do—and, on occasion, what you have been asked *not* to do! If your supervisor says, "Now I know you think the Wight Widget campaign was a stupid idea from the start, but please don't ride *that* hobby horse in your report," or your professor says, "Please stick to the quantitative impact of plus/minus grading and don't launch into a diatribe on 'Teachers Who Done Me Wrong' "—keep those limits in mind as you contemplate your purpose.

Consider Your Audience

As you think about the issue about which you will write, you must keep constantly in mind the image of the intended and potential readers of your paper. Those readers offer at once a curb and a spur to invention and development of argument; as you write, you must take into account both what the readers are likely to know and not to know about the subject, and what biases and misconceptions they are likely to harbor about the subject and possibly about you, the writer. Keeping the readers in mind, along with your purpose in addressing them, keeps you on the path and out of the underbrush of tangential issues and unnecessary pleas and explanations.

Who are your readers? For papers written for this course, one will generally be the instructor. But not just the instructor: Another may be your roommate or spouse or a friend to whom you will read a preliminary draft. Then, too, at some point members of your composition class are likely to read the essay or hear it read. For papers written as part of your job, one reader nearly always will be your boss. But your boss's boss may be another reader, your colleagues both in and outside the company a collective third. The potential audience for your essay is both large and uncertain—the identity, biases, knowledge, and frame of mind of them all impossible to know for certain as you write. And yet some consideration of just those matters—the identity, biases, knowledge, and disposition of the readers—is essential to successful writing of any kind. If you bore your readers by explaining terms they already understand, or condescend to them, or baffle them with unfamiliar terms, you will probably not convince them that you are a person whose opinions they should value.

This is the paradox of the writer's situation: To know the audience is both crucial to establishing an effective persona and apparently nearly impossible. Even if you know the identity of at least one reader positively—your rhetoric instructor, for example—what do you really know about him? He is college educated, with one or more advanced degrees from a large midwestern university (according to diplomas on the wall in his office); tall, Anglo, with sandy hair and hazel eyes; married, with a couple of children (judging from the wedding band he wears and the snapshots of children on his office desk). And even if you know these things about your instructor, what do you know about the extent of his knowledge or about his values? How much is he likely to know about the pros and cons of nuclear energy, U.S. Central American policy, the need for government subsidy of Olympic contenders or of the fine arts, or the advantages of hiking? What are his biases likely to be concerning the issue at hand?

Stereotypes, however noxious the term may be in other contexts, offer some help to you in search of your reader. **Stereotypes** are conventional characteristics of groups as perceived by outsiders or by members of the group themselves. They can be misleading and unfair, and even at best they overlook individual variations. Carefully considered, however, they can offer a starting point in reader analysis. Your instructor, for example, because of his education, is likely to have a good vocabulary and at least a basic understanding of nuclear energy. He probably knows, too, that American athletes operate at a financial disadvantage compared to Eastern European Olympic hopefuls who are supported by their governments. He is likely to be reasonably well informed about current events, though his knowledge of literature may surpass his knowledge of Latin America. These generalizations, stereotyped though they are, are probably sound. So you have some idea, by considering the stereotypical characteristics of a college instructor, of which terms you will need to explain and which you may take for granted. You also have some idea, although here we tread upon uncertain ground, of what his preconceptions about the subject might be.

However, you may pursue stereotypes too far. College instructors are a notoriously liberal bunch, so you might decide that yours probably opposes the use of nuclear power to develop weapons and perhaps even to produce energy. He may well be a pacifist, and thus may oppose American military intervention in troubled Central American countries. He is bound to be bookish and may regard hiking as a pastime suitable only for the hardy simple-minded. He probably likes symphonic music and considers country-and-western lyrics maudlin. Chances are, he is bored with football and considers fraternities a waste of time. And so on.

Stereotypes of this more particular sort differ from the preceding generalizations about education and familiarity with certain subjects. The more you pinpoint characteristics, the more likely you are to be wrong. Such stereotypes are more likely to shut off thought than to open up possibilities for developing arguments. Your instructor may very well be a fan of both football and Willie Nelson, and somewhere in his dark past he may have joined a fraternity. If you write an essay opposing scholarships for football players simply in an attempt to "write what sells," you may find the attempt self-defeating. You may also run into trouble with classmates or other readers who like football and support the concept of athletic scholarships, by your casual assumption that anyone who reads your paper is opposed to them. Besides, if your instructor is fair-minded, he will give high marks to a well-written essay on *any* side—there are often more than two sides—of an issue.

The writer is at best always a bit uncertain of the reader, even if the two are the closest of friends. If the reader is unknown, or multiple, the difficulty is compounded. But one cannot type away in a vacuum as if there will be no reader, or behave as if the reader is a passive sponge that will soak up the writer's ideas, however messily she spills them out on the page. Nor can one assume that there will be but a single reader, even for a class assignment or a confidential report. Nor that any single reader has but one dimension. Rhetorician F. L. Lucas has claimed (in "What Is Style?") that a spoken or written encounter between two minds involves six identities:

1. A's real self
2. A's perception of himself
3. A's perception of B
4. B's real self
5. B's perception of himself
6. B's perception of A

And that six-way encounter is for an audience of one. If twenty members of your rhetoric class are reading copies of your essay, you may marvel that the room can hold all the operating personas. Certainly you cannot hope to hold them all in mind at once as you write. The resulting essay would be overly cautious—or confused.

The Invented Reader

What you as a writer must do, finally, is to visualize an appropriate reader for the argument you propose. The actual readers will accommodate themselves to what rhetorician Walter Ong has termed the "invented reader" insofar as they are comfortable doing so. For example, the appropriate invented reader for an essay on hiking to be submitted for a composition course might be a person with a high school education (or more) who has never tried hiking, but would at least be willing to consider the idea. For this reader a certain level of vocabulary, knowledge, and experience can be assumed: You will not need to identify the Alps, but you may need to identify the location of the less well known Davis Mountains if your discussion centers on hiking there. You will not need to define *knapsack*, but you may want to indicate desirable features in a backpack. You will not need to convince your reader that mountains are beautiful or that the country is more healthful than the city, but you may need to offer some convincing arguments that hiking offers the best way to enjoy the outdoors.

This "invented" reader helps you to determine which topics to explore for her benefit and your own, and what arguments to offer in support of your conclusion; she also saves you from needlessly agonizing over whether or not your instructor (and possibly classmates) likes hiking. Of course, if you *know* that your actual reader despises any setting more rural than Central Park or any activity more strenuous than hailing a taxi, your arguments may need to be fuller and stronger than if you know that reader to be not only a hiker but also a proficient technical climber who has scaled Mt. McKinley. Should the latter be true, on the other hand, you hardly need persuade her at all. Try an essay on racquetball.

The point at which real and invented reader meet is the moment of actual reading: a moment and place at which you may not be present to explain, interpret, or defend what you have written and why you have chosen to argue as you have. So the invented reader must be a comfortable fit for the actual reader: The latter is appealed to as a reasonable, well-educated, and informed person, and indeed wants to be just that sort of individual. She accepts the voice that regards her so highly and is favorably disposed toward its assertions. She begins to regard the issue through the selective filter of your persona.

As you think about your subject and jot down ideas for developing it, invent an appropriate and plausible reader for a discussion of the issue at hand, and consider, treading lightly on the stereotypes:

1. How much is the reader likely to know about the subject?
2. How much, in the way of background and explanation, does the reader need to know?
3. What are the reader's biases and misconceptions about this issue likely to be?
4. How does the reader regard the writer (if at all) before reading the paper?

The fourth question, as discussed earlier, matters if the reader's opinion of the writer is very strong—especially if it is strongly negative. In this case, the writer must take special pains to be diplomatic, convincing, and thorough. Ideally, that care would be taken in any event. If you have considered the issue, your purpose in writing about it, and the nature and needs of your intended audience, you will discover what you need to say, and how much. In so doing, you will also create a persona that will add to the persuasiveness of your essay. You will, without being cynical or manipulative about it, write what really sells.

EXERCISE 2–1

Write down all the stereotypical characteristics (including fields of knowledge, likes and dislikes) you can deduce from your observations of your rhetoric classmates. Limit yourself to characteristics that seem typical of a majority of the students. Also list probable characteristics and areas of knowledge for your instructor. Discuss your "audience analysis" with the rest of the class. Are most people in agreement?

WORKING TOWARD A THESIS

Having marked some boundaries by preliminary thinking about the rhetorical context of purpose and audience, you will find that the subject at hand has assumed a more manageable size. Your specific *thesis* should be your next concern if the purpose and audience or the assignment itself has not already suggested the thesis. **The thesis of any organized expository or argumentative paper is the statement of its controlling idea, the main thrust of the argument.** This thesis defines the scope and limitations of the topic you propose to address. It states what is important to you—what you will show your readers to be important—about your subject. It should anticipate and promise answers to a reader's bored or skeptical "Why?" or "So what?"

Your complete thesis statement, which will consist of a conclusion and its main supporting points, may appear at the beginning of your paper, at the end of the introductory paragraph or section, or in the conclusion. It is even possible that the complete form of the thesis (including the supporting points) may not be written out as such in the finished essay. Instead, only its main clause, the asserted claim, may be stated. In that case, the supporting points still are spelled out, but separately, as topic sentences within the essay. But, regardless of the final form and placement of the thesis, a well-formulated thesis is always limited sufficiently and precisely enough to be stated in a single, declarative sentence. It thereby serves as a guide for the writer developing an essay and assures unity in the argument.

Once you have your purpose and audience clearly in mind, various invention strategies can help you formulate a workable thesis—one that will make clear just what ideas your argument needs to develop. We will look at three kinds of invention strategies in this chapter: using topical checklists, finding and resolving contradictions, and examining influences and consequences. These strategies are not mutually exclusive; on occasion you will need all three—and perhaps the muse as well.

Invention Strategy: Topical Checklists

Discovering possibilities and developing a thesis that will permit their realization is the creative part of even the most prosaic assignment. Paradoxically, one kind of stimulus for argumentative creativity may be

found in formulaic lists of stock issues, or **topics:** not lists of essay assignments to which we sometimes apply the term *topics,* but lists of
possibilities for developing different kinds of subjects.

The classical rhetoricians divided the topics into "common" and
"special" categories, according to whether the subject was an ordinary
one or a matter for public deliberation. As an example of the latter, a
speech presenting a choice between possible courses of action—perhaps
whether or not to grant diplomatic recognition to Cuba—would take up
the overriding topic of advantage: Which course of action would be more
advantageous to us? The arguer would then consider whether to develop
the argument according to advantages of security or those of honor, or
perhaps both. (If the United States were to recognize Cuba, perhaps that
closer relationship with a neighboring country would lead to strategic
advantages over the USSR. Or perhaps we should consider the humani-
tarian and diplomatic obligations a large and powerful country owes to
one smaller and weaker.) Subcategories of the topics of security and honor
then stimulate the discovery of further supporting arguments. These categories were set down in the anonymous *Rhetorica ad Herennium* some
two thousand years ago, and yet they are still relevant. When arguing in
favor of one course of action over others, we still work from the topic of
advantage to discover ways in which the action we favor will serve the
interests of our audience. And, as we address the interests and needs of
our audience, we create a considerate and empathetic persona, increasing
the ethical appeal of our arguments.

The topics can serve as aids to *invention* of arguments, not merely
as aids to uncovering some preexisting arguments of superior merit.
Rarely is there but one way to make a point; by mulling over a topical
checklist, the writer can circumvent the writer's block of having "nothing to say" and can discover a number of possibilities for developing a
thesis. The important thing is to ask questions. The following list of
topical questions may help you formulate a preliminary thesis or may
suggest to you still other questions about your subject.

1. **Exactly what is my subject?** Do I need to define it more clearly? Has
   my subject been misunderstood or misconstrued?
2. **Do I need or want to emphasize positive or negative aspects of my
   subject?** What are those aspects?
3. **Can my subject be divided up into parts?** Is one aspect more important
   or more relevant than others? What do I need or want to stress?
4. **Just what does my subject remind me of?** What associations does it have
   for me? Is my subject, whether a thing, a person, or an event, similar to
   another thing, person, or event that is probably familiar to my readers?
   Are there any unexpected and enlightening similarities? Is the comparison favorable or unfavorable? Does the comparison make my subject
   easier to understand?

5. **What caused or created my subject, if an event or a thing?** Would understanding the cause or precedent make it easier to understand my subject?
6. **What effects has my subject had or is it likely to have?** Are the effects important or unexpected?

An example will illustrate the usefulness of asking questions to generate content for a paper. Suppose that you have been asked to write an argumentative essay on rock music. Specifically, you are asked to defend or attack some aspect of rock to an audience of your peers, most of whom enjoy at least some rock music. You, too, like rock music, but you draw a blank or your response seems to you self-evident and not in need of justification: "Well, I like it. . . . So who doesn't?" What *about* rock music? Looking at the list of questions above and adding to it further questions as they occur to you, you consider what rock music is and what associations it brings to mind. The checklist questions elicit the following responses from you:

Beatles. Stones. Electric instruments. Repetition, heavy beat. Most effective played at full volume. Soul music influence (according to Mick Jagger). Less twangy than country; faster beat than soul or folk; lyrics less sentimental than other popular music forms—more inclined to the bizarre or even the humorous. Less associated with protest than is folk music. Does have connotative associations with youth, rebellion, desire to shock, intense sexuality. Often associated with the youth rebellion and "free love" movement of the '60s. I don't like ALL forms of rock—'70s acid rock, for instance, or the really mindless primitivism of some punk rock groups.

Of your responses to the questions, one may touch a chord of interest and of memory: Perhaps it is rock music's debt to soul. You remember reading an interview with Mick Jagger in which Jagger acknowledged the great influence soul music has had on his own work. That creative transformation of older forms—didn't rock owe something to country music as well?—would support a strong defense of rock, especially against the charge that "it all sounds just alike," that rock music lacks creativity. Once you have narrowed your ideas and found specific threads that tie them together, you are well on your way to a thesis, and to an essay.

Other possible essays could have been generated from your answers: You might have defended the social relevance of rock by discussing the development of its lyrics of protest. You might have contrasted "classic" rock with what you regard as inferior and transient forms evolved from it, such as acid or punk rock. The whole point of the topics, or "stock issues," as they are also known, is to break the vacuum of the writer's first response to an assigned topic: "So what?" If you can come up with an approach that you can believe in, that you find worth developing, the ethical appeal of your argument will be strong.

In breaking the vacuum, you also begin to work toward what rhetorician Sheridan Baker has called the "argumentative edge" of your thesis—giving your paper a reason for being, an answer to the "So what?" question. Your thesis will have an argumentative edge if it takes a stance toward its subject: "Rock music is a popular form of music" is no more than a statement of the obvious, but "The appeal of rock music will endure into the next century" has some meat on its rhetorical bones. You have asserted a claim in the latter sentence; you have something to prove to your reader.

Analyzing your subject through considering topical questions is especially useful in narrowing a broad subject to manageable proportions for a short paper. "Rock music" is broad enough to serve as the subject of an entire book; "the relationship of rock music concerts to hearing loss" or "logistical problems in staging outdoor rock concerts" might be developed in a research paper; and "the artistic impact of the Beatles' *Abbey Road* album" could serve as the subject for a shorter argument.

Once the subject is narrowed appropriately, it still must be focused; to do so, you will need to develop a "because" clause—a *premise*—to show your reasons for making the thesis assertion. Finding the support you need will send you back to the topical checklist and perhaps to the library. The kinds of theses likely to emerge from this process of narrowing and focusing will center on questions of *fact* and questions of *definition:* What is X? What does X mean? In both cases, the "because" clause will explain and much of the body of the paper will illustrate the thesis assertion.

EXERCISE 2-2

A. Apply questions in the topical checklist on pages 38–39 to three or four of the following subjects. What additional questions occur to you for these subjects? Based on the answers you develop, suggest two or three tentative thesis assertions for each subject. Your audience is your rhetoric classmates, and your purpose is to persuade them to take some kind of action—you must decide what kind. You wish to project an honest, believable, and convincing persona, which you will do by looking hard at the subject and kindly at the readers.

The insanity defense for accused criminals
Jogging
The results of the next presidential (or congressional) election
Academic cheating
Keeping dogs as pets in apartments
The Motion Picture Academy's rating system for movies

B. For each of the thesis assertions developed in part A, answer the following questions about your audience:

1. How much are my readers likely to know about this subject? For what aspects of it will I need to provide background information, and in what detail?
2. How interested are my readers likely to be in this subject? If their interest is likely to be low, how can I generate greater interest? What kinds of appeals are they likely to respond to?
3. Are my readers likely to agree with my position on the issue(s), or disagree? If they are likely to disagree, with what kinds of arguments and illustrations might I convince them to hear me out, and perhaps even to change their minds?
4. Are the readers likely to regard me as trustworthy and knowledgeable on this subject? If not, how can I win their confidence?

C. Modify your "because" clause (or add one if you have none) for each of the assertions developed in part A after considering what arguments will most effectively reach your audience, based on your analysis in part B.

Invention Strategy: Finding and Resolving Contradictions

Sometimes, of course, narrowing a topic to a component element will not satisfy your purpose; and sometimes a topical checklist will not help you discover the most compelling and relevant aspects of a particular problem. A second invention strategy—finding and resolving contradictions in the subject—can supplement or replace the topical checklists in those cases. This strategy begins with a close and critical look at the subject with a specific objective in mind: contradictions. Look for the claims that don't quite mesh, the experiments that reach different conclusions, the experts who disagree with each other, the "facts" that are in some way incompatible with other "facts" about the subject.

Take, for example, the subject of smoking. Suppose that, as an employee of Medicare, you've been asked by your boss to prepare a report on the economic costs to American society of tobacco smoking. A preliminary thesis assertion would probably come immediately to mind: The economic costs of smoking are enormous. But you reserve judgment and do some research. You find that the Surgeon General's 1979 report on smoking estimated the economic impact of smoking at $27 billion, including the cost of "decreased work productivity" due to cigarette breaks, absences due to smoking-induced respiratory ailments, and the like. You also skim a report from the U. S. Public Health Service that attributes to tobacco use medical costs of $23 billion each year and "another $30 billion lost to society because of illness and premature death."

So far, so good. But then you turn up a more recent study made by an esteemed group of Stanford University researchers, sponsored by the National Bureau of Economic Research. This group of researchers argues that the comparatively large number of smokers who die before reaching retirement age help fund Social Security and Medicare through the taxes they pay during their working years—while those same smokers die too soon to receive many (or any) benefits in return. Seventeen percent fewer smokers live to age 65 than do nonsmokers, thereby actually *saving* the system from $10,000 to $20,000 apiece, for a total of some $14.5 billion in benefits uncollected by smokers born in 1920 alone. *Now* you have a problem to solve, and that problem will help you define both the scope of your thesis and the content of your argument. Is smoking an economic drain on society or, in a perverse and surprising way, an economic boon? Resolving the contradiction between the studies becomes your purpose; your thesis will remain an unanswered question—but far from a directionless or unfocused one—as you suspend judgment and work out the problem.

In using this approach to the invention of arguments, you will find that the contradictions typically fall into one of three categories, each of which will lead to a particular kind of argument:

1. *Real contradictions* concerning questions of fact. Where you find factual error, your thesis offers a corrective to the error, and your argument resolves the contradiction through *evidence* and *explanation.*
2. *Apparent contradictions* centering on verbal misunderstandings and differing constructions of key concepts. Where you find verbal misunderstanding, your thesis offers clarification, and your argument resolves the contradiction through *redefinition* and *illustration.* *
3. *Apparent contradictions* involving paradox.† Where you find paradox, your thesis unites the supposedly incompatible elements, and your argument resolves the contradiction through *synthesis*, reconciling the incompatible ideas through a deeper understanding of the subject.

You may determine that the smoking problem demonstrates a real contradiction between incompatible "facts." You resolve it as you examine the evidence closely and determine that a number of the dollar figures reached in the various studies are essentially unknowable statistics. How, for example, can we put an accurate dollar figure on the pro-

---

*Chapter 3, "Definition in Argument," discusses in more detail the central role definition plays in argument.

†A paradox is an apparent contradiction that is nonetheless true.

ductivity lost to smoking breaks on the job? You may decide that the Stanford researchers' numbers make more economic sense than the doomsayers' figures.

Or you may conclude, after looking at the various reports, that the contradictory conclusions stem from verbal disagreement only: Most of the studies focus on costs demonstrably incurred (such as medical bills); some focus on costs presumably incurred (such as decreased work efficiency); and the Stanford study focuses on costs presumably avoided by the premature deaths of smokers. Therein may lie the problem: These studies reflect different senses of *cost*. Pinpointing those differences may well show that the contradictory results are only apparent, not real. The problem is a matter of definition, not substantive disagreement.

Then, too, the Stanford study may turn out to illuminate a paradox rather than a factual contradiction. You may conclude that smoking both costs the system and saves the system. The net result may be a negligible economic impact, and such may be the conclusion of your report.

Searching out and resolving contradictions in your subject has several advantages to the writer of argument. It is a strategy that compels you to postpone judgment—and premature judgment, as semanticist S. I. Hayakawa and others have noted, closes the mind and makes developing arguments more difficult. Moreover, this approach provides a focus, a goal, and a direction to pursue that goal. It gives new life to the subject, new interest for both writer and reader. We all enjoy seeing a thorny problem solved—and even more, solving it!

EXERCISE 2–3

A. Identify two or three contradictory notions, either inherent or merely apparent, in the following subjects:

pornography (For example: Some say it is "victimless" crime; some say it victimizes women and children.)
euthanasia
equal pay for women
electing, rather than appointing, judges
"pot luck" roommates
television ads for beer and wine
careers in the military
government subsidies to tobacco farmers
surrogate mothers' bearing children for others
organ transplantation
bilingual education

B. Choose three of the contradictions you have discovered and identify them as primarily factual, verbal, or paradoxical.
C. Develop thesis sentences that propose a resolution to each of the three contradictions identified in part B.
D. Suppose that you will write a paper using one thesis developed in part C. How might you need to modify it to reach an audience consisting of the members of your rhetoric class? Discuss briefly.

Invention Strategy: Examining Influences and Consequences

A third strategy for developing arguments focuses on what has influenced your subject and what your subject in turn has influenced.* After all, in this world nothing but a writer facing a blank sheet of paper exists in a vacuum. Considering influences and consequences can reveal important and overlooked aspects of a subject as you identify those influences and distinguish relationship from mere coincidence.

And, in fact, such an examination will help you develop an argument much more satisfactorily than will approaching your subject from two other perspectives that we asssociate with argument even more frequently. The first of these is the question of **policy:** "What should be done?" or "What stance should be taken?" The second is the question of **value:** "What is X worth?" Two examples will illustrate the developmental difficulties policy and value theses create for a writer. Returning to the problems posed a student writer and a fund-raiser earlier in the chapter, we might develop theses such as the following:

A standardized syllabus and final exam should not be adopted for English 101, because standardization interferes with academic freedom and inhibits the flexibility needed to address the individual needs of classes and to reflect the individual teaching styles of professors.

The Children's Hospital, because it has a computerized central supply and planning office, does a superb job of using funds efficiently.

Both of these proposed theses seem all right. The first one in particular sounds full of developmental possibilities—or at least of long-winded

---

*And I, in turn, have been greatly influenced in my thinking on this particular strategy by Lawrence D. Green's thought-provoking "Enthymemic Invention and Structural Prediction" in *College English* (41.6: 623–34) and by the excellent classroom handouts generously shared with me by Carol Ann Britt of the University of Texas at San Antonio and Barbara J. Biasiolli of St. Mary's University.

phrases. But, surprisingly, both have problems that will hinder their development into full, well-reasoned arguments.

First, the student's proposed thesis about a standardized syllabus presents a complex developmental problem. It sets up a question of policy—that is, a discussion of what *should* be done—and what kind of issue could be more suitable to argument? But the student writer can't persuade an uninformed or skeptical audience to support a policy until she has established the values on which the policy is to be based and considered the influences leading to and consequences following from that policy. Then, too, there are some slippery terms to define and illustrate: *standardization, academic freedom, flexibility.* And all of this should *precede* the writer's declaration of the thesis, unless she is addressing people who already fully agree with her assertions—and if so, what need is there for persuasion?

Next, the fund-raiser's argument centers on evaluation: The Children's Hospital does a great job. The problem again will lie in development. Just what constitutes a "great job"? Theses centering on questions of value tend to get sidetracked into clarification and defense of the writer's chosen criteria of value rather than the specific issue at hand. For instance, *does* computerization alone automatically make an organization efficient?

It is the matter of audience that makes policy and value questions risky choices for theses if we truly wish to persuade. Both of these sample arguments are headed for trouble once the writers recall their rhetorical context and consider their audience—each with its probable questions, preconceptions, and doubts—and attempt to develop a convincing paper. If the audience does not share the writer's hierarchy of values, the paper is doomed to rhetorical failure; if it does share those values, the argument may be unnecessary and therefore seem trivial.

All the same, the point is *not* that you should avoid all questions of policy or value; they are important to argument. Value and policy arguments may develop naturally in conclusions to papers. And in appropriate contexts (when you are addressing an audience already predisposed to agree with you) either can serve as theses. Rather, the point is that such statements can lead you to a dead end; they provide little help in generating and developing the basic structure of a written argument. So, unless your assignment specifies a policy or value thesis, **avoid creating theses centering on questions of policy or questions of value.**

But theses centering on questions of influence can lead to well-developed arguments on the same subjects. And because they have greater persuasive possibilities, they can even enable you to steer the reader toward policy and value conclusions that follow from the influences and consequences you demonstrate. If, for example, you believe that athletes should be tested regularly for drug use, what kinds of reasons could you offer in support of that policy? Some possibilities: "Drugs are bad" (value statement); "Public health is more important than privacy" (value statement); "People in public life should be compelled to set a good example for the rest of us" (policy statement). But each of these claims would immediately and unproductively alienate part of your audience, and each would be difficult to "prove." Instead, you might try a different approach to both subject and audience:

Testing athletes for drug use leads to improvement in the overall quality of athletics because precautionary procedures of this kind encourage athletes to maintain their health and fitness.

This thesis focuses on influences and consequences rather than values or policy. If you can demonstrate that the relationships you claim here do indeed exist, you can persuade your reader of the validity of your conclusion: "Testing athletes for drug use leads to improvement in the overall quality of athletics." It then becomes much easier to further assert, by way of conclusion to your essay, that if we grant that drug abuse is undesirable (an easily accepted value claim) and if you have demonstrated that testing athletes really does lead to greater health and fitness among athletes (the main thrust of your argument), we cannot deny the reasonableness of the policy claim that athletes *should* be so tested.

THE ENTHYMEME AS THESIS

To demonstrate that the relationships you claim do exist, you should first express your thesis as an **enthymeme.** *The enthymeme is a core argument consisting of an assertion and a "because" clause justifying that assertion.* The assertion is the conclusion to the argument, and the "because" clause is a premise. An enthymeme has three component elements, or **terms:** the subject term of the conclusion (A, restated in the premise as A'), the predicate term of the conclusion (B), and the predicate term of the premise (C). There must be three terms—that is, B and C must be distinct concepts, not restatements of each other. Without three terms, as we shall see later, you have an assertion, not an argument. For the purpose of developing a thesis, an enthymeme takes the following form:

—A—   ———————B———————
Subject   Active, Transitive Verb   Object   (CONCLUSION)
                        BECAUSE

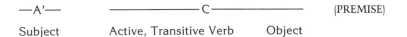

—A'—	———————C———————	(PREMISE)
Subject	Active, Transitive Verb Object	

In any enthymeme, an implicit relationship between B and C underlies the two expressed relationships between A and B and between A' and C. The implicit premise, C ↔ B, should express an idea that the audience can reasonably be expected to grant without argument.

The argument about drug abuse fits the enthymemic model:

(A) Testing athletes for drug use (B) leads to quality athletic performance BE-CAUSE (A') precautionary measures of this kind (C) promote health and fitness.

It makes a claim—"Testing athletes for drug use leads to quality athletic performance"—based on a supporting claim about the influence of fear on athletes' behavior: "Precautionary measures of this kind promote health and fitness." The conclusion is further based on an implicit idea linking those two:

(C) What promotes health and fitness (B) leads to quality athletic performance.

The implicit part of the argument should be, and here is, the kind of statement that your audience can be relied on to grant. It is the shared ground, the **major premise,** from which you will base and develop your explicit argument.

The expressed premise, known as the **minor premise,** should make an association between ideas for which an audience will expect further argument and explanation. Here, the statement that "precautionary measures such as drug testing promote health and fitness" expresses an idea that not everyone shares. Some say that such measures promote only cheating. Some say that such measures lead to paranoia among athletes, a state hardly likely to promote health and fitness. Others might assert that no positive correlation can be shown between the absence of drugs in the system and good physical condition. Still others might question just what the arguer means by *health* or *fitness*. So the writer here has some defining and explaining to do, and needs to muster evidence and examples to support the premise.

If the major premise is granted and the minor premise is demonstrated persuasively, the final business of an argument is to make the assertion that is your thesis. And, if you have done your job well, that thesis will appear inevitable and incontrovertible to a reasonable reader.

Guidelines for Developing a Thesis Enthymeme

1. The thesis must have three terms: The stated premise must not just restate the conclusion in different words, but must share one term with the conclusion.

   - Two terms constitute an assertion only, not an argument, and thus lead to rhetorical dead ends.
   - Four terms cannot be linked logically in a *single* unified argument.

2. The thesis should be expressed as a main clause and a dependent ("because") clause.

3. The verbs in both clauses should be active transitive verbs that show *influence* (such as verbs of *consequence*).

   - Avoid passive verbs; they obscure the true agent of an action.
   - Avoid copulative ("to be") verbs; they lead to redundant arguments with only two terms.
   - Avoid verbs of policy ("should," "must," "ought to," etc.); they lead to arguments with only two terms.
   - Avoid verbs of evaluation; they lead to vague claims or arguments that defend the chosen values more than they discuss the intended subject.

4. The complete enthymeme need not appear as a single sentence in the essay, though its conclusion (the thesis assertion) and minor premise will be stated at the points where they are demonstrated. The major premise may or may not be stated explicitly.

SHAPING THE ARGUMENT

In your written argument, the shared idea of the major premise makes an effective introduction, enhancing your ethical appeal to your readers. Making a case for the minor premise is the primary work of the essay, and you may organize that case in a number of ways. You need to accomplish the following, however you arrange the essay:

1. Show that the terms A′ and A are indeed redefinitions of the same term.
2. Define and illustrate B and C. The enthymeme tells you how to limit and focus your explanations of the terms:

   a. C in terms of its relation to A′.
   b. B in terms of its relation to C.

3. Establish the relationships C ↔ B and A′ → C through explanation and illustration.

You may begin with any of the three terms except A, since the whole thrust of the argument is to move toward establishing the relationship A ≅ B. One way—though by no means the only way—to organize an argumentative essay based on an enthymeme is to move from major premise (defining terms B and C and relating B to C) to minor premise (defining A′ and C and relating A′ to C) to conclusion (defining A, showing that it is but a restatement of A′, and relating it to B).

Major Premise	Introduction	C ↔ B
Minor Premise	Body of Essay ("Because" Clause)	A′ → C
Conclusion	Thesis Assertion	A → B

An example will illustrate how this process works. As an intern for a U. S. Senator from a northeastern state, you have been asked to prepare a paper on the subject of farm subsidies. The Senator is undecided whether or not to vote in favor of an upcoming bill eliminating most of those subsidies in an effort to balance the federal budget. You do some research and decide, to your surprise, that farm subsidies actually hurt farmers in the long run. But, although from a heavily industrialized state, the Senator has a number of farmers in his constituency; he will need some persuading to see the issue as you now understand it. So you work on a core enthymeme that will help you find the strategy you need. It develops along these lines:

Farm subsidies should be eliminated.

No—only two terms and a policy assertion. The Senator would never accept that right off the bat. Besides, this is in passive voice and obscures the agent: The Senate has to act, though I don't want to dwell on that unpleasant fact until I've made my case.

Farm subsidies are harmful in the long run.

Not enough—only two terms and a value assertion. "To be" verb doesn't point toward any specific action.

Farm subsidies are harmful in the long run and therefore should be eliminated.

No—still nothing specific to work with; just combines value and policy claims.

OK: Time out. Just what *is* so bad about farm subsidies? They hurt farmers. *How?* Well, all the data I've found suggests a kind of rebound effect from the huge imbalances subsidies create in supply and demand. But how can I convince the Senator that's so? He would probably grant that imbalances in supply and demand are bad for farmers. Perhaps he would accept the notion that artificial manipulation of the marketplace leads to imbalances—I could show a lot of evidence for that. And aren't farm subsidies artificial manipulation of the marketplace? So:

(A) Farm subsidies ultimately (B) hurt farmers because (A') this artificial manipulation of the farm economy (C) creates huge imbalances between production and demand.

This should work. I'll first discuss the general point that farmers are important contributors to this country's economy, so the last thing we want to do is lessen farmers' ability to make a livelihood (B). No; better leave that point out. The Senator already is convinced of it, and I'll just annoy him by spelling it out for him. I'll begin with the idea that imbalances in production and demand hurt the farm economy and thereby tend to hurt farmers (C → B).

Next I should argue that artificial manipulation of the farm economy— better define and illustrate this term (A')—leads to such undesirable imbalances (A' → C). I'll need some strong statistics here and authoritative statements from a couple of leading economists. Some illustration of manipulation creating problems would help here, too.

Then my conclusion: First, show that farm subsidies constitute artificial manipulation of the agricultural economy (A → A'); then, my thesis: Farm subsidies really hurt farmers in the long run (A → B).

The enthymeme, by compelling you to keep the rhetorical context of purpose and audience in mind, helps you to discover what your ar-

---

Evaluating a Thesis Enthymeme

1. Reconstruct and evaluate the implied premise (C ↔ B).

   - It should be believable, likely to be readily accepted by the reader.
   - It should not be trivial.

2. Evaluate the expressed premise (A' → C).

   - It should sum up the major thrust of your argument, including the major point(s) you intend to develop.

3. Evaluate the conclusion (A → B).

   - It should be a statement that the intended audience either does not yet know, does not yet understand, or does not yet accept.

4. Be prepared to modify the thesis enthymeme as you work through the process of writing the paper.

gument needs to accomplish and even how to go about developing it. An essay begins to take shape. You have considered your subject and your stance toward it, you have considered your audience and its needs and interests, and you have generated a rough framework of ideas that is solid and honest—and therefore likely to be convincing. Additional research may be necessary, depending on the topic, the potential readers, and your purpose in addressing them, but you are ready to write.

EXERCISE 2–4

A. Each of the following statements concerns a question of influence, value, or policy. Identify each accordingly, then comment on the problems and/or possibilities it presents as a thesis for an article that you, as a summer intern for the National Park Service, might write for the Park Service employees' newsletter at Rocky Mountain National Park in Estes Park, Colorado. Which seems to hold the greatest potential for development? Briefly discuss why. Modify that statement into a thesis enthymeme appropriate to your own beliefs, purpose, and audience.

B. What definitions and relationships will your article need to discuss or prove, based on the thesis enthymeme you have developed?

Injured hikers should bear the cost of their rescue because they undertook hiking with full awareness that it entailed risks.

Hiking permit fees to enable the Park Service to fund the rescue of injured hikers will lead to fewer hiking injuries because the act of paying into a rescue fund impresses on hikers the dangers of back country trekking and the need to take precautions.

The lives of injured hikers are less valuable than those of people who attempt to rescue them because the hikers were probably careless.

Requiring injured hikers to bear the cost of their rescue will maintain national park operating funds because making people assume responsibility for their own actions decreases unnecessary risk-taking.

Hikers get injured because they take unnecessary risks.

Other ways of generating an essay are possible; there may be as many strategies for invention as there are writers. Some writers begin by creating a formal outline—and stick to it. Some simply sit down and write everything that comes to mind regarding the topic, and later rework what they have written into a coherent whole. Some wait for inspiration to strike—but many who wait for the muse to speak wait in vain. Katherine Anne Porter claimed, "I always write my last line, my last paragraphs, my last page first." Many writers of arguments (notably those developing enthymemes) write their conclusion first, then look for evidence to support that conclusion. Do what works for you. But when you find yourself up against that wall with no opening, writer's block, *begin by asking questions, by looking for gaps and contradictions, by considering your subject in its context with its attendant influences and consequences.* And always consider your purpose and your audience. You will find that you can go over the wall, or around it. Or knock it down.

As you write a rough draft developing the thesis you have worked out, defining key terms and providing evidence to support your assertions become important considerations. The next two chapters will offer some suggestions for those elements of your essay. Then, Chapter 5 will discuss the finishing (such as ideas for introductions and conclusions) and revising of draft into essay; and Chapter 6 will give you pointers for polishing your style. With hard work and a good ear for language, you will find that out of the rubble of that wall of writer's block you can construct a strong and persuasive essay.

GROUP DISCUSSIONS ARE BENEFICIAL

(Student Draft)

1   A study entitled *The American Freshman—national norms for fall 1986* shows that first-year college students aren't studying as much as in the past. The study asked 204,000 freshmen numerous questions, including how much time they spend studying each week. The startling response is that almost half of the freshmen, 48.2 percent, study less than five hours each week. That's less than one hour per week per class, folks. Only about 20 percent said they study more than 10 hours each week.

2   It's only natural to question whether our future leaders will treat major problems with the same energy as they do their studies. Is the "Ward Cleaver effect" taking its toll?

3   Our generation has been raised on television. Studies show that, by the time they graduate from high school, young adults have spent more time watching television than they have spent in the classroom. For most, TV is the perpetual teacher. Witness the problem of Ward Cleaver.

4   In the first few minutes of any *Leave it to Beaver* episode, Theodore or Wally does something reprehensible (like calling someone a "stinker" or blowing up the Dairy Queen). Twenty minutes into the show, Ward finds out about the mischief and resolves the crisis within the half hour. After removing the commercials, Beave's crisis is presented, discovered and resolved in 22 minutes of show time.

5   Unfortunately, many Americans come to expect their answers quickly—whether it be answers to the quiz on *Silas Marner* or answers to the *Contra* funds diversion. It is apparent that current college students think one scant hour a night of studying is more than enough. One hour a day of thinking, however, is not going to solve the problems of this nation, present or future.

6   Therein lies the problem: College has become too much memorization and not enough thinking.

7   I want to sharpen my critical thinking skills, not merely learn a trade. Had I wanted just a "job license," I would have gone to one of those technical schools that advertise on late night TV. Instead, I came to college to get a diploma—to learn how to reason, how to interpret and how to think.

8   Unfortunately, too many professors teach as if college is an extention of high school. They lecture for three hours and assign hundreds of pages of reading each week. At the end of six weeks, they give tests that include so many questions that there is no time to both think about the

answers and finish the test. The only way for a student to maximize his or her grade is to memorize facts and spit them back out just as they are offered in the teachers' lectures. The student who takes the time to think about the questions will never finish.

9   What challenge is there in rote?

10   Of course, this does not apply to all professors, but in my experience at this university, it includes more than half.

11   Students are also to blame. Very few are willing to participate in discussion groups outside of classtime. They attend the lectures, take the tests and stop thinking once the bell rings.

12   Discussion groups are the best way to learn. Most of the facts needed to answer test questions today can easily be relearned years from now at any library. The opinions of my peers, however, cannot be learned from any text or reference book.

13   Remember, I am here to sharpen my critical thinking skills as well as to learn how to operate a TV camera. There is no better way to learn about my own thought processes than to hear how others reach decisions. I wish I had more of an opportunity to exchange ideas with other students, both inside and outside the classroom.

QUESTIONS AND IDEAS FOR DISCUSSION

1. The author of this material, a member of a campus newspaper writing staff, was told he needed to write a column of about 1,000 words. The intended audience is comprised of college students and faculty. Does the author have a clear sense of his purpose in addressing them? Comment.

2. What is the author's main point? Does he have a thesis? If so, what is it? Does it cover the argument's actual content? Could you suggest an improved version? If you find no apparent thesis, suggest one that might give a firmer shape to the essay.

3. What idea(s) in this draft would have to be eliminated in an essay developed from your suggested thesis statement?

4. What idea(s) in this draft would need to be developed more fully in a well-thought-out essay developed from your suggested thesis statement?

5. Do you find any gaps in the reasoning in this argument? If so, how might they be remedied?

6. Comment on the appropriateness of the title.

PAY EQUITY IS UNFAIR TO WOMEN

Linda Chavez

1   Striking secretaries at Yale recently threatened to bring the 284-year-old university to a standstill over what they saw as discrimination in wages favoring men over women. Female workers in Washington State won a discrimination suit in a federal district court that may cost the state government nearly $1 billion in back pay and increased wages. The U.S. House of Representatives passed a bill in the last session of Congress that required all federal jobs to be reevaluated, with the aim of raising the pay for jobs held mainly by women.

2   All these actions were taken in the name of comparable worth, a controversial theory that jobs have an intrinsic, measurable value that should dictate the wages paid. Sounds like a great deal for women trapped in underpaid occupations, doesn't it? In the short run it may be: women in jobs directly affected by the strikes, suits, and legislation could get higher wages. But in the long run all women will lose. If the proponents of comparable worth succeed in their quest, they will bring about the most radical alteration of our economy in the nation's history, replacing the market system with a system of administered wages. Why, then, have so many otherwise sensible people endorsed comparable worth?

3   The answer lies partly in the ability of comparable worth advocates to cloak themselves in the rhetoric of fairness. They have even coined a phrase to describe their goal: pay equity. Mimicking the strategy of the civil rights movement, they point to the statistical disparity between the average earnings of men and women and conclude that discrimination must exist. They note the high concentration of women in certain occupations and claim job segregation. But equal pay for equal work is the law of the land, as is the guarantee that any woman has the right to any job for which she is qualified. What pay equity requires is not the fairness of equal opportunity, but something disturbingly different.

4   In recent years the courts have held that government ought to remedy any disparities in the success achieved by various groups in society. Courts routinely find, for example, that discrimination exists when an employer's work force has fewer blacks in it than their proportion in the local labor market. With people conditioned to think this way, comparable worth advocates have only to prove that women earn less than men to convince many that discrimination is the cause. The fact that women earn 72 cents for every dollar that men earn, based on their average hourly wages, leads few people to ask why. Instead, they ask what we can do about it.

5   The wage gap between men and women is a complex phenomenon. No single explanation suffices. Women continue to work at different jobs

than men, with fully half of all women concentrated in three occupations, despite strides in opening up positions that have been male enclaves. These female occupations—sales, clerical, and professional—command salaries in the market commensurate with the supply and demand of people able and willing to perform the work.

6   Earnings clearly play only a partial role in women's decision to work in a limited number of jobs. Of far greater importance is the need that most women have to balance the demands of a job with the responsibilities of family life. Working mothers may be willing to take less pay to get other benefits—a job that doesn't penalize the woman who intermittently interrupts her career for childbearing, or a job that provides regular working hours and proximity to a telephone in case of a child-related emergency.

7   Comparable worth advocates want no part of such complexities. It is as if they cannot conceive that women are capable of acting in their self-interest. Instead, they depict working women as victims of conspiracy and oppression, incapable of making rational decisions about their needs and desires. The fact that women continue to seek employment primarily in low-paying, female-dominated jobs despite expanded opportunity in higher-paying, traditionally male occupations does not suggest to comparable worth advocates that the non-monetary benefits of certain jobs may have appeal. Rather, it suggests to them that women need protection from the consequences of their choices.

8   While espousing feminist ideology, the comparable worth advocates offer up protectionist legislation to insulate women from the demands of the market. But like so much of what passes for protection, comparable worth may make victims of its intended beneficiaries. Women will ultimately be the biggest losers.

9   If comparable worth becomes the law of the land, higher salaries almost certainly will mean fewer jobs in traditionally female occupations. Employers forced to pay higher wages with no concomitant rise in productivity have to raise prices or reduce the number of jobs. What manager, faced with a decision between losing his competitive edge by hiking prices or making do with fewer secretaries, will choose the former, particularly in the age of computers and word processors?

10   Australia has had a variation of comparable worth in both the public and private sectors since 1972. Within five years of enactment of its law, female unemployment in Australia rose, the number of women working part time increased, and the growth of female participation in the labor force slowed.

11   What the comparable worth advocates always ignore is who will bear the costs of the pay increases their system would mandate. The costs will not be borne by some elite band of larcenous employers. They will be borne mainly by women.

QUESTIONS AND IDEAS FOR DISCUSSION

1. What is the main point—the thesis conclusion—of this essay? Where is it stated? Why do you think Chavez expresses it at the point at which she does?
2. What are the major supporting points for the thesis? Is each supporting point itself supported by adequate and persuasive explanation, examples, and/or definition? Identify any points that seem to warrant further development or modification to be convincing.
3. Discuss your response to this essay. Did you agree with Chavez's basic position before reading? If so, how did that affect the closeness with which you considered her actual argument? Whether or not you disagreed with the author's basic position before reading, were you put off by any unsupported value statements or assumptions? If so, identify them.
4. Chavez centers much of her argument on contradictions she finds in the movement toward "comparable worth" pay in the job market. Describe the contradictions she finds. Are they, in her judgment, real or only apparent? Do you agree? Comment.
5. Chavez also offers an enthymeme in her essay. We might restate that enthymeme (found in paragraph 9) as follows:

A comparable worth policy leads to higher salaries in traditionally female jobs.
Higher salaries, however, lead to fewer traditionally female jobs.
So, a comparable worth policy leads to fewer traditionally female jobs.

Does Chavez fully develop and convincingly prove this argument? Comment.
6. Is Chavez trying to do too much in this essay? Should she have focused more specifically on either persuading us of the contradiction she finds in the whole notion of comparable worth, or persuading us of the argument expressed in the enthymeme in paragraph 9? Whether or not you agree with her position, create a thesis that would limit her argument clearly and that would be "provable" in a short essay such as this one.

SUGGESTIONS FOR WRITING AND FURTHER DISCUSSION

1. Develop a thesis, using any of the methods discussed in this chapter, on the subject of grading. Assume that your purpose is to convince the Faculty Senate (to change/not to change) the grading system at

your school. Evaluate the thesis, perhaps in a small group discussion with members of your writing class. After making whatever changes are needed in the thesis, write an essay developing its argument through explanation, examples, and other detail.

2. Develop a thesis and, from it, an essay arguing that all this talk about considering readers is just so much insincere hot air (we won't worry just now about the improbability of that metaphor): No writing is worth reading—indeed, no writing is *possible*—that is not written for oneself first and foremost.

3. What underrated musical artists of the twentieth century will people listen to in the twenty-first century? Convince your readers (members of your writing class) to take seriously a particular composer/performer/group you admire.

4. Write an essay from one of the theses you developed in Exercise 2–2. Suggestions for purpose and audience are given in the exercise, but you may stipulate others instead.

5. What do you think about the expanding movement to ban smoking in public places? Write a letter to your city or town council putting forward your views in hopes of affecting local policy. (Then, mail it!)

6. Write an essay from the thesis you developed in Exercise 2–3.

7. Colleges and universities have recurring problems with two kinds of abuses within athletic programs: play-for-pay and drug use among athletes. Given the readers of your alumni magazine as an audience, decide on a purpose for addressing them about some aspect of one of these problems and develop a thesis and then an essay suitable for the magazine to print.

8. If you are from a farming region or are otherwise knowledgeable about farming, write an essay that will enlighten your classmates about a particular aspect of the farm economy and its problems in this country.

9. Write an essay from the thesis you developed in Exercise 2–4. Suggestions regarding purpose and audience are given in the exercise.

10. Write an essay from the thesis and supporting ideas you developed in response to questions following the student draft about college academic problems. Your essay should be appropriate for an audience of your own campus community. Your purpose should be to compel that community's recognition of a problem—and perhaps thereby to shame its members into doing something about the problem.

11. Whether or not you are presently employed, you undoubtedly intend to be employed following your academic studies—so what Linda Chavez is concerned about in "Pay Equity Is Unfair to Women" concerns you as well. Write an essay (one that would be even more suitable for publication in *Fortune* than Chavez's) that argues either the thesis you developed in response to the questions following the essay or a contrary or otherwise modified position on the same issue.

3

Definition in Argument

"When I use a word," Humpty Dumpty said, in rather a scornful tone, "it means just what I choose it to mean—neither more nor less."

"The question is," said Alice, "whether you can make words mean so many different things."

"The question is," said Humpty Dumpty, "which is to be master—that's all."

Lewis Carroll, *Through the Looking-Glass*

To be master or not to be master of the words we use in any communication (but especially argument) is all the choice we have; we have no alternative as to whether we will or will not use language. Wordless communication and wordless persuasion are possible, of course: One photograph of a starving child may move people to contribute their money or their time to a refugee cause more quickly than an hour's cajoling would do, or a well-placed fist to the jaw may dissuade one person from continuing to argue politics with another. But nonverbal persuasion is particularly vulnerable to misinterpretation, and it is difficult to sustain for long. Nonverbal persuasion speaks directly to the emotions; argument at least purports to address the intellect.

So if we are to construct arguments, we must use words. And, lest we be misunderstood, we are obliged to use those words carefully and precisely, aware not only of their denotations—literal meaning—but also of their connotations and possible ambiguities. Through the careful selection of words and the definition of key terms, we assure our readers' comprehension and affect our readers' reception of our arguments.

With language we make sense of the world as we see it and dwell in it. To the extent that we live, with the poet Wallace Stevens, the life of the imagination, words define our reality. We can give form to the concept of Spain for someone who has never traveled there, give meaning to the idea of tact for someone who hasn't any, or make a suggestion for producing better widgets believable in an employer's imagination. And to the extent that we use language to shape experience and to communicate with other people, we rely on definition. Definition is essential to any use of language, but especially to written argument. If we express the issue fuzzily, very often our thoughts are also fuzzier than they should be. Defining the issue and the pertinent terms will help to ensure that we have a clear idea of our subject and our stance toward it, and that the reader will have a clear understanding of both subject and stance.

HOW TO DEFINE

Reportive Definitions

Just as definitions have several uses in argument—whether to clarify a term or to control the scope of a discussion—they are of several kinds, according to our various purposes. Definition may be *reportive* or *stipulative:* The first, as rhetorician Gerald Runkle succinctly puts it, states "how society uses the term"; the second, "how I use the term." A reportive definition may indicate an historical or current, general or technical, use of a term, and may do so in a number of ways, including

Giving synonyms: An impeachment is an accusation, charge, or indictment.

Giving examples: Andrew Jackson was the subject of an impeachment.

Giving conditions for use of the term: We normally use the term *impeachment* only in reference to public officials.

Putting the term in a class and stating the features that distinguish it from other members of the class (*genus* plus *differentiae*): An impeachment is an accusation of misconduct in office made before an appropriate tribunal.
—Adapted from *Random House Dictionary*

Comparing or contrasting the term with others: An impeachment is not a conviction.

Showing the etymology, or historical derivation, of the term: The term *impeachment* comes from the Latin word for *trap.*

Combining any of the methods above.

All of these ways of defining help explain how a word is used. The "class-plus-distinguishing characteristics" definition may be the most complete method, but sometimes we need to know as well what uses of a term are *not* appropriate: An impeachment is *not* a conviction, after all.

Stipulative Definitions

A stipulative definition may assign meaning arbitrarily to a new term (*wabe,* as Alice correctly guesses in her conversation with Humpty Dumpty, means "the little grass-plot round a sundial"); restrict narrowly the meaning of an extant term; or even assign a new meaning to an old term—though the latter should be done for some good reason and not, as Humpty Dumpty claims, simply to show "which is to be master." Stipulative definitions may be expressed in the same ways reportive definitions are expressed. For example, one might stipulate by synonym a secondary meaning of *impeachment* for a given context: "a discrediting of someone." A cynic might stipulate a harsher synonym: "the modern equivalent of a lynching." Or the same observer might use an example: "Richard Nixon was the subject of impeachment—by the press, which seems to have designated itself the appropriate tribunal for such action." Another stipulative definition (from a different viewpoint) might give an unusual condition for the use of the term: "In an impeachment no bail is required of the individual impeached, however dangerous to the public weal that person may be."

As these examples show, how you as a writer define your terms makes apparent your attitude toward your subject and even toward your audience. Many people forget that *impeachment* does not mean *conviction,* and they may need to be reminded of that fact for purposes of clarity. Even if your readers can be expected to understand the term, you may need to define it in order to control their attitudes toward what the word represents. In any case, one caution is in order: Definitions should not be used in desperation as a starting point for an essay, or as filler. Dictionaries are available to readers as well as to writers; you risk seeming condescending to your readers if you define common words, just as you risk alienating them if you offer only cryptic quotations from dictionaries to define rare or difficult terms.

HOW TO JUDGE DEFINITIONS

A definition, whether reportive or stipulative, should adhere to certain standards of clarity and completeness:

1. **It should avoid circularity.** The tautology "Business is business" enlightens us not at all; "A good movie is one you like" is little better.

2. **It should not employ ambiguous or metaphorical language, or terms more difficult or obscure than the term to be defined.** Dr. Johnson is notorious for his definition of *net:* "anything reticulated or decussated, at equal distances, with interstices between the intersections."

3. **It should be exact, neither too broad nor too narrow.** The problem with saying that "a president of the United States must be a citizen of the United States" is that the statement, while true, is too broad; more than two hundred million people are U.S. citizens. "A president of the United States must be a man who is a native-born citizen of that country, and at least thirty-five years old," on the other hand, is too narrow, for a woman is also entitled to hold that position. A really thorough and exact definition will be reversible, so that both "x is y" and "y is x" are true statements.

4. **It should indicate connotative values if they are significant.** *Rhetoric,* for example, is often used in a pejorative sense: We may speak of "empty rhetoric" or "mere rhetoric" in dismissing the argument of one with whom we disagree. Writers who intend to use the term in a neutral or favorable way would do well to define the term, perhaps in the classical sense: "the art of persuasion." They should indicate that the negative connotations do not apply to the term as they use it.

You will notice the injunction above against using metaphorical language in a definition. The reason is that we are here concerned with definition that focuses, at least nominally or partially, on either how a term is used or how the writer wishes it to be used in written or oral discussion. A metaphorical definition—as, for instance, Marx's famous definition of religion as "the opium of the people"—focuses less on such practical concerns than on the reader's imagination, by specifically linking the term in question to something quite unlike it in any literal sense. Metaphor can be a powerful persuasive tool, and even an illuminating one—helping readers to visualize a concept that in more pedestrian prose might elude them. Chapter 6 will have more to say about the uses of metaphor in argument.

EXERCISE 3-1

Identify the following definitions as reportive or stipulative, and indicate which term is being defined and which method or methods (from the list above) are used in defining. Do any of the definitions seem wholly or partially metaphorical?

1. Crampons are metal soleplates bearing a number of sharp teeth and designed to be strapped to the soles of hiking shoes and to grip the ice as the hiker traverses glaciers.

2. Faith is the substance of things hoped for, the evidence of things not seen.
   —Hebrews 11.1
3. Let Rhetoric be defined, then, as the faculty of discerning in every case the available means of persuasion.
   —Aristotle, *Rhetoric*
4. To be accepted as a paradigm, a theory must seem better than its competitors, but it need not, and in fact never does, explain all the facts with which it can be confronted.
   —Thomas Kuhn, *The Structure of Scientific Revolutions*
5. We are gorged with papers, reports, memos, the random and miscellaneous ingredients of information. Knowledge, says Boorstin, is "orderly and cumulative," the province of books that disperse the "enduring treasure of our whole human past."
   —Hugh Sidey, also quoting Daniel Boorstin, in *Time*, 3 Aug. 1987, 21.
6. Success is a red Porsche—or a blue Jaguar.
7. In the same way that the income-tax system does not exist simply to collect money, but also to provide incentives for various sorts of economic activities, so grading is not simply an evaluation process; it is a way of providing incentives for various sorts of intellectual behavior.
   —Miles Pickering, "Are Lab Courses a Waste of Time?"
8. Secularization is the wonderful mechanism by which religion becomes nonreligion. Marxism is secularized Christianity; so is democracy; so is utopianism; so are human rights.
   —Allan Bloom, *The Closing of the American Mind*
9. The Census defines as "urban" any city or town or village having at least 2,500 residents.
   —Andrew Hacker, ed., *U/S: A Statistical Portrait of the American People*
10. Wrestling: a sport in which each of two opponents struggles hand in hand in an attempt to force the other down.
    —*Random House Dictionary*
11. Wrestling is not a sport, it is a spectacle. . . .
    —Roland Barthes, "Wrestling," *Mythologies*
12. Biosynthesis is the production of complex substances from simple ones by or with living organisms.
    —*The American Heritage Dictionary*
13. Crime control means gun control.
    —Sen. Edward Kennedy
14. We shall call the absolute square of a wave function that cannot be normalized its *intensity*.
    —Siegmund Brandt and Hans Dieter Dahmen, *The Picture Book of Quantum Mechanics*

15. A "boomerang divorce" is a divorce after which the couple continues to live together.

    —*Jeopardy*, Merv Griffin Enterprises, 16 July 1987.

16. Definition always consists, as being a dialectical animal, of a body which is the genus, and a difference which is the soul of the thing defined.

    —Andrew Marvell

EXERCISE 3-2

Judge the definitions in Exercise 3-1 according to the standards listed on page 62. Then pick two that you find incomplete or confusing and write a more exact and clearer definition for the term in question. (To do so, you will probably need to look up some words in a good dictionary and possibly need to talk to a class member who knows more about, say, quantum mechanics than you do.)

EXERCISE 3-3

Use three different means of defining (chosen from the list on page 60) each of the following:

history	myth	enormity
mental health	plastic	argument
language	detente	genius

THE ROLES OF DEFINITION IN ARGUMENT

A certain agreement between writer and reader about definitions is necessary for clear communication. Where the possibility exists that definitions are not shared, meanings must be spelled out. Definitions of any sort, reportive or stipulative, have two functions in argument: They may be used informatively, to clarify the issue and the terms pertinent to it; and they may be used persuasively, to control the scope of the argument and the readers' responses. They may even fulfill both purposes at once, as we shall see.

Using Definition to Clarify

The first goal of definition is to achieve clarity. One benefit of a clearly defined issue and clearly defined terms is that the audience may thereby determine whether its own conclusions and beliefs coincide with or differ from the writer's; or if they differ, whether the disagreement is merely a verbal misunderstanding centering on an equivocal (ambiguous) or vague term, or one that reflects a fundamental difference of opinion. For example, if I should argue that the United States ought to intervene in El Salvador, much hinges upon how broadly or narrowly I use the term *intervene*. If I mean "to send civilian advisors to mediate between the government and the revolutionaries, and to send food and medical supplies," and you understand the term as meaning "to send military troops to defeat the rebels," our verbal misunderstanding could lead to your rejecting my argument. If I define my terms, you still may reject my conclusion, but at least we will understand each other. And we might even find that we agree—if civilian advisors, food, and medical supplies are a form of "intervention" that is acceptable to you. To define ambiguous or vague key terms is to clarify the substance and extent of our disagreement, and perhaps to show that we have no real disagreement at all.

In the late 1970s, two separate landmark legal cases hinged largely on the definition of the term *racial quota*. These two were the reverse discrimination suits brought by Allan Bakke and Marco DeFunis, Jr., against the University of California at Davis Medical School (UCDMS) and the University of Washington Law School (UWLS), respectively. The problem of definition in these cases is described by Allan P. Sindler:

There were a few things about quotas on which all sides to the dispute saw eye to eye, and this helped to narrow the areas of disagreement a bit. First, they agreed that it would be unsound policy and also illegal to limit the admittance of highly qualified minorities to professional school when, if they had been non-minority persons, they would have been admitted. This would be, of course, the old-fashioned restrictive racial quota, outlawed by the courts. Second, they agreed that the intent of the preferential practices at issue was to expand, not constrict, minority admissions. The problem context was an affirmative desire to increase minority enrollment (At least X number wanted. Welcome!), in contrast to the negative purpose of the old-style discriminatory quota (No more than X number wanted. Keep out!). Finally, they also agreed that explicit race preference was the most direct and effective means to achieve, with predictability and certainty, designated levels of increased minority admissions.

A fourth item of seeming agreement turned out, when probed, to be the key object of dissension. Proponents and opponents alike shared the view that a positive racial quota in selective admissions voluntarily adopted by a professional school was an unwise policy and most probably illegal as well. It would constitute "reverse discrimination," which would prejudice the opportunities of nonminority students and which a school would find difficult to justify as reasonably consistent with its educational mission. Clearly, then, the position of supporters of UWLS and of UCDMS was that the admissions policies of these two institutions were quite different from an unsound and forbidden racial quota. But those who identified with Marco DeFunis, Jr., and Allan Bakke were no less adamant in asserting that the special admissions practices for minorities were variants of a racial quota, regardless of what other name they chose to go by. Both semantically and substantively, therefore, the disagreement turned on divergent conceptions of what a racial quota meant.

Here the disagreement was real enough, but only careful definition pinpointed it. It was agreed by all parties that limiting the number of minority students would be illegal and undesirable; the substantive issue hinged on whether requiring *at least* a certain number or percentage of minority students constituted a racial quota of an equally undesirable sort—one that limited the numbers of white students illegally. All were opposed to any condition that might be labeled a racial quota; the question was, just what *is* a racial quota?

Using Definition to Control

The second goal of definition is to control the scope of the argument by defining its limits. In the argument about military intervention in El Salvador, if I define what I mean by intervention, I narrow the limits of my thesis to what I am willing and able to support. If I am opposed to using military force, definition enables me to establish the limits within which I am prepared to argue my case. In the legal argument concerning reverse discrimination, Bakke's and DeFunis's lawyers defined *racial quota* in a way that the courts accepted as applying to their cases. They were able, through skillful definition, not only to clarify the question at hand but also to control its scope. This use of definition is of central importance to successful argument. It is no mere formality that the first (affirmative) speaker in a debate is responsible for defining the terms of the proposition.

Controlling the scope of the argument can also enable a writer to control the audience's responses. If you are the one to establish the issue and to make the issue clear, you can disarm a hostile audience by compelling it to deal with the issue on terms you have established. As psychiatrist Thomas Szasz has observed, definition is power:

The struggle for definition is veritably the struggle for life itself. In the typical Western two men fight desperately for the possession of a gun that has been thrown to the ground; whoever reaches the weapon first, shoots and lives; his adversary is shot and dies. In ordinary life, the struggle is not for guns but for words: whoever first defines the situation is the victor; his adversary, the victim. For example, in the family, husband and wife, mother and child do not get along; who defines whom as troublesome or mentally sick? Or, in the apocryphal story about Emerson visiting Thoreau in jail, Emerson asks: "Henry, what are you doing over there?" Thoreau replies: "Ralph, what are *you* doing over there?" In short, he who first seizes the word imposes reality on the other: he who defines thus dominates and lives; and he who is defined is subjugated and may be killed.

Has Szasz overstated the power and importance of definition? Even if he has, we know that definitions have power. The question then arises, how do we employ this power? How ethical is it to use definition to manipulate a reader's response, to "impose reality on the other"? Consider your own experience: Surely, at some time, you have been placed at a disadvantage in a dispute because the other party first defined the issue in terms favorable to his or her own position. If your parents proclaimed, as you filled out college applications, "You're free to go to any college you choose. Of course, if you go to our alma mater, we'll pay your expenses," you may have sensed some damage done to the usual meaning of *free choice*. If a person you were dating declared, "If you go to that party without me, you don't love me. You don't know what it means to love!", you no doubt found yourself at a disadvantage in the discussion. With *love* defined as "not going to a party without me," that lovers' quarrel became a problem of definition. And just as surely, on other occasions you have been the one to define a situation to your own advantage: "Sure, I said I'd work out last weekend, Coach, and I did. Dancing *is* a workout." Whether right or wrong, the use of definition to control (handicap?) audience response is frequent, and one of which you should be aware—and wary.

Persuasive Definitions

Usually a definition is intended to be informative, but to the extent that it is designed to control the scope of the argument and the responses of the audience, its purpose is also to be persuasive, whether it is reportive or stipulative. Persuasive definitions, as Irving Copi explains in *Introduction to Logic* (6th ed.), are "phrased in emotive language and . . . intended to influence attitudes as well as to instruct" (153). Take the everyday term *writer*, for instance. We might define it reportively as "a person who produces literary, journalistic, or technical compositions." A cynic, however, might attempt to influence our attitude toward what the term represents by defining *writer* as "a person possessed of a typewriter and an independent income." An obviously persuasive definition of *writer* is Cornelius Register's: "The writer has taken unto himself the former function of the priest or prophet. He presumes to order and legislate the people's life. There is no person more arrogant than the writer."

In the same vein, Professor Copi cites a parody of letters from members of Congress to constituents that illustrates the diverse ends that persuasive definitions can be made to serve.

Dear Sir:

You ask me how I stand on abortion. Let me answer forthrightly and without equivocation.

If by abortion you mean the murdering of defenseless human beings; the denial of rights to the youngest of our citizens; the promotion of promiscuity among our shiftless and valueless youth and the rejection of Life, Liberty, and the Pursuit of Happiness—then, Sir, be assured that I shall never waver in my opposition, so help me God.

But, Sir, if by abortion you mean the granting of equal rights to all our citizens regardless of race, color or sex; the elimination of evil and vile institutions preying upon desperate and hopeless women; a chance to all our youth to be wanted and loved; and, above all, that God-given right for all citizens to act in accordance with their own conscience—then, Sir, let me promise you as a patriot and a humanist that I shall never be persuaded to forego my pursuit of these most basic human rights.

Thank you for asking my position on this most crucial issue and let me again assure you of the steadfastness of my stand.

As you can see, it is all in how you define your terms!

THE RIGHT STUFF

Tom Wolfe

1   A young man might go into military flight training believing that he
was entering some sort of technical school in which he was simply
going to acquire a certain set of skills. Instead, he found himself all
at once enclosed in a fraternity. And in this fraternity, even though
it was military, men were not rated by their outward rank as ensigns,
lieutenants, commanders, or whatever. No, herein the world was
divided into those who had it and those who did not. This quality,
this *it*, was never named, however, nor was it talked about in any
way.

2   As to just what this ineffable quality was . . . well, it obviously
involved bravery. But it was not bravery in the simple sense of being
willing to risk your life. The idea seemed to be that any fool could
do that, if that was all that was required, just as any fool could throw
away his life in the process. No, the idea here (in the all-enclosing
fraternity) seemed to be that a man should have the ability to go up
in a hurtling piece of machinery and put his hide on the line and
then have the moxie, the reflexes, the experience, the coolness, to
pull it back in the last yawning moment—and then to go up again
the next day, and the next day, and every next day, even if the series
should prove infinite—and, ultimately, in its best expression, do so
in a cause that means something to thousands, to a people, a nation,
to humanity, to God. Nor was there *a test* to show whether or not
a pilot had this righteous quality. There was instead, a seemingly
infinite series of tests. A career in flying was like climbing one of
those ancient Babylonian pyramids made up of a dizzy progression
of steps and ledges, a ziggurat, a pyramid extraordinarily high and
steep; and the idea was to prove at every foot of the way up the
pyramid that you were one of the elected and anointed ones who had
the right stuff and could move higher and higher and even—ultimately, God willing, one day—that you might be able to join that
special few at the very top, that elite who had the capacity to bring
tears to men's eyes, the very Brotherhood of the Right Stuff itself.

3   None of this was to be mentioned, and yet it was acted out in
a way that a young man could not fail to understand. When a new
flight (i.e., a class) of trainees arrived at Pensacola, they were brought
into an auditorium for a little lecture. An officer would tell them:
"Take a look at the man on either side of you." Quite a few actually

swiveled their heads this way and that, in the interest of appearing diligent. Then the officer would say: "One of the three of you is not going to make it!"—meaning, not get his wings. That was the opening theme, the *motif* of primary training. We already know that one-third of you do not have the right stuff—it only remains to find out who.

4   Furthermore, that was the way it turned out. At every level in one's progress up that staggeringly high pyramid, the world was once more divided into those men who had the right stuff to continue to climb and those who had to be *left behind* in the most obvious way. Some were eliminated in the course of the opening classroom work, as either not smart enough or not hardworking enough, and were left behind. Then came the basic flight instruction, in single-engine, propeller-driven trainers, and a few more—even though the military tried to make this stage easy—were washed out and left behind. Then came more demanding levels, one after the other, formation flying, instrument flying, jet training, all-weather flying, gunnery, and at each level more were washed out and left behind. By this point easily a third of the original candidates had been, indeed, eliminated . . . from the ranks of those who might prove to have the right stuff.

5   In the Navy, in addition to the stages that Air Force trainees went through, the neophyte always had waiting for him, out in the ocean, a certain grim gray slab; namely, the deck of an aircraft carrier; and with it perhaps the most difficult routine in military flying, carrier landings. He was shown films about it, he heard lectures about it, and he knew that carrier landings were hazardous. He first practiced touching down on the shape of a flight deck painted on an airfield. He was instructed to touch down and gun right off. This was safe enough—the shape didn't move, at least—but it could do terrible things to, let us say, the gyroscope of the soul. *That shape!—it's so damned small!* And more candidates were washed out and left behind. Then came the day, without warning, when those who remained were sent out over the ocean for the first of many days of reckoning with the slab. The first day was always a clear day with little wind and a calm sea. The carrier was so steady that it seemed, from up there in the air, to be resting on pilings, and the candidate usually made his first carrier landing successfully, with relief and even *élan.* Many young candidates looked like terrific aviators up to that very point—and it was not until they were actually standing on the carrier deck that they first began to wonder if they had the proper stuff, after all. In the training film the flight deck was a grand piece of gray geometry, perilous, to be sure, but an amazing abstract shape as one looks down upon it on the screen. And yet once the newcomer's two feet were on it . . . *Geometry—*my God, man, this is a . . .

skillet! It *heaved,* it moved up and down underneath his feet, it pitched up, it pitched down, it rolled to port (this great beast *rolled!*) and it rolled to starboard, as the ship moved into the wind and, therefore, into the waves, and the wind kept sweeping across, sixty feet up in the air out in the open sea, and there were no railings whatsoever. This was a *skillet!*—a frying pan!—a short-order grill!— not gray but black, smeared with skid marks from one end to the other and glistening with pools of hydraulic fluid and the occasional jet-fuel slick, all of it still hot, sticky, greasy, runny, virulent from God knows what traumas—still ablaze!—consumed in detonations, explosions, flames, combustion, roars, shrieks, whines, blasts, horrible shudders, fracturing impacts, as little men in screaming red and yellow and purple and green shirts with black Mickey Mouse helmets over their ears skittered about on the surface as if for their very lives (you've said it now!), hooking fighter planes onto the catapult shuttles so that they can explode their afterburners and be slung off the deck in a red-mad fury with a *kaboom!* that pounds through the entire deck—a procedure that seems absolutely controlled, orderly, sublime, however, compared to what he is about to watch as aircraft return to the ship for what is known in the engineering stoicisms of the military as "recovery and arrest." To say that an F-4 was coming back onto this heaving barbecue from out of the sky at a speed of 135 knots . . . that might have been the truth in the training lecture, but it did not begin to get across the idea of what the newcomer saw from the deck itself, because it created the notion that perhaps the plane was gliding in. On the deck one knew differently! As the aircraft came closer and the carrier heaved on into the waves the plane's speed did not diminish and the deck did not grow steady—indeed, it pitched up and down five or ten feet per greasy heave—one experienced a neural alarm that no lecture could have prepared him for: This is not an *airplane* coming toward me, it is a brick with some poor sonofabitch riding it (*someone much like myself!*), and it is not *gliding,* it is *falling,* a fifty-thousand-pound brick, headed not for a stripe on the deck but for *me*—and with a horrible *smash!* it hits the skillet, and with a blur of momentum as big as a freight train's it hurtles toward the far end of the deck—another blinding storm!— another roar as the pilot pushes the throttle up to full military power and another smear of rubber screams out over the skillet—and this is nominal!—quite okay!—for a wire stretched across the deck has grabbed the hook on the end of the plane as it hit the deck tail down, and the smash was the rest of the fifteen-ton brute slamming onto the deck, as it tripped up, so that it is now straining against the wire at full throttle, in case it hadn't held and the plane had "boltered" off the end of the deck and had to struggle up into the air again. And already the Mickey Mouse helmets are running toward the fiery monster . . .

6   And the candidate, looking on, begins to *feel* that great heaving sun-blazing deathboard of a deck wallowing in his own vestibular system—and suddenly he finds himself backed up against his own limits. He ends up going to the flight surgeon with so-called conversion symptoms. Overnight he develops blurred vision or numbness in his hands and feet or sinusitis so severe that he cannot tolerate changes in altitude. On one level the symptom is real. He really cannot see too well or use his fingers or stand the pain. But somewhere in his subconscious he knows it is a plea and a beg-off; he shows not the slightest concern (the flight surgeon notes) that the condition might be permanent and affect him in whatever life awaits him outside the arena of the right stuff.

7   Those who remained, those who qualified for carrier duty—and even more so those who later on qualified for *night* carrier duty—began to feel a bit like Gideon's warriors. *So many have been left behind!* The young warriors were now treated to a deathly sweet and quite unmentionable sight. They could gaze at length upon the crushed and wilted pariahs who had washed out. They could inspect those who did not have that righteous stuff.

8   The military did not have very merciful instincts. Rather than packing up these poor souls and sending them home, the Navy, like the Air Force and the Marines, would try to make use of them in some other role, such as flight controller. So the washout has to keep taking classes with the rest of his group, even though he can no longer touch an airplane. He sits there in the classes staring at sheets of paper with cataracts of sheer human mortification over his eyes while the rest steal looks at him . . . this man reduced to an ant, this untouchable, this poor sonofabitch. And in what test had he been found wanting? Why, it seemed to be nothing less than *manhood* itself. Naturally, this was never mentioned, either. Yet there it was. *Manliness, manhood, manly courage* . . . there was something ancient, primordial, irresistible about the challenge of this stuff, no matter what a sophisticated and rational age one might think he lived in.

QUESTIONS AND IDEAS FOR DISCUSSION

1. Wolfe gives an arbitrary stipulative definition for a term he has coined: "the right stuff." How does he develop his definition? Can it be expressed in a single sentence? (Try it.) What is the advantage of an extended definition to a reader?

2. Is Wolfe's a persuasive definition? Is it an argument? Explain.

3. Wolfe's style of writing has been described as flamboyant. Certainly his use of language is anything but dull and dry. This lengthy definition of "the right stuff" holds a reader's attention, as any persuasive definition must. Give some examples of passages that particularly engage your interest: What about them makes them particularly interesting and readable?

4. Does reading this excerpt from *The Right Stuff* make you want to read the book? Explain why or why not, as specifically as possible.

ARS POETICA

Archibald MacLeish

A poem should be palpable and mute
As a globed fruit,

Dumb
As old medallions to the thumb,

Silent as the sleeve-worn stone
Of casement ledges where the moss has grown—

A poem should be wordless
As the flight of birds.

A poem should be motionless in time
As the moon climbs,

Leaving, as the moon releases
Twig by twig the night-entangled trees,

Leaving, as the moon behind the winter leaves,
Memory by memory the mind—

A poem should be motionless in time
As the moon climbs.

A poem should be equal to:
Not true.

For all the history of grief
An empty doorway and a maple leaf.

For love
The leaning grasses and two lights above the sea—

A poem should not mean
But be.

QUESTIONS AND IDEAS FOR DISCUSSION

1. MacLeish's poem is argumentative. Where is its thesis most directly stated? What support does MacLeish give for his thesis? Discuss the irony inherent in the thesis: The poem is an argument against argument, so to speak.
2. MacLeish's definitions are metaphorical; that is, they define by comparing essentially unlike things in order to create visual images and emotional, rather than logical, understanding. Paraphrase MacLeish's metaphorical definitions in everyday English. What do they gain and what do they lose in the process?
3. Do we ordinarily read a poem expecting that we are going to be convinced or persuaded? Or do we expect a poem simply to remind us of things half-forgotten, to show us a fresh way of looking at the world? Do some poems do both? Try to find some examples of poems with persuasive aims. Are they "good" poems? Comment.

ON MORALITY

Joan Didion

1   As it happens I am in Death Valley, in a room at the Enterprise Motel and Trailer Park, and it is July, and it is hot. In fact it is 119°. I cannot seem to make the air conditioner work, but there is a small refrigerator, and I can wrap ice cubes in a towel and hold them against the small of my back. With the help of the ice cubes I have been trying to think, because *The American Scholar* asked me to, in some abstract way about "morality," a word I distrust more every day, but my mind veers inflexibly toward the particular.

2   Here are some particulars. At midnight last night, on the road in from Las Vegas to Death Valley Junction, a car hit a shoulder and turned over. The driver, very young and apparently drunk, was killed instantly. His girl was found alive but bleeding internally, deep in shock. I talked this afternoon to the nurse who had driven the girl to the nearest doctor, 185 miles across the floor of the Valley and three ranges of lethal mountain road. The nurse explained that her husband, a talc miner, had stayed on the highway with the boy's body until the coroner could get over the mountains from Bishop, at dawn today. "You can't just leave a body on the highway," she said. "It's immoral."

3   It was one instance in which I did not distrust the word, because she meant something quite specific. She meant that if a body is left alone for even a few minutes on the desert, the coyotes close in and eat the flesh. Whether or not a corpse is torn apart by coyotes may seem only a sentimental consideration, but of course it is more: one of the promises we make to one another is that we will try to retrieve our casualties, try not to abandon our dead to the coyotes. If we have been taught to keep our promises—if, in the simplest terms, our upbringing is good enough—we stay with the body, or have bad dreams.

4   I am talking, of course, about the kind of social code that is sometimes called, usually pejoratively, "wagon-train morality." In fact that is precisely what it is. For better or worse, we are what we learned as children: my own childhood was illuminated by graphic litanies of the grief awaiting those who failed in their loyalties to each other. The Donner-Reed Party, starving in the Sierra snows, all the ephemera of civilization gone save that one vestigial taboo, the provision that no one should eat his own blood kin. The Jayhawkers, who quarreled and separated not far from where I am tonight. Some of them died in the Funerals and some of them died down near Badwater and most of the rest of them died in the Panamints. A woman

who got through gave the Valley its name. Some might say that the Jayhawkers were killed by the desert summer, and the Donner Party by the mountain winter, by circumstances beyond control; we were taught instead that they had somewhere abdicated their responsibilities, somehow breached their primary loyalties, or they would not have found themselves helpless in the mountain winter or the desert summer, would not have given way to acrimony, would not have deserted one another, would not have *failed*. In brief, we heard such stories as cautionary tales, and they still suggest the only kind of "morality" that seems to me to have any but the most potentially mendacious meaning.

5   You are quite possibly impatient with me by now; I am talking, you want to say, about a "morality" so primitive that it scarcely deserves the name, a code that has as its point only survival, not the attainment of the ideal good. Exactly. Particularly out here tonight, in this country so ominous and terrible that to live in it is to live with antimatter, it is difficult to believe that "the good" is a knowable quantity. Let me tell you what it is like out here tonight. Stories travel at night on the desert. Someone gets in his pickup and drives a couple of hundred miles for a beer, and he carries news of what is happening, back wherever he came from. Then he drives another hundred miles for another beer, and passes along stories from the last place as well as from the one before; it is a network kept alive by people whose instincts tell them that if they do not keep moving at night on the desert they will lose all reason. Here is a story that is going around the desert tonight: over across the Nevada line, sheriff's deputies are diving in some underground pools, trying to retrieve a couple of bodies known to be in the hole. The widow of one of the drowned boys is over there; she is eighteen, and pregnant, and is said not to leave the hole. The divers go down and come up, and she just stands there and stares into the water. They have been diving for ten days but have found no bottom to the caves, no bodies and no trace of them, only the black 90° water going down and down and down, and a single translucent fish, not classified. The story tonight is that one of the divers has been hauled up incoherent, out of his head, shouting—until they got him out of there so that the widow could not hear—about water that got hotter instead of cooler as he went down, about light flickering through the water, about magma, about underground nuclear testing.

6   That is the tone stories take out here, and there are quite a few of them tonight. And it is more than the stories alone. Across the road at the Faith Community Church a couple of dozen old people, come here to live in trailers and die in the sun, are holding a prayer sing. I cannot hear them and do not want to. What I can hear are

occasional coyotes and a constant chorus of "Baby the Rain Must Fall" from the jukebox in the Snake Room next door, and if I were also to hear those dying voices, those Midwestern voices drawn to this lunar country for some unimaginable atavistic rites, *rock of ages cleft for me*, I think I would lose my own reason. Every now and then I imagine I hear a rattlesnake, but my husband says that it is a faucet, a paper rustling, the wind. Then he stands by a window, and plays a flashlight over the dry wash outside.

7   What does it mean? It means nothing manageable. There is some sinister hysteria in the air out here tonight, some hint of the monstrous perversion to which any human idea can come. "I followed my own conscience." "I did what I thought was right." How many madmen have said it and meant it? How many murderers? Klaus Fuchs said it, and the men who committed the Mountain Meadows Massacre said it, and Alfred Rosenberg said it. And, as we are rotely and rather presumptuously reminded by those who would say it now, Jesus said it. Maybe we have all said it, and maybe we have been wrong. Except on that most primitive level—our loyalties to those we love—what could be more arrogant than to claim the primacy of personal conscience? ("Tell me," a rabbi asked Daniel Bell when he said, as a child, that he did not believe in God. "Do you think God cares?") At least some of the time, the world appears to me as a painting by Hieronymous Bosch; were I to follow my conscience then, it would lead me out onto the desert with Marion Faye, out to where he stood in *The Deer Park* looking east to Los Alamos and praying, as if for rain, that it would happen: ". . . *let it come and clear the rot and the stench and the stink, let it come for all of everywhere, just so it comes and the world stands clear in the white dead dawn.*"

8   Of course you will say that I do not have the right, even if I had the power, to inflict that unreasonable conscience upon you; nor do I want you to inflict your conscience, however reasonable, however enlightened, upon me. ("We must be aware of the dangers which lie in our most generous wishes," Lionel Trilling once wrote. "Some paradox of our nature leads us, when once we have made our fellow men the objects of our enlightened interest, to go on to make them the objects of our pity, then of our wisdom, ultimately of our coercion.") That the ethic of conscience is intrinsically insidious seems scarcely a revelatory point, but it is one raised with increasing infrequency; even those who do raise it tend to *segue* with troubling readiness into the quite contradictory position that the ethic of conscience is dangerous when it is "wrong," and admirable when it is "right."

9   You see I want to be quite obstinate about insisting that we

have no way of knowing—beyond that fundamental loyalty to the social code—what is "right" and what is "wrong," what is "good" and what "evil." I dwell so upon this because the most disturbing aspect of "morality" seems to me to be the frequency with which the word now appears; in the press, on television, in the most perfunctory kinds of conversation. Questions of straightforward power (or survival) politics, questions of quite different public policy, questions of almost anything: they are all assigned these factitious moral burdens. There is something facile going on, some self-indulgence at work. Of course we would all like to "believe" in something, like to assuage our private guilts in public causes, like to lose our tiresome selves; like, perhaps, to transform the white flag of defeat at home into the brave white banner of battle away from home. And of course it is all right to do that; that is how, immemorially, things have gotten done. But I think it is all right only so long as we do not delude ourselves about what we are doing, and why. It is all right only so long as we remember that all the *ad hoc* committees, all the picket lines, all the brave signatures in *The New York Times*, all the tools of agitprop straight across the spectrum, do not confer upon anyone any *ipso facto* virtue. It is all right only so long as we recognize that the end may or may not be expedient, may or may not be a good idea, but in any case has nothing to do with "morality." Because when we start deceiving ourselves into thinking not that we want something or need something, not that it is a pragmatic necessity for us to have it, but that it is a *moral imperative* that we have it, then is when we join the fashionable madmen, and then is when the thin whine of hysteria is heard in the land, and then is when we are in bad trouble. And I suspect we are already there.

QUESTIONS AND IDEAS FOR DISCUSSION

1. Didion describes the process of *trying* to define an abstraction. Does she actually offer a definition of *morality?*
2. If you conclude that Didion does not actually define *morality*, what is her thesis here, and why does she title the essay "On Morality"? If you conclude that Didion does define the word, is that definition reportive or stipulative? Is it a persuasive definition? How would you go about defining *morality?*
3. What does Didion mean by "wagon-train morality"?
4. Why does Didion object to words like *morality?* Evaluate her argument.

SUGGESTIONS FOR WRITING AND
FURTHER DISCUSSION

1. What is the effect on an angry prisoner when police officers refer to themselves as *pigs* before the prisoner has a chance to do so? Why do antiabortionists insist on being called prolife advocates instead? Write an essay in which you support Thomas Szasz's assertion that "he who first seizes the word imposes reality on the other: he who defines . . . dominates." Support your argument with vivid and appropriate examples. You may choose to modify or qualify Szasz's thesis.

2. Write a paper, addressed to an audience of white, black, Hispanic, and Oriental college students, in which you argue in favor of or in opposition to affirmative action programs designed to ensure that a certain percentage of minority students be included in graduate programs. Bear in mind that both you and the members of your audience have a stake in the question.

3. Write an extended *nonsexist* definition (that is, one not succumbing to stereotypes of what is masculine or feminine) of "the right stuff."

4. MacLeish's "Ars Poetica" defines poetry. Write a brief essay, perhaps a page in length, in which you define something more concrete than *poetry* in metaphorical and persuasive terms. Try *lettuce, toothpicks, bicycle, marshmallow, rain,* or *pencil.* Define the word by conditions for use, comparison with another word, or by any of the other methods that may lend themselves to metaphorical expression. To describe your subject effectively, find images that are fresh and appropriate.

5. Write an essay in which you redefine in a favorable light some quality or condition that is normally viewed unfavorably, such as *laziness, quarrelsomeness, evasiveness, obesity,* or *hypochondria.* Assume that your readers regard the state or condition in the usual way; attempt to win them over with a careful and persuasive redefinition.

6. Joan Didion shares with us her distrust of the word *morality,* a distrust resulting from the misapplications and distortions of the word's meaning. Think of a word that you object to or regard as misused or fuzzily abstract. Then write an essay in which you show your readers what is wrong with the usual meaning or use of the word, and what, in more concrete terms, it means or ought to mean. You might try one of the words that both ordinary people and courts of law have a lot of trouble defining, such as *decency.*

7. Suppose you were compelled to give up—to forget all the words you know except seven—what are the words you would keep?

   —Kahlil Gibran

   Write an essay in which you argue the reasons for your seven choices.

8. Write an essay—directed toward your classmates who you believe may not understand the term as they should—in which you argue an

extended definition for one of the terms you may have defined in Exercise 3–3:

history   myth
mental health   genius
language   detente

4

Research and the Uses of Evidence

Learn, compare, collect the facts!
In your work and in your research there must always be
passion.

Ivan Petrovich Pavlov

CREATIVITY IN RESEARCH

While the arguments you develop for many purposes and occasions will not require support beyond your own knowledge, experience, or expertise, others will require such support. And finding support for arguments means research. Unfortunately, the very word *research* puts many students off, bringing to mind visions of notecards, outlines, and what often seems the pointless rehashing of ideas and information that other people already have stated sufficiently well. But the same students may be people who enjoy puzzles, mysteries, or controversy; and true research, as opposed to cut-and-paste work, addresses those interests admirably. Effective, creative research involves solving puzzles: historical, political, scientific, economic, technical, or literary. Creative research does not come with conclusions and solutions ready-made; the researcher must be not only a worker of puzzles but also a sleuth—finding the evidence, distinguishing the valuable source or witness from the unreliable one, using imagination to reach a sound but not foregone conclusion. Creative research involves as well the awareness that sources of evidence often

82

disagree with each other, sometimes radically. The researcher must sort through conflicting dates, theories, interpretations, and predictions in order to determine where the truth lies.

As you research and write documented essays, then, you will find that a large part of what makes research enjoyable and creative stems from your willingness to go beyond the obvious and superficial elements of your subject. In the words of G. K. Chesterton, "There is no such thing on earth as an uninteresting subject; the only thing that can exist is an uninterested person." You must take an interest in finding out what is interesting in your subject.

An important first step is to find an aspect of your subject with potential for development and with potential for more than one possible solution or interpretation. The invention strategies discussed in Chapter 2 should help you here. And if you have been assigned a subject or a limited number of options, choose the road less traveled. For a paper in Medieval English history, for example, opt for the Coronation Charter of Henry I rather than the Magna Charta if your purpose is to show the influence some significant English document had on the development of the common law. A quick check in the card catalog and in an encyclopedia will show you whether or not enough material is likely to be available for developing a paper on the Coronation Charter. When you are working on a subject about which you have little prior knowledge, *make your preliminary thesis a question to be explored.* By doing so, you will keep your mind and your options open. And make it a question worth exploring. Of "Just what was the Coronation Charter of Henry I?" and "Did the Coronation Charter have any lasting effect on the government or the history of England?" the latter is more likely to offer a variety of possible responses and interpretations and, therefore, is more likely to stimulate creative analytical thinking.

Once you have a preliminary thesis question in mind, begin your search for evidence that will provide both answers and support for those answers. After some preliminary investigation (a number of possible sources are listed on pages 89–95), you will acquire enough basic material and evidence to begin to work your research question into a preliminary thesis. As we discussed in Chapter 2, be sure that your thesis, or controlling concept, is specific and limited and that it has, in rhetorician Sheridan Baker's words, an "argumentative edge." It should take a stand on the issue under investigation. And, as always, you must be willing to modify your stand if further research reveals flaws or misconceptions in it.

With your investigation initiated and your preliminary thesis formulated, determine key terms and define them if necessary (as discussed in Chapter 3). Then work out an outline or bare-bones draft of your proposed argument. Even if you have outline-phobia and usually write assigned outlines *after* writing essays, I urge you to write at least a list of major supporting points for your thesis, jotting down beneath each point any evidence you already have found to support that point. Doing so will give you a sense of direction: making clear what points need support and further research, revealing imbalances in development (too many points developing the causes, not enough on the results, perhaps) or inconsistencies in organization, exposing tangential points not strictly tied to your thesis. This step will make your writing a less complicated task, particularly if the paper is to be lengthy, and will help you to be more efficient in your further research. You will spend your time looking for evidence that is needed rather than overworking points for which you already have adequate support.

Except for the length of the paper and the use of outside sources, the actual writing and revision of the documented essay is much the same process involved in any essay or report. Properly and effectively using evidence to reach and support conclusions about your subject is likely to be your greatest challenge as researcher. For evidence presents some difficulties: First, you must locate it; second, you must evaluate it, for if the facts are unreliable, they are of little use; and third, you must cite it accurately, incorporate it into your own text smoothly, and credit its source. Discussing ways to meet these challenges will be our primary concern in this chapter.

FINDING EVIDENCE FOR ARGUMENTS

Evidence used to develop an argument can be of many kinds. Facts—examples, statistics, personal and authoritative testimony, and an assortment of bits of information—are used to provide supporting evidence for conclusions. In this chapter and elsewhere, the term *evidence* is used broadly, including under that heading everything from scientific data to personal anecdotes. Such evidence differs in kind, but not necessarily in merit, if the material is appropriate to the context in which it is used and if more is not claimed for it than is warranted. Some of the major kinds of evidence you will need to support your theses include examples (including even personal experiences and analogies), authoritative testimony, and statistics. We will consider these in turn.

Kinds of Evidence

Examples These are the specific instances of a phenomenon or members of a class that lead us to hypotheses or to generalizations about the entire class. The beautiful sunset today is in part an example of the effects of atmospheric pollutants. The Granny Smith apple I hold in my hand is an example of the class of apples. Examples are concrete and illustrative; they can be very persuasive in support of arguments. But examples should be representative of their class, and even then they do not *prove*. I cannot conclude from my examples here that the effects of atmospheric pollution are attractive, or that all apples are green and tart. More representative examples might be soot-covered buildings or people suffering from respiratory illnesses, and some red variety of apple, such as Red Delicious.

However, we should never underestimate the value of examples to argument, despite their limitations. With an example we cease to tell our readers about our idea and begin to *show* it to them so that it can become theirs. Furthermore, examples create images that are far more likely to be retained by a reader than are long loops of abstract reasoning. Finally, examples help to make complex theories plainer.

Authoritative Testimony   Arguments are frequently supported by the assertions of authorities. Such support enables the writer to make a persuasive case without having to enumerate all the data supporting the claim. You will recall arguments from authority from your childhood: "Why must I?" "Because I said so!" And you may recall resenting arguments of that ilk. To be acceptable, testimony first must be specific and limited—no vague and hollow verbal flourishes such as "Disarmament is a splendid idea." Second, it must be given by reputable authorities speaking within their areas of expertise. Margaret Mead may be cited in anthropological arguments; any comments she may have made about physics, on the other hand, do not carry the weight of authority. Linus Pauling is an accepted authority in chemistry, but a controversial one in nutrition and medicine. And third, the statements should be cited fairly and not out of context. Supreme Court Chief Justice Taney has been unfairly condemned as a racist for having written in the Dred Scott decision in 1857 that the Negro has "no rights which a white man [is] bound to respect." Justice Taney did use those words, but in a context that showed how much he deplored the idea and how wrong he considered it to be.

If authoritative testimony fulfills these three criteria, it is no fallacy to offer it as support for a relevant conclusion. To refuse to use such testimony imposes an unnecessary burden on the arguer, as columnist Ann Landers points out in her reply to a do-it-yourself reasoner:

Dear Ann Landers:

    Regarding the person who wanted to know if cold water boils faster than hot water and if hot water freezes faster than cold, you said you believe in going to the top and [that you had] contacted Dr.

Jerome Weisner, Chancellor of Massachusetts Institute of Technology.

Dr. Weisner said a problem of such extraordinary dimensions should be handled by an expert, so he turned the letter over to the dean of science, John W. Deutch. Deutch said neither statement was true.

Even though Dr. Deutch gave the correct answer, that procedure is called argument by authority and has absolutely no place in science. I was able to come to the same conclusion by using a pan of hot water, a thermometer, a stove, a refrigerator, and a watch with a second hand.

You, Ann Landers, exemplify what is wrong with our society. Too many bozos are too lazy to find the answers for themselves. It is easier to call on an "authority." How much more satisfying to rely on one's intelligence.

[Signed] Self-Reliant in Riverside

Dear Self-Reliant:

When a reader asks such a question, I am not about to tell him to do a home experiment, nor would I do one myself. I assure you that Dr. Deutch didn't boil any water, either. He *knew* the answer—which is the beauty of having a battery of top consultants.

In fairness to "Self-Reliant," we cannot discount the value of observation in reaching conclusions. But many questions do not lend themselves to such inductive tests and observation: How far away is the sun? Do cigarettes really cause lung cancer? What might Napoleon have done differently at Waterloo?

The use of expert testimony can provide valuable and convincing information in written argument as long as it fulfills the three requirements of specificity, relevance, and accuracy. To support some kinds of assertions, testimony can offer more appropriate premises than can most other kinds of evidence. For example, if I want to convince you that the English major provides excellent career preparation, quotations from professional school officials and employers would be likely to carry considerable weight. I might quote, for instance, this lament from an executive of the Prudential Insurance Company: "One of the chief weaknesses of many college graduates is the inability to express themselves well. Even though technically qualified, they will not advance far with such a handicap."

Statistics We are often distrustful of statistics, and rightly so—but we love to cite them. And for all our sophistication, we tend to believe statistics unless they strike us as outrageous or unpleasant. Only when the conclusions suggested by statistical information surprise or offend us do we ask for more evidence. However, in all cases it is well to be wary of statistics. Few forms of evidence are more susceptible to manipulation and distortion.

First, we cannot judge statistics adequately unless we know the way the data were collected and the procedures used to arrive at the results. And, even then, only a professional statistician is able to evaluate the conclusions. However, we nonstatisticians can use a few guidelines to help us make reasonable judgments about statistics. If a sample, including polls, is used to compile the statistics, we need to know something about the sample in order to determine whether it is representative and sufficient. If we know how a question on a poll was worded and how the respondents were selected, we can determine the probable fairness of the results. If we know who compiled the statistics and for what objective, we have a further determinant of their value. In a thorough study of the uses of evidence, appropriately entitled *Evidence,* Robert Newman and Dale Newman offer basic criteria for evaluating statistics:

1. Who wants to prove what?
2. What do the figures really represent?
3. What conclusion do the figures support?

Do both the following statements involving statistics use them fairly, as far as you can tell?

"The average age of our dancers is 28," says Biff Liebbe at Studebaker's, which plays no music of more recent vintage than 1970. "Jitterbug music like 'Rock Around the Clock' really packs the dance floor."
—Marty Primeau, "Dallas Dancing," in *Dallas Life Magazine,* 7 Aug. 1983

We evidently have enough *medical* knowledge to reduce prematurity rates to very low levels, but we lack the *social* ability to make such care accessible and acceptable to all women. Currently, the net result is that about 7% of all babies born in the United States—250,000 each year—weigh less than 2,500 grams (5.5 pounds), and about 100,000 of them weigh less than 1,500 grams (3.3 pounds). Interestingly, the chance of survival at any weight is highest for a black female, lowest for a white male.
—*Harvard Medical School Newsletter,* Aug. 1983

In the first quotation the manager of a nightclub offers a statistic—that "the average age of our dancers is 28"—which is probably a guess in the guise of statistical "fact." Did the manager verify each patron's age? It is more than likely that this number represents the manager's guess, based on the customers' apparent age or sheer wishful thinking—the manager's desire to attract customers in their late twenties. In the second quotation the statistics cited are seemingly trustworthy: Births are recorded, along with birthweight, sex, and race of the babies. The statistics here are not offered as being more precise than they actually are: "*about* 7% of all babies" and "*about* 100,000 of them." And the reporter of the statistics, Harvard Medical School, has a good reputation for dispensing reliable information. With reason, we are likely to accept the statistics from Harvard and question those from the nightclub.

The value of carefully determined statistics—and of evidence generally—is dramatically underscored by the disastrous Bay of Pigs invasion of 1962. As Charles W. Roll and Albert H. Cantril explain in *Polls: Their Use and Misuse in Politics*, a missing piece of evidence might have averted the whole fiasco:

During April and May 1960, Lloyd A. Free conducted an opinion survey in Cuba for the Institute for International Social Research. . . . A report was prepared based upon 1,000 carefully executed interviews in Havana and other urban areas throughout Cuba—where about 60 percent of the Cuban people live. The report showed that far from despair, the Cuban people backed Castro overwhelmingly, were enthused [sic] about the revolution Castro had brought to Cuba, were relieved that the days of Batista were over, and were optimistic about the future of the country. . . . Nonetheless, in the transitional days between the Eisenhower and Kennedy Administrations the report got buried and forgotten. It surfaced only after the ill-fated invasion attempt. When it was later learned that the report's findings directly contradicted the assumption of the invasion—that the Cuban populace would join the handful of invaders in an overthrow of the Castro regime—Arthur Schlesinger wrote poignantly that he only wished a copy had come to his attention earlier.

Accurate information and valid statistics can do more than support arguments; they can save face—and lives.

Locating Background and Historical Evidence

Where do you locate the examples, statements from authorities, statistics, and other facts your writing assignment requires? In the preliminary stages of researching a topic that may well be new and unfamiliar to you, you probably will turn to encyclopedias and bibliographies of books that provide an overview of your subject. The general information available in encyclopedias will help you formulate questions to pursue in arriving at a working thesis and then developing your arguments. And if your assignment is historical in nature—that is, having to do with an event, a work, or an issue not recently in the news—you may well find all the material you need in books and back issues of periodicals and newspapers. An annotated list of some of the best sources of background and historical data follows. Under each category the most general works are listed first, followed by specialized works in alphabetical order.

Encyclopedias   In addition to the following, you can find specialized encyclopedias by identifying the subject heading for your research topic in the *Library of Congress Subject Headings* (two volumes; the reference librarian can direct you to it) and then looking in the card catalog under "[Subject]: ENCYCLOPEDIAS."

New Encyclopedia Britannica. 15th ed. 30 vols. Chicago: Encyclopedia Britannica, 1980. General encyclopedia. Signed articles with bibliographies. Use the "Micropaedia" index to locate your subject in the 19-volume "Macropaedia."

Encyclopedia Americana. 30 vols. with annual supplements. New York: American Corporation, 1978. General encyclopedia. Use the index volume to locate your subject.

Britannica Encyclopedia of American Art. Chicago: Encyclopedia Britannica, 1973. Includes short articles on all fields of art with bibliographies, glossary, and information on museums.

Casell's Encyclopedia of World Literature. John Buchanan-Brown, ed. 3 vols. Rev. ed. New York: William Morrow & Co., 1973.

Daniel, Howard. *Encyclopedia of Themes and Subjects in Painting: Mythological, Biblical, Historical, Literary, Allegorical and Topical.* New York: Harry N. Abrams, 1971.

Encyclopedia of Business Information Sources. 3rd ed. Detroit: Gale Research Co., 1976. Lists sourcebooks, periodicals, organizations, handbooks, and bibliographies on business topics.

Encyclopedia of Philosophy. 8 vols. New York: Macmillan Publishing Co., 1967. Articles covering Eastern and Western philosophy from ancient times to the present.

Encyclopedia of Sociology. Guilford, Conn.: Dushkin Publishing Group, 1974. Covers terms, theories, and important theorists in the field.

Harper Encyclopedia of the Modern World. New York: Harper & Row, Publishers, 1970. Covers historical events from 1760 to late 1960s.

International Encyclopedia of the Social Sciences. D. L. Sills, ed. 17 vols. New York: Macmillan Publishing Co., 1968. Articles in anthropology, economics, history, law, political science, psychology, and sociology.

McGraw-Hill Encyclopedia of Science and Technology. 4th ed. 15 vols. with supplementary yearbooks. New York: McGraw-Hill Book Co., 1977. Written for the nonspecialist.

The New Illustrated Encyclopedia of World History. William L. Langer, ed. 2 vols. New York: Harry N. Abrams, 1975.

Bibliographies   Bibliographies list books and periodical articles covering a particular field or, as in the *Bibliographic Index* below, a number of fields of study. For additional bibliographies in these and other fields, consult the library card catalog for "[Subject]: BIBLIOGRAPHIES" listings.

The Bibliographic Index. New York: Wilson, 1938 to present. Issued twice a year and cumulated annually. A bibliography of bibliographies. Indexes bibliographies in both books and periodicals.

Ballou, Patricia K. *Women: A Bibliography of Bibliographies.* Boston: G. K. Hall, 1980. Women's studies issues.

Bibliographic Guide to Business and Economics. Boston: G. K. Hall, 1975 to present.

Day, Alan E. *History: A Reference Handbook.* Hamden, CT: Linnet Books, 1977. A guide to bibliographies, handbooks, dictionaries, and other sources.

Dyment, Alan R. *The Literature of the Film: A Bibliographic Guide to the Film as Art and Entertainment, 1936–1970.* London: White Lion, 1975.

Ehresmann, Donald L. *Fine Arts: A Bibliographic Guide to Basic Reference Works, Histories & Handbooks.* 2nd ed. Littleton, CO: Libraries Unlimited, 1979.

Guerry, Herbert. *A Bibliography of Philosophical Bibliographies.* Westport, CT: Greenwood Press, 1977. Includes entries on subjects and on particular philosophers.

Harmon, Robert B. *Political Science Bibliographies.* 2 vols. Metuchen, NJ: Scarecrow, 1973, 1976. A bibliography of bibliographies.

MLA International Bibliography of Books and Articles on Modern Language and Literature. New York: Modern Language Association of America, 1921 to present.

Van Fleet, David D. *An Historical Bibliography of Administration, Business & Management.* Monticello, Ill.: Vance Bibliographies, 1978.

Woodbury, Marda. *A Guide to Sources of Educational Information.* Washington, D.C.: Information Resources Press, 1976. Annotated.

Locating Current Evidence

Encyclopedias and books listed in specialized bibliographies or gathered directly from the card catalog are an excellent source of information for subjects that are not recent or are given to changes over time, and of background information for almost any subject. But all too often beginning writers *end* their quest for evidence at just this point, with encyclopedias and a stack of dusty books. The advantage books offer the researcher is considerable, for books often provide comprehensive, indepth treatment of important issues in the subject of your research. In addition, books often include bibliographies that refer you to still more sources of information and ideas. But the time required for writing and publishing books makes much of the information available in them at least five years old. This limitation may be of little or no consequence if your subject is literary or historical (including past scientific and technical issues), but it is a drawback if you need current, up-to-the-minute data—as is the case with all arguments about current events and controversies and most professional research done for employers.

If you need updated or recent information on your subject, turn to the periodical indexes. The most well-known of these is the *Reader's Guide to Periodical Literature*, which is reasonably up-to-date (supplements are issued biweekly) and can provide adequate resources for many subjects and occasions for writing. However, the *Reader's Guide* suffers a limitation as well. The more than 160 periodicals referenced therein are largely "general interest" magazines and journals which may not offer the specialized information you require for some projects and papers.

Writers of argument sometimes need just what the card catalog and the *Reader's Guide* cannot always offer us: current or specialized information. Fortunately, some resources are available that can provide recent and even up-to-the-moment bibliographic and reference material, while others can offer information as specialized as *Nineteenth-Century Literature Criticism* and *Bibliography of North American Geology*. Recent material may be gathered from a number of sources, as the following samples indicate:

Indexes, Abstracts, and Almanacs Updated Annually

Book Review Index. Detroit: Gale Research Co., 1965 to present. Covers literature, art, business, economics, religion, and current affairs. Useful in evaluating sources.

Computer Yearbook. Detroit: Computer Yearbook Co., 1952 to present. Developments and applications described for the nonexpert.

Statistical Abstracts of the United States. Washington, D.C.: Bureau of the Census, 1878 to present. Summarizes social, political, economic, and cultural statistics, with sources identified. Some regional, state, and metropolitan information included.

World Almanac & Book of Facts. New York: Newspaper Enterprise Assn., 1868 to present. Useful detailed index of wide range of subjects.

Indexes Updated Quarterly or Monthly

Art Index. New York: Wilson, 1929 to present. Issued quarterly. Indexes art periodicals, museum bulletins, and related materials; covers both European and English-language publications.

Biological and Agricultural Index. New York: Wilson, 1964 to present. Issued monthly. Notes the inclusion of bibliographies, charts, illustrations, and the like for each item indexed.

Book Review Digest. New York: Wilson, 1905 to present. Issued monthly. Includes excerpts from reviews.

Business Periodicals Index. New York: Wilson, 1958 to present. Issued monthly. Covers (by subject) periodicals in accounting, advertising, banking, finance, insurance, labor, and taxation.

Current Biography. New York: Wilson, 1940 to present. Issued monthly. Useful articles about people recently in the news. Monthly issues and annual yearbook are both indexed.

Editorials on File. New York: Facts on File, 1970 to present. Issued monthly and cumulated bimonthly. Covers U.S. and Canadian newspapers. Reprints editorials, arranged by subject.

Education Index. New York: Wilson, 1929 to present. Issued monthly. Covers all subjects related to education.

Film Literature Index. Albany, N.Y.: SUNY-Albany, 1973 to present. Issued quarterly. Indexed by author and subject. Includes television.

Humanities Index. New York: Wilson, 1965 to present. (Before 1974 entitled *Social Sciences and Humanities Index.*) Issued quarterly. Covers archaeology and classical studies, area studies, folklore, history, language and literature, literary and political criticism, performing arts, philosophy, religion and theology, and related subjects.

Music Index. Detroit: Detroit Information Service, 1949 to present. Issued monthly. Lists articles by author, subject, composer, and famous performers.

New York Times Index. New York: New York Times, 1913 to present. Issued bimonthly. Alphabetically cross-referenced by subjects, persons, and organizations. Helpful in locating articles in unindexed newspapers in that it provides researcher with dates under which to look.

Social Sciences Index. New York: Wilson, 1965 to present. (Before 1974 entitled *Social Sciences and Humanities Index.*) Issued quarterly. Covers anthropology, economics, environmental sciences, geography, law and criminology, public administration, political science, psychology, social aspects of medicine, sociology, and related subjects. Includes separate author listing of book reviews.

Indexes and Bulletins Updated Biweekly and Weekly

Reader's Guide to Periodical Literature. New York: Wilson, 1900 to present. Issued biweekly. Indexes about 100 general, nontechnical magazines. Articles are cross-referenced by author and subject.

Congressional Quarterly Weekly Report. Washington, D.C.: Government Printing Office, 1945 to present. Issued weekly with quarterly index. Describes congressional actions of the preceding week and reprints important texts and speeches. Provides charts showing the progress of major legislation through committee and floor sessions.

Facts on File. New York: Facts on File, 1941 to present. Issued weekly, indexed annually. Digest of world news.

Public Affairs Information Service Bulletin. New York: P.A.I.S., 1915 to present. Updated bimonthly with quarterly cumulations and an annual. Covers books, government publications, pamphlets, and periodical articles relating to economic and social conditions, public administration, and international relations.

Vital Speeches of the Day. Stronghold, L.I.: City News Publishing Co., 1934 to present. Issued biweekly and indexed in *Reader's Guide.* Full texts of recent addresses by prominent individuals, mostly American.

Weekly Compilation of Presidential Documents. Washington, D.C.: Government Printing Office. Updated weekly. Texts of presidential speeches, press conferences, and other presidential materials.

Still, if you are interested in a current issue not having to do with American national politics and policy, even these sources may not provide facts and opinions appropriate to or recent enough for your purposes. A raging controversy about last month's state elections, the newest treatment for cancer, an innovative soil additive for drought-stricken regions, or a just-released, best-selling exposé of the plastics industry—subjects like these require information that has not yet reached the compilers of indexes, let alone the writers of books. For such needs resources are available that writers sometimes overlook: the Postal Service, the telephone, a car or public transportation, and myriad computer networks that may be available through your college library. You can write directly to the sources of much information; you can telephone when you need immediate verification of facts; you can interview people locally who have knowledge of particular local (and sometimes state or national) issues; and you can query computer database networks for almost any imaginable current data.

Using databases to locate up-to-date material is a relatively new option for the researcher, but computerized information services are available in an increasing number of university and college libraries. The possibilities for gathering current material quickly and accurately from computer search networks is almost limitless, and expanding daily. A small sampling of the databases presently available includes those in the accompanying list. Many of these databases, such as the *National Newspaper Index,* are updated daily. Some of them are based on bibliographic indexes also available in print; the database versions can locate the exact information you need in a fraction of the time you might spend thumbing through the printed volumes. Many more offer information that might otherwise be difficult or impossible to locate quickly. Your reference librarian can inform you about the availability of and charges for the computerized services.

Selected Database Sources

Multidisciplinary and Current Affairs

ASI (American Statistics Index)
CIS (Congressional publications)

Comprehensive Dissertation Index
Conference Papers Index (Scientific and technical conference reports)
Encyclopedia of Associations (Descriptions and directory information)
Foundation Grants Index
GPO Monthly Catalog (U.S. government publications)
Grants Database
Magazine Index (Popular magazines)
National Newspaper Index (*The Christian Science Monitor, The New York Times, The Wall Street Journal*)
Newsearch (Magazine and newspaper articles, past month)
NTIS (Government-sponsored research reports)
PAIS International (Articles, books, documents on public policy)

Sciences

Biosis Previews (Biological Abstracts, Biological Abstracts/RRM)
CA Search (Chemical Abstracts)
Chemsearch (Dictionary listing of most recently cited substances in CA Search)
Georef (Earth science publications)
INSPEC (Physics Abstracts, Electrical and Electronics Abstracts, Computer and Control Abstracts)
Medline (Index Medicus, Index to Dental Literature, International Nursing Index)
Scisearch (Science Citation Index)
SPIN (Searchable Physics Information Notices)

Applied Sciences and Technology

Compendex (Engineering Index)
Energyline (Energy Information Abstracts)
Enviroline (Environmental information)
ISMEC (Information Service in Mechanical Engineering)
Pollution Abstracts
Selected Water Resources Abstracts

Social Sciences and Humanities

America: History and Life
Artbibliographies Modern
ERIC (Research in Education, Current Index to Journals in Education)
Historical Abstracts
Language and Language Behavior Abstracts
MLA Bibliography (Literature and linguistics)
Philosopher's Index
Population Bibliography
Psychinfo (Psychological Abstracts)

RILM Abstracts (Music)
Social Scisearch (Social Science Citation Index)
Sociological Abstracts

Business and Economics

ABI/INFORM (Business journals)
Disclosure (Corporate financial reports to the SEC)
Economics Abstracts International
EIS Industrial Plants (Information on manufacturing establishments)
Management Contents (Business journals, proceedings)
PTS F&S Indexes (Company, product, and industry information)
PTS International Forecasts (Predicasts)
PTS U.S. Forecasts (Predicasts)
Standard & Poor's News (S&P's Daily News and Cumulative News)
Trade Opportunities (Export opportunities for U.S. businesses)

Gathering first-hand and up-to-the-minute facts and testimony through letter and telephone queries, interviews, and computer searches has two drawbacks: It takes time and tenacity, and it can be expensive. It can also be fruitless: You may receive no reply to your letter, and the computer may not turn up anything you can use. To decide whether or not to pursue such sources of information, consider the importance to your argument of the evidence you hope to get and the importance of your argument itself. For a short, informal essay, such an investment of time and money may not be worthwhile or even necessary. Your own knowledge and experiences may suffice. For a term paper or a major presentation to your company, however, the investment may be essential.

EVALUATING EVIDENCE

Facts are stubborn things; and whatever may be our wishes, our inclinations, or the dictates of our passions, they cannot alter the state of facts and evidence.
—John Adams

But one must not be misled by the evidence.   —Sigmund Freud

John Adams was quite right: Facts are stubborn things, and it requires tremendous mental agility to avoid dealing with them or to escape the conclusions they point toward. But Freud was right as well, for facts are also slippery and elusive things; they can be misleading, so that we sometimes hardly know whether to accept them or to denounce them as frauds. Not long ago our ancestors accepted as fact the notions that the earth was flat and that witches could not drown. And more recently it was settled fact that the atom could not be split nor could human beings be conceived in a Petri dish. What is presented as fact—and believed—is sometimes conceived in error or ignorance or falsehood. Some people hesitate to use the word *fact,* so slippery is it. But whether we use the word or not, much reasoning relies on data we call, from preference or habit, **facts**—that is, beliefs we hold about our world based on evidence we have chosen to attend to.

Evidence cannot be gathered indiscriminately; in deciding what sources to use and in assessing the material gathered from them, we must make judgments about the quality and appropriateness for our purposes of the evidence we are searching for and the evidence we find. Pertinent evidence provides premises that support conclusions. Since the conclusions to such arguments are never more than probable,* their persuasiveness depends on evidence that is

1. *recent* (or contemporaneous, in historical arguments);
2. *primary,* if possible ("eyewitness" evidence);
3. *unbiased* (as far as humanly possible);
4. *representative* of its class;
5. *sufficient* in quantity to carry conviction.

Recent Evidence

Always note the dates of evidence offered in support of a writer's thesis. Recent evidence is often desirable—as the emphasis in the previous section on ways of gathering current material reflects. If you are writing about the sciences (natural, social, or political), business, or technology—all fields in which new developments and discoveries occur almost daily, often invalidating or modifying previous thought—you must use the most recent evidence available on your subject, if your argument is to be credible. For this reason periodicals, newsletters, news reports, and computer databases will provide valuable evidence. Because of the time required for publishing, books in these fields may be somewhat dated by the time they appear in print. They provide useful background information, however, and their bibliographies may lead you to further sources.

On the other hand, if you are writing about history, philosophy, the fine arts, or literature—all fields in which a little distance from the subject can add context and perspective to your evaluation of it—books and periodicals can be equally useful. Even if your topic is, say, the recent work of Jasper Johns, books dealing with his earlier works or with twen-

---

*These kinds of arguments use inductive reasoning, which we will discuss more fully in Chapter 7.

tieth-century artists in general can provide a context for comparison and evaluation, while contemporary art journals such as *Artforum* or *Art in America* can offer a counterpoint to your own judgments of Johns's recent paintings.

Primary Evidence

Evidence is *primary* if it comes from the original source. It is *secondary* if it comes from someone else's report on or evaluation of the original source. For example, Jasper Johns's actual paintings (or, less satisfactorily, prints of them) are a primary source; Meyer Shapiro's discussion of them is a secondary source. Marx's *Communist Manifesto* is a primary source; Edmund Wilson's discussion of the impact of Marxist socialism in *To the Finland Station* is a secondary source. Froissart's account of the Hundred Years' War is an interesting case, for he was not on hand for many of the events he reports in the *Chronicles*. In relative terms, however, the *Chronicles* offer primary information while Geoffrey Brereton's assessment of them and their author (in Brereton's introduction to the Penguin edition, 1968) is secondary material.

The advantage of primary evidence is obvious: Using primary evidence, you make your own assessment without having to judge through the filter of someone else's vision—a filter which might be inaccurate or otherwise distorted. Herein lies the advantage, too, of reading foreign-language material in the original tongue, for inaccuracies can occur and biases creep into translations. It is ideal to know German if you are reading Freud or Marx, French if you are reading Froissart, classical Greek if you are reading Aristotle. If you cannot read German or French or classical Greek, it is well to know the relative merits and demerits of the translators. Consult your instructor or reference librarian for help in choosing the most accurate translations. Also note which translations your secondary sources seem to favor.

Secondary source material should always be reviewed and assessed in light of whatever primary evidence is available. Unfortunately (but life—and research—would be dull otherwise), you will find that the authors of secondary sources frequently disagree with each other, sometimes in minor details and sometimes in major conclusions. However, the more secondary material you accumulate, the better able you will be to assess the reliability of each source, balancing one claim against a contradictory one in order to identify and eliminate as many inaccuracies and biases as possible.

This is not to suggest that all primary evidence is superior to all secondary evidence. Even the eyewitnesses to events or the developers of new processes and products or the discoverers of previously uncharted geographical and astronomical bodies are human and subject to all kinds of prejudices, biases, and misperceptions—particularly about themselves and their own observations, discoveries, inventions, or pet subjects. You must evaluate written primary evidence as you would any other. In doing so, recall the discussion of emotional appeals and slanting in Chapter 1. As with secondary sources, try to find more than one primary source in order to weigh their relative merits.

Unbiased Evidence

First principle: Nothing that is written is totally without bias—even recipes. (For years I was intimidated by a pound cake recipe that sternly instructed, "Use butter *only*." Margarine, it turns out, works fine.) So in evaluating evidence in others' arguments or for your own, consider first what the biases are and then whether they are strong enough to affect the value of the evidence. Sometimes the writer's bias is obvious: "Belying her petite good looks, soft-spoken Lucy White is not only a suburban wife and mother but a highly successful plaintiff's attorney." Sometimes the bias is more subtle: "Mrs. Lucy White has successfully combined careers as wife of Henry White and mother of twin sons and as a plaintiff's attorney." This statement might at first appear congratulatory rather than condescending, but its bias becomes apparent when we try a different version: "Mr. Henry White has successfully combined careers as husband of Lucy White and father of twin sons and as an economics professor." Has the writer a reputation for fairness, or, if she is unknown to you, has she created a trustworthy persona in what she has written? A careful reading and comparison with other material written on the same subject will help you to determine what biases are reflected in the material at hand.

Just as you consider your own rhetorical stance in preparing to write an argumentative paper, you need to consider the rhetorical stance of the authors of both primary and secondary source material in order to assess the material's merit as evidence. In evaluating evidence and arguments, consider the writers' point of view about the subject matter and their purpose in writing about it. For instance, an author who is interested in how Henry James's work is connected with his life will approach *The Portrait of a Lady* differently from one who is interested in the development of the American novel. One point of view is no more valid than the other, but each affects the scope and emphasis of the respective work. A writer's purpose—the thesis, or whole aim in writing—also affects the content of the argument and reflects the author's biases about the particular subject. Read the preface or "author's note" of a book to get an immediate idea of both the writer's point of view and purpose in writing. In his concluding note to *The Best and the Brightest*, for example, author David Halberstam states both:

At that point I was looking for a new assignment, and my colleague at *Harper's*, Midge Decter, suggested that I do a piece on McGeorge Bundy, who was after all the most glistening of the Kennedy-Johnson intellectuals. It would be a way not only of looking at him—very little was known about what he really did and stood for—but also of looking at that entire era. . . . When the article was finished I had a feeling of having just started. . . . I wanted to find out the full reasons why it [the escalation of the war in Vietnam] had all happened, I wanted to know the full context of the decisions, as well as how they were made. Why had they crossed the Rubicon? . . . The question that intrigued me most was *why*, why had it happened. So it became very quickly not a book about Vietnam, but a book about America, and in particular about power and success in America, what the country was, who the leadership was, how they got ahead, what their perceptions were about themselves, about the country and about their mission.

Halberstam spells out, more fully than this excerpt can suggest, just what his subject is and what his purpose in writing about it is. Not incidentally, he shows us the excitement creative research—research that is discovery and not just recapitulation—can generate. He is frank about his own biases, his belief that the men in power at the time were intelligent people who made some incredibly irrational decisions. Of his own position regarding the war, Halberstam writes, "[I]n the fall of 1963 I came to the conclusion that it was doomed and that we were on the wrong side of history." Such frankness is of help to us as we evaluate the evidence any writer offers. When frankness is not forthcoming or the book or article includes no prefatory note, the prose itself almost always provides clues. What, for example, are the apparent biases of the *Newsweek* reporter who wrote the following excerpt on the enduring appeal of Nancy Drew mysteries?

Stereotyped ethnic dialect, like automobile running boards, has been eliminated by rewriting the early books, but blacks are still about as common as Martians; if it weren't for her protofeminist pluck, Nancy, with her cleancut friends, country-club membership and limitless leisure, would be as ideal a heroine for the Reagan era as she was for the glamour-hungry Depression years.

—26 Mar. 1984

Representative Evidence

If you want to argue that blue jays are the most obnoxious of creatures, you cannot observe and catalogue every blue jay. A handful of examples and anecdotes will suffice. But the blue jays you describe should be typical of their class; that is, they should not be blue jays raised by hand and kept in cages. The same is true of weightier matters: Any evidence you cite should be typical of the class about which the conclusion is drawn. If you question eighty students at a wealthy, church-related university about their political preferences in order to support a generalization that college students in the United States are politically conservative, you may draw conclusions that are unreliable—your sampling (besides being relatively small and limited to a single campus) is not representative of American college students in general. Since the constraints of time, good sense, and space usually preclude using all the available examples of a class, those you cite should be typical.

Sufficient Evidence

What constitutes "sufficient" evidence to carry conviction will vary. As a rule, one example can illustrate, but not convince. A thousand examples can convince, but readers are likely to doze off long before they reach the end of the litany. Readers really do not want to hear about every flamingo in captivity or about every single play in a soccer match, however brilliantly played. Generally, the greater the controversy or the more unexpected the conclusion drawn, the more evidence needed. Regardless of the audience, more evidence would be required to make a convincing case on either side of the gun control issue or the insanity defense for murder than would be required to support an argument on the educational and ecological value of zoos. Or flamingos.

EXERCISE 4–1

For each of the following topics, indicate whether current information and evidence (no more than three to four months old) would be essential, important, useful, or not necessary.

1. Race relations in South Africa since 1985
2. The justness of the insanity defense for murder
3. The rise and fall (and rise and fall) of OPEC (Organization of Petroleum Exporting Countries)
4. The difficulties of living with a roommate
5. Whether Fascism is more dangerous to world peace than is Communism
6. Possible cures for AIDS
7. The viability of NATO
8. The claim that Austrian President Kurt Waldheim was guilty of Nazi war crimes in World War II
9. The health of the Social Security system
10. The relationship, if any, between legal drinking age and the number of serious traffic accidents in this state

EXERCISE 4-2

First, identify the type of evidence offered in each item below: example, testimony, statistic, or other kind of "fact." If the evidence is not common knowledge, a source will be mentioned; indicate your assessment of the source as likely to be accurate and fair, not likely to be accurate and fair, or unknown to you and impossible to evaluate. Then evaluate the evidence according to the first four standards described earlier: Does it appear to be recent (or contemporaneous) or outdated, primary or secondary, unbiased or biased, and representative or unrepresentative of its class?

1. One of the first black American businesswomen to become a millionaire was Sarah Breedlove Walker, who lived from 1867 to 1919.
   —*Notable American Women*,
   The Belknap Press of Harvard University Press, 1971

2. Debussy's *Pelleas et Melisande* is "the only significant opera that impressionism has produced."   —*Harvard Dictionary of Music*,
   2nd ed., 1969

3. As someone who has spent six months in Spain (in 1972), I can state from experience that relations between the Guardia Civil (state police) and the university students are anything but cordial.

4. Philomel is the name poets give to nightingales, but in the myth it was Procne who became a nightingale; Philomel was transformed into a lark.

5. The two movies to cinematographer Albert Lamorisse's credit are *White Mane* (1953) and *The Wonderful Adventure of Nils* (1962).
   —*The New York Times Dictionary of the Film*, 1974

6. Table salt is not a salt at all, but sodium chloride.

7. Professor Barney Slocum of Cambridge College Department of Mechanical Engineering says that Canadian and American bridges built before 1917 should be examined annually for structural defects.

8. More people in the West than in any other region of the United States approve of abortion during the first trimester of pregnancy.
   —*Gallup Poll of Public Opinion*, 1981

9. *Albion* is the poetic name for England.

10. Both men and women agree that a woman's life is more difficult than a man's.   —*Gallup Poll of Public Opinion*. 1935–1971.
    This statement is based on a
    poll taken in April 1946.

11. Among John Updike's poetic works are "Ex-Basketball Player," "Insomnia the Gem of the Ocean," and "Tao in the Yankee Stadium Bleachers."
    —*Granger's Index to Poetry*,
    Columbia University Press, 1982

12. Burundi and Cameroon are two African nations.
13. "Adrian IV is recognized as the first, and so far only, Englishman to
    have been pope."   —*The People's Almanac #3,* 1981
14. Illinois raised its legal drinking age from nineteen to twenty-one in
    1980 and saw a drop in the number of traffic accidents among drivers
    under twenty-one.
15. Anthony Trollope, the novelist, invented the mailbox.
                            —John Kenneth Galbraith, noted economist,
                                        in *A View from the Stands*
16. According to Census records, "1980 marked the first increase in the
    foreign-born proportion [of the U. S. population] since the 1900–1910
    decade."
                                            —Andrew Hacker, ed.,
                    U/S: A Statistical Portrait of the American People

---

EXERCISE 4–3

Revise each of the following generalizations (or one of the variations
suggested in parentheses) to a statement precise and limited enough to
be supported in a short essay (three to five pages). Write out your revised
generalization, and then discuss briefly the kinds of support—examples,
testimony (including your own knowledge and experiences), statistics,
and other kinds of "facts" that would be effective in an argument addressed to the other members of your rhetoric class.

1. Fraternities are inherently a bad (good) idea.
2. Politicians should (should not) be independently wealthy.
3. Math (any other major) is a useful college major.
4. Video games are interesting.
5. Soccer (any other sport) is superior to football.
6. The number of law school graduates should be restricted; there are
   too many lawyers.
7. Motorcycles (speedboats, snowmobiles) are a public hazard and
   should be outlawed.
8. Travel to foreign countries is fun and educational.
9. Abortion is murder (a woman's right).
10. The income tax amounts to creeping socialism (keeps needy people
    from dying for lack of food, shelter, or medical care).

USING EVIDENCE IN
DOCUMENTED ESSAYS AND
RESEARCH PAPERS

Summarizing, Paraphrasing, Quoting

Once you return from the library, armed with all sorts of ammunition with which to demolish the opposition in your written argument, two temptations and two difficulties arise. The first temptation is to use every bit of the material you have worked so hard to find, even if some of the evidence is tangential to your thesis, or even if you have so much material that to summarize or quote from all of it will leave you no room or energy to develop your own ideas in response to it. The second temptation occurs when the source material is written so well and so clearly that you cannot imagine expressing the information in any other way. This usually unwarranted humility can result in an unattractive patchwork of a paper largely made up of lengthy quotations seamed together with transitional remarks—or in plagiarism, whether unconscious or deliberate.

Therefore, your first task must be to test your working outline and your evidence against each other. Your research may have turned up additional points to support your thesis, or it may have exposed flaws in your thesis that require you to modify your stance. Some fascinating material may not fit anywhere in your outlined argument, and you must let that material wait for another day and another essay. Then, too, what you have learned may suggest a more logical way of ordering the points you propose to make. And inadequacies in the support you have gathered will become apparent as you briefly identify the evidence you have found under each entry in your outline or bare-bones draft (if you use notecards, simply arrange them according to the major points they support). Where support appears inadequate, you must decide whether to modify or eliminate that particular point, or return to the library.

Now, how do you record the supporting material in such a way that you avoid that second temptation? Summarize most of it; paraphrase what is important but difficult to grasp in the original; and quote what is crucial, brief, and clear. If you are using a general or research handbook, these three ways of recording your research are explained in some detail therein. Briefly, to **summarize** is to express another's ideas *in your own words* and to do so in many fewer words than the original. To **paraphrase** is to express another's ideas *in your own words* and to do so in about the same number of words or even more words than the original. To **quote** is to express another's ideas *in that person's own words* and to indicate clearly that you have done so. In each case, you credit the source in your paper.

Even after you have put temptation behind you and have summarized most of your source material and have put aside all of it that is not directly relevant to your argument, the two difficulties remain to be dealt with. The first difficulty is that fitting source material into your own prose may be difficult to manage without ending up with something that reads as if it had been cut and pasted; the second, that the punctuation, pronouns, and verb tenses in the source material may not mesh well with your own writing. When the latter is the case, the quotations seem obtrusive even if they are introduced properly.

In order to overcome or avoid these difficulties, keep in mind a few points:

1. Direct quotations should be few and significant. The paper is to be your essay and your argument, after all. Too many other voices overpower your own. Instead, rely on restatement, summary, and evaluation of much of the source material in your own words.
2. Quotations (and paraphrases and summaries) must be accurate. An inaccurate quotation is careless and can be misleading, and a quotation taken out of context can be distorted.
3. Quotations ordinarily should be preceded or followed by comment or analysis. If a passage does not merit comment or analysis, it usually does not merit direct quotation. (In which case, summarize instead.)
4. Quotations must be grammatically and logically incorporated into the paragraph in which you use them. They should fit into, not just be appliqued on, your own argument.
5. All sources, whether quoted, paraphrased, or summarized, must be properly cited.

To accomplish these aims, first, take most of your notes in your own words. This bit of advice is time-worn but still valuable. Taking notes in your own words has the initial advantage of requiring that you read closely and truly understand what you are reading, a requirement not exacted by a Xerox machine. In addition, understanding the material will facilitate your use of it in your own argument; and because it will be recounted in your own words, you will avoid the patchwork effect of excessive quotations. (Of course, citations still will be required.) Save direct quotations for brief, brilliant comments, controversial statements, statistics, and personal testimony you feel will strengthen your argument. Always indicate directly quoted material with quotation marks and page references in your notes so that you will avoid confusion later as you write and revise.

Incorporating Quotations

Second, as you write the essay, incorporate quoted material grammatically and logically into your own paragraphs. Quotations should not crop up unannounced, without evident context. Those running longer than three lines of typescript should be indented ten spaces (and instructors may prefer that you also single-space them) and should be introduced by an entire sentence or by a clause and a colon. Shorter quotations also must be given a context that fits them grammatically and logically into your argument and your words. Brief quotations may be incorporated in an almost limitless number of ways, as the following examples indicate:

(1)

Mark Antony uses irony in his funeral oration for Caesar. "I come to bury Caesar, not to praise him" (3.2.79–80) asserts just the opposite of what he intends to do. Mark Antony uses the oration to praise Caesar backhandedly and to attack Caesar's murderers while pretending to applaud them.

(2)

Mark Antony's funeral oration for Caesar uses irony effectively, for after claiming, "I come to bury Caesar, not to praise him" (3.2.79–80), Mark Antony goes on to attack Caesar's murderers through the irony of his repeated reference to "the noble Brutus." As the whole context of his speech makes clear, Caesar's ally means the opposite of what he says here.

(3)

Never was a funeral oration used to better political effect than that of Mark Antony over the body of the dead Caesar. He begins with a disclaimer: "I come to bury Caesar, not to praise him" (3.2.79–80). Having lulled Caesar's enemies, Mark Antony then turns the crowd against them through the heavy irony of his repeated praise of them, "all honorable men."

In the first example the quotation serves as the subject of a sentence explaining its meaning. In the second the same quotation is grammatically imbedded within a sentence that gives it a context in the play and in the student writer's argument. The quoted phrase, "the noble Brutus," is incorporated without punctuation because it functions as the object of a preposition. And in the third selection the quotation is introduced by a clause and a colon as is typical of longer quotations, and the quoted phrase "all honorable men" serves as an appositive describing the murderers.

But suppose that the quotation is written in the past tense, and your paragraph is written in the present; or that the quotation begins with a capital letter, but a capital letter is not needed at the point in your own sentence at which you quote another's words; or that you want to omit words or sentences preceding, following, or in the middle of what you plan to quote—what then? The following pointers should help you resolve most dilemmas of this sort.

Changes   Generally, avoid changes in the quoted material. If you must have them, put brackets around the altered letter or word. Do not alter punctuation except as noted below.

1. If the quoted material begins with a capital letter and its placement in your own sentence requires a lower-case letter, change the initial letter to lower case. Conservative usage dictates brackets around the altered letter, but brackets can be distracting. Try to rephrase your own sentence so that the quotation can be incorporated without such changes. (If your typewriter has no bracket keys, you must ink in any brackets required, for parentheses do not indicate added or altered words.) Make the same kind of change if the original quotation begins with a lower-case letter and your grammatical context for it requires a capital.

Original Statement: The one function that TV news performs very well is that when there is no news, we give it to you with the same emphasis as if there were news.   —David Brinkley

As Quoted: David Brinkley has observed that "[t]he one function that TV news performs very well is that when there is no news, [newscasters] give it to you with the same emphasis as if there were news."

2. If the quoted material uses present tense and you would prefer to have it in past tense, avoid making a change in the quoted material by wording your introduction in such a way that the shift in tense is accounted for without changing the original. In brief quotations involving only a single verb, you may change the tense and bracket the altered word, but try to avoid the need to do so by reworking your own sentence or by omitting from the quotation the part containing the troublesome verb.

Original Statement: Those who make peaceful revolution impossible will make violent revolution inevitable.   —John Kennedy

As Quoted: The United States was culpable in the Iranian revolution of 1979 to the extent that it did all in its power to keep the Shah in sole control of the government, despite the widespread opposition to many of the Shah's policies. The U.S. failed to heed John Kennedy's warning made almost two decades earlier: "Those who make peaceful revolution impossible will make violent revolution inevitable."

Original Statement: Boswell is the first of biographers.   —Macauley

As Quoted: In the nineteenth century Macauley declared Boswell to be "the first of biographers."

3. Commas, semicolons, colons, and periods ending quotations may be changed to the punctuation mark that fits your own grammatical context (usually a period, comma, or no punctuation). Do not end a quotation with double punctuation (the original writer's and then your own).

Original Statement: If the life of a human being is more valuable than the life of, say, a cabbage, this must be because the human being has qualities like consciousness, rationality, autonomy, and self-awareness which distinguish human beings from cabbages. How, then, can we pretend that the life of a human being with all these distinctive qualities is of no greater value than the life of a human being who, tragically, has never had and never will have these qualities?
—Peter Singer and Helga Kuhse, rev. of Robert and Peggy Stinson, *The Long Dying of Baby Andrew*

As Quoted: As Singer and Kuhse observe, it is pointless to "pretend that the life of a human being with all these distinctive qualities [such as rationality and self-awareness] is of no greater value than the life of a human being who, tragically, has never had and never will have these qualities" (16).

4. Change double quotation marks (" ") within quotations to single marks (' ') unless the whole passage is set off from the text.

Original Statement: Apparently, now that he knew he was in trouble, his thoughts had turned to his God. "Have mercy!" they heard him shouting indignantly. "I say have mercy, damn it!"   —Clarence Day, *Life With Father* (Knopf, 1935) 26

As Quoted: Day's father was a man not to be trifled with, even by Almighty God. On the rare occasion when the senior Day felt the need to call upon his Maker, it was as if he called upon an equal: " 'Have mercy!' they heard him shouting indignantly. 'I say have mercy, damn it!' " (26).

Omissions   Whenever you omit parts of a quoted passage, make sure that what you do quote still shows grammatical continuity and logical sense. For example:

Original Statement: Singer and Kuhse (above).

Unclear Abridgement: As Singer and Kuhse cogently argue, "a human being is more valuable than the life of a cabbage . . . because . . . these distinctive qualities are of . . . greater value than the life of a human being who, tragically, has never had and never will have these qualities" (16).

Effective Abridgement: As Singer and Kuhse cogently argue, "the life of a human being is more valuable than the life of a cabbage [primarily because of] . . . qualities like consciousness . . . and self-awareness" (16).

1. If you omit words, phrases, or sentences in the middle of a quoted passage, indicate the omission with ellipses (. . .). Use four dots if the words on either side of the ellipses are both grammatically complete sentences or if a sentence ends and another begins in the omitted section.

Original Statement: The cult of "reason," so widely applied in the course of the last three centuries, has come to seem to me in a sense a blind alley. Our thoughts and actions may be controlled by but they do not spring from what we call reason.

—Edmund Wilson, *The Dead Sea Scrolls, 1947–1966* (Oxford UP, 1969) 277

As Quoted: Logic is not the source of ideas, Wilson reminds us: "The cult of 'reason' . . . has come to seem to me in a sense a blind alley. Our thoughts and actions may be controlled by but they do not spring from what we call reason" (*Dead Sea Scrolls* 277).

[An abbreviated form of the title is included in a reference to one of several works written by the same author(s).]

2. If you omit sentences before the quoted material (as you ordinarily will), do not use ellipses. If you omit words or sentences following the quoted material, and the next words in the sentence are your own, do not use ellipses. But if you end your own sentence with quoted words that do *not* end a sentence in the original, you must use ellipsis dots following the quotation.

Original Statement: Her long, black hair, always drawn and braided in the day, lay upon her shoulders and against her breasts like a shawl. I do not speak Kiowa, and I never understood her prayers, but there was something inherently sad in the sound, some merest hesitation upon the syllables of sorrow.

—N. Scott Momaday, *The Way to Rainy Mountain*

As Quoted: His grandmother's reverence touched him: "I do not speak Kiowa, and I never understood her prayers, but there was something inherently sad" in her quiet chanting.

As Quoted: His grandmother's reverence touched him: "I do not speak Kiowa, and I never understood her prayers, but there was something inherently sad in the sound. . . ." He would never forget it.

Additions   Always make sure that it will be clear to a reader that anything you have added is not in the original quotation. Added words are bracketed. Never confuse brackets with parentheses; if words appear in parentheses, they are assumed to be part of the original quotation.

1. If you insert words of your own into a quoted passage for transition or explanation, put them in brackets.

Original Statement: Wilson's, above.

As Quoted: Logic is not the source of ideas, Wilson reminds us: "The cult of 'reason' . . . [is] in a sense a blind alley. Our thoughts and actions may be controlled by but they do not spring from what we call reason" (*Dead Sea Scrolls* 277).

2. If you put some of the quoted words in italics (indicated in a typewritten paper by underlining), follow the quotation with "(emphasis added)."

Original Statement: And love is an impediment to marital happiness. Founded on projection, abetting the quest for indirect self-acceptance, love can contribute neither to candid intimacy nor to self-acceptance.

—Snell Putney and Gail J. Putney,
The Adjusted American (Harper, 1966) 118

As Quoted: Many psychologists have argued that what we call *love* is a destructive emotion: "Founded on projection, abetting the quest for *indirect* self-acceptance, love can contribute neither to candid intimacy nor to self-acceptance" (Putney and Putney 118; emphasis added).

3. If the quoted material contains an error, follow the error with "[sic]" so that your readers will know the error is not yours.

Original Statement: In reviewing its provisions, we could not determine how the bill might effect future Supreme Court rulings.

—John Q. Legislator, letter to constituents

As Quoted: Senator Legislator wrote that the committee "could not determine how the bill might effect [sic] future Supreme Court rulings."

CITING SOURCES

Avoiding Plagiarism

As you write your essay, you must cite your sources of evidence whether you are quoting directly, paraphrasing, or summarizing. You must also cite the sources of ideas that are not your own. The only statements that do not require citation are common-knowledge statements, put into your own words, and your original ideas, interpretations, and conclusions. Failure to cite sources, and cite them accurately, constitutes plagiarism—a kind of theft that violates every aim of scholarship and integrity that academic institutions hold dear.

For the following thorough definition of plagiarism I am indebted to Nancy Hilts Deane, *Teaching with a Purpose,* 5th ed. (New York: Houghton Mifflin, 1972):

Plagiarism is the presentation of the words, ideas, or opinions of someone else as one's own. A student is guilty of plagiarism if he submits as his own work a part or all of an assignment copied or paraphrased from a source, such as a book, magazine, or pamphlet, without crediting the source; the sequence of ideas, arrangement of material, or pattern of thought of someone else, *even though he has expressed it in his own words* [emphasis added]. Plagiarism occurs when such a sequence of words or ideas is used without having been digested, integrated, and reorganized in the writer's mind, and without acknowledgement in the paper.

Similarly, a student is an accomplice in plagiarism and equally guilty if he allows his paper, in outline or finished form, to be copied and submitted as the work of another; if he prepares a written assignment for another student and allows it to be submitted as that student's work; or if he keeps or contributes to a file of papers or speeches with the clear intent that they be copied and submitted as the work of anyone other than the author.

One difficulty students encounter in avoiding plagiarism is deciding whether some statements are common-knowledge information or the intellectual property of a particular writer. Certainly it is easy to see that you need not cite a source for the dates of wars or of reigns, or the names of presidents, princes, and publishing companies. But what about the formula for making ordinary glass or the fact that *Albion* is a poetic name for England? What about the name of the first black professional baseball player, or his batting average? What about a brief identification of the First Law of Thermodynamics? All these bits of information are, just like the name of the first president of the United States, part of the **body of common knowledge.** Common knowledge is information common to any person informed in a given field. Any textbook on the subject, any specialized (and sometimes general) dictionary or encyclopedia is likely to contain such information.

As you begin your study of a particular field of knowledge, of course, almost everything you learn will be new to you. Initially, then, you may cite sources unnecessarily. You will begin to identify the common knowledge in the field as you read more widely. But when in doubt, cite your source. Better too many citations than too few.

Citing sources accurately and appropriately not only shows you to be an honest scholar but also adds the weight of authoritative testimony to arguments concerning subjects on which you cannot speak personally as an authority. In both ways, proper citation adds to the persuasiveness of your paper. But endless numbers of footnotes do not add to any paper's persuasiveness; they distract readers by continually sending them to the bottom of the page or the end of the paper. Accordingly, the Modern Language Association (MLA)* has revised its guidelines for citations in order to eliminate most purely bibliographic notes (notes giving only publication information and page references). The one exception occurs

---

*The MLA citation system is used for papers written in the humanities. Other disciplines have slightly different rules for citations. In the social sciences, the APA citation system briefly summarized on pages 114–115 is the norm. In the natural sciences, the preferred citation system varies. Some references for scientific citations are given on pages 115–116. (This, by the way, is a discursive footnote.)

when you want to cite several sources simultaneously, which would require a long and obtrusive parenthetical citation. Discursive notes (notes commenting on, but not strictly part of, the text of the paper) cannot always be eliminated but should be few in number.

As you take notes for your research paper, record all the following information that is applicable for each source. All numbers (except page numbers for prefaces and other front matter in books, which are distinguished from the text proper by the use of lower-case Roman numerals) should be given in Arabic numerals.

Books

> *Author(s)*
>
> *Editor(s)* of anthologies of essays, stories, poems, and the like
>
> *Translator* (if any)
>
> *Title of Chapter or Part of Book* (if only part is used; also note page numbers of chapter or part used, if it constitutes an identifiable unit of the book; put title in quotation marks)
>
> *Title of Book* (including subtitle, if any; both underlined)
>
> *Name of Series* (if work is part of a series; series name neither underlined nor put in quotation marks)
>
> *Number of Volumes with This Title* (if work is in more than one volume; and number of this particular volume)
>
> *Place of Publication*
>
> *Publisher*
>
> *Year of Publication*

Periodicals

> *Author(s) of Article*
>
> *Title of Article* (in quotation marks)
>
> *Name of Periodical* (underlined)
>
> *Volume Number and Year* (for scholarly journals)
>
> *Month and Year* (for general circulation magazines; include day of month for weekly or biweekly magazines)
>
> *Page numbers* for the entire article (separately record *specific* page numbers with passages to be cited within your paper)

Recording all the applicable information on a notecard for each source will help you avoid return trips to the library when you prepare your "Works Cited" list.

Citations in the Humanities

In order to meet both the goal of properly citing all source material and that of eliminating purely bibliographic footnotes, follow one general principle: **Give the least amount of information needed to send the reader**

to the appropriate point in the appropriate text. Most of the identifying information about each work cited will be given in a list of works cited at the end of the paper. Citations in the text itself will direct the reader to a specific page (or line, if the reference is to a poem or play) in that work; they will not repeat the complete information given in the list of works cited.

Some additional guidelines follow.

What to Include in Parenthetical Citations

1. Do not repeat in parentheses what you have already said in the text proper.
2. Put as little as possible in parentheses to keep interruptions to a minimum. Author's* surname and page number will suffice if you have only one work by that author in your list of works cited. Page number alone will suffice if you mention the author's name in the text proper, and you have used no other work by that author.

   If your paper largely concerns works by a single author, you need not repeat the author's name each time you quote or refer to what is obviously one of his or her works.
3. If you have used more than one work by the same person or persons, include an abbreviated form of the title in the citation.
4. If you have used works by different authors with the same surname, give first name or initial as well to distinguish the works from each other.
5. If a work has two authors, include both names in the citation. If it has three authors or more, you may use the first author's name and the Latin abbreviation "et al." (meaning "and others").
6. If you are using an indirect reference—for example, you are referring to a statement by Smith as quoted in a work by Jones—make clear that you are not using the original source by using the abbreviation "qtd. in" (for "quoted in").
7. If your reference is to a poem, indicate line numbers rather than page numbers. Do not use the abbreviations *l* or *ll.*, which could be confused with numbers. Instead, write out *line* or *lines* until the reference to lines is clearly established; thereafter, just give the numbers.
8. If your reference is to a play, indicate act, scene, and line(s), using Arabic numbers and periods: 3. 2. 112 would direct a reader to Act 3, scene 2, line 112.
9. The abbreviations *p., pp.,* and *vol.* are no longer used when the reference is clearly to page numbers or volume number.

How to Punctuate Parenthetical Citations

1. Use no punctuation between author's name and page number: (Smith 268)
2. Use no punctuation between title and page number: (*Ideas* 268)

*References to *author* also apply to *editor* when you are referring to entire anthologies and other compilations.

3. Put a comma between author's name and title (if title is needed): (Smith, *Ideas* 268)
4. Place parenthetical citations after the closing quotation mark and before the period except in the case of long, blocked quotations. Then they follow the period at the end of the quoted passage.

Basic Forms for Lists of Works Cited

Entries in the list of Works Cited are alphabetical. For each, the author's surname is given first, flush against the left margin. Subsequent lines, if any, are indented five spaces from the left margin.

Examples of Basic Forms for Entries in List of Works Cited (Alphabetically)

Books

Galbraith, John Kenneth. *The Anatomy of Power.* Boston: Houghton, 1983.

Collections and Anthologies

Groutz, Samuel, ed. *Moral Problems in Medicine.* Englewood Cliffs, NJ: Prentice-Hall, 1976. (reference to entire book)

Szasz, Thomas. "The Right to Health." In *Moral Problems in Medicine,* ed. Samuel Groutz. Englewood Cliffs, NJ: Prentice-Hall, 1976. (reference to component part of book)

Barthelme, Donald. "Lightning." *Overnight to Many Distant Cities.* New York: Putnam's 1983. (reference to component part of book all by one author)

Computer Data

"The Decade Ahead: Plan for the Oil Industry." Diskette 4. Marietta, NM: Petroleum Resources, Inc., 1984.

Congressional Documents

United States, 94th Congress, second session, 2 June 1976. *Congressional Record* 112 (15): 20343. Soybean price supports debate.

Films

The Dresser. Columbia Pictures, 1984.

Interviews

Durning, Thomas P. Vice-President, Have a Heart Foundation. Personal interview. Chicago, IL, 14 Nov. 1984.

Journal Articles

Doig, A. "Watergate, Coulson, and the Reform of Standards of Conduct," *Parliamentary Affairs* 36 (Summer 1983): 316–33.

Legal Citations

U. S. Constitution. Art. 1, sec. 3.

United States v. *Mudge et al.* U. S. District Court. 252 Federal Supplement (10 Dec. 1965): 806.

Letters, Personal

Stephen, Lydia. Letter to author. 20 June 1988.

Magazine Articles

Taubes, Gary. "Waiting for the Protons to Die." *Discover* Apr. 1984: 52–55.

Musical Compositions

Vivaldi, Antonio. *Nisi Dominus.* The Academy of Ancient Music. Editions de L'Oiseau-Lyre, Decca DSLO 506.

Newspaper Items

Germani, Clara. "Team of Middle-Aged Rowers May Stroke Its Way to the Olympics." *Christian Science Monitor* 1 Mar. 1984: 1.

Margolis, Jon. "Showdown 84: Who Has 'Ammo' to Beat Reagan?" *Chicago Tribune* 18 Mar. 1984, late ed., sec. 5: 1.

Reviews, Critical

Reinart, Otto. Rev. of *Ibsen: The Open Vision,* by John S. Chamberlain (Atlantic Highlands, NJ: Humanities Press, 1982). *Modern Drama.* 26.4 (Dec. 1983): 570–72.

Citations in the Social Sciences

The *Publication Manual of the American Psychological Association* explains in detail the most common citation system in the social sciences. The following summary of APA documentation is reprinted with the kind permission of Lynn Quitman Troyka from the *Simon and Schuster Handbook for Writers* (Prentice Hall, 1987) 648–49.

What to Include in Parenthetical Citations

1. If a parenthetical citation comes at the end of your sentence, place the sentence's period after the parentheses.
2. If you are paraphrasing or summarizing material and you do *not* mention the name of the author in your text, do this: (Jones, 1982).
3. If you are quoting and you do *not* mention the name of the author in your text, do this: (Jones, 1982, p. 65).
4. If you are paraphrasing, summarizing, or quoting material and *do* mention the name of the author in your text, do this: (p. 65).

5. If you use more than one source written in the same year by the same author(s), assign letters (a, b, etc.) to the works in the References list and do this for a parenthetical reference: (Jones, 1983a).
6. If you refer to a work more than once, give the author's name and year only the first time; then use only the name.
7. If you cite several sources in one place, put them in alphabetical order by authors' last names and separate the sources with a semicolon: (Bassuk, 1984; Fustero, 1984).

Guidelines for the Reference List

1. Arrange the list of sources cited alphabetically by author's last name. For two or more works by an author, arrange the works by date, most recent first.
2. Start with an author's last name, followed by initials for the author's first and middle names. If there is more than one author, name them all (up to six authors)—again starting with the last name and using initials for first and middle names. If there are over six authors, use only the first author and the words *et al.*
3. Put the date of publication in parentheses immediately after the author's name. If you list two works by the same author published in the same year, assign letters (a, b, etc.) to the year: (1984a), (1984b).
4. Put the title after the year of publication. Capitalize only the first word and any proper names in a title or subtitle. Do not put articles in quotation marks. Underline titles.
5. Put the city of publication and the publisher next. Use short forms for the names of well-known publishers: New York: Harper.
6. Put page numbers next, but use *p.* or *pp.* only for page numbers of articles in newspapers or popular magazines. Do not use *p.* or *pp.* with page numbers of articles in professional journals. In contrast, parenthetical references to specific pages always include *p.* or *pp.*—no matter what type of source.
7. Start each item at left margin, but if the item has two or more lines, indent all lines after the first line five spaces.

Citations in the Natural Sciences

The following sources will show you the correct documentation methods for various sciences.

Biology

Council of Biology Editors' Style Manual Committee. *CBE Style Manual.* 5th ed. Bethesda, MD: Council of Biology, 1983.

Chemistry

American Chemical Society. *Handbook for Authors of Papers in American Chemical Society Publications.* Washington, DC: American Chemical Society, 1978.

Geology

U.S. Geological Survey. *Suggestions to Authors of Reports of the United States Geological Survey.* 6th ed. Washington, DC: Department of the Interior, 1978.

Physics

American Institute of Physics. *Style Manual for Guidance in Preparation of Papers.* 3rd ed. New York: American Institute of Physics.

In all these ways even the immortal words of Shakespeare and the far-reaching ideas of Wernher von Braun may be used to support and made to fit congruently into your arguments. Finding, evaluating, and incorporating reliable evidence in your essays and reports is a necessary skill if you wish to avoid reinventing the wheel each time you set out to examine an issue, an event, a proposal, a poem, or a life. Evidence is the meat of argument that fleshes out the skeletal framework of your thesis. And it is research, creatively undertaken and carefully interpreted, that provides the evidence for arguments.

REPORTS, INFERENCES, JUDGMENTS

S. I. Hayakawa

1   For the purposes of the interchange of information, the basic symbolic act is the *report* of what we have seen, heard, or felt: "There is a ditch on each side of the road." "You can get those at Smith's Hardware Store for $2.75." "There aren't any fish on that side of the lake, but there are on this side." Then there are reports of reports: "The longest waterfall in the world is Victoria Falls." "The Battle of Hastings took place in 1066." "The papers say that there was a smash-up on Highway 41 near Evansville." Reports adhere to the following rules: first, they are *capable of verification*; second, they *exclude*, as far as possible, *inferences and judgments*. (These terms will be defined later.)

Verifiability

2   Reports are verifiable. We may not always be able to verify them ourselves, since we cannot track down the evidence for every piece of history we know, nor can we all go to Evansville to see the remains of the smash-up before they are cleared away. But if we are roughly agreed upon the names of things, upon what constitutes a "foot," "yard," "bushel," "kilogram," "meter," and so on, and upon how to measure time, there is relatively little danger of our misunderstanding each other. Even in a world such as we have today, in which everybody seems to be quarreling with everybody else, *we still to a surprising degree trust each other's reports*. We ask directions of total strangers when we are traveling. We follow directions on road signs without being suspicious of the people who put them up. We read books of information about science, mathematics, automotive engineering, travel, geography, the history of costume, and other such factual matters, and we usually assume that the author is doing his best to tell us as truly as he can what he knows. And we are safe in so assuming most of the time. With the interest given today to the discussion of biased newspapers, propagandists, and the general untrustworthiness of many of the communications we receive, we are likely to forget that we still have an enormous amount of reliable information available and that deliberate misinformation, except in warfare, is still more the exception than the rule. The desire for self-

preservation that compelled men to evolve means for the exchange of information also compels them to regard the giving of false information as profoundly reprehensible.

3   At its highest development, the language of reports is the language of science. By "highest development" we mean greatest general usefulness. Presbyterian and Catholic, workingman and capitalist, East German and West German *agree* on the meanings of such symbols as *2 × 2 = 4, 100° C, HNO₃, 3:35* A.M., *1940* A.D., *1,000 kilowatts, Quercus agrifolia,* and so on. But how, it may be asked, can there be agreement about even this much among people who disagree about political philosophies, ethical ideas, religious beliefs, and the survival of my business versus the survival of yours? The answer is that circumstances *compel men to agree,* whether they wish to or not. If, for example, there were a dozen different religious sects in the United States, each insisting on its own way of naming the time of the day and the days of the year, the mere necessity of having a dozen different calendars, a dozen different kinds of watches, and a dozen sets of schedules for business hours, trains, and television programs, to say nothing of the effort that would be required for translating terms from one nomenclature to another, would make life as we know it impossible.

4   The language of reports, then, including the more accurate reports of science, is "map" language, and because it gives us reasonably accurate representations of the "territory," it enables us to get work done. Such language may often be dull reading: one does not usually read logarithmic tables or telephone directories for entertainment. But we could not get along without it. There are numberless occasions in the talking and writing we do in everyday life that *require that we state things in such a way that everybody will be able to understand and agree with our formulation.*

Inferences

5   Not that inferences are not important—we rely in everyday life and in science as much on *inferences* as on reports—in some areas of thought, for example, geology, paleontology, and nuclear physics, reports are the foundations; but inferences (and inferences upon inferences) are the main body of the science. An inference, as we shall use the term, *is a statement about the unknown made on the basis of the known.* We may *infer* from the material and cut of a woman's clothes her wealth or social position; we may *infer* from the character of the ruins the origin of the fire that destroyed the building; we may *infer* from a man's calloused hands the nature of his occupation; we

may *infer* from a senator's vote on an armaments bill his attitude toward Russia; we may *infer* from the structure of the land the path of a prehistoric glacier; we may *infer* from a halo on an unexposed photographic plate its past proximity to radioactive materials; we may *infer* from the sound of an engine the condition of its connecting rods. Inferences may be carefully or carelessly made. They may be made on the basis of a broad background of previous experience with the subject matter or with no experience at all. For example, the inferences a good mechanic can make about the internal condition of a motor by listening to it are often startlingly accurate, while the inferences made by an amateur (if he tries to make any) may be entirely wrong. But the common characteristic of inferences is that they are statements about matters which are not directly known, made on the basis of what has been observed.

6   The avoidance of inferences . . . requires that we make no guesses as to what is going on in other people's minds. When we say, "He was angry," we are not reporting; we are making an inference from such observable facts as the following: "He pounded his fist on the table; he swore; he threw the telephone directory at his stenographer." In this particular example, the inference appears to be safe; nevertheless, it is important to remember, especially for the purposes of training oneself, that it is an inference. Such expressions as "He thought a lot of himself," "He was scared of girls," "He has an inferiority complex," made on the basis of casual observation, and "What Russia really wants to do is to establish a communist world dictatorship," made on the basis of casual reading, are highly inferential. We should keep in mind their inferential character and . . . should substitute for them such statements as "He rarely spoke to subordinates in the plant," "I saw him at a party, and he never danced except when one of the girls asked him to," "He wouldn't apply for the scholarship, although I believe he could have won it easily," and "The Russian delegation to the United Nations has asked for *A, B,* and *C.* Last year they voted against *M* and *N* and voted for *X* and *Y.* On the basis of facts such as these, the newspaper I read makes the inference that what Russia really wants is to establish a communist world dictatorship. I agree."

7   Even when we exercise every caution to avoid inferences and to report only what we see and experience, we all remain prone to error, since the making of inferences is a quick, almost automatic process. We may watch a car weaving as it goes down the road and say, "Look at that *drunken driver,*" although what we *see* is only *the irregular motion of the car.* I once saw a man leave a dollar at a lunch counter and hurry out. Just as I was wondering why anyone should leave so generous a tip in so modest an establishment, the

waitress came, picked up the dollar, put it in the cash register as she punched up ninety cents, and put a dime in her pocket. In other words, my description to myself of the event, "a dollar tip," turned out to be not a report but an inference.

8   All this is not to say that we should never make inferences. The inability to make inferences is itself a sign of mental disorder. For example, the speech therapist Laura L. Lee writes, "The aphasic [brain-damaged] adult with whom I worked had great difficulty in making inferences about a picture I showed her. She could tell me what was happening at the moment in the picture, but could not tell me what might have happened just before the picture or just afterward." Hence the question is not whether or not we make inferences; the question is whether or not we are aware of the inferences we make. . . .

Judgments

9   . . . By judgments, we shall mean *all expressions of the writer's approval or disapproval of the occurrences, persons, or objects he is describing.* For example, a report cannot say, "It was a wonderful car," but must say something like this: "It has been driven 50,000 miles and has never required any repairs." Again, statements such as "Jack lied to us" must be avoided in favor of the more verifiable statement, "Jack told us he didn't have the keys to his car with him. However, when he pulled a handkerchief out of his pocket a few minutes later, a bunch of keys fell out." Also a report may not say, "The senator was stubborn, defiant, and uncooperative," or "The senator courageously stood by his principles"; it must say instead, "The senator's vote was the only one against the bill."

10   Many people regard statements such as the following as statements of "fact": "Jack *lied* to us," "Jerry is a *thief*," "Tommy is *clever*." As ordinarily employed, however, the word "lied" involves first an inference (that Jack knew otherwise and deliberately misstated the facts) and second a judgment (that the speaker disapproves of what he has inferred that Jack did). In the other two instances, we may substitute such expressions as, "Jerry was convicted of theft and served two years at Waupun," and "Tommy plays the violin, leads his class in school, and is captain of the debating team." After all, to say of a man that he is a "thief" is to say in effect, "He has stolen *and will steal again*"—which is more of a prediction than a report. Even to say, "He has stolen," is to make an inference (and simultaneously to pass a judgment) on an act about which there may be

difference of opinion among those who have examined the evidence upon which the conviction was obtained. But to say that he was "convicted of theft" is to make a statement capable of being agreed upon through verification in court and prison records.

11   Scientific verifiability rests upon the external observation of facts, not upon the heaping up of judgments. If one person says, "Peter is a dead-beat," and another says, "I think so too," the statement has not been verified. In court cases, considerable trouble is sometimes caused by witnesses who cannot distinguish their judgments from the facts upon which those judgments are based. Cross-examinations under these circumstances go something like this:

WITNESS: That dirty double-crosser ratted on me.
DEFENSE ATTORNEY: Your honor, I object.
JUDGE: Objection sustained. (Witness's remark is stricken from the record.) Now, try to tell the court exactly what happened.
WITNESS: He double-crossed me, the dirty, lying rat!
DEFENSE ATTORNEY: Your honor, I object!
JUDGE: Objection sustained. (Witness's remark is again stricken from the record.) Will the witness try to stick to the facts.
WITNESS: But I'm telling you the facts, your honor. He did double-cross me.

This can continue indefinitely unless the cross-examiner exercises some ingenuity in order to get at the facts behind the judgment. To the witness it is a "fact" that he was "double-crossed." Often patient questioning is required before the factual bases of the judgment are revealed.

12   Many words, of course, simultaneously convey a report and a judgment on the fact reported, as will be discussed more fully in a later chapter. For the purposes of a report as here defined, these should be avoided. Instead of "sneaked in," one might say "entered quietly"; instead of "politician," "congressman" or "alderman," or "candidate for office"; instead of "bureaucrat," "public official"; instead of "tramp," "homeless unemployed"; instead of "dictatorial set-up," "centralized authority"; instead of "crackpot," "holder of nonconformist views." A newspaper reporter, for example, is not permitted to write, "A crowd of suckers came to listen to Senator Smith last evening in that rickety fire-trap and ex-dive that disfigures the south edge of town." Instead he says, "Between 75 and 100 people heard an address last evening by Senator Smith at the Evergreen Gardens near the South Side city limits". . . .

How Judgments Stop Thought

13   A judgment ("He is a fine boy," "It was a beautiful service," "Baseball is a healthful sport," "She is an awful bore") is a conclusion, summing up a large number of previously observed facts. The reader is probably familiar with the fact that students almost always have difficulty in writing themes of the required length because their ideas give out after a paragraph or two. The reason for this is that those early paragraphs contain so many judgments that there is little left to be said. When the conclusions are carefully excluded, however, and observed facts are given instead, there is never any trouble about the length of papers; in fact, they tend to become too long, since inexperienced writers, when told to give facts, often give far more than are necessary, because they lack discrimination between the important and the trivial.

14   Still another consequence of judgments early into the course of a written exercise—and this applies also to hasty judgments in everyday thought—is the temporary blindness they induce. When, for example, a description starts with the words, "He was a real Madison Avenue executive" or "She was a typical hippie," if we continue writing at all, we must make all our later statements consistent with those judgments. The result is that all the individual characteristics of this particular "executive" or this particular "hippie" are lost sight of; and the rest of the account is likely to deal not with observed facts but the stereotypes and the writer's particular notion (based on previously read stories, movies, pictures, and so forth) of what "Madison Avenue executives" or "typical hippies" are like. The premature judgment, that is, often prevents us from seeing what is directly in front of us, so that clichés take the place of fresh description. Therefore, even if the writer feels sure at the beginning of a written account that the man he is describing is a "real leatherneck" or that the scene he is describing is a "beautiful residential suburb," he will conscientiously keep such notions out of his head, lest his vision be obstructed.

QUESTIONS AND IDEAS FOR DISCUSSION

1. Is it possible to write an argument using only reports? Explain.
2. Is Hayakawa correct in the statement, "Reports are verifiable" (paragraph 2)? Can you think of a nonverifiable report? Discuss.
3. Consider the map analogy Hayakawa uses in paragraph 4 and elsewhere. Map is to territory as the language of reports is to what?

4. Discuss the points at which it becomes more difficult to distinguish among reports, inferences, and judgments than this excerpt suggests. Do inferences ever underlie judgments? Do judgments ever underlie reports? If you believe so, give examples.
5. How do judgments stop thought? What is the implication of this problem for writers?

Mark Alsop

Professor Spurgin

English 1302

April 14, 1988

The Problem of Bias

in Television News Reporting

Since its development in the 1920's, television has grown into one of the largest industries in the United States. For a number of years confined to the laboratory, television now can be found in nearly every home in the country. Television can take its viewers to any place in the world, and even to the moon and beyond. Accordingly, one of its important functions has become to keep viewers informed about world affairs, and one of the largest divisions of each of the networks is the news department. Television news is so important and so competitive now that annual contracts in excess of one million dollars have been offered to a handful of the broadcasters who read the news. Television news is powerful, too: Most people rely on television to provide them with all the information they will receive about current events. Through their presentation of the news, television newspeople affect and direct the opinions of millions of people each evening. It is important that we who watch television news recognize both its power and its potential for abuse of that power. Bias in television news may be subtle in a cynical post-Watergate America, but it is no less present. When powerful influence is colored with bias, the combination can be problematic.

The history of television news reporting is a history of steadily increasing power and influence. In the early days of commercial television, as recounted by Edward Jay Epstein in <u>News from Nowhere</u> (87), the news divisions

This and the next page show the Student Essay on page 126 typed in MLA format.

124

were the network stepchildren, well behind the quiz shows in budget and prestige. News presentations were limited to fifteen minutes. News took on a
bigger role "only when the quiz show scandals prompted the networks to take
their public service function more seriously" (Schudson 109). Not surprisingly, when the time slot was doubled to thirty minutes, the news department's
prestige rose as well. Then, too, technical improvements in television and
the imminent use of satellites to provide near-instant transmission of news
added to the excitement.

And the newspeople determined to take advantage of their position. David
Halberstam notes in an _Atlantic_ article on CBS that "by 1961, the people at
CBS News knew that they were at a threshold, about to make a breakthrough in
technology that would almost surely mean a comparable jump in power and influence" (52). Nor were the people at CBS mistaken. Television news each
evening is now the primary source of news for more than 64 percent of the
American public, according to a Roper Poll (cited in "TV News" 49).

The degree of influence television reporters have on the public is therefore not surprising. When Walter Cronkite was selected to "anchor" the then-
new half-hour news program, he was a fairly well-known radio announcer. After
a few years on the CBS evening news, he was voted "Most Trusted American" in
several polls (Sobol 322). In fact, Stephan Lesher goes so far as to claim
that Walter Cronkite singlehandedly orchestrated American opposition to the
war in Vietnam. Lesher argues that in the evening newscast on 27 February
1968, Cronkite,

> unelected by anyone to anything, not privy to any comprehensive,
> analytical reports by America's military or intelligence resources
> . . . decided unilaterally that United States policy in Vietnam

THE PROBLEM OF BIAS
IN TELEVISION NEWS REPORTING

Mark Alsop
(Student Essay)

1   Since its development in the 1920's, television has grown into one of the largest industries in the United States. For a number of years confined to the laboratory, television now can be found in nearly every home in the country. Television can take its viewers to any place in the world, and even to the moon and beyond. Accordingly, one of its important functions has become to keep viewers informed about world affairs, and one of the largest divisions of each of the networks is the news department. Television news is so important and so competitive now that annual contracts in excess of one million dollars have been offered to a handful of the broadcasters who read the news. Television news is powerful, too: Most people rely on television to provide them with all the information they will receive about current events. Through their presentation of the news, television newspeople affect and direct the opinions of millions of people each evening. It is important that we who watch television news recognize both its power and its potential for abuse of that power. Bias in television news may be subtle in a cynical post-Watergate America, but it is no less present. When powerful influence is colored with bias, the combination can be problematic.

2   The history of television news reporting is a history of steadily increasing power and influence. In the early days of commercial television, as recounted by Edward Jay Epstein in *News from Nowhere* (87), the news divisions were the network stepchildren, well behind the quiz shows in budget and prestige. News presentations were limited to fifteen minutes. News took on a bigger role "only when the quiz show scandals prompted the networks to take their public service function more seriously" (Schudson 109). Not surprisingly, when the time slot was doubled to thirty minutes, the news department's prestige rose as well. Then, too, technical improvements in television and the imminent use of satellites to provide near-instant transmission of news added to the excitement.

3   And the newspeople determined to take advantage of their position. David Halberstam notes in an *Atlantic* article on CBS that "by 1961, the people at CBS News knew that they were at a threshold, about to make a breakthrough in technology that would almost surely mean a comparable jump in power and influence" (52). Nor were the people at CBS mistaken. Television news each evening is

now the primary source of news for more than 64 percent of the American public, according to a Roper Poll (cited in "TV News" 49).

4   The degree of influence television reporters have on the public is therefore not surprising. When Walter Cronkite was selected to "anchor" the then-new half-hour news program, he was a fairly well-known radio announcer. After a few years on the CBS evening news, he was voted "Most Trusted American" in several polls (Sobol 322). In fact, Stephan Lesher goes so far as to claim that Walter Cronkite singlehandedly orchestrated American opposition to the war in Vietnam. Lesher argues that in the evening newscast on 27 February 1968, Cronkite,

> unelected by anyone to anything, not privy to any comprehensive, analytical reports by America's military or intelligence resources . . . decided unilaterally that United States policy in Vietnam was wrong, that the war must end in stalemate, and that the United States must negotiate with humility. (5)

While Lesher's claims may overstate Cronkite's influence on the American public, by the early 1970's Cronkite was widely perceived as "your favorite uncle with a world statesman's demeanor" (producer Fred Friendly; quoted in Diamond 71). Cronkite ultimately became perhaps the most trusted man in America.

5   Walter Cronkite's zoom to popularity and trust was paralleled by that of the television news industry as a whole. By the mid-seventies, pollster Lou Harris found that TV news had "made by far the greatest gains in public confidence since 1965—overtaking the military, organized religion, the Supreme Court, the house of Representatives, and the executive branch of the federal government" (qtd. in Barrett, *Moments of Truth* 137). In the mid-eighties, public confidence in TV news reporters is at a ten-year high ("Honesty" 13), and the popularity of news programs is, if anything, greater than a decade ago. CBS's *60 Minutes* news program consistently is at the top or near the top of the Nielson ratings—according to *U.S. News & World Report* ("TV News" 49), forty-three million people watch *60 Minutes* regularly—and Ted Turner's Cable News Network and other cable channels now offer round-the-clock news programs that draw large audiences. Incredibly, if we are to believe the usually reliable Harris polls, the average American has more confidence in television news than in his religion or his government (Barrett 137).

6   Television news today is powerful, and so it is fortunate that the networks were from the beginning aware of the possibilities for abuse of their power. The National Association of Broadcasters de-

veloped a Television Code in order to insure high quality broadcasting in programming and advertising (Fang 220). This code governs all networks and all broadcasters appearing on television. In addition to the code, each network has its own Code of Ethics, with certain sections devoted exclusively to the news department. These codes are intended to sustain the integrity of television news by providing for the strict neutrality of news reporters. According to Thomas Griffith of *Time* magazine, "As the CBS News code defines the job, the analyst is 'to help the listener to understand, to weigh, and to judge, but not to do the judging for him. . . . the audience should be left with no impressions as to which side the analyst himself actually favors'" (48). Many newspeople believe that the aims of the news codes are attainable, and that bias is not a factor in TV news reporting. *Nightline* anchor Ted Koppel claims that

> [a]nyone who has strong opinions and who allows them to be reflected probably won't last long as an anchor. There's a curious paradox about television. Anyone who appears on it for half an hour five nights a week has influence, but the moment you use it you lose it. If viewers come to the conclusion that I'm pronuke or anti-Reagan and I am using the program as a soapbox, I've lost it all. (qtd. in Hennessee 52)

7   This admirable aim of fairness is not always realized, however. What people see and hear on the news is not always what actually took place. Whether deliberate or inadvertent, bias and distortion in the news is commonplace. The causes of distortion are many; only a few will be considered here.

8   First, although television news shows on-the-scene film of current events, many things are inevitably cut from the footage shown. Merely making the choice of what to put on the air and what to cut constitutes a self-censorship that may reflect a particular news editor's bias. In his discussion of the history of bias in television news reporting, Edward Epstein acknowledges that the limitations of time and the need for "order, time, and logic . . . [make it impossible] in most cases to record from beginning to end the natural sequence of events, with all the digressions, confusions, and inconsistencies that more often than not constitute reality" (153). If the editors favor what the news cameras have caught, they may edit out confusion and turmoil that they would perhaps leave in in another circumstance. One political party's convention, for example, may seem to the viewers at home to be a more orderly and well-conducted event than the other, while in truth both were equally chaotic. A recent CBS news story about an arts festival in Miami came under fire for including

irrelevant and "unsavory" footage of Miami slums ("TV News" 49).
CBS formally apologized to the city. And a study of the content of
news stories on Arab and Israeli matters has shown a decided shift
from pro-Israeli to neutral or even pro-Arab news presentation between 1973–1979 (Asi 71). The shift began after Egyptian President
Anwar Sadat's historic visit to Israel, a move viewed favorably by
Western reporters.

9   Videotaped reports are subject to other forms of distortion as
well. The use of "reverses"—filming a reporter asking questions and
posing in a number of different ways and then splicing the posed
footage into the actual interviews—is a common practice (Griffith
48). While it is true that reverses are done only with the consent of
the person being interviewed, what the television audience sees is
not the actual interview but rather an adulterated version of it. In
the reverse, the reporter can be portrayed as cool, angry, or intrigued—and such simple things as facial expression or tone of voice
can have an editorial effect on viewer responses. If the reporter sounds
suspicious, the viewers half-consciously begin to feel suspicious as
well. In any event, the reporter in a reverse is not being shown the
way she or he really acted at the time of the interview.

10   News reporters can distort not only the physical context and
content of their reports but the facts themselves. One of the most
common sources of distortion is the unattributed quotation, as described by Edith Efron in *The News Twisters:* "Newsmen hide behind anonymous sources of opinion. Scattered throughout news stories are such phrases as critics feel . . . , experts believe . . . , the
police feel. . . . These sources are totally uncheckable and must be
taken on blind faith" (106). An audience cannot accurately evaluate
information without knowing the source. Who are the "source close
to the investigation" and the "experts" saying all these things? It is
possible—and should not be—for a reporter to offer his or her personal judgments while appearing to be quoting an authority.

11   Another way in which reporters can offer personal judgments
without quite appearing to do so is to slant the story in the powerful
"last word," as Efron puts it:

> After reporting on conflicting opinions on a controversial issue,
> the reporter climaxes the story with a quotation or a paraphrase
> or an endorsement of one side—omitting all recapitulation of
> the other side. Thus, after reporting on the conflicting opinions
> of the black militants and New York Teachers Union in the New
> York school strike of 1968, a reporter summed up with the black
> militant position only—effectively endorsing it. (109)

The reporter who uses the "last word" in this way may not be consciously aware of the slanting in such conclusions, but its effect on a television audience is not mitigated by the reporter's innocence. We television viewers owe it to ourselves, of course, to listen carefully to the conclusions to news reports, for even when both sides in a dispute are recapitulated at the end, one side inevitably must be presented last, and what we hear last tends to stay with us if we are giving the report but half our attention.

12   The push to adopt "action news" formats has led to problems of its own. Television news has become dramatized, with helicopters and minicams making possible on-the-scene coverage of fire and famine. However, as W. Lance Bennett notes in *News: The Politics of Illusion,* "As a result of this built-in bias in favor of action reporting, a new breed of news stories has begun to appear: stories that have less to do with the importance or meaning of an event than with the capacity to use costly equipment and convey images of drama and action" (16).

13   Perhaps the best way to assess news distortion and bias is to compare the length and content of actual news presentations. The 1984 Democratic primary race offers a good opportunity to assess the comparative fairness of TV news reporting, for airtime alone offers candidates the advantage of publicity. During the period of 9 January–9 March, according to *Dallas Morning News* television reporter Ed Bark ("Comparing" 1E+), CBS devoted more airtime to Walter Mondale and less to Gary Hart than did either ABC or NBC. ABC gave better than 25% more airtime to John Glenn than did the other two major networks, while NBC gave slightly more airtime to Jesse Jackson than did the others. The significance of some of these figures may be slight, but a viewer watching only ABC might have been more surprised at Glenn's withdrawal from the race than one who watched the other networks. Glenn was substantially more visible on ABC. By the same token, a viewer watching only CBS might have been even more surprised than the rest of the country when Hart upset Mondale in New Hampshire, for CBS consistently gave Mondale twice as much coverage as Hart.

14   However, during the five-day period of 5 March–9 March, following the New Hampshire primary and Hart's surprise upset, coverage of Hart increased dramatically, equalling coverage of Mondale on ABC and nearly doubling coverage of Mondale on NBC (Bark, "Comparing" 1E+). Airtime for John Glenn dropped off substantially, down to a paltry nine seconds in five days. And George McGovern, never regarded by the networks as a serious contender, disappeared entirely from NBC. During the same period, Jesse Jackson received twice as much coverage on ABC as he did on NBC.

15   Of course, the *kind* of news presentation matters nearly as much as its length. The extended coverage of Gary Hart after the New Hampshire primary is a case in point. NBC's close look at Hart was largely negative. Roger Mudd spent several minutes examining what he called "the mysteries of Gary Hart," focusing his attention on such matters as Hart's legal name change, "John Kennedy" affectations, and apparent uncertainty about age. (Hart, 47, had said he was 46.) Mudd's comments included the declaration that Hart is "making his living off the politically rootless in America, the World War II baby-boomers who were weaned on television, grew up with computers, but have lost their appetite for political ideology" (Bark, "Comparing" 1E+). ABC, on the other hand, gave no air time to Hart's age discrepancy and CBS gave the matter a half-minute's attention.

16   The problem of possible bias became even more interesting a few weeks later in the campaign. A Jesse Jackson supporter, Louis Farrakhan, threatened the life of a reporter who wrote a story showing Jackson in an unfavorable light. Jackson refused to repudiate the statements made by Farrakhan. And the networks downplayed and delayed reporting on the entire incident (Bark, "Jackson" 3E). CBS reporter Bob Faw commented on the situation:

> Given what Farrakhan said, was the press responsible, cautious, or gunshy? . . . Reporters travelling with Jackson, black and white, insist that they are as tough on him as are reporters assigned to Mondale and Hart. But they do concede Jackson is a different kind of candidate and that sometimes he *is* treated differently.
>
> (Qtd. in Bark, "Jackson" 3E)

17   These are but a handful of examples of the subtle slanting that goes on daily in news broadcasts. I could have offered many more, and I could have offered a number of examples of scrupulously unslanted reports as well. I certainly do not mean to imply that newspeople deliberately attempt to manipulate and deceive the American public; quite the contrary. But some striking and disturbing characteristics of national news broadcasts do stand out. The three networks report virtually the same major stories each day, and the facts of each story are almost invariably identical. However, the presentation and interpretation of these facts differ remarkably; I sometimes have found myself changing my mind about an issue after watching it discussed first on one network and then on another. Certainly bias cannot be avoided, but given the enormous audience and the strong impact television news has on that audience, we who comprise it owe it to ourselves to balance television news with that presented in newspapers and news magazines; to watch news re-

porting consciously and carefully, noting especially any bias in the "last word"; and to make a habit of watching all three networks in turn, rather than allowing a single network to influence our opinions.

Works Cited

Asi, Morad. "Arabs, Israelis, and TV News: A Time-Series, Content Analysis." Television Coverage of the Middle East. Ed. William C. Adams. Norwood, NJ: ABLEX, 1981, 67–75.

Bark, Ed. "Comparing Hart and Mondale." Dallas Morning News 13 Mar. 1984: 1E+.

———. "Jackson treatment a media issue." Dallas Morning News 10 Apr. 1984: 3E.

Barrett, Marvin, ed. Moments of Truth. New York: Crowell, 1975.

Bennett, W. Lance. News: The Politics of Illusion. New York: Longman, 1983.

Diamond, Edwin. Sign Off: The Last Days of Television. Cambridge, MA: MIT, 1982.

Efron, Edith. The News Twisters. Los Angeles: Nash, 1971.

Epstein, Edward Jay. News from Nowhere. New York: Random, 1973.

Fang, I. E. Television News. New York: Hastings House, 1968.

Griffith, Thomas. "Television's Necessary Neuters." Time 19 Dec. 1977: 48.

Halberstam, David. "CBS: The Power and the Profits." Atlantic Jan. 1976: 33–71.

Hennessee, Judith Adler. "The Man Who Wouldn't Be King." Esquire Jan. 1984: 50–56.

"Honesty and Ethical Standards of TV Reporters and Commentators." Gallup Report July 1983: 13.

Lesher, Stephan. Media Unbound: The Impact of Television Journalism on the Public. Boston: Houghton, 1982.

Schudson, Michael. "The Politics of Narrative Form: The Emergence of News Conventions in Print and Television." Daedalus 111.4 (1982): 97–112.

Sobel, Robert. The Manipulators. New York: Doubleday, 1976.

"TV News Gets Bigger, But Is It Better?" U.S. News & World Report 21 Feb. 1983: 49–50.

SUGGESTIONS FOR WRITING AND
FURTHER DISCUSSION

1. "Even in a world such as we have today, in which everybody seems to be quarreling with everybody else, we still to a surprising degree trust each other's reports."   —S. I. Hayakawa

   Write a documented essay in which you demonstrate the truth of the above statement by offering examples from what you have read and from what you have experienced personally. In working for an argumentative edge, consider whether we are wise or unwise to be so trusting, and whether our trust is symptomatic of health or of an apathy that makes us unwilling to investigate things for ourselves.

2. "The one function that TV news performs very well is that when there is no news, we give it to you with the same emphasis as if there were news."   —David Brinkley

   David Brinkley's wry comment on the news industry—in which thirty minutes must be filled daily whether or not anything has happened in the world that day—pinpoints one of the problems inherent in the rigid structure of television news: a half-hour every day devoted to international and national news, weather reports, and sports. Watch national and local news programs for a week and take notes on the content, length, and presentation of "nonnews" human interest and idle-curiosity stories. Are such stories treated "with the same emphasis" as elections, coups, and natural disasters? Based on your observations and accumulated data, write one of the following: an essay addressed to one of the national networks or your local television station in which you argue the dangers or the benefits of such indiscriminate treatment; an essay addressed to David Brinkley in which you argue that emphasis on the unimportant is no longer commonplace in television news reporting; or an essay addressed to the national networks in which you argue in favor of a variable-length news broadcast, perhaps supplemented (to even out the time-slots) with educational programming when needed.

3. Use one of the following questions to generate a working thesis and ultimately a documented essay.*

   What did Benjamin Franklin accomplish in France?
   What were the reasons for Gerald Ford's defeat in 1976? (or Jimmy Carter's defeat in 1980? or Lyndon Johnson's decision not to run for a second full term in 1968?)
   What are the reasons for the decline in SAT scores?
   What was Yoko Ono's influence on John Lennon's work?
   What were the reasons for race riots in Watts?
   Is "The Pill" really dangerous?

---

*I am indebted to my colleague Virginia White Oram, now of Richland College, for suggesting many of these topics for research and argument.

What was the significance of the Boxer Rebellion?

Why was Churchill defeated in his bid to become Prime Minister after World War II?

How important have been Ingmar Bergman's contributions to movie making?

Are the benefits of liver transplants worth the costs?

Should the United States involve itself in any way in El Salvador? (in Lebanon and the rest of the Middle East?)

What should be done about Three Mile Island? What compensation, if any, should people living near it receive?

Should criminal trials be televised?

Are labor unions still needed in the United States?

Should adoption records be open?

What is the current state of the Communist party in the United States?

What effect do pets have on their owners' health?

What was Alfred Hitchcock's contribution to the art of the film?

Should the insanity defense be allowed for major crimes?

How has the BART public transportation system worked out in California?

Did Lizzie Borden kill her parents?

What was the importance of the voyage of the *Beagle*?

What should be done about veterans who were exposed to Agent Orange during the Vietnam War?

How did Thomas Jefferson treat the Indians?

Is the Social Security System doomed?

Is jogging harmful?

Are women with young children discriminated against in the workplace?

Should the tenure system in American colleges be changed?

What can be done to improve public education in America?

What applications for computers will we see within the next ten years?

5

Revising

I understand a fury in your words.
But not the words.

Othello, 4.2.31-32

Once you have roughed out a thesis and have developed it into a draft, with key concepts defined and evidence mustered in support of your argument, you are likely to find that what you have before you is still far from a polished essay. Perhaps there are gaps where you've failed to make smooth transitions between points; perhaps you have no strong conclusion and the argument trails weakly off; or perhaps you see that you've failed to provide examples to illustrate a crucial point.

Fortunately, however, an essay need not begin as a unified, complete, coherent and clear piece of writing, even though it should end up as just that. Writing is not the art of setting down fluidly what you already knew, nor is it simply a matter of justifying conclusions previously reached. As many writers and teachers of writing have reminded us, writing is often the process of discovering what you do know and learning things you may not have known before you began to write. Good writers usually learn as they go. They begin with certain ideas, but they are not afraid to modify or change them. If you set your ideas in cement before you begin to write ("Lying can never be justified," "This law is reprehensible," "Requiring foreign language study in college is futile"), do not be surprised to find a wall of concrete blocking your way at some point in the process of writing. You will come to an abrupt and premature halt, because assertions stop thought if they are regarded as settled truths.* Besides, why write about what is obvious and irrefutable?

Thoughtful prewriting will reduce the time you spend rewriting but will not eliminate it. The writers who appear not to revise generally proceed very slowly, mentally casting and recasting each sentence before it goes on the page and continually checking the development of thought. The rest of us tear through—or plod through—a succession of drafts, adding, deleting, changing, reordering, and polishing what we have written. Revision is usually necessary because the first thing that comes to mind is rarely the best idea a writer will have; because ideas often come to mind by free association and later require rearranging in order to make sense to a reader; and because the sentence style of the first draft tends to be monotonous and convoluted. After all, the writer is concerned at that point more with getting the ideas down on the page than with expressing them in the clearest and most elegant prose possible.

THE AIMS OF REVISION

All writers feel a parental attachment to the words we have created—an attachment that makes revision difficult. But however difficult to inflict, the slashes from our own red pens bleed less than those from a professor's or an editor's. The thesis that we struggled to generate may turn out to need a shift in emphasis, an additional qualification, or—on occasion—a complete reversal. Some of the notes we took in researching the topic may turn out to be irrelevant to the emphasis the paper develops as it takes shape. Whole paragraphs may have to be shifted from one point in the essay to another. A writer must be willing to do a little verbal surgery.

In revising a draft, a writer tries to

1. **Unify and complete** the argument by eliminating tangential and unrelated ideas and evidence from the essay and adding material when needed.
2. **Organize** sentences and paragraphs so that related ideas are expressed together or in sequence, and so that points are ordered and expressed logically.
3. **Improve the coherence** of the writing by checking for (and perhaps adding) subordinated sentence structures for ideas related in hierarchical or causal ways; parallel sentence structures for coordinate ideas; and appropriate transitions.

*Recall S.I. Hayakawa's discussion of the dangers of judging hastily—"Reports, Inferences, Judgments"—in the readings for Chapter 4.

4. **Improve the clarity** of the writing by eliminating wordiness, checking the precision and appropriateness of word choices, and proofreading for grammatical and mechanical correctness.

Revision involves other matters as well, but these four are central to the process. You may have noticed that the first two points largely concern the *content* of the essay or other written message, and the last two its *style*—the way in which it has been written. The distinction is somewhat artificial, for style and content are nearly inseparable. If an idea is fuzzily expressed, as noted in Chapter 3, the idea itself is probably fuzzy as well. Nevertheless, we can—and do—talk about content and style as separate concerns of the writer, however intrinsically related they are. It *is* possible to write banal ideas in clear phrases, and it *is* possible to phrase a brilliant idea in muddy, muddled language. But in the latter case, the brilliance is usually obscured by the mud.

In this chapter we will consider just how you can revise to improve the content of your arguments and the clarity of your prose style, and, in so doing, enhance the persona—or *ethos*—created through your words. We will first look at large-scale elements of the essay (macro-revision) and then at paragraphs, sentences, and words (micro-revision). Then, in the next chapter, we will examine more sophisticated features of style, such as the use of figures of speech and the ways in which style can affect in positive ways the emotional appeal—*pathos*—of what you write.

MACRO-REVISION: THE DRAFT AS A WHOLE

Once you have worked out a rough draft from your notes, look critically at the argument you have developed to make sure that the paper is not poorly organized or sketchy in parts of its development. Just as you did in your prewriting considerations, ask questions:

- Have the logical relationships among the parts of my thesis transferred from my head to the actual paper?
- Have I considered as much of the subject as my knowledge and curiosity permit and my thesis demands?
- What have I left undefined or undefended?
- Where have I failed to be concrete when I might have given specific examples?
- Have I considered all the possible dimensions of this problem, or all its possible solutions?
- Have I taken for granted anything the reader might not readily understand or accept?

And the first question of all at this point:

- Is the argument unified—does the essay discuss a *single* issue?

Testing for Unity and Completeness

An essay is unified if it has a clearly defined thesis concept and if all the points and illustrations in the essay are related to and support that thesis. If you have worked out your thesis with care, according to the guidelines in Chapter 2, your draft is likely to be unified in support of that thesis. But minds work through associations that are not always logical, and random or tangential ideas can stray into arguments without the writer's realizing that they are unrelated to the thesis at hand. In revising, test each supporting point, the topic of each paragraph, against the thesis. Points that do not further the argument must be dropped, however much they interest you.

But making sure that your paper is unified does not assure that the points you have made are in the most logical, interesting, or easy-to-follow order, or that you have all the supporting details needed to carry conviction. Effective writing provides enough support for the writer's conclusions to be convincing; at the same time, it does not belabor the obvious or overwhelm readers with needless detail. In practice, it is easier to accept that bit of advice than to implement it, for how is the writer to know when a piece of writing contains "just enough" reason and detail? Good sense and the stipulations of the assignment, if the writing has been assigned, usually will provide the answers. What constitutes "completeness" in any piece of writing will vary with the rhetorical context of audience and your purpose in addressing it. A report on your recent sociology project will be much more detailed in the formal essay submitted to your instructor than in a letter to your grandmother, yet both may be fully developed for the audience and for your purposes.

In working on the organization and development of your formal argument, you may find it helpful to test what you have written against the five parts of classical rhetorical argument: *introduction, exposition, confirmation, refutation,* and *conclusion.* Consider whether or not you have presented a fully developed argument in classical terms. The organization of your essay may well differ from the classical model, but if you have eliminated any of the parts, such as the exposition or refutation, be sure you have done so purposefully and not carelessly.

Introduction   An introduction may range in length from a single sentence to a paragraph, a longer passage, or an entire chapter—depending on the length of the work and the complexity of the subject matter. Regardless of its length, every introduction has two functions that cannot be dispensed with: It must *interest* and it must *inform* the readers. The introduction must establish an appealing persona and make the readers want to read further; all your work is in vain if they do not.

How do you gain the readers' trust and interest? You establish the common ground you share with them (the "major premise" discussed in Chapter 2), arouse their curiosity, intrigue them with a little-known or unusual fact, show that your subject has been long misunderstood or neglected, or offer a thesis that turns on end commonly held attitudes about your subject. You must, in short, find something new and important to say, or find a clearer and simpler way of discussing something often considered complex and tedious, or find a vivid example with which to pique your readers' interest.

Richard Whately, a nineteenth century theologian, identified several categories of introductions to arguments, among them the *preparatory, inquisitive, narrative, corrective,* and *paradoxical* introductions. To this list we will add the *major premise* introduction, the *concession,* the *contradiction exposed,* and the *autobiographical* introduction. Below you will find examples of each to show you some of the possible approaches you might try in completing your own essays.

In the **preparatory** introduction the writer explains or defines the subject before discussing it in detail in the body of the essay. The preparatory introduction often culminates in the thesis statement. While it certainly has its uses, too many writers think of this kind as the *only* form introductions take.

A respected businessman with whom I discussed the theme of this article remarked with some heat, "You mean to say you're going to encourage men to bluff? Why, bluffing is nothing more than a form of lying! You're advising them to lie!"

I agreed that the basis of private morality is a respect for truth and that the closer a businessman comes to the truth, the more he deserves respect. At the same time, I suggested that most bluffing in business might be regarded simply as game strategy—much like bluffing in poker, which does not reflect on the morality of the bluffer.

—Albert Z. Carr, "Is Business Bluffing Ethical?"

In the **inquisitive** introduction the writer asks provocative questions to stimulate the readers' interest.

Is there an ever-present past? Are there permanent truths which are forever important for the present? Today we are facing a future more strange and untried than any other generation has faced. The new world Columbus opened seems small indeed beside the illimitable distances of space before us, and the possibilities of destruction are immeasurably greater than ever. In such a position can we afford to spend time on the past? That is the question I often asked. Am I urging the study of the Greeks and Romans and their civilizations for the atomic age?

—Edith Hamilton, "The Ever-Present Past"

In the **narrative** introduction the writer begins with an anecdote that illuminates the thesis in some way and draws the reader in. It can be a most effective introduction, for even adults enjoy a good story.

A woman I know worked for a time in one of those prestigious sweatshops in which the imposing abodes of America's corporations are designed. A mean woman with an X-Acto knife, she was given the job of constructing the little presentation models with which her firm coaxed its clients even further into the frontiers of modern architecture. But she could stand the subsistence pay, the stiff neck, and the enforced veneration for the firm's presiding genius only long enough to complete a single model: a one-inch-to-one-foot cardboard and Mylar prototype of a huge building slated for construction somewhere in downtown Houston.

A few years after she quit the firm she found herself at the Houston airport and decided to kill the two hours she had between planes by taking a cab downtown and finding the building over whose embryo she had labored so long. Though she couldn't remember what company had commissioned it, she figured she had been so intimately acquainted with its design that she could spot it without any trouble.

But after an hour's search up and down the city streets, she could not for the life of her find it, and had to assume, as she boarded her plane, that the design had been changed or the project had been canceled just after she had quit. Then, suddenly, looking down at the retreating city as her plane rose in the sky, she saw her building standing right smackdab in the middle of Houston. During her search she must have passed it half a dozen times, but only now, with a bird's-eye view of it on a cardboard and Mylar scale, could she recognize it.

I think my friend may have stumbled upon what's wrong with modern architecture: it is best appreciated from a couple of thousand feet off the ground. It is conceived from an aerial point of view, from the Olympian perspective of a god, an angel, a chairman of the board.
—Andrew Ward, "The Trouble with Architects"

In the **corrective** introduction the writer shows how the subject has been misunderstood and then indicates how it will be regarded in the essay at hand. Stipulative definitions often figure in corrective introductions.

Metaphor is for most people a device of the poetic imagination and the rhetorical flourish—a matter of extraordinary rather than ordinary language. Moreover, metaphor is typically viewed as characteristic of language alone, a matter of words rather than thought or action. For this reason, most people think they can get along perfectly well without metaphor. We have found, on the contrary, that metaphor is pervasive in everyday life, not just in language but in thought and action. Our ordinary conceptual system, in terms of which we both think and act, is fundamentally metaphorical in nature.
—George Lakoff and Mark Johnson, *Metaphors We Live By*

In the **paradoxical** introduction the writer shows that both parts of an apparent contradiction regarding the subject are nonetheless true.

What are we to make of Jesus Christ? This is a question which has, in a sense, a frantically comic side. For the real question is not what are we to make of Christ, but what is He to make of us? The picture of a fly sitting deciding what it is going to make of an elephant has comic elements about it. But perhaps the questioner meant what are we to make of Him in the sense of "How are we to solve the historical problem set us by the recorded sayings and acts of this Man?" This problem is to reconcile two things. On the one hand you have got the almost generally admitted depth and sanity of His moral teaching, which is not very seriously questioned, even by those who are opposed to Christianity. In fact, I find when I am arguing with very anti-God people that they rather make a point of saying, "I am entirely in favour of the moral teaching of Christianity"—and there seems to be a general agreement that in the teaching of this Man and of His immediate followers, moral truth is exhibited at its purest and best. It is not sloppy idealism, it is full of wisdom and shrewdness. The whole thing is realistic, fresh to the highest degree, the product of a sane mind. That is one phenomenon.
—C.S. Lewis, "What Are We to Make of Jesus Christ?"

In the **major premise** introduction the writer establishes the ground shared between writer and reader by discussing the basic assumptions that will give rise to the thesis. This introduction is particularly effective when the thesis itself is likely to prove somewhat controversial and is best expressed at a later point in the essay.

Nowadays . . . we have to be a little more vague in our meaning of Christianity [than were people in former times]. I think, however, that there are two different items which are quite essential to anybody calling himself a Christian. The first is one of a dogmatic nature—namely, that you must believe in God and immortality. If you do not believe in those two things, I do not think that you can properly call yourself a Christian. Then, further than that, as the name implies, you must have some kind of belief about Christ. The Mohammedans, for instance, also believe in God and in immortality, and yet they would not call themselves Christians. . . .
—Bertrand Russell, "Why I Am Not a Christian"

In the **concession** the writer acknowledges whatever merit can be granted an opposing viewpoint. This kind of introduction establishes a thoughtful, reasonable persona and is well suited to arguments that are likely to elicit some opposition from the anticipated audience. The concession tends to diffuse hostilities and make readers more amenable to a differing viewpoint.

While confined here in the Birmingham city jail, I came across your recent statement calling my present activities "unwise and untimely." Seldom do I pause to answer criticism of my work and ideas. If I sought to answer all the criticisms that cross my desk, my secretaries would have little time for anything other than such correspondence in the course of the day, and I would have no time for constructive work. But since I feel that you are men of genuine good will and that your criticisms are sincerely set forth, I want to try to answer your statement in what I hope will be patient and reasonable terms.
—Martin Luther King, Jr., "Letter from Birmingham Jail"

In the **contradiction exposed** form of introduction the writer points out the wrinkles in what on the surface appears to be an uncomplicated and straightforward idea. This is a good way to heighten a reader's interest in what might be expected to be a boring subject.

> Man will never conquer space. Such a statement may sound ludicrous, now that our rockets are already 100 million miles beyond the moon and the first human travelers are preparing to leave the atmosphere. Yet it expresses a truth which our forefathers knew, one we have forgotten—and our descendants must learn again, in heartbreak and loneliness.
> —Arthur C. Clarke, "We'll Never Conquer Space"

In the **autobiographical** introduction the writer tries to establish a rapport with readers through personal details or anecdotes, often identifying his or her expertise in the subject or giving particular reasons for being interested in it. A note of humor or humility is usually in order in such introductions.

> I write of nuclear power as a self-confessed coward in the face of all massive concentrations of energy. Lightning frightens me. A surge in the wind's strength makes me uneasy in an airplane. And I cannot stand at the base of a 200-foot dam without thinking of the force of gravity stored up behind it, waiting to sweep everything before it.
> —Roger Starr, "The Case for Nuclear Energy"

As the foregoing examples show, a wide variety of effective introductions is possible. A few kinds of introductions can lead to problems, however, and are best avoided.

1. **Sweeping Declarations.** These are statements so broad you can have no hope of dealing with them adequately in a short essay—or short book. "Dawn of civilization" introductions ("Since prehistoric times humankind has fought wars for economic reasons") are of this ilk, as are broad moral claims ("Killing is always wrong"). Such introductions are unprovable and distract readers from your specific argument.

2. **Filler.** Also known as "throat-clearing" introductions, these wordy and desperate attempts to get something—*anything*—down on paper are typified by vague statements ("Education in a heterogeneous society presents interesting problems"), obvious statements ("It is hard to understand a different culture without experiencing it firsthand"), and pointless definitions ("Propaganda is a form of persuasion").

3. **Alienating Pronouncements.** Statements that insult, offend, or otherwise alienate your readers are, for obvious reasons, deadly in introductions (and dangerous elsewhere). If you are writing about the challenge of hunting wild turkey for an audience that includes bird watchers and gun-control advocates, for instance, there is little point in starting out with the assertion that "Nothing can match the thrill of shooting a wild turkey after a long day of stalking the wily bird."

Exposition   At some point, often after the introduction but sometimes as part of it, you may need to provide expository information about your subject, defining key terms and giving background information readers will need in order to understand the subject correctly. This part of the essay can be long or short or dispensed with altogether, depending on the familiarity of the subject matter to the intended audience. Here you must judge (as we discussed in Chapter 2) the extent of the audience's probable knowledge about your subject. For example, an article about the use of a new drug to fight multiple sclerosis will require less general background information (and more technical detail and review of previous scholarship on the subject) if it is to be published in the *Journal of the American Medical Association* for an audience of doctors than if it is to be published in *Time* for the general public. In the latter case, the writer will probably explain the disease itself as well as the drug and its effects.

While the exposition is not an overtly persuasive part of an argument, it can help win readers' good will by reducing the potential for confusion or indifference about the subject matter. And, because all that we write is necessarily selective, the exposition can help win readers' sympathies by the information it includes.

Confirmation   This is the rhetorical term for the core of the argument: the reasons, examples, and evidence the writer offers in support of the thesis. Make sure you offer no reason (for drawing your thesis conclusion) without explanation and no explanation without example, and you will be unlikely to leave weak links in the development of your argument.

The problem then becomes making sure you have organized your points clearly and logically. Now, there is no magic formula for organizing your points. The supporting points for most subjects can be offered in almost any imaginable order—as long as you have a rationale for the ordering that makes sense and enables you to move easily and naturally from one point to the next. The ordering of points frequently changes in the process of writing, as new and previously unsuspected connections between ideas become apparent to you. No matter what order is finally determined, keep in mind the analogy of relay race strategy: End with the strongest runner, and don't begin with the weakest.

Whatever order you settle on, however, one cardinal rule does apply: If you set up reader expectations for a particular ordering of ideas—perhaps by itemizing your main points early in the essay—you are bound to discuss those points in the same order in which you first identify them.

Refutation   You must always consider other possible ideas and viewpoints about the subject besides your own. To show that you have done so enhances your persona substantially by demonstrating that you are both well informed and reasonable. If you argue that the federal government is right to give tax credit for private school tuition, you must remember that many people oppose such credits, and you must speak to this opposition either directly or indirectly. If you claim that aliens from outer space have visited Syracuse, New York, you must bear in mind that many people do not believe that life exists elsewhere in the universe. Investigating opposing viewpoints helps you determine which points will best support your own thesis—and occasionally, if you are open-minded, will cause you to modify your own position to reflect what truth you see in the opposition.

The placement of the refutation depends on two factors: the nature of the subject matter and your sense of your audience. If the subject is controversial, it is well to put the refutation early, since the opposing viewpoint will be on the readers' minds anyway. If the subject is not particularly controversial for your audience, the refutation may precede or follow the confirmation or, rarely, be dispensed with entirely. In "Surrogate Motherhood: An Ethical Dilemma," reprinted in Chapter 10, William E. May begins with the refutation. In "On Morality" (Chapter 3), on the other hand, Joan Didion refutes the prevailing notion of morality after explaining her own sense of it. For some complex and controversial subjects, the confirmation and refutation may alternate point by point. Clarence Darrow elects this method in "Why I Am an Agnostic" (Chapter 10).

Conclusion   The conclusion can be the most difficult part of an essay for a beginning writer—and is often so for an experienced writer. After struggling with an argument for some days—or hours, at least—you may be sorely tempted just to stop, rather than conclude. As a result, the essay will either drop off abruptly at its end or mindlessly repeat for the readers what they already have been told. If your essay turns out to be long, ten to fifteen pages or more, and complex, you are justified in repeating the major points you have made to support your thesis. But if your essay is less than five pages, you insult your readers' intelligence and attention span by reiterating what you have just finished saying. Instead of reinforcing the argument, such conclusions undercut it.

A few other pointers: The rhetorical (open-ended) question—admittedly my favorite type of conclusion during my high school years—grows tiresome with overuse. So, too, the concluding quotation can be effective, but ending your argument with someone else's words can weaken the power of your own persona and, therefore, also should be used with restraint. And unless the essay is very long, and the conclusion itself more than just a single paragraph, the writer should avoid all temptations to begin the conclusion with the words, "In conclusion. . . ." Most readers are bright enough to see the white space at the bottom of the page and to realize that the end is near.

With all these injunctions in mind, what remains for you to do in a conclusion?

You may **omit a formal conclusion,** if your essay is quite short (perhaps no more than a page or two). A single summing-up sentence (often your thesis) will probably suffice.

I'll put it bluntly: if you care for the quality of life in our American democracy, then you have to be for censorship.
    —Irving Kristol, "Pornography, Obscenity, and the Case for Censorship"

You may **end with a final illustration or metaphor** that epitomizes your thesis or ties the conclusion to the introduction by returning to and completing an image or anecdote begun there.

Of course, if McGuffey were to compile his readers now he would alter some selections. Each generation needs to draw differently from the reservoir of our cultural heritage. My regret is to see so much of it left out of sight, out of mind.

I mean no implication that today's college students are less intelligent. As a group they are impressive young people. After I had told the story of that night in Athens in 399 B.C. there was a lively discussion prompted by this man who had so far survived 2,000 years.

I just wish I could have put aside the wonder whether the occasion was at last a funeral service.
    —Vermont Royster, "The Death of Socrates"

You may **point toward a solution** if your argument has focused on identifying and discussing a problem. Or you may **assess the value of your subject,** or **advocate a policy toward it.**

These are but a handful of examples of the subtle slanting that goes on daily in news broadcasts. I could have offered many more, and I could have offered a number of examples of scrupulously unslanted reports as well. I certainly do not mean to imply that newspeople deliberately attempt to manipulate and deceive the American public; quite the contrary. But some striking and disturbing characteristics of national news broadcasts do stand out. The three networks report virtually the same major stories each day, and the facts of each story are almost invariably identical. However, the presentation and interpretation of these facts differ remarkably; I sometimes have found myself changing my mind about an issue after watching it discussed first on one network and then on another. Certainly bias cannot be avoided, but given the enormous audience and the strong impact television news has on that audience, we who comprise it owe it to ourselves to balance television news with that presented in newspapers and news magazines; to watch news reporting consciously and carefully, noting especially

any bias in the "last word"; and to make a habit of watching all three networks in turn, rather than allowing a single network to influence our opinions.
—Mark Alsop, "The Problem of Bias in Television News Reporting"

You may **indicate a preference or final judgment** if your argument has focused on comparing two or more things or events.

A more sensible alternative is possible. Do not do away with Santa Claus or presents or Christmas trees—simply do away with the lies and evasions. Like little Virginia, many years ago, children today will find the truth just as enchanting as the fibs and fallacies. The spirit of sharing and giving at Christmastime is represented by a "pretend" figure known as Santa Claus. Real people do the giving, and children can be part of that giving: Those with more toys than they need can select one or more that they might have received to take to the Salvation Army or another charitable organization so that little Sally can have some toys at Christmas, too. No enjoyment is lost to the child who learns about Santa as a symbol and who reads "The Night Before Christmas" for what it is—a delightful fairy tale. And no loss of innocence occurs at age seven or eight in children who have known the truth all along. Santa is just too wonderful a part of Christmas to be put in the position of being exposed as a lie.
—T.J. Stone, "Lies, Fallacies, and Santa Claus"

You may **state your thesis** and discuss or illustrate it if your argument develops an enthymeme according to the model of Chapter 2.

The newspapers yield only as much as the reader brings to his reading. If the reader doesn't also study foreign affairs, or follow the money markets, or keep up his practice of foreign languages, then what can he expect to learn from the papers?
—Lewis Lapham, "Sculptures in Snow"

EXERCISE 5-1

Evaluate the following introductory paragraphs from student essays. Comment specifically on weaknesses and strengths you find. Which paragraph or paragraphs do you find most promising? Why?

Note: These essays were written after the students had read a Melville story and some of the writings of philosopher Jeremy Bentham. The two main characters in the Melville story are the narrator, an attorney, and his "wayward copyist," or clerk, Bartleby. Bartleby is a passive resister; his usual reply when asked to do something is, "I would prefer not to." But the attorney finds himself strangely drawn to the useless Bartleby.

(1)

Jeremy Bentham developed a philosophical and political theory called Utilitarianism. Utilitarianism states that all decisions should be made by deciding what gives the greatest good to the greatest number. Herman Melville's short story "Bartleby the Scrivener" has characters who support and attack Utilitarianism.

(2)

The narrator in Herman Melville's short story "Bartleby the Scrivener" is confounded by the presence of his employee Bartleby. The character of Bartleby is an enigma, a man who refuses to conform to the narrator's notions of what "ought" to be done. Bartleby opposes his employer wholeheartedly, although passively, and "prefers not to" do anything the narrator asks of him. While considering the narrator's actions and his philosophies concerning Bartleby, one can also consider Jeremy Bentham's principles of utilitarianism and notice the similarities between the two men's views on Life and Human Nature. Bentham's theories are directly applicable in the case of the narrator.

(3)

There are only two characters that undergo any form of development in "Bartleby the Scrivener," a short story by Herman Melville. Of these two, Bartleby and the narrator, the latter is more complex in his action and decisions.

(4)

After reading "Bartleby the Scrivener" one would agree that Bartleby is no ordinary law clerk and that he is indeed an eccentric. But upon considering the narrator as a main character, one may also agree that he is no ordinary narrator. Not only does he report his experiences with a wayward copyist, but he acts as a moral agent. Faced with the problem of Bartleby, the narrator seeks some reasonable means through which he may understand Bartleby's resistance. In doing so, the narrator soon discovers that it is not just his curiosity that must be satisfied but his sense of moral responsibility as well.

EXERCISE 5–2

Which of the following subjects—regardless of your purpose or your specific thesis—would be likely to require extensive exposition for an audience of your rhetoric class? Which would require brief exposition? Is there any subject here for which you could dispense with the exposition entirely? Explain.

Writing letters of complaint to landlords
Deer hunting
Commodities trading
The requirements at this college for a liberal arts degree
The requirements at this college for an engineering degree
The relative merits of *WordPerfect* and Microsoft *Word*
The need for expanded mass transit in this community

The need for expanded mass transit in Miami, Florida

African photo safaris

The Nicaraguan economy

Fraternity grade requirements at this college

Ethics in argumentation

The psychological needs reflected in slang usage among high school students

The "Theory of Everything" (TOE) in physics

The enduring appeal of the game of *Monopoly*

EXERCISE 5-3

Based on the thesis idea that obscenity laws cannot be made specific enough to serve any useful purpose, you have written a draft that includes the following points. Order them in a way that seems appropriate to your purpose of persuading your state legislators not to pass some pending legislation on obscenity. Add any additional points that would improve the argument, and take out any that do not work. Then, in a paragraph or two, explain why you made the choices you did and ordered the points as you did.

Obscenity is an inherently nebulous concept, dependent on the viewpoint of each beholder.

A survey of students in a mass media class showed no consensus regarding whether five slides showed indecent subjects. One of those slides was a photo of a woman being electrocuted; another was of a scene from an X-rated movie.

Juries that try obscenity cases are made up of ordinary citizens with no training in psychology or ethics. It is often impossible for them to reach decisions in such cases, thus wasting tax money and accomplishing nothing.

It might be more useful to promote ethics education in schools than to pass obscenity laws.

Many times obscenity has violent rather than sexual overtones.

What is obscene to one person is art to the next person; the key question is whether either is demonstrably harmed.

EXERCISE 5-4

Suppose that you have written drafts for essays based on the following thesis conclusions. For which of them, if any, would extensive refutation be advisable? For which, if any, would a brief refutation be sufficient? Indicate for each whether you would put the refutation before, following, or alternating point-by-point with your own arguments. Assume that your audience is your rhetoric classmates, and your purpose is to persuade them to adopt your viewpoint on a subject about which they have relatively little knowledge but may have biases or preconceptions.

WordPerfect's extensive user support system will make it the dominant word processing program for some time to come.

Fear of the AIDS epidemic in Africa will make African photo safaris by wealthy North Americans a thing of the past.

Playing *Monopoly* promotes acquisitive behavior in children.

EXERCISE 5-5

Evaluate the following concluding paragraphs from student essays as specifically as you can without having the entire essays before you. Comment on particular weaknesses and strengths.

(1)

In conclusion, this essay has demonstrated that eliminating smoking on most airline flights has increased safety and made flying more pleasant for all concerned. In the words of Homer Coombs, the frequent flyer mentioned earlier, "Let them [the smokers] eat cake—at least now I'll be able to taste mine!"

(2)

If you do all the above and you still get no response, forget about it and just don't tell any more jokes. Now you know that telling a joke well really can be hard to do. However, if you have the drive, the spirit, and the stupidity, you will probably tell a joke anyway.

(3)

Scientific evidence that contradicts certain religious beliefs shows that it is time for some of the devout to rethink their interpretation of the Bible. If the evidence of evolution conflicts with the idea that humans were instantaneously created by God, perhaps a more valid theory could encompass the significant aspects of both beliefs: God created humans in a period that, although long to finite minds, was only a day out of eternity. Is it not the Bible that says (in 2 Peter 3.8) that "a thousand years [is] as one day" with the Lord?

(4)

Thus, I find the symbol of my philosophy of life: the eternal cockroach. Although such a choice may be irreverent, it does, nevertheless, direct my path. The roach's survival throughout the ages—and throughout many people's houses—reminds me not to focus entirely on one goal. Instead, the best move is to diversify my interests and skills and thereby be prepared for whatever opportunities I encounter. In this way, I will never be forced into a small niche, like the Smilodon,* where I might face failure. Instead, I will always succeed. It is amazing that from such a small insect can come such a valuable lesson.

(5)

I wonder if SMU is not making a mistake in its course requirements—its devotion to the core curriculum. When we graduate, we will be competing with people who were able to decline to take an art course in preference to one in their own chosen specialty. Being well-rounded in the past meant knowing more; now, it means knowing less.†

We have just spent several pages considering different ways of developing introductions and conclusions to the argument that you have spent time and care developing out of your thesis idea. The reason for emphasizing such finishing touches is that they are important to the persuasiveness of what you write, but too often become mere hurried afterthoughts and the dullest parts of an essay. By comparison, only a few paragraphs here have dealt with the main work of writing—the exposition, confirmation, and refutation that constitute the body of argument. That disproportion is deliberate, but it should not mislead you: You must spend your greatest time and care developing the body of your argument. However, if you have worked out a thesis with care, as suggested in Chapter 2, you have in the process discovered what shape your particular argument needs to take. The possibilities are countless. The work of writing and revising the body of the essay becomes a matter of filling out that shape through reflection, research, discussion, and, always, writing.

That done, the argument may well be unified and complete but still a bit ragged around the edges. It is time to look more closely at each paragraph, sentence, and even individual word choices.

*The smilodon, this essay explains earlier, was the "sabre-toothed tiger" of the Oligocene period. It overspecialized in its hunting methods and thus died out when its prey did.

†I cannot resist a footnote here: The student who concluded his essay with this paragraph made a near-perfect score on the MCAT exam this year and will soon begin study in his "own chosen specialty" at the Johns Hopkins Medical School. Apparently he was undamaged by the core curriculum.

MICRO-REVISION: PARAGRAPHS, SENTENCES, WORDS

Paragraph Completeness

Full development or completeness within each individual paragraph—from the first to the last—involves much the same considerations, on a smaller scale, as does completeness in the entire essay. The one- or two-sentence paragraph often serves well for transition or for emphasis, but for making a complex point such a length is inadequate. Even the three-sentence paragraph can be cursory. At any length, the underdeveloped paragraph leaves readers fidgeting: What does this have to do with the rest of the paper? Why does the writer draw this conclusion? How does this point fit in? What does this mean? or (worst of all), So what? Complete paragraphs may raise such questions in the reader's mind, but they also answer most of those questions. And anticipating and answering the reader's questions about the topic rarely can be accomplished in a couple of sentences.

Certainly, completeness is not determined by number of sentences or number of lines alone, but few sentences and few lines can be symptomatic of poor development. Always look closely at short paragraphs. Do they develop the topic idea thoroughly, or do they take for granted knowledge the reader may not have? Do they define key terms? Do they break down the topic idea into its component parts, if any? Do they use evidence, examples, and analogies to make clear the relationships between ideas and the reasons for the conclusions they draw? Ask these questions in evaluating any paragraph, especially the last: Does it give an example? Any paragraph benefits from an illustration.

Accordingly, I offer a few examples to illustrate how a paragraph might be tested for completeness:

1. **Does the paragraph define key terms?** Readers do not appreciate writers who casually introduce terms important to their argument, but pertinent only to a very specialized field of knowledge, without giving the slightest hint what the words mean. In the essay from which the following paragraph has been taken, the writer traces the development of laser technology from science-fiction dreams to reality. This paragraph defines the key term *laser:*

The acronym "laser," coined by scientist Gordon Gould in 1957, describes in shorthand form how the device works: Light Amplification by Stimulated Emission of Radiation. In 1916 Einstein predicted that electrons in an atom could be deliberately stimulated to emit photons (light energy) of a certain wavelength. He was right. The laser must first be "pumped" with energy in a variety of ways—from Maiman's flash tube to a nuclear explosion—so that the electrons are excited into higher energy states. But these high energy electrons are unstable—and fall back to a lower energy level. On the way down, their extra energy is released as light. That light is captured inside the laser and amplified by bouncing it back and forth between mirrors. The laser beam that emerges is amplified, monochromatic, coherent light—and it shines with an unearthly power.

—"The Dazzle of Lasers," *Newsweek*, 13 Jan. 1983

Bear in mind, however, that if a reader's vocabulary is limited, the writer cannot be faulted for using words the reader does not understand. Dictionaries serve as useful intermediaries between writer and reader in such cases. As writer, be careful to use only words that you understand and that fit the context precisely. As reader, when you don't know the meaning of a word, look it up.

2. **Does the paragraph break down the topic into its component parts, if any?** All writing involves analysis—the breaking down of a subject or a problem into its component parts. Many paragraphs are devoted to the detailing of such components. Always consider the possibility that the topic of a given paragraph could be better understood if it were broken down and explained analytically, as in the following case:

As a Wasp, the mildest thing I can say about the stereotype emerging from the current wave of anti-Wasp chic is that I don't recognize myself. As regards emotional uptightness and sexual inhibition, modesty forbids comment—though I dare say various friends and lovers of mine could testify on these points if they cared to. I will admit to enjoying work—because I am lucky enough to be able to work at what I enjoy—but not, I think, to the point of compulsiveness. And so far as ruling America, or even New York, is concerned, I can say flatly that (a) it's a damn lie because (b) if I *did* rule them, both would be in better shape than they are. Indeed I and all my Wasp relatives, taken in a lump, have far less clout with the powers that run this country than any one of the Buckleys or Kennedys (Irish Catholic), the Sulzbergers or Guggenheims (Jewish), or the late A. P. Giannini (Italian) of the Bank of America.

—Robert Claiborne, "A Wasp Stings Back," *Newsweek*, 30 Sept. 1974

3. **Does the paragraph provide evidence, examples, or analogies?** If it does not, add an example or two, or compare your topic to something simpler or more concrete. If the paragraph is not improved and made more interesting, take the example or analogy (or both) out. You will find, however, that you will usually want to keep it. The example of a specific book makes this paragraph more convincing than it would have been had it made only general assertions:

It's often the best books that draw the beadiest attention of the censors. These are the books that really have the most to offer, the news that life is rich and complicated and difficult. Where else, for example, could a young male reader see the isolation of his painful adolescence reflected the way it is in *Catcher in the Rye*, one of the *most* banned books in American letters. In the guise of fiction, books offer opportunities, choices, and plausible models. They light up the whole range of human character and emotion. Each, in its own way, tells the truth and prepares its eager readers for the unknown and unpredictable events of their own lives.

—Loudon Wainwright, "A Little Banning Is a Dangerous Thing," *Life*, 1982

Revising for Coherence

Beginning writers usually are willing to accept the precept that every paragraph in a paper should be clearly related to the paper's thesis and that every sentence in a paragraph should be clearly related to the topic sentence. But they are sometimes incredulous of the notion that each sentence must also be directly connected to the sentences immediately preceding and following it. Each sentence must logically follow from or be parallel in value to the sentence before it; it must have a logical link to the idea expressed in the sentence after it. If these conditions are met, and the connections between ideas reinforced by transitions and parallelism, the writing will be coherent. If these conditions are not met, the writing will be incoherent. We will look at examples of both.

The biggest single flaw in most writing is incoherence; and incoherence is caused largely by failure to recognize the need to justify assertions logically or failure to recognize that relationships between ideas are not necessarily obvious or self-evident. The solution to both problems lies in thinking through and then spelling out such relationships—no easy task.

The relationships between ideas in the sentences in a paragraph are made clearer by the use of subordination, repetition (of sentence structures, words, or pronouns), and appropriate transitions—but the relationships between ideas must first exist, or coherence devices create only a mockery of coherence and add to the confusion. Consider a baffling example of such mock coherence:

Among the most liberal of educations is that received at a prep school such as the one I attended. However, prep schools offer a student the opportunity to get to know students from all over the country and from several foreign countries. This variety of students has been very interesting. For example, we had to study three foreign languages in order to graduate. Foreign languages were not difficult for me, but math certainly was hard. For that matter, the beds were hard, too. Accordingly, Sweetly Prep did not believe in coddling students. We therefore, as you can see, received a liberal and thorough education.

—Student draft

What this writer has done is to freely associate ideas: liberal education⟩ variety of students, including foreign students⟩ study of foreign languages⟩ hard studies and hard beds⟩ students not coddled⟩ students received liberal education. As he rambles, he loses sight of his real topic (what makes a prep school education "among the most liberal of educations"?) but not of the injunction to be coherent. So he ties together the argument, which he senses is getting away from him, with a string of inappropriate transitional words and repeated phrases. The attempt is no more successful than attempting to giftwrap a bicycle: The unwieldy paragraph, like the Schwinn, cannot be contained. But no paragraph is utterly beyond hope, once we recognize both its problems and its possibilities. We will return to this one.

Subordination   All ideas are not created equal, and one task of revising is to make sure that what matters most is given most prominence in your argument. This is true on the large scale, where you give most attention and greatest space to developing your strongest points. It is equally true on the sentence level, where you make sure that major points are expressed in independent clauses and minor details about those points are subordinated into dependent clauses, phrases, or even words. The importance of choices you make about what to emphasize and what to subordinate can be illustrated by the following sentences combining three bits of information: "Davis quit in disgust," "Davis flew to Tahiti," and "Stafford hired a new accountant."

After Stafford hired a new accountant, Davis quit in disgust and flew to Tahiti.

Just before Davis quit in disgust and flew to Tahiti, Stafford hired a new accountant.

Davis flew to Tahiti where, disgusted that Stafford had hired a new accountant, he wired the company his resignation.

Having quit the company in his disgust that Stafford had hired a new accountant, Davis flew to Tahiti.

In one of these sentences, what seems to matter most is that Davis quit. In another, it is the fact that Stafford hired a new accountant. In others, Davis's flight to Tahiti is prominent. None is "right" or "wrong," but in each sentence the emphasis is slightly different. When you write, make sure that the information you want to emphasize is expressed in main clauses: Never bury a key point in a dependent clause.

Repetition: Key Terms, Parallel Structure, and Pronouns   Repetition of key terms, repetition of grammatical patterns (parallelism), and the use of pronouns as links back to nouns mentioned earlier also provide useful aids to coherence. Each of these three coherence devices serves to remind the reader of the relationship between the sentence he or she is reading and the ideas in previous sentences. The first, *the repetition of key terms*, keeps before the reader the paragraph topic under consideration and the connection between ideas expressed in different sentences. (Notice that the use of many synonyms in a misguided attempt to add variety leads only to confusion.) The second, *the repetition of grammatical patterns*, or parallel structure, reinforces the equivalent importance of ideas by putting them in grammatically equivalent patterns. A pair or more of nouns, adjectives, verbs, or adverbs creates a minor parallelism; a pair or more of phrases, dependent clauses, or independent clauses with nearly identical grammatical patterns creates a major parallelism. (Be careful, however, not to confuse parallelism with Dick-and-Jane sentence structure, composed of endless series of short subject-verb-complement clauses.) The third, *the use and repetition of pronouns,* enables the writer to avoid continually renaming subjects under discussion. The pronoun is necessarily a coherence device, for it always refers back to some previously mentioned noun, and the reference needs to be completely clear and unambiguous (not "Sam told Peter he was likely to be fired"—the intended reference in this case might be to either man). The following paragraph from Alfred North Whitehead's "Universities and Their Functions" illustrates the use of these three devices to reinforce the interweaving of ideas within a paragraph.

The justification for a university is that it preserves the connection between knowledge and the zest of life, by uniting the young and the old in the imaginative consideration of learning. The university imparts information, but it imparts it imaginatively. At least, this is the function which it should perform for society. A university which fails in this respect has no reason for existence. This atmosphere of excitement, arising from imaginative consideration, transforms knowledge. A fact is no longer a bare fact: it is invested with all its possibilities. It is no longer a burden on the memory: it is energizing as the poet of our dreams, and as the architect of our purposes.

Avoiding Repetitiousness.   The careful writer, of course, uses repetition and reminder with restraint, taking care not to use the devices so much that they call attention to themselves rather than to the ideas they link. The writer of the following paragraph (written before mandatory retirement was outlawed) has failed to heed this caution.

As we grow older, many of us begin to realize just how absurd it is to set the specific age of 65 for mandatory retirement. Why must we have mandatory retirement in the first place? Why, if we must have mandatory retirement, must retirement occur at age 65? What makes age 65 the "right" age for retirement? Why not retire at 49, or at 72? What is the significance of age 65? The truth is that during the German worker revolts of the late nineteenth century, Bismarck's advisors determined that setting mandatory retirement at age 65 would pacify most of the laborers. Why not? In the late nineteenth century, few people even lived to age 65; the new mandatory retirement law really meant that most people could work their entire adult lives. Today, the average lifespan has increased markedly, but retirement at age 65 is still the rule at most companies. Why do employers persist in following Bismarck on the issue of mandatory retirement at 65?

Such heavy-handed repetition only annoys a reader, creating a distraction rather than the intended reinforcement of ideas. The writer repeats words and phrases pointlessly where combining clauses could make such repetition unnecessary. He repeats rhetorical questions so often that they lose their rhetorical force and begin to sound merely querulous. And surely the phrases "mandatory retirement" and "age 65" could be reduced in number for the sake of the reader. Problem repetition may be avoided in these ways:

1. Combine related sentences, subordinating less important ideas to more important ideas, and putting equally important ideas into parallel structure. In this way the number of repeated terms can be reduced. For example, certain points in the following sentences could be subordinated to others:

The city council will vote on the proposed commercial development north of the Loop. The vote will take place next week, by which time the city council must resolve the question of conflict of interest. The possible conflict of interest stems from the fact that five of the seven city council members own property north of the Loop.

As it stands, this paragraph contains pointless, rather than emphatic or coherent, repetition. The sentences could be combined:

The city council will vote next week on the proposed commercial development north of the Loop, by which time the council members must resolve the question of conflict of interest stemming from the fact that five of the seven members own property in the area in question.

If the resulting single sentence leaves the reader a bit breathless, it could easily be made into two sentences: ". . . north of the Loop. By that time the council. . . ." In either case, some needless repetition is avoided, and the relationship between ideas made clear by the use of grammatical subordination.

When ideas are equal in value, parallel structure can eliminate unnecessary repetition and make unity and coherence more apparent, as demonstrated by the following paragraph and its revision.

Original Version: The provost has proposed several actions for the university to take in order to achieve its goal of increasing its prestige nationally. The university should raise the standards for admission. It should improve the caliber of the faculty. It should improve the physical facilities for the natural sciences. Also, new computer science equipment and refurbishing the building in which it is housed would strengthen the computer science program. All academic courses should be made more rigorous to combat grade inflation. All these actions will require the support of the board of trustees and the support of the alumni if they are to succeed. The trustees and the alumni will need to provide funds to accomplish the provost's aims for the university. They must also provide enthusiasm if the undertaking is to succeed.

Revised Version: To further the university's goal of increasing its prestige nationally, the provost has recommended that the standards for admission be raised and that the courses of study be made more rigorous. To complement those aims, he has also recommended that the caliber of the entire faculty and the quality of facilities and equipment for the natural sciences and computer science be improved. And to make possible such extensive changes, he has asked for financial and moral support from the board of trustees and the alumni.

The careless repetition of words and sentence patterns in the first version has been eliminated in the second, while the real parallelism of ideas and syntax is made clearer. Notice, too, that similar ideas have been grouped together: the quality of the academic program and of those admitted to it, the quality of the instructors and of the facilities that make possible a respected academic program, and the money and the enthusiasm that make implementing all these improvements possible. Grouping together similar ideas in similar grammatical units has improved the coherence of the paragraph and made its unity more apparent. Pronouns and transitional words underscore that coherence: *those* aims, *also, and, such* . . . changes.

2. Vary repeated words and grammatical units slightly. Instead of repeating a term exactly, use an occasional synonym, where appropriate, or pronoun. A thesaurus may help you to find synonyms, but remember: There are few exact synonyms. *Home* has connotations of warmth and family that *house* lacks. A *partisan* may not be a *patriot*, or vice versa. In order to decide whether you need to use a synonym for a repeated word or phrase, try reading the passage aloud. If any term seems annoyingly frequent, use a synonym in one or two places if the synonym carries the same denotation and connotation.

The parallelism of words, phrases, and clauses is not broken but is softened by adding modifiers. For example, the sentence

Finding a need, learning about it, and acting upon what is learned are the principles of effective community service.

contains parallel structures (three gerund phrases), but the first gerund is modified by a direct object, the second by a prepositional phrase, and the third by a prepositional phrase in which the object of the preposition is itself a clause. That variety within the same basic structure maintains parallelism while avoiding monotony.

You also may vary parallel structures by using *ellipsis*—the omission of clearly understood words, often in parallel phrases or clauses. Look at the next-to-last sentence of the preceding paragraph: "The first gerund is modified by a direct object, the second [gerund is modified] by

a prepositional phrase, and the third [gerund is modified] by a prepositional phrase. . . ." The clauses would be tedious if the words in brackets
had been repeated each time. Ellipsis serves to avoid that needless repetition while preserving the parallel structure of the sentence.

Transitions   Both subordinate and parallel relationships among ideas
are strengthened by the appropriate use of transitions. *Appropriate* is a
key word here. The sentences in the "prep school" paragraph you read
on page 153, for example, are not clearly related to one another and
certainly are not related in the ways implied by the transitions. Transitional words and phrases are not freely interchangeable; they have mean-

---

Transitions

Logical outcome: therefore, thus, it follows that, consequently,
hence, so, as a result, then, for this reason, accordingly

Logical cause: to this end, with this object, for this reason, because

Time sequence: first (second, third, etc.), next, later, afterward, then,
finally, at last, previously, earlier, until, when, in the meantime,
meanwhile, immediately, now, formerly, subsequently, thereupon,
at that time, the following day (week, month, etc.)

Spatial relationship: here, nearby, farther away, above, below, opposite, on the left (right, top, bottom), between

Additional information: and, also, in addition, moreover, furthermore, similarly

Examples: for example, in particular, specifically, for instance, to
illustrate

Comparison: similarly, by the same token, likewise, in the same
way, just as

Contrast or qualification: but, however, in contrast, on the other
hand, for all that, nevertheless, still, yet, notwithstanding, in spite
of

Concession: admittedly, it must be granted, it is true, of course,
naturally, although, granted that, no doubt, even though

Emphasis or restatement: indeed, truly, of course, chiefly, principally, in other words, in short, that is, in effect

Summary or conclusion: finally, when all is considered, at last, in
conclusion, to summarize, in short, in brief

ings, and those meanings state different relationships. They may appear at the beginnings of sentences or as parenthetical elements within sentences (as in the sentence "The difficulty, *however,* came not so much in arranging the trip as in recruiting the passengers"). The chart below lists some of the common transitions and the relationships they indicate. And the following paragraph, from Walter Lippmann's "The Indispensable Opposition," illustrates the uses of simple transitions in making clear the relationships among ideas.

The opposition is indispensable. A good statesman, like any other sensible human being, always learns more from his opponents than from his fervent supporters. For his supporters will push him to disaster unless his opponents show him where the dangers are. So if he is wise he will often pray to be delivered from his friends, because they will ruin him. But, though it hurts, he ought also to pray never to be left without opponents; for they keep him on the path of reason and good sense.

—*The Atlantic,* August 1939

Coherence is a basic requirement of effective writing. It is essential to persuasion. The best way to achieve coherent writing is to put yourself, as far as possible, in the position of your own reader. After you finish the draft of an essay, put what you have written aside, for a day or two if possible, and then try to read the piece as if you have never seen it before. Try to see only the logical connections on the page, not the ones in your head. Listen for the droning sound of pointless repetition and for the satisfying balance of parallel structure. Make sure that you mean *thus* when you say it, and not *afterward.* By putting yourself in your reader's position, you will produce writing that a reader can follow and therefore can appreciate. In so doing, you help create a persona a reader can trust.

EXERCISE 5–6

Revise the following paragraph, using subordination to bring the elements of the paragraph into appropriate relationship to each other. You must first decide which points are primary, which subordinate. Reorder clauses or sentences if you find a need to do so.

Garlic gets bad press (for causing bad breath) that it does not deserve. This problem must have arisen because people do not know enough about garlic. Garlic is a member of the lily family. It is cousin to the onion. It was long grown in the Mediterranean basin. Dioscorides was a first-century Greek physician. He believed that garlic could cleanse the body of toxins, restore energy, and increase male virility. In the centuries since, it has been claimed as a cure for everything from dandruff to athlete's foot. During World War I, children wore garlic around their necks. They did so to ward off the dreaded Spanish Influenza. British soldiers in World War I used sphagnum moss soaked in garlic juice to dress wounds when hospital gauze ran out. In Mexico, garlic soup is a folk remedy for digestive problems and intestinal parasites. Garlic may not have all the powers people have attributed to it over the years. Garlic does taste good.

—Adapted from Stuart and Lawrence Teacher,
The Teacher Brothers Modern-Day Almanac, 1983

EXERCISE 5-7

Revise the student paragraph on page 155 by eliminating or varying some of the heavy-handed repetition of syntax and pronouns.

EXERCISE 5-8

Revise the following paragraph (a corrupted version of a paragraph in Joseph Epstein, "The Virtues of Ambition," *Harper's,* October 1981) by improving the parallel structure of phrases and clauses.

We do not choose to be born. Also, our parents are not chosen by us. We have no say as to our historical epoch, in what country we are born, or any say about the circumstances of our upbringing. Then, too, we do not, most of us, choose to die, or select the time or conditions of our death. But within all this realm of choicelessness, we do determine how we shall live. We can live courageously or in cowardice, act honorably or dishonorably. Also, we can live with purpose or in drift. We decide what is important in life, and what is trivial in life is our decision as well. We make the decision that what makes us important either is what we do or what we refuse to do. But no matter how indifferent the universe may be to our choices and what we decide, they are ours to make. We decide. We make choices. And as we decide and things are chosen by us, so are our lives formed. In the end, forming our own destiny is what ambition is about.

EXERCISE 5–9

Improve the coherence of the following paragraphs by adding transitions where they are needed and combining clauses where appropriate.

(1)

After fighting the mountain for another eight hours, I managed to pass the other climbers. I reached the peak of Fremont first. I took my final step to reach the top. I realized that Mount Fremont had won the battle. I did not feel the glory I had anticipated feeling. I felt uncomfortable. I had invaded a sacred place. The mammoth mountains and their ring of clouds were serenely oblivious of my accomplishment. The vastness of all I could see made me feel as inconsequential as the little pikas squeaking defiance at me from the rocks and boulders.

(2)

All students should study abroad at some point in their academic careers. The contact with a foreign culture, even one similar to our own, provides a remedy for American insularity. We tend to think that the world revolves around the United States. We are as provincial as the people of the Middle Ages who believed the sun and planets revolved around the earth. Study abroad remedies this provincialism. It makes history, geography, and political science come to life for students. It makes us appreciate our own country and the freedom and conveniences it offers. It promotes understanding among peoples of different cultures and beliefs. Study abroad offers the most efficient and memorable way to complete a liberal education.

EXERCISE 5–10

A. Look carefully at the student paragraph on "liberal education in prep school" on page 153. Explain the logical problems in the writer's choices of transitions. Comment on the contexts in which the writer uses *however, for example, accordingly,* and (that most abused of all transitions) *therefore.*

B. One topic that finds its way into this jumble of ideas and sentences is "Prep schools offer liberal educations." Another is "Sweetly Prep did not believe in coddling students." Identify two others.

C. Develop a coherent paragraph stemming from one of the topics you have identified. Use subordination to avoid purposeless repetition; use ellipsis to vary some sentence patterns.

Improving Clarity

Eliminating Wordiness   As we have seen, an important question writers must ask as we reread and relish the fruits of our toil is this: Have I said all I should? And the corollary to that question is this one: Where have I used more words than I needed to express a point? Paradoxically, it is possible for writing to be both underdeveloped and wordy. Consider the following passage, for example. It drones on like the next-door neighbor's home movies, full of sound but signifying nothing:

> Poetry is written in many forms and meters, and sometimes in arrangements that appear meterless and very nearly formless as well. Of course, that variety of form and meter, even the lack of both, makes poetry what it is. Every poet is entitled to his or her own artistic freedom, as long as he or she is true to the vision that inspires a particular poem. Variety is naturally a feature of this freedom. Any poet can write any length of line or any variety of stanzaic patterns, and many succeed in writing good poems in a variety of forms, with and without meter. Variety is important in poetry.
>
> —Student essay

Do you hear the pointless reiteration of words and thought? This writer says almost nothing (what she does say amounts to "Variety in form and meter, and even the lack of both, are important elements of the poet's artistic freedom of expression," repeated aimlessly) while missing the chance to illustrate her point with examples that would make it clearer and more convincing than mindless repetition does.

To eliminate underbrush of this sort from your own prose, look for wordiness and strike out unnecessary words, phrases, or sentences (even entire paragraphs, perhaps). Wordiness is not determined by number of words, but by number of useless words: verbal deadwood. It can take several forms, ranging from needless repetition (of words, phrases, or clauses) to unnecessary passive voice. (The passive voice—"The bill *was voted on* at the last Student Senate meeting"—is wordier than the active—"The Student Senate *voted on* the bill at its last meeting.") Samuel Johnson's advice has helped many a writer to discard wordy verbal flourishes: "Read over your compositions and, when you meet a passage which you think is particularly fine, strike it out." Strike out anything that appears to be merely decorating the page or taking up space, for it will not add to the persuasiveness of your prose. Beware of wordy sentences such as these:

Ann told Ryan the way in which to convince the boss to offer him a transfer to San Diego. (Avoid wordy connectors: "How" would be simpler and clearer than "the way in which.")

Art is different things to different people. (This sentence really has no meaning beyond superficial and self-evident observation. Avoid words like *different, various,* and *diverse.* They can make you think you have said something when you haven't.)

Without a doubt, the single factor among many that has meant the most to my understanding of the complexities and vagaries of contemporary urban society has been my mother. (Here pompous, wordy diction disguises a simple observation: "More than anyone else, my mother has helped me understand the complex and sometimes frightening world around me.")

There are many people who form and develop opinions about others that are very wrong. (Several kinds of wordy constructions mar this sentence. First, it begins with an expletive, *there are*. Expletives are inherently wordy and often ineffectual. Just say, "Many people form. . . ." Second, *form* and *develop* here are redundant. Drop one. Third, the last subordinate clause is inadequately subordinated. It can be reduced to a single adjective. And fourth, weak intensifiers like *very* and *so* are unnecessary and therefore wordy. They usually dilute the impact of what they modify rather than strengthen it. The core sentence now stands revealed as "Many people form wrong opinions about others.")

The student who wrote the paragraph about the poet's freedom of form and meter later revised it to a less wordy and more specific passage:

How could both e. e. cummings and John Milton be called by the same designation, poet? How could Lord Tennyson, Geoffrey Chaucer, and Gerard Manley Hopkins share it as well? Some of these poets, notably Milton, use strict stanzaic patterns and formal meter; their sonnets always look and sound like sonnets and their odes are recognizably odes. Others, like Hopkins, depart from standard meters, and some, like William Carlos Williams, seem to abandon meter altogether. And yet they are all poets, for what makes a poem is not wholly form, nor is it meter. What makes a poem is a special perspective of life, or of a red wheelbarrow, that strikes a chord of recognition—even reverence—that the reader had not known he possessed.

And this writer had ideas she had not known *she* possessed, until she stripped away the undergrowth of wordiness in her first version and confronted the need for real content.

Choosing the Right Words   Precise and careful word choices make writing clear. When joined with a pleasing style and logical, thoughtful development of ideas, they also make writing interesting. As you revise your drafts of reports and essays, ask yourself whether or not your word choices reflect the following priorities.

1. **Write with verbs and nouns.** Use verbs of action (thereby avoiding the overuse of *to be, to have, to make,* and *to do*) and specific nouns (avoiding *thing* and other vague, abstract words), so that the rhetorical weight of your sentences is not borne by adjectives and adverbs. Action verbs and specific nouns are rhetorically "strong" words; adjectives and adverbs are weaker. The difference is easily illustrated by a pair of sentences:

The crucially important point is to do as much as possible to get the bill passed.

We must work, with all the energy and determination we can muster, to see Senate Bill 1234 made law.

The first version is colorless and nearly weightless; it gives us no sense of action or of any person acting. The subject is *point* and the verb, *is*. Even the adverb and adjective modifying *point* add no real intensity to the sentence. The second version, while only slightly more specific (naming the particular bill in question), speaks with greater force and conviction: *we work, we can muster*. This sentence speaks of people, people acting. The adjectival modifiers give way to nouns: *energy* and *determination*. Even *to get* in the first version becomes *to see*, a more graphic verb, in the second.

2. **Prefer the concrete to the abstract, the specific to the general.** Although all words are abstractions, some are even further removed from concrete reality than others. *Head of government* is more abstract than *dictator*, for *heads of government* names a bigger and more vaguely defined class, including queens, pontiffs, prime ministers, and presidents. *Dictator* is in turn more abstract than *Castro, Franco,* or *Mussolini*—names that refer to specific dictators. The tendency of language is toward ever greater abstraction: It is like some great helium balloon always trying to slip away into the stratosphere as we either watch it sail away or try to pull it back down nearer earth. It is tempting just to let our language go, to say, "The movie was pretty interesting," because saying so is nearly effortless. It may take a conscious effort to pull our words down to the specific and concrete: "What I liked about the movie was the cinematography, which gave most of the scenes the appearance of paintings." And we could, of course, be still more concrete, describing in physical detail the artistic quality of particular scenes. Both specificity (identifying particular instances and features) and concreteness (creating images of tangible things) can clarify and illuminate an assertion. We cannot avoid the abstract, but we will support it with the specific and concrete if we wish to be clear.

3. **Be aware of connotative as well as denotative meanings.** A word's *denotation* is its meaning in the most neutral sense possible—its "dictionary" meaning. Its *connotation* is the emotional baggage the word carries. In the United States, for example, *democracy* carries positive connotations and *discrimination* carries both negative and positive connotations, depending on whether we are discussing the unfair treatment of minority groups or the ability to select a fine wine. Writers must be concerned with those societal connotations, selecting words that avoid unintended or undesirable connotations.

4. **Choose words that are consistent and appropriate in level of diction.** That is, be careful not to use slang in one sentence and pompous

diction in the next, let alone both kinds of language in a single sentence. We do well to avoid such peculiar hybrids as this one: "It is imperative that the proponents of both sides of the question get their acts together and resolve this problem." Most of the sentence is unduly pompous, while "get their acts together" is ludicrously colloquial in contrast.

The level of diction in any piece of writing—whether formal, informal, or colloquial—should also be appropriate to the rhetorical situation of a writer addressing a particular audience for a particular purpose. A treaty, a judicial decision, or even a letter of application for a job requires a level of formality that would be out of place in a note to a friend or an informal column in a college newspaper. Notice the difference in persona created by the different levels of diction in these examples.

Formal Diction: I trust that my experience in claims analysis will prove useful in helping your company set up a risk management program. I enjoyed meeting the members of your executive committee and look forward to hearing from you as soon as you have made a decision regarding my application.

Informal Diction: I believe that my work in claims management will help me get the job with Xavier Corporation, Mr. Matthews. I appreciate your letter of recommendation.

Colloquial Diction: I've got the right stuff for the job at Xavier, Joel, and if they aren't completely crazy, I'm pretty sure they'll hire me. Wish me luck!

Each of these levels of diction is appropriate to its rhetorical context, and each is internally consistent in diction.

The stiff formality of impersonal constructions ("it appears to this writer that") and unwieldy third-person constructions when you are using personal illustrations and comments ("one sees that" in place of "we see that," or "one goes to the first classes of the semester" when you mean "I go to the first classes of the semester") does nothing for the appeal of your persona or the clarity of your argument. Some students adopt this pseudoformality in the mistaken belief that academic writing requires that the writer shun the word *I*. What those students confuse is the use of personal illustration and the personal voice of the writer—both of which are appropriate to much academic writing—and I-centered prose, the self-indulgent, self-centered writing that offers opinions in place of reasons. I-centered prose makes statements like "I feel that the Russo-Japanese War of 1904 was a disaster from start to finish." Content-centered prose, on the other hand, makes statements like "The Russo-Japanese War was a disaster for the Russians because they underestimated both the strength and the tenacity of their Japanese adversaries."

Another typical feature of pseudoformal prose is **jargon** used to impress the reader. Jargon is the vocabulary peculiar to a given profession, trade, or other group, and it has value in some applications. It allows two doctors to communicate specifically about the nature of a medical problem without going into elaborate descriptions of the case. It enables an attorney to write a contract that will stand up to legal challenges, because many of the convoluted phrases of legal jargon have been court-tested and their precise meaning established. But jargon has earned a bad name because too often it is used not by people sharing the same vocabulary but by people trying to impress or bewilder outsiders, those not privy to the specialized vocabulary. When doctors use medical jargon to talk over the heads of their partients, and when attorneys use legal jargon in order to perpetuate a need for their services (since nobody but other lawyers can make sense of the language), then "myocardial infarction" and "whereas the aforementioned party of the first part" amount only to so much gibberish. The abuse of jargon defeats the aim of clarity.

Checking Grammar and Mechanics   Even lapses of grammar and spelling, let alone clarity and coherence, can damage the *ethos* a writer desires to convey. A friend recently received the following letter from a real estate agent in response to an inquiry about a lake house the agent had listed for sale.

Allen Bilbo
8734 Medders
Pittsburg, PA

Dear Mr. Bilbo,

Sending you the description on the home at Trevernon Lake. There is approx. 2000 pluss sg. ft. of living space and is nine years old all in excellent condition. The home is on 3 water front lots, The garage has 4 storage closets, The garage has a ginie door opener. 70 ft. antena. All of the window treatments stay with the house, there are so maney extra you must see this to appreshate it.

Sinncerly,

Pete [surname deleted]
[name of realty company deleted]

Do you think Pete made the sale? Certainly that was his ultimate goal: first, to get Allan (whose name he misspelled) to see the house; then, to get him to buy it.
    But Allan declined even to see the house after receiving this letter.

His reasons had to do with the ethos—though he did not use that term—the letter projected. It seemed to be the work of a careless and not-too-bright individual, not a person with whom Allan had any interest in doing business. Pete's persona was damaged and his argument defeated largely because his letter showed almost complete disregard for the conventions of spelling, grammar, and mechanics. Even the ZIP code was missing. Either Pete did not know better or he did not care—and either would have been fatal to his persuasive aims. Would you depend on Pete to get all the details of a real estate sale and title transfer taken care of properly? Even without knowing him, most of us would decide against dealing with Pete, simply on the basis of his careless and unclear writing.

Pete's ignorance of grammar and mechanics is remarkable and unfortunate. However, we cannot take too much comfort in knowing that we would never write a business letter as terrible as this one, for writing problems need not be as dramatic as Pete's to affect adversely our powers of persuasion.

One Problem: Illogical Predication   A number of excellent handbooks are available to guide writers in checking for correct usage and grammar. However, one problem that is both overlooked by many handbooks and directly related to the clarity of written argument is sentence logic or *predication*. In every sentence, the predicate says something about the subject—and the relationship must be both grammatical and logically possible. "Tom caught the flu" and "Tom was the flu" are both grammatical sentences: The first takes the form noun–transitive verb–object (N-TV-O), and the second takes the form noun–linking verb–predicate nominative (N-LV-PN). But the second sentence is nonsense; what the predicate says about the subject is not logically possible. Less obvious, but just as illogical, is the following sentence:

My future career will be an astronaut.

A career cannot be an astronaut; only a person can be. The sentence is faultily predicated. An acceptable, logical version would be:

My future career will be astronautics.

Both sentences take the form N-LV-PN, but only the second one makes sense. *Career* and *astronautics* are logically balanced. Astronautics can be a career. An astronaut can *have* a career, but not *be* one.

Faulty predication most often occurs in sentences linking subjects and predicate nominatives with *to be* verbs, as in the sentences above about astronauts and astronautics. This form of faulty predication is sometimes called *faulty equation*, for the elements on either side of a *to be* verb must be "equal"—either a subject noun (or pronoun) and a predicate noun, or a subject noun and a predicate adjective describing the subject noun. In the following sentences, linking verbs join elements that are neither grammatically nor logically "equal."

Waiting   for my roommate   is   when   I get impatient.
SUBJECT NOUN   LINKING VERB   ADVERB

His poor attitude   is   why   he is failing physics.
 SUBJECT NOUN   LINKING VERB   ADVERB

The reason we can't go now   is   because the car won't start.
SUBJECT NOUN   LINKING VERB   ADVERB

The easiest way to avoid faulty equations is to shun noun-linking verb-adverb predications unless the subject is a unit of time or date ("Five o'clock is when they will arrive" is correct, though wordy; "They will arrive at five o'clock" is better). The sentences above might be revised as

Waiting for my roommate, I always get impatient.

He is failing physics because of his poor attitude.

We can't go now because the car won't start.

And these versions are less wordy as well.

But, as the first "astronaut" sentence shows, even noun-linking verb-noun or noun-linking verb-adjective combinations are not foolproof. Here's another example of a grammatical but illogical sentence:

The thought of cloning higher life forms, such as primates, is impossible at this time.

The *thought* cannot be impossible, for I just stated it; the *deed* might be impossible. A revision says what the writer really intended:

To clone higher life forms, such as primates, would be impossible at this time.

Though faulty predication may be most common in sentences employing linking verbs, it can occur with any verb:

The ball, stolen from a U.Va. running back, allowed a North Carolina safety to score a touchdown.

Balls cannot "allow" anything to happen; they are inanimate objects. But

Stealing the ball from a U.Va. running back enabled a North Carolina safety to score a touchdown.

makes sense—to North Carolina, at least. Can you spot the illogic in the next sentence?

The science requirement in the College of Humanities urged me to change my major to business.

The dean, your advisor, or your parents might so urge you, but requirements are abstractions and cannot speak. A more sensible version:

My fear of the science requirement in the College of Humanities prompted me to change my major to business.

EXERCISE 5-11

Reduce the following paragraph to its core meaning by eliminating all the deadwood and other wordy constructions. Then add real content.

Freshmen in college probably should not attempt to declare a major during their freshman year. The first year is a year of beginnings, so a student should not feel forced to make such an important decision at that time. There is plenty of time for declaring a major later; the freshman should not feel pressure to do so too soon.

After you have eliminated the deadwood, and perhaps even sooner, the inadequacy of the paragraph's development will be obvious. What may have appeared to the writer to be a decent paragraph turns out to be an idea flimsily dressed—rather like the emperor in his new clothes. The paragraph topic itself—"Freshmen in college probably should not attempt to declare a major"—is worth considering; the writer simply has yet to design and stitch up something of real substance.

EXERCISE 5-12

Arrange the following groups of words in a hierarchy of abstraction and generality, beginning with the most concrete and specific.

1. government employee, diplomat, person, ambassador, Mr. Pomeroy, worker, citizen, Ambassador to Mallingua

2. laws, controversial issues, *Roe* v. *Wade,* legal decisions on abortion
3. lives, is, exists
4. female, woman, person, Jane Jones, computer technician
5. machine, aircraft, Boeing 747, airplane, transport vehicle

---

EXERCISE 5–13

After consulting a good dictionary, explain the denotative and connotative differences among the words within the following groups.

1. agree, acquiesce, endorse, go along with, support, favor
2. idea, wild guess, speculation, theory, conjecture, hypothesis
3. ok, acceptable, essential, desirable, advantageous, beneficial, commendable
4. criminal, crook, jailbird, felon, prisoner, inmate, parolee
5. diplomacy, reticence, cowardice, reluctance, diffidence, uncertainty

---

EXERCISE 5–14

Rewrite the following paragraph, making word choices more specific where appropriate. Also add concrete supporting detail where needed to enhance the paragraph's clarity and persuasiveness. Your audience is one of the local television stations; your purpose, to persuade its managers to eliminate the movie reviews they presently feature.

Movie reviewers really do not do much good. They see a lot of free movies, praise the ones they like, and pan the ones they dislike. But their tastes are no better than anyone else's. Nor are they immune to influences of various kinds. Their job is interesting for them but seems pointless to me.

EXERCISE 5–15

Correct the faulty predication in the following sentences.

1. My job next summer will be a lifeguard at a girls' camp.
2. His ambition was Mt. Everest.
3. Janie's idea was eager to get started.
4. Your ability is unable to get the job.
5. The cases currently before the Honor Council include Ralph Lawrence and Peter Cardin.
6. Not only did her action steal pages from a book that wasn't hers, but she denied others access to the material.
7. The reason why Edward is only a clerk is because he cannot get along with his superiors.
8. By stopping in Memphis and changing planes enables us to save fifty dollars on the airfare.
9. Little Jessica McClure, who fell into a well in October 1987, is an example of why all inactive wells should be capped.
10. The stock market's volatility told Avery to put most of his money into bonds.

EXERCISE 5–16

Correct all faulty predication in the following paragraph. Do not change any sentences that are predicated logically.

Television reflects a bad effect on sports. For one thing, television makes colleges illegally recruit to get better players. A second bad effect shows the inconvenience of scheduling athletic competition in order to get optimum television coverage. Third, limited television coverage is why minor sports, not often shown on TV, are being neglected. And finally, the huge revenues generated by television coverage encourage greed in the participants, so that professional basketball players earn more annually than their fans are likely to make in a decade.

When you look over a rough draft of an essay, check it first for the large matters of unity, completeness, and logical organization. Then look at each paragraph's internal unity, completeness, and coherence. Finally, check the individual sentences for word choices and spelling and for logical predication and good grammar in all respects: subjects agreeing with verbs, modifiers logically placed and clearly worded, possessives correctly formed, sentences appropriately punctuated. Using good grammar shows your concern for your readers, your desire to express your ideas clearly for them. It also affects your persona positively: You show yourself to be an exact and educated writer. And bear in mind that the positive effect of good grammar is slight compared to the negative impact bad grammar has on readers. Good grammar is invisible; bad grammar is an eyesore. Don't be concerned about correctness as you write your rough draft, but do give it attention as you revise.

Heed your word choices as well. Check your essay for helium-filled vocabulary: Wherever possible, change abstract nouns and colorless verbs to more concrete nouns. Change lofty phrases to simpler words. Change some verbs of stasis (*be, have, do*) to stronger and more precise verbs. Use adjectives and adverbs with restraint; put the weight of your words into verbs and specific, concrete nouns. Your writing will be not only clearer but also more readable after such changes.

All these concerns and all this close examination of an essay, report, or important letter may seem like a great deal of trouble, and so they are. But if you would persuade, the trouble is well worth taking. You have written; you have revised. You have given attention to the individual sentences, the paragraphs, the entire composition. You have taken your reader into account; you have expressed yourself clearly and well. In short, you have created a credible persona. And your argument is all the more likely to persuade your reader.

CONFORMITY AND NONCONFORMITY:
THE PRICES PAID FOR EACH

(Rough Draft)

1 My high school had a tight hierarchy of social groups, and I think that was the biggest problem anyone faced who was not part of a "popular" group. If you weren't in a group, you were labeled a misfit, a social deviant. Every person longed to be accepted by his peers, so almost every person chose to belong to a group. Each group had a certain underlying interest—drinking, surfing, etc. But within each group was a secret code, an idea that every other group was an enemy to be ridiculed and pushed aside as inferior. The group I belonged to resulted from this rigid social system of jeering ridicule and ostracism. We contrasted with the other cliques in many ways, and I think, really, that we ultimately benefited from our various differences.

2 Our group was comprised of those who could not quite squeeze into the tightly knit groups. We were tired of being misfits, so we came to the decision to form our own group in defiance. Also in retaliation, we refused to acknowledge the endless social customs of school life. Because we had been cast aside, we looked down on these supposedly trivial practices and drowned ourselves in a search for "higher meaning." We went to any extreme to differentiate ourselves from the other groups.

3 These differences were, at first, looked down upon condescendingly by the others. We were considered peculiar, weird, odd. We were resented because our nonconformity magnified their own over-conformity. Our supposed individualism was a cause of discomfort for them, for they had given up much of theirs in favor of conformity. But as time wore on, we were seen as creatures of interest. They wondered at our refusal to comply to their standards. They even began to see some worth in our attempts, although we didn't see it. They began to admire our uniqueness, even though we did not see ourselves as unique.

4 Our revolt was one of defense, one of comfort. We clung together for the support we had not found in the other cliques. We were not nonconformists, even though we conformed to a guise of nonconformity. We thought of ourselves as rebels without a cause, a '60's generation reborn. We gained security by throwing ourselves into a facade of superiority. We were in revolt against the school and

anything else that, if adhered to, would take away our supposed individuality. We put on the mask of young intellectuals, but it was really only a mask. As time passed, we realized that our attempts to be different only had made us aware of the high school fun we had missed: the football games, the homecoming dances, and endless other social activities. But we also came to realize that, because we had refused to adhere to these social customs, we had gained a perseverence that would enable us to stand up against any demands that would strip us of our individual character.

5   It is this individuality that must be guarded closely. In his lifetime, a person will be invited to join an immeasurable number of social groups that will inevitably have conflicting interests. Even though some comfort may be gained through acceptance into any one of them, if their underlying interest is not his, the security gained is not worth the loss of his uniqueness.

QUESTIONS AND IDEAS FOR DISCUSSION

1. What is the paper's thesis? Is it clearly defined and restricted? Does it indicate the interest and importance of the controlling idea of the essay? Rewrite the thesis, restricting it appropriately and making it clear and interesting.
2. How well do the essay's supporting points actually support the thesis? Comment on the organization and completeness of the argument.
3. Identify any fuzzy or apparently contradictory statements in the essay.
4. At what points would examples or additional detail add interest and clarity to the essay?
5. Give several examples of wordy constructions and wordy phrases from the essay. Suggest less wordy, more direct ways of stating the ideas.
6. Could any sentences be combined effectively? Give three examples, rewritten as compound, complex, or compound-complex sentences.
7. Edit the essay for grammar, mechanics, and spelling. What problems— if any—recur frequently?
8. Is the working title appropriate for the essay that takes shape here? Explain.

NONCONFORMITY:
THE PRICE AND THE PAYOFF

Kathy Taylor
(Student Essay)

1   High school is a time for laughter and romance, parties and football games, homecoming and pep rallies—but it is also a time of conflict and distress, lost identities and bitter rivalry. My high school was structured in such a tight hierarchy of social groups that a person was labeled a misfit, a social deviant, if he chose not to belong to one. Since every adolescent longs to be accepted by his peers, almost every person belonged to some identifiable group. Each group had a unifying interest, whether drinking, surfing, toking, or dating every eligible member of the opposite sex in the school. But within each group was a secret code, a hushed understanding that every other group was to be ridiculed and its members shunned as inferior human beings. The group I belonged to was a clique-by-default, comprised of the social castoffs and so-called misfits. We should have been the most miserable of creatures, but we were not. In retrospect, I think we benefited in some curious ways from our pariah status.

2   Our group consisted of those who could not quite squeeze into the tightly knit cliques and those who had been tried out and quickly discarded because of some barely discernible difference, such as long hair or pimples, out-of-style clothing, or a horsey laugh. Tired of being misfits, we rallied together in defiance; we became reverse snobs who refused to participate in or even acknowledge the endless rites of high school. We neither gave nor accepted homecoming mums; we did not deign to adorn our lockers with spirit ribbons and posters; we made a point of not wearing the school colors on the days of football games. Scorning such trivial and meaningless customs, we drowned ourselves in a search for "deeper meaning." Instead of cheering at football games, we spent endless hours arguing over Carlos Castaneda's *Don Juan*, the poetry of Leonard Cohen, and the advantages of socialism. Instead of conforming to the tailored, conservative dress of our peers, we wore ragged blue jeans and t-shirts, cowboy hats and overalls. The girls wore no make-up; the boys kept their hair long and ragged. We went to any extreme that we could devise to differentiate ourselves from the other groups.

3   Naturally, the other groups at first regarded us with revulsion or, at best, condescension. They thought us peculiar and they resented the fact that our nonconformity magnified their own conformity. Our individualism made them uncomfortable, for they had surrendered their own to status knit shirts, khaki pants, A-line skirts,

and deck shoes. But as time passed, they grew used to us: We became creatures of interest to them, exotic and alien. They marveled at our refusal to conform to their standards, and a number of them, unknown to us, began secretly to admire us for what they considered our uniqueness.

4   We did not see ourselves as unique, or special. The truth was that we clung together for the solace of feeling that we belonged somewhere. We were not true nonconformists—our efforts to be different were successful because we conformed as much as the other groups did, but in our case, to a guise of nonconformity. We felt secure because we appeared to be above all the petty high school customs, but I, for one, secretly would have loved to sit in the football stadium, a ridiculous beribboned mum dusting glitter all over my A-line skirt, cheering my halfback boyfriend on to victory. Denying those feelings was a defensive ruse. If we could not have popularity, we did not want it.

5   Or so we told ourselves. We revolted against the school, against all social customs, against anything that might take away our supposed individuality. We wore the mask of young intellectuals, secretly fearing all the while that we might be unmasked. I was not the only one in our group who sensed that we were missing something valuable, not so much school dances and locker decorations for their own sake, but a bridge between childhood and adulthood. But in another sense, we had made something positive out of the hurtful experience of being excluded. We had made friendships that were deep and have lasted; we had learned to persevere in the face of ridicule and to stand up for our own and others' right to be different. We were tuned in to the world of ideas and the real world around us while our classmates saw no further than their next date. Time will tell whether our losses or our gains were greater. I believe it will be the latter, even if I never do wear a mum.

QUESTIONS AND IDEAS FOR DISCUSSION

1. Comment on the changes from the rough draft to the final draft of this essay. What change strikes you as the most important one? Why?
2. Compare the thesis of the final draft with that of the original draft and with the revision you had proposed for the latter. Which most effectively sums up the controlling idea of this essay?
3. What are the main points of this argument? Do they seem logically arranged and adequately developed?

4. Comment on the use of coherence devices such as transitions, parallel structure, and repetition of key terms in this essay. How well does Taylor use such devices? Where would you suggest changes or additional transitions?

5. Describe Taylor's persona in the final draft of the essay. Does it differ at all from the persona of the original draft? Explain. How does Taylor avoid sounding self-pitying—or does she avoid self-pity?

SUGGESTIONS FOR WRITING
AND FURTHER DISCUSSION

Use the following sentences, some of which are taken from sample passages reprinted in this chapter, to stimulate ideas for potential essays addressed to an audience of your rhetoric classmates. The following offer possibilities for reaction or further development. Feel free to modify any thesis as you see fit; instead of maintaining that "thin people are crunchy and dull, like carrots," you might prefer to argue that "smart people are sharp and pointed, like ice picks" or that "beautiful people are boring; they all look alike."

Lying can never be justified.

Inheritance laws [or any other law] are reprehensible.

Requiring foreign language study in college is futile.

Fraternities help students balance the academic and social demands of college life.

"[Thin people] are crunchy and dull, like carrots." (Suzanne Britt Jordan)

Bilingual education prevents children from becoming fully part of their society.

"It's often the best books that draw the beadiest attention of the censors." (Wainwright)

"The university should impart information imaginatively." (Whitehead)

Mandatory retirement at age 65 is both wasteful and cruel.

Professional sports have gotten out of hand largely because of television.

"[B]luffing is nothing more than a form of lying!" (Carr)

"[C]an we afford to spend time on the past?" (Hamilton)

"[M]etaphor is pervasive in everyday life, not just in language but in thought and action." (Lakoff and Johnson)

"Man will never conquer space." (Clarke)

"I'll put it bluntly: if you care for the quality of life in our American democracy, then you have to be for censorship." (Kristol)

"If the [newspaper] reader doesn't also study foreign affairs, or follow the money markets, or keep up his practice of foreign languages, then what can he expect to learn from the papers?" (Lapham)

Freshmen in college probably should not attempt to declare a major.

6

The Power of Style

He who has nothing to assert has no style and can have none: he who has something to assert will go as far in power of style as its momentousness and his conviction will carry him.

George Bernard Shaw

WHAT IS STYLE?

Writers can enhance the power of their arguments by giving attention to the ethical and the emotional appeal of style. In Chapter 5 we discussed some of the basic elements of style that affect writers' ethical appeal; in this chapter we will examine more sophisticated elements of style, such as metaphor, that can affect an argument's emotional appeal. Chapter 6 centers on ways of expressing ideas that will create the emphases writers want, in language that will keep most readers' attention.

But style is an elusive concept. Few words have been defined as variously as this one, or with as much accompanying—often contradictory—advice. "Style is the dress of thoughts," Lord Chesterfield said, but it is not mere adornment; we don't simply "dress up" our ideas with rhetorical flourishes. Style is "proper words in proper places," according to Swift, but what *are* proper words, and where are the proper places for them? "Style is the man himself," wrote Buffon, pointing toward the intrinsic relationship between style and creation of the persona, but failing to show us how best to apply that truth to writing.

Style is that which distinguishes us from everybody else, or fails to, depending on its merit and distinctiveness. If style is not the whole person, it is certainly that part of you or me that the world first sees and assesses. To the degree that our style is felicitous, readers are inclined to be receptive to our arguments. Consider, for example, the relative persuasiveness of the following arguments:

To the Editor of the *Denver Post:* Colorado is overrun by tourists. They bring money, but they leave trash behind them. They are not concerned with ecology. Also, they are not interested in preserving the beauty of our state. The worst ones are the ones in the big campers. They are a hazard on our mountain roads, and besides, people who stay in campers don't support our hotel industry. The best way to reduce crowding and protect our natural resources would be to engender a stiff gasoline tax. This would also bring needed revenue to the state.

[Signed] Gib Murphey

To the Editor of the *Denver Post:* Despite the revenues they bring to Colorado, tourists are arriving in such numbers that our state's natural resources are endangered. The National Parks and Forests are being polluted by trash and exhaust fumes from countless automobiles, and the mountains trampled and eroded by countless feet in lugsoled boots. While granting the importance of the tourist industry, I propose that it be contained in a way that would also provide revenue to replace that lost to reduced numbers of tourists: a new gasoline tax. We would then see fewer campers and trailers; we would see more of our mountain wildflowers again.

[Signed] Bill Lewis

The point made in these two letters is essentially the same: Reduce the glut of tourists and the problems they bring to Colorado by instituting a higher gasoline tax. Which of the two is more likely to impress the voters and legislators reading the *Post?*

The difference between the two letters is a difference in style and in the voice (persona) that speaks through the words. In characterizing the styles of the two letters, we might be struck first by the tone of the writing: The first writer sounds belligerent; the second, reasonable and sincere. We might also talk about the elements of style that create tone: diction and the length and structure of sentences.

First, the writers' diction, or choice of words. Murphey uses short, abstract or nonspecific words (*beauty, natural resources*) for the most part; when he tries to use "big" words, he uses them incorrectly (*engen-*

der), redundantly (ecology *is* the science concerned with "preserving the beauty" of nature), or inconsistently (*engender* is a "formal" word; *stiff*, following it, is used colloquially). Murphey repeats pronouns frequently: lots of *they*'s and a vague *this*. Lewis uses formal language ("I propose that it be contained") but relieves his abstractions ("natural resources are endangered") with concrete images ("trampled by countless feet in lugsoled boots").

Second, the writers' sentence lengths and structure. Murphey uses a total of ninety words in eight sentences of 5, 9, 6, 12, 10, 20, 19, and 9 words, respectively. The sentences vary from five to twenty words in length, but twenty words is not a long sentence, and most of the sentences are closer to half that length. Here is concrete evidence that Murphey's sentence style is short and choppy. There is more evidence: Of the eight sentences, six are grammatically simple, one is compound, and one, surprisingly enough, is compound-complex. But the latter is really two sentences expressing different thoughts, haphazardly joined together: "They are a hazard on our mountain roads, and besides, people who stay in campers don't support our hotel industry." All but one of Murphey's sentences begin with the subject; the single exception begins with a transitional word, *also*.

Lewis, on the other hand, uses ten more words than Murphey in half as many sentences. His four sentences contain 20, 28, 35, and 17 words, respectively. A little more variety might be preferable, but notice that the last sentence is really two independent clauses joined by a semicolon and so has the effect of varying sentence length with two very short sentences of eight and nine words each. The short clauses following the long preceding sentences give those last words particular emphasis. Lewis's sentence patterns are complex, compound, complex, and compound. His first sentence begins with a dependent clause, his third with an adverbial phrase, and the second and fourth with the subjects. The variety in sentence openers relieves the second letter from the monotony of the first, as does the variety in sentence structure.

This close look at specific features of style shows how two paragraphs on the same topic can be almost totally different in the way they sound and in the way they affect a reader. The characteristics of Lewis's style that help to make his letter more persuasive than Murphey's are the use of specific words to illustrate his generalizations; the variety of his sentence patterns; the rhythm of his sentences (especially the parallel phrases and parallel clauses in the second and last sentences); and, most importantly in terms of logic, the combination of related ideas into sentences, with less important ideas grammatically subordinated to more important ideas (for example, Lewis's first sentence: The introductory clause is a concession which Lewis regards as less important than what he says in the main clause). We will consider each of these elements of style and how you may employ them to good effect in your own arguments.

THE ELEMENTS OF STYLE

In written language, then, style consists largely of our **word choices** and **grammatical choices,** which together set the tempo of our prose, and which stem in part from our logical choices: the kinds of relationships we draw between ideas. In responding to style, we respond in general terms to the tone, the degree of complexity, and the distinctiveness of a piece of writing. In more specific terms we speak of a writer's word choices, or **diction,** as being typically

Short or long	(*list* or *enumerate*)
Concrete or abstract	(*letter* or *correspondence*)
Specific or general	(*bull terrier* or *dog*)
Metaphorical or literal	(*love is a fire* or *love is a feeling*)
Everyday or technical	(*cancer* or *carcinoma*)

We describe the writer's grammatical choices in terms of

Sentence types	(simple, complex, and so on)
Sentence openers	(transitional words, dependent phrases or clauses, or the subject of the sentence)
Sentence length	(varied by joining or subordinating clauses and phrases)
Distinctive syntactical patterns	(such as parallelism or anastrophe)

Grammar in the sense of "good" and "bad" is a feature of style only when it is faulty and thereby calls attention to itself. As noted in Chapter 5, good grammar is invisible.

EXERCISE 6–1

A. In a few paragraphs or less, describe the writers' verbal and grammatical stylistic choices in each of the following passages. Give specific examples from the paragraphs to support your assertions. Then summarize the key elements of each writer's style in these passages in a single declarative sentence for each.

B. Which of the writers' styles is most congenial to you and most like the way you would like to sound in your own writing? As an exercise of your options in prose style, write a paragraph of your own following that writer's sentence structure and paragraph development exactly. Aim also for the same degree of formality or informality, and the same tone, whether serious, humorous, ironic, or otherwise. Your sentences need not have exactly the same number of words as those in the model passage, but they should be of comparable length and structure. Pick a topic completely different from that discussed in the model passage. For example, using paragraph 2 as a model, your first sentence might be "Not all freshmen recognize what a terribly stressful situation this can be, this first year of college." The pattern of this sentence is the same as Pirsig's original, but the topic is entirely different.

C. In a paragraph describe the experience of attempting to write in another person's style. Did the differences between that writer's characteristic means of expression and your own make the undertaking difficult? Having finished the exercise, does what you have written sound alien to you, or is the style enough like your own that you can still hear your own voice?

(1)

This change in the angle of vision was in itself a daring innovation. Hitherto, the traveller had observed certain laws of proportion and perspective. The Cathedral had always been a vast building in any book of travels and the man a little figure, properly diminutive, by its side. But Sterne was quite capable of omitting the Cathedral altogether. A girl with a green satin purse might be much more important than Notre-Dame. For there is, he seems to hint, no universal scales of values. A girl may be more interesting than a cathedral; a dead donkey more instructive than a living philosopher. It is all a question of one's point of view. Sterne's eyes were so adjusted that small things often bulked larger in them than big. The talk of a barber about the buckle of his wig told him more about the character of the French than the grandiloquence of her statesmen.

—Virginia Woolf, "The 'Sentimental Journey,' "
The Second Common Reader

(2)

Not everyone understands what a completely rational process this is, this maintenance of a motorcycle. They think it's some kind of a "knack" or some kind of "affinity for machines" in operation. They are right, but the knack is almost purely a process of reason, and most of the troubles are caused by what old time radio men called a "short between the earphones," failures to use the head properly. A motorcycle functions entirely in accordance with the laws of reason, and a study of the art of motorcycle maintenance is really a miniature study of the art of rationality itself. . . .

—Robert M. Pirsig,
Zen and the Art of Motorcycle Maintenance

(3)

Miss Groby taught me English composition thirty years ago. It wasn't what prose said that interested Miss Groby; it was the way prose said it. The shape of a sentence crucified on a blackboard (parsed, she called it) brought a light to her eye. She hunted for Topic Sentences and Transitional Sentences the way little girls hunt for white violets in springtime. What she loved most of all were Figures of Speech. You remember her. You must have had her, too. Her influence will never die out of the land. A small schoolgirl asked me the other day if I could give her an example of metonymy. (There are several kinds of metonymies, you may recall, but the one that will come to mind most easily, I think, is Container for the Thing Contained). The vision of Miss Groby came clearly before me when the little girl mentioned the old, familiar word. I saw her sitting at her desk, taking the rubber band off the roll-call cards, running it back upon the fingers of her right hand, and surveying us all separately with quick little henlike turns of her head.

—James Thurber,
"Here Lies Miss Groby," *My World—And Welcome to It*

EXERCISE 6–2

Write two paragraphs each requesting a loan so that you can buy a car. Address the first paragraph to your parents, the second to a local bank. Then write a third paragraph, analyzing the differences in style, content, and persona in the two requests. Which of the two do you believe would have greater persuasive power? Why?

FIGURES OF SPEECH

Figures of speech are words and arrangements of words that are employed other than in their ordinary meanings or usual order, for emphasis or variety. Figures of speech, unlike correct grammar, are by their very nature visible features of style. However, they should never be self-consciously or obtrusively visible, but rather made to serve the writer's rhetorical ends. They are not of value in themselves, as Thurber's Miss Groby believed, but in their contribution to the memorable expression of ideas and images. **Tropes** are the figures that play on the meanings of words; **schemes** are the figures that alter the usual arrangements of words in sentences.

Tropes

Metaphor and Simile. These are comparisons of unlike things that unexpectedly share certain characteristics. Normally a metaphor compares one thing that is likely to be familiar to readers with another that is less familiar in order to illuminate the less-understood idea or entity. Metaphors and similes create images in readers' imaginations.

Laws are like cobwebs, which may catch small flies, but let wasps and hornets break through.
        —Jonathan Swift, "A Critical Essay Upon the Faculties of the Mind"

. . . a writer, like an acrobat, must occasionally try a stunt that is too much for him.
        —E. B. White, "The Ring of Time"

True art is a conduit between body and soul, between feeling unabstracted and abstraction unfelt.
        —John Gardner, *On Moral Fiction*

Paradox. A paradox (which we discussed on a larger scale in Chapter 2) is an apparent contradiction, both parts of which are nevertheless true.

Last fall I had an advanced graduate student, bright, energetic, well-informed, whose papers were almost unreadable.
        —Wayne Booth, "The Rhetorical Stance"

Absolute seriousness is never without a dash of humor.
        —Dietrich Bonhoeffer,
        Letters and Papers from Prison

Being frustrated is disagreeable, but the real disasters in life begin when you get what you want.   —Irving Kristol

Irony. Irony takes a number of forms, but typically it involves saying one thing while clearly implying the opposite.

Although students in past years have received generous help from their instructors in maintaining and developing poor writing habits, the current clamor for "writing across the curriculum" threatens to make poor writing passé.
        —John Keenan, "A Professor's Guide to
        Perpetuating Poor Writing Among Students"

The new outdoor swimming pool and six more tennis courts were important additions to the Wilson University campus, even though the library funds had to be cut back. After all, the students, accustomed as they are to a country-club life, would have been at a loss without their little luxuries.

Understatement. Also called *litotes,* understatement is a form of irony, for it describes something as minor or unimportant that the writer evidently considers significant.

If we do nothing to stop the escalation of nuclear armament worldwide, we are going to find ourselves in a bit of a fix.

Winters can be chilly here on the North Sea.

I tried to save the world, but it didn't work out.
—Richard Selzer, *Mortal Lessons*

Overstatement. Also called *hyperbole,* overstatement calls attention to a point through obvious exaggeration.

You might have to go back to the Children's Crusade in A. D. 1212 to find as unfortunate and fatuous an attempt at manipulated hysteria as the Women's Liberation movement.
—Helen Lawrenson, "The Feminine Mistake"

The war on poverty, that monstrous insult to the rippling muscles in a black man's arms, is an index of how men actually sit down and plot each other's deaths, actually sit down with slide rules and calculate how to hide bread from the hungry.
—Eldredge Cleaver, "Domestic Law and International Order"

Four hostile newspapers are more to be feared than a thousand bayonets.
—Attributed to Napoleon Bonaparte

Rhetorical Question. The rhetorical question is asked to make a point, not to seek information. It does not really question; it asserts.

Was it for this—these computer markings on a slip of paper—that I gave up a social life and buried myself in the library for a semester?

Can we hope to learn if we dare not question?

Have I not as good a right to be free as you have?
—Frederick Douglass,
The Life and Times of Frederick Douglass

Schemes

Parallelism. Parallelism is the arranging of equivalent images or ideas in pairs or series of grammatically identical words, phrases, or clauses. Minor variations among the elements (the addition of an adjective to one, for instance) are acceptable and sometimes even desirable—to prevent the parallelism from becoming monotonous.

It [the declaration that standards for evaluating works of art do not exist] pleases those resentful of disciplines, it flatters the empty-minded by calling them open-minded, it comforts the confused.
—Marya Mannes,
"How Do You Know It's Good?"

(This sentence also employs anaphora, described below.)

In many ways writing is the act of saying *I*, of imposing oneself upon other people, of saying *listen to me, see it my way, change your mind.*
—Joan Didion, "Why I Write"

Anaphora. A kind of parallelism, anaphora creates emphasis through the repetition of the same word or words at the beginning of successive clauses.

Let us work together toward our common goal, and let us persevere in the face of all discouragement.

Death is fearsome; death is shadowy and unknowable; death is inescapable.

Antithesis. Antithesis is a form of parallelism in which contrasting ideas are expressed in parallel clauses or phrases. The grammatical parallelism calls attention to the contrast.

How much the world asks of them [clergy and teachers], and how little they can actually deliver!
—H. L. Mencken, "Education"

They [people of middle age] neither trust everybody nor distrust everybody, but judge people correctly.
—Aristotle, *Rhetoric*, Book II

We observe today not a victory of party but a celebration of freedom—symbolizing an end as well as a beginning—signifying renewal as well as change.
—John F. Kennedy, Inaugural Address

Ellipsis. In order to prevent monotony, parallelism is sometimes modified through ellipsis, the omission of clearly implied words to avoid repeating them unnecessarily.

Words can be more powerful, and more treacherous, than we sometimes suspect; communication more difficult than we may think.
—F. L. Lucas, "What Is Style?"

Reform is affirmative, conservatism negative; conservatism goes for comfort, reform for truth.
—Ralph Waldo Emerson, "The Conservative"

(This sentence also includes antithesis.)

Anastrophe. Ordinary word order in English sentences is Subject-Verb-Complement. Anastrophe is the inversion of usual word order, such as

Verb-Subject or Complement-Verb-Subject. Anastrophe calls attention to the idea a sentence expresses by virtue of its unusual syntax.

Cool was I and logical.   —Max Shulman, "Love Is a Fallacy"

From this alienation of personal power comes the sense of resignation with which we accept the political dispensations of a powerful government whose hold upon us continues to increase.
—William F. Buckley, "Why Don't We Complain?"

Out of its [the circus's] wild disorder comes order; from its rank smell rises the good aroma of courage and daring; out of its preliminary shabbiness comes the final splendor.
—E. B. White, "The Ring of Time"

Climax. Climax is the arranging of phrases or clauses in order of increasing importance, for dramatic impact.

And for the support of this Declaration, with a firm reliance on the protection of Divine Providence, we mutually pledge to each other our Lives, our Fortunes, and our sacred Honor.
—Thomas Jefferson, The Declaration of Independence

For if we ever begin to suppress our search to understand nature, to quench our own intellectual excitement in a misguided effort to present a unified front where it does not and should not exist, then we are truly lost.
—Stephen Jay Gould, "Evolution as Fact and Theory"

EXERCISE 6-3

A. Identify the figures of speech in the following sentences and passages. Some may contain more than one figure of speech.
B. Read aloud the sentences and passages in the list. Pick ten that particularly appeal to your ear and write sentences of your own, with completely different subject matter, that mimic the same schemes and/or tropes as those in the list. For example, if you choose the first sentence as a model, you will write a sentence of your own that employs anaphora: "Friends neither ask nor expect favors; friends do not think first of what you can do for them; friends take pleasure in your company alone."

1. We neither gave nor accepted homecoming mums; we did not deign to adorn our lockers with spirit ribbons and posters; we made a point of not wearing the school colors on the days of football games.
—Student essay

2. Papa was not only a gentleman; he was a gentle man, compassionate and strong.

3. A slight injection of knowledge may hurt our feelings, but it may save our lives.
   —Sinclair Lewis, "Gentlemen, This Is Revolution"

4. Foolish indeed we would be, to accept such a compromise.

5. God would have us know that we must live as men who manage our lives without him.
   —Dietrich Bonhoeffer, *Letters and Papers from Prison*

6. Our high school colors were purple and gold, a combination so garish the colors were no doubt chosen to startle our athletic opponents into dropping the ball.

7. Lawton "borrowed" paper, pencil, and paper clips from the office; he "forgot" to return the change when a clerk gave him too much; he claimed as business expenses his lunches with his best friend; and he lectured his son regularly on the importance of honesty.

8. Walking in a spring rain is delightful; it is like being pelted with marshmallows.

9. What more could anyone desire?

10. He arrived at college a farmboy; he departed, eight years later, a nuclear physicist.

11. The board of directors is stifling the president's successor in her attempts to make changes; they should give the heir some air—and a little room in which to breathe it.

12. To the state the proposed highway is a convenience for travelers; to the city it is an important link between the east and the west areas; to our neighborhood it is a lifeline to the rest of the community.

13. In modern times, it has become fashionable for a young woman, upon reaching the age of eighteen, to signify her membership in adult society by announcing that she refuses to make a debut.
    —Judith Martin, *Miss Manners' Guide to Excruciatingly Correct Behavior*

14. The situation is grave, the remedy painful.

15. Some recent work by E. Fermi and L. Szilard which has been communicated to me in manuscript form leads me to expect that the element uranium may be turned into a new and important source of energy in the immediate future.
    —Letter from Albert Einstein to Franklin Roosevelt, August 2, 1939

16. "Even if her frosting gets stale, I'll always love my cupcake."
    —"Michael" on *Newhart*, CBS, 10 Oct. 1987

17. "Joanna, if you need me, I'll be locked in my room for eternity."
    —"Stephanie" on *Newhart*, CBS, 10 Oct. 1987

18. He will never furnish the house of his own mind.

—John Ciardi

19. I was no longer simply a member of the proud graduating class of 1940; I was a proud member of the wonderful, beautiful Negro race.

—Maya Angelou, "Graduation"

20. Women are like tea bags—you never know how strong they are until you get them into hot water.

—Nancy Reagan, qtd. in *Ladies Home Journal*, Sept. 1987

The Power of Metaphor

Figures of speech have particular value to the writer of argument because of their distinctive quality—if you wish to call attention to an idea, a metaphor or a climactic sentence order can help toward that end. Of all the figures, the most familiar—and one of the most effective—is metaphor. Metaphor (including its variant, simile) centers on relationships, but the relationships, unlike those in literal analogies, surprise the reader with unexpected and figurative connections. Metaphor is:

If the writing of history resembles architecture, journalism bears comparison to a tent show. The impresarios of the press drag into their tents whatever freaks and wonders might astonish a crowd; the next day they move their exhibit to another edition instead of to another town four miles farther west.

—Lewis Lapham, "Sculptures in Snow"

Metaphor is not:

The writing of history is like the writing of fiction in that both history books and novels depend heavily upon the selective imaginations of their authors, and both contain fiction and reality in very nearly equal doses.

In the first case the writing of history is compared to something completely unlike it in every sense except a symbolic or pictorial one: a traveling tent show. In the second the writing of history is compared to another form of writing, and the resemblances, however cynically depicted, are offered as being literal resemblances.

The following statements contain metaphor. The first metaphor is as much an argumentative assertion as it is an image: History is the story of violence, death, and war. The metaphor is powerful for all its brevity. The second metaphor also hints of militarism, but it is familiar stuff, not fresh and no longer particularly vivid. The third offers a visual image—the sand-bank, which, although daily buffeted by the tide, steadily increases in size and strength nonetheless—an image which clarifies the abstract relationship between reason and prejudices.

History is a bath of blood.   —William James, "The Moral Equivalent of War"

With this new line of attack, we should gain ground against the competition.

Appealing to reason as we do, we are in a sort of a forlorn hope situation, like a small sand-bank in the midst of a hungry sea ready to wash it out of existence. But sand-banks grow when the conditions favor; and weak as reason is, it has the unique advantage over its antagonists that its activity never lets up and that it presses always in one direction, while men's prejudices vary, their passions ebb and flow, and their excitements are intermittent.
                            —William James, "War and Reason"

How effective do you find the next four metaphorical passages? Why?

But the first quality that attracts us is not his [the poet John Donne's] meaning, charged with meaning as his poetry is, but something much more unmixed and immediate; it is the explosion with which he bursts into speech.
                        —Virginia Woolf, "Donne after Three Centuries"

At his death in 1979 he [S. J. Perelman] had been writing steadily for more than half a century, putting the language through some of its most breathtaking loops, and in both America and England the woods are still full of writers and comics who were drawn into the gravitational pull of Perelman's style and never quite got back out.
                            —William Zinnser, On Writing Well

Police brutality is only one facet of the crystal of terror and oppression.
            —Eldredge Cleaver, "Domestic Law and International Order"

Humor can be dissected, as a frog can, but the thing dies in the process and the innards are discouraging to any but the pure scientific mind.
                        —E. B. White, as quoted in Zinnser

Since the power of metaphor lies in its ability to suggest fresh and unexpected figurative associations between unlike things, beware the metaphor that has grown stale with overuse—the cliché. The first metaphor that suggests itself often will be a cliché:

I think we ought to hire McDuff. He's fit as a _____ and eager as a _____ to work. Your objections amount to nothing more than a _____ in a teapot, because I know he'll keep his shoulder to the _____ and get the job done as fast as greased _____ .

We are all occasionally tempted to write, "That was the straw that broke the camel's back," or "He had the Midas touch," or others among a host of tired metaphors that come so trippingly to the tongue. Worse yet, because such metaphors have lost their visual quality in our imaginations, we can easily toss two or three incompatible metaphors in together to create "a real kettle of fish"—smelly ones. During the Democratic presidential primary campaign of 1984, candidate Gary Hart was ridiculed in the press for declaring, "We have brought the [Walter] Mondale juggernaut to its knees." Such mixed metaphors can damage a writer's credibility with readers and can render a serious argument ludicrous, as the following letter illustrates.

To the Editor: It is imperative that the state attorney general be called before a grand jury to testify about the alleged illegal contributions he received during the last campaign. We cannot foul the waters of the office which is the cornerstone of our state government with the forked tongue of an unscrupulous politician.

Humorous writing can be made merely silly by mixing metaphors:

My most enduring memory of college is that of typing essays at three o'clock in the morning. Somehow it was always 3:00 a.m. when I sailed into my dorm room, armed with a whole battalion of books on the subject of my paper and lots of grist for the mill. My brain came alive in the small hours, a veritable garden for the plucking. I honestly believed I was smarter between the hours of 1:00 a.m. and 6:00 a.m.; the typewriter was my Matterhorn, and I was ready to climb. Some evenings, I would have let out a yodel or two from sheer exuberance, but my roommate only barely tolerated the clatter of the typewriter alone. As it was, he occasionally threw a book at me, but I put that down to bad dreams.

Mixed metaphors can occur when writers are careless or unconscious of their embedded metaphors—metaphorical comparisons only hinted at by verbs, nouns, and modifiers. When an embedded metaphor is used, the reader may not recognize the imagery it suggests until a word or phrase further on reinforces it. In the preceding paragraph *sailed* is an embedded metaphor that creates no image until the writer either reinforces it ("I sailed into my dorm room, head into the storm of my roommate's wrath") or jars against it. As the paragraph was actually written, the military metaphor might recall warships, but few of those vessels could carry a battalion, much less "grist for the mill"—a cliché that springs alarmingly back to life in the company of so much incongruous imagery. The following embedded metaphors, on the other hand, are brought to life with compatible images. *Strain* is reinforced by *exercising:* Exercising can strain muscles, so why not words? And the growth of friendship is like the growth and branching of a strong and beautiful tree.

He's talking about how much strain you can put on the word "right" when you say you're exercising one.
                    —Alistair Cooke, "Justice Holmes and the Doffed Bikini"

They were trained together in their childhoods, and there rooted between them such an affection which cannot choose but branch now.
                    —Shakespeare, *The Winter's Tale*, 1.1.21–23.

What makes embedded metaphors sometimes difficult to spot is that language is so suffused with metaphor that we may fail to note those not on the surface; the poet Theodore Roethke observed that "almost all language is dead metaphor." Last year's metaphor was yesterday's cliché and is today's ordinary word, useful but colorless until the juxtaposition of it with another metaphor (dead and buried or newborn) restores the blush of life to it. When the embedded metaphors are incompatibly mixed with other metaphors, the results can be unintentionally funny or just baffling:

We gained security by throwing ourselves into a facade of superiority.

To "throw oneself into a project" no longer creates an image; the metaphor is dead and has become merely an idiomatic expression. But when the phrase is juxtaposed with another metaphor that we ordinarily read past—*façade* (in architecture, a false front on a building; used metaphorically to speak of persons)—a suicidal image is unwittingly created. The subjects of the sentence appear to have had the habit of throwing themselves against metaphorical walls, hardly the usual way to gain a sense of security. Careful writers are forever plucking clichés and mixed metaphors from their own prose, and still, like weeds, the pesky things pop up again in unexpected places.

Despite these cautions, do not let the fear of looking ridiculous with inappropriate, clichéd, or mixed metaphors deter you from experimenting with metaphor in your own arguments. The ability to write with fresh and effective metaphors may well be, as rhetorician F. L. Lucas has suggested, the single greatest skill a writer can cultivate. Just keep plucking the weeds.

EXERCISE 6–4

Create persuasive metaphors to describe the following:

1. The sound of chalk scraping across a blackboard
2. Telephone solicitors
3. An old person's hands
4. A five-year-old in a toy store
5. The last snow before spring
6. The difference between writing and typing
7. Social Security
8. Making a first job application

9. The current political situation in the Middle East (or Central America)
10. The stock market

EXERCISE 6–5

The following paragraphs are taken from the same editorial, "The Purpose of Presidents," which appeared in *The Wall Street Journal* on November 21, 1986. Both paragraphs use metaphor. Which uses it more effectively? Explain why.

(1)
President Reagan's occasionally disjointed performance at his news conference Wednesday evening appears to have caused dissatisfaction all around. The president quickly became enveloped by a miasma over who did what, where, when, with whom and by the way how does all this square with the National Security Act of 1977? This vaporous bog was predictable and partly of the president's own making. Mr. Reagan and his staff understand well enough the geostrategic importance of Iran, but by failing to elaborate this crucial point in his opening remarks he effectively made it a nonsubject.

(2)
Nobody is in fact being shut out of the foreign-policy process. Washington is a vast funnel of diverse opinions about what the foreign policy of this country ought to be. At the bottom of the funnel, someone has to act, someone has to decide what U.S. policy will be. Our reading of Article II of the Constitution says that the president is the person at the bottom of the foreign policy funnel. And when the president decides or acts, some of the people in the funnel become winners and some become losers.

REVISING FOR STYLE

A pleasing style will enhance the persuasiveness of any argument, but style cannot be "acquired" instantly, any more than a person can acquire taste simply by purchasing a house already furnished and decorated by someone else. Style can be improved in a number of ways, but (just like the development of the persona) the improvement must be accomplished by indirection. As William Strunk asserts in *The Elements of Style*, "To acquire style, begin by affecting none." Do not "decorate" your prose.

Instead, first consider the elements of the rhetorical situation that we have taken up: audience, purpose, persona. If you have a clear sense of the rhetorical situation, your style will be appropriate to that context. Second, look closely at the style of writers you admire. Observe the measurable, quantifiable elements of their style: How long are their sentences? What verbs do they use? What sorts of metaphors occur, and how often? How much variety in sentence lengths and patterns is evident? Consider, too, the overall impression that each piece creates: What kind of tone is conveyed, and how is it achieved? How appropriate is the writing's degree of complexity to its subject and its intended audience?

Third, if you keep a journal, try imitating the styles of writers with distinctive and diverse styles, good and bad. Recognizable mimicry demands a thorough understanding of the thing imitated. If you enjoy this sort of exercise, and do it often enough, you will absorb such elements of others' styles as are congenial to your own developing style, and you will begin consciously to reject poorly constructed patterns of expression.

Fourth, apply what you learn about effective prose style as you revise throughout the writing process. Don't set out to write a sentence using metaphor, parallelism, or an introductory adverbial clause. But as you revise, consider whether a metaphor might illustrate a dull or unclear assertion more pointedly, whether two equally important ideas might be better expressed in parallel clauses, or whether an introductory clause or phrase might provide appropriate subordination of one idea to another, or a transition from one sentence to another. *Read aloud what you have written:* If you stumble over the words (or doze off while reading them), you may need to hone your words and polish your sentences. Make a conscious effort as you revise to use some of the suggestions in the following checklist, which briefly summarizes the major stylistic elements covered in Chapter 5 and this chapter.

1. **Revise word choices to make diction more effective.**

    Write with verbs and nouns. Adjectives and adverbs are weaker than verbs and nouns and should not carry the weight of meaning in the sentence. Changing some *be, have,* and *do* verbs to more descriptive verbs will help you avoid overreliance on modifiers. Consider the difference in the following sentences:

    Poor: Resolution of the problem as soon as possible is extremely important.

    Better: We must resolve the problem immediately.

    Be specific and concrete. At the same time, choose the simplest word that is also exact.

    Call a spade a spade and not a digging implement.

"I never write *metropolis* when I can get the same price for *city*."
—Mark Twain

Avoid vague words like thing **and** interesting. What *makes* the "thing" (whether a rutabaga or a theory) interesting? Whenever possible, *show* the readers rather than tell them: Provide examples.

Vague: For something of that sort, it was an interesting theory.

Specific: He argued that the crisis in the stock market arose solely from computerized automatic "sell" orders.

Use fresh and appropriate metaphors. *Appropriate,* of course, is just as important as *fresh.* Not every paragraph calls for a metaphor.

Stale: The law school's rules form the cornerstone and foundation of the great edifice of legal education.

Bizarre: At best, the law school's rules lend substance to our thoughts, becoming the fabric that is added to society to form the garment of dignity that shields us from our animal nakedness.
—Student Essay

Better: The law school's rules were never intended to bind the well-intentioned, only to restrain the unscrupulous with what fetters we can manage.

2. **Work for variety and appropriate emphasis in sentence patterns. Eliminate pointless repetition of words or patterns.**

Use subordination to show the logic of relationships within sentences and to avoid the monotony of "Dick and Jane" style.

Inappropriate: War is forced upon us. An enemy's injustice leaves us no alternative. A war is now thought permissible.

Appropriate: Only when forced upon us, only when an enemy's injustice leaves us no alternative, is a war now thought permissible.
—William James, "War and Reason"

Use sentence openers other than the subject to add variety and improve coherence by providing transitions between sentences. Such openers may be single words (*actually*), phrases (*in the meantime*), or clauses (*although the directors overlooked Marcomb's objection*). Try not to overuse your favorite openers (*therefore,* for example). The following show the difference a sentence opener can make in both style and sense.

Poor: Owen King is tall, fair, and quiet; James King is short, dark, and outspoken. The brothers think alike on most subjects.

Better: Owen King is tall, fair, and quiet; James King is short, dark, and outspoken. But for all their apparent differences, the brothers think alike on most subjects.

Use parallel structure to emphasize coordinate relationships within sentences and paragraphs, and to improve the rhythm, or euphony, of the prose.

Nonemphatic: If we do nothing but stand where the forties have left us, we will inevitably become something other than what we once were. In that case the founders of the republic would not recognize us as the nation they created. Only by affirmative moral recommitment to the revolution of the individual with which our national life began can we regain ourselves.

—adapted from the paragraph below

Emphatic: If we do nothing, if we continue to stand where the forties have left us, we will have taken one decision, we will have ceased to be what we were and we will inevitably become something else, something very different, something the founders of the republic would not recognize and surely would not love. Only by action, only by moral action, only by moral action at the highest level—only by affirmative recommitment to the revolution of the individual which was the vital and creative impulse of our national life at the beginning of our history—only by these means can we regain ourselves.

—Concluding paragraph of Archibald MacLeish,
"The Conquest of America"

Eliminate pointless repetition of words by combining clauses and using synonyms and pronouns. Pronouns themselves can be overdone, and the nouns to which the pronouns refer should be apparent. The best way to test for overused words in your drafts is, as always, to read them aloud. What lulls your eye may annoy your ear. (A caution: Some repetition is preferable to sounding like a thesaurus. I once had a student who, in writing about her home, felt obliged to call it a domicile, a house, and an edifice all in the same paragraph.)

Repetitious: Many claims have been made for *Moby Dick*'s being the Great American Novel. But I doubt that more than six people have read *Moby Dick* all the way through. I doubt that more than four of that select group can honestly say that they enjoyed the experience. I would like to see the signatures of that many people able to make such a statement. Having read the Classic Comic Book version does not count. Having seen Gregory Peck in the movie version does not count, either. Surely, to earn the laurels of greatness, a book should be a pleasure to read, but *Moby Dick* is drudgery to read. A few moments of excitement occur, sure, but hundreds of pages of tedium occur as well. The Great American Novel should center on great American themes. Westward expansion would be a good choice. The emancipation of the slaves in the Civil War would also be effective, or a story about the immigration of people from every corner of the globe. How the immigrants were assimilated into American society is a truly American theme. The nineteenth-century whaling industry has nothing to do with the making of this country we call America. Melville's collected misfits are hardly great Americans. The Great American Novel is a book—or many books—yet to be written. It is not *Moby Dick.*

Effective: Despite all the claims made for its being the Great American Novel, I defy anyone to gather the signatures of more than six people who have read *Moby Dick* all the way through, or more than four of that select group who can honestly say that they enjoyed the experience. Having read the Classic Comic Book version or having seen Gregory Peck in the movie version does not count—nor does the signature of anyone who skipped over the chapters on how to use whale blubber. Surely, to earn the laurels of greatness, a book should be a pleasure to read; *Moby Dick* is drudgery. A few moments of excitement do not compensate for hundreds of pages of the tedious recounting of shipboard life. Second, the Great American Novel should center on great American themes—westward expansion, for example, or the emancipation of the slaves in the Civil War, or the immigration and assimilation of people from every corner of the globe. What has the nineteenth-century whaling industry or Melville's collection of misfits to do with the making of this country we call America? The Great American Novel is not *Moby Dick* but a book—or many books—yet to be written.

EXERCISE 6-6

Try your hand at combining the following material (which is given in no particular order) into a coherent and persuasive paragraph. Combine, subordinate, and rephrase clauses as you see fit, as long as you preserve their meaning. You may add to what is given here, but you must include all this information. Then write a paragraph explaining the reasons for your choices of arrangement and emphasis, and detailing your stylistic choices.

This is not to say that white-collar criminals should not be closely monitored.

Imprisoning people convicted of white-collar crimes is senseless.

People who have written hot checks or embezzled money are no threat to the physical safety of others.

Imprisonment does not rehabilitate such criminals.

Imprisonment does not pay back the victims of white-collar crime.

White-collar crime usually involves money.

Such criminals should be compelled to work to pay back their victims.

They should do work that brings income to the state, and their victims should receive part of the pay from their work.

Prison externships could offer a solution.

Imprisoning white-collar criminals in minimum security facilities only costs the taxpayer.

Convicted persons could work in government facilities or in private facilities, such as factories and hospitals, under state government contract.

They should pay for their crime.

Imprisoning white-collar criminals does nothing for the victims.

Imprisoning white-collar criminals is a waste of the inmates' abilities.

Those abilities could be put to profitable use by the state.

EXERCISE 6–7

Read the letters to the editor in several recent daily editions of a local newspaper or your campus newspaper. Select a letter that seems to you to have merit in its argument but also to fail in its expression of that argument. Improve the style of the letter by rewriting it. Add and delete material as necessary, but retain the essential argument of the original. Attach the original letter to your revision of it. What kinds of stylistic improvements (clause combining, elimination of pointless repetition, and so on) did you make?

EXERCISE 6–8

Describe your room, house, or apartment in such a way that the reader will be persuaded of its attractiveness, shabbiness, inconvenience, or menace to public health. Optional: Assume the distinctive style of Ernest Hemingway, William Faulkner, J. D. Salinger, James Joyce, or another writer with whose work you are acquainted.

Style is, on the one hand, a potentially powerful component of the emotional appeal of argument. But insofar as writers' individual styles help to create their personas on paper, style is a component of the ethical appeal. And to the extent that sound and sense are (as Alexander Pope reminds us) intrinsically related, style is even a component of the logical appeal. We may speak of style as something distinct from the content of our argument, but it is no mere "dress of thoughts." Style is of the very fiber of thought.

WAR AND REASON

William James

1 I am only a philosopher, and there is only one thing that a philosopher can be relied on to do. You know that the function of statistics has been ingeniously described as being the refutation of other statistics. Well, a philosopher can always contradict other philosophers. In ancient times philosophers defined man as the rational animal; and philosophers since then have always found much more to say about the rational than about the animal part of the definition. But looked at candidly, reason bears about the same proportion to the rest of human nature that we in this hall bear to the rest of America, Europe, Asia, Africa, and Polynesia. Reason is one of the very feeblest of Nature's forces, if you take it at any one spot and moment. It is only in the very long run that its effects become perceptible. Reason assumes to settle things by weighing them against one another without prejudice, partiality, or excitement; but what affairs in the concrete are settled by is and always will be just prejudices, partialities, cupidities, and excitements. Appealing to reason as we do, we are in a sort of a forlorn hope situation, like a small sand-bank in the midst of a hungry sea ready to wash it out of existence. But sand-banks grow when the conditions favor; and weak as reason is, it has the unique advantage over its antagonists that its activity never lets up and that it presses always in one direction, while men's prejudices vary, their passions ebb and flow, and their excitements are intermittent. Our sand-bank, I absolutely believe, is bound to grow,—bit by bit it will get dyked and break-watered. But sitting as we do in this warm room, with music and lights and the flowing bowl and smiling faces, it is easy to get too sanguine about our task, and since I am called to speak, I feel as if it might not be out of place to say a word about the strength of our enemy.

2 Our permanent enemy is the noted bellicosity of human nature. Man, biologically considered, and whatever else he may be in the bargain, is simply the most formidable of all beasts of prey, and, indeed, the only one that preys systematically on its own species. We are once for all adapted to the military *status*. A millennium of peace would not breed the fighting disposition out of our bone and marrow, and a function so ingrained and vital will never consent to die without resistance, and will always find impassioned apologists and idealizers.

3   Not only men born to be soldiers, but non-combatants by trade and nature, historians in their studies, and clergymen in their pulpits, have been war's idealizers. They have talked of war as of God's court of justice. And, indeed, if we think how many things beside the frontiers of states the wars of history have decided, we must feel some respectful awe, in spite of all the horrors. Our actual civilization, good and bad alike, has had past wars for its determining condition. Greatmindedness among the tribes of men has always meant the will to prevail, and all the more so if prevailing included slaughtering and being slaughtered. Rome, Paris, England, Brandenburg, Piedmont,—soon, let us hope, Japan,—along with their arms have made their traits of character and habits of thought prevail among their conquered neighbors. The blessings we actually enjoy, such as they are, have grown up in the shadow of wars of antiquity. The various ideals were backed by fighting wills, and where neither would give way, the God of battles had to be the arbiter. A shallow view, this, truly; for who can say what might have prevailed if man had ever been a reasoning and not a fighting animal? Like dead men, dead causes tell no tales, and the ideals that went under in the past, along with all the tribes that represented them, find to-day no recorder, no explainer, no defender.

4   But apart from theoretic defenders, and apart from every soldierly individual straining at the leash, and clamoring for opportunity, war has an omnipotent support in the form of our imagination. Man lives *by* habits, indeed, but what he lives *for* is thrills and excitements. The only relief from Habit's tediousness is periodical excitement. From time immemorial wars have been, especially for non-combatants, the supremely thrilling excitement. Heavy and dragging at its end, at its outset every war means an explosion of imaginative energy. The dams of routine burst, and boundless prospects open. The remotest spectators share the fascination. With that awful struggle now in progress on the confines of the world, there is not a man in this room, I suppose, who doesn't buy both an evening and a morning paper, and first of all pounce on the war column.

5   A deadly listlessness would come over most men's imagination of the future if they could seriously be brought to believe that never again *in saecula saeculorum* would a war trouble human history. In such a stagnant summer afternoon of a world, where would be the zest or interest?

6   This is the constitution of human nature which we have to work against. The plain truth is that people *want* war. They want it anyhow; for itself; and apart from each and every possible consequence. It is the final bouquet of life's fireworks. The born soldiers want it hot and actual. The non-combatants want it in the back-

ground, and always as an open possibility, to feed imagination on and keep excitement going. Its clerical and historical defenders fool themselves when they talk as they do about it. What moves them is not the blessings it has won for us, but a vague religious exaltation. War, they feel, is human nature at its uttermost. We are here to do our uttermost. It is a sacrament. Society would rot, they think, without the mystical blood-payment.

7   We do ill, I fancy, to talk much of universal peace or of a general disarmament. We must go in for preventive medicine, not for radical cure. We must cheat our foe, politically circumvent his action, not try to change his nature. In one respect war is like love, though in no other. Both leave us intervals of rest; and in the intervals life goes on perfectly well without them, though the imagination still dallies with their possibility. Equally insane when once aroused and under headway, whether they shall be aroused or not depends on accidental circumstances. How are old maids and old bachelors made? Not by deliberate vows of celibacy, but by sliding on from year to year with no sufficient matrimonial provocation. So of the nations with their wars. Let the general possibility of war be left open, in Heaven's name, for the imagination to dally with. Let the soldiers dream of killing, as the old maids dream of marrying. But organize in every conceivable way the practical machinery for making each successive chance of war abortive. Put peace-men in power; educate the editors and statesmen to responsibility;—how beautifully did their trained responsibility in England make the Venezuela incident abortive! Seize every pretext, however small, for arbitration methods, and multiply the precedents; foster rival excitements and invent new outlets for heroic energy; and from one generation to another, the chances are that irritations will grow less acute and states of strain less dangerous among the nations. Armies and navies will continue, of course, and will fire the minds of populations with their potentialities of greatness. But their officers will find that somehow or other, with no deliberate intention on any one's part, each successive "incident" has managed to evaporate and to lead nowhere, and that the thought of what might have been remains their only consolation.

8   The last weak runnings of the war spirit will be "punitive expeditions." A country that turns its arms only against uncivilized foes is, I think, wrongly taunted as degenerate. Of course it has ceased to be heroic in the old grand style. But I verily believe that this is because it now sees something better. It has a conscience. It knows that between civilized countries a war is a crime against civilization. It will still perpetrate peccadillos, to be sure. But it is afraid, afraid in the good sense of the word, to engage in absolute crimes against civilization.

QUESTIONS AND IDEAS FOR DISCUSSION

1. James uses not only the logical appeal of reason to support his argument in this essay but also the emotional appeal of style. Characterize the features that distinguish James's style, giving examples from the text. For example, James's sentences are often heavily parenthetical and subordinated, as in the second sentence of the second paragraph: "Man, biologically considered, and whatever else he may be in the bargain, is simply the most formidable of all beasts of prey, and, indeed, the only one that preys systematically on its own species." What is the stylistic effect of so much subordination?

2. Do you agree that the analogy between war and love is startling—and attention-getting? James limits the analogy to one element; might a cynic add others?

3. Comment on James's proposed solution to the problem of war. Do you find the solution reasonable?

SCULPTURES IN SNOW

Lewis Lapham

1   At random intervals in the nation's history one or another of the liberal occupations attracts a claque of admirers eager for simple answers. In the 1950s it was thought that psychoanalysis could resolve the enigma of human nature; in the 1960s it was the physicists who were going to steal the fires of heaven and the lawyers who were going to reform the laws and manage the nation's foreign policy; the most recent surge of hyperbole has placed the mantle of omniscience on the profession of journalism. For the last fifteen years journalists have enjoyed a reputation for knowing how the world works. This is silly. Reporters tend to show up at the scenes of crimes and accidents, and they take an imbecile's delight in catastrophe. Few of them know enough about the subject under discussion—whether politics, music, or the structure of DNA—to render a definitive opinion about anything other than the menu at the nearest Marriott Inn. But to concede the shallowness and ignorance of the press does nothing to diminish its usefulness or importance. Even the most mean-spirited criticisms fail to answer the question as to why anybody would bother to read or write the news. Why not wait a hundred years, until the archives have been opened and the historians have had time to arrange events in an orderly and patriotic sequence?

2   Any plausible defense of journalism rests on a modest presumption of what it provides. As follows:

3   • If the writing of history resembles architecture, journalism bears comparison to a tent show. The impresarios of the press drag into their tents whatever freaks and wonders might astonish a crowd; the next day they move their exhibit to another edition instead of to another town four miles farther west. Their subject matter is the flux of human affairs, and they achieve their most spectacular effects by reason of their artlessness and lack of sentiment.

4   The press makes sculptures in snow; its truth dwells in the concrete fact and the fleeting sound of the human voice.

5   • Journalists hire themselves out as journeymen, not as immortal artists. It would be fair to compare them to a troupe of medieval stonemasons traveling the circuit of unfinished cathedrals with a repertoire of conventional forms. They can carve figures of the saints fifty feet above the nave, but nobody would expect them to impart expression to the face.

6   Or, to take a metaphor more likely to recommend itself to the Republicans now in Washington, journalists possess the social graces of Pony Express riders—resolution, ingenuity, punctuality. They bring the news from Ghent or California, and they do their readers no favor if they try to shape it into a work of literature. Maybe this is why the books that journalists feel compelled to write, about the war in Algeria or last year's election campaign, so often read like a definitive study of a formation of clouds.

7   • The critics of the press complain about its pessimism, its cynicism, its unwillingness to recommend a program of political advancement. Every now and then a reader of *Harper's* writes to say that the magazine should publish sermons. "Be more positive," says a correspondent in Oklahoma. "Imagine that you have been proclaimed king," says a correspondent in Florida, "and submit your blueprint for Utopia."

8   They send their requests to the wrong address. The reader in hope of inspiration can study the collected works of St. Augustine or Bishop Paul Moore; he can listen to Billy Graham defy the foul fiend or sit in rapturous contemplation of an elm tree or a whale.

9   William Randolph Hearst once complained to Dorothy Parker that her stories were too sad. To this objection (not very different from the admonitions circulated by vice presidents in charge of public relations), Miss Parker replied:

10   "Mr. Hearst, there are two billion people on the face of the earth, and the story of not one of them will have a happy ending."

11   If a man drinks too much and his doctor tells him that one of these days he will fall down dead in the club car on the way to Westport, is the doctor a pessimist? Is Israel a pessimistic nation because it bombs the Iraqi nuclear installation southeast of Baghdad, or is it an optimistic nation because it accepts the conditions of its existence? Is it pessimism to say that the theories of supply side economics have little basis in fact, or that American novelists don't write very good novels?

12   Journalism, like history, has no therapeutic value; it is better able to diagnose than to cure, and it provides society with a primitive means of psychoanalysis that allows the patient to judge the distance between fantasy and reality.

13   The question is never one of optimism or pessimism. It is a question of trying to tell the truth, of the emotions required of the teller and of the emotions the attempt calls forth in the reader. If the news, no matter how bad, evokes in the reader a sense of energy and hope, then it has done as much as can be said for it. The unctuous recitation of platitudes usually achieves the opposite effect, instilling in the reader a feeling of passivity and despair.

14   Great power constitutes its own argument, and it never has much trouble drumming up friends, applause, sympathetic exigesis, and a band. In his commencement address at West Point last May, President Reagan was pleased to announce that the American "era of self-doubt" had come to a satisfactory end. The rest of his speech could have been accompanied by a fanfare of trumpets and drums.

15   But a democracy stands in need of as much self-doubt as it can muster and as many arguments as possible that run counter to the governing body of opinion. The press exerts the pressure of dissent on officals otherwise inclined to rest content with the congratulations of their retainers. From the point of view of the Soviet authorities the Soviet press is admirably optimistic; the era of self-doubt ended with the revolution of 1917.

16   • The press in its multiple voices argues that the world of men and events can eventually be understood. Not yet, perhaps, not in time for tomorrow's deadline, but sooner or later, when enough people with access to better information have had an opportunity to expand the spheres of reference. This is an immensely hopeful and optimistic assumption. Defined as means rather than an end, journalism defends the future against the past.

17   • The media offer for sale every conceivable fact or opinion. Most of these objects possess a dubious value, but it isn't the business of the journalist to distinguish between the significant and the worthless.

18   During World War II British raiding units pressed far behind German lines in the North African desert in search of stray pieces of metal. The patrols collected anything that came to hand—a shell casing, a broken axle, a button torn from the uniform of a dead corporal. The objects were sent to Cairo for analysis, and by this means British intelligence guessed at the state of German industry.

19   So also with journalism. The data are always fugitive and insufficient. To treat even the most respectable political ideas as if they were the offspring of pure reason would be to assign them, in Lewis Namier's phrase, "a parentage about as mythological as that of Pallas Athene."

20   • Without an audience, the media would cease to exist. Even if people don't read the same papers and periodicals, the media provide the connective tissue holding together the federation of contradictory interests that goes by the name of democracy. How else except through the instruments of the media could the surgeon and the labor leader, the ballerina and the stock-car driver form even a dis-

torted image of one another? The media present a spectacle infinitely more crowded than Balzac's *Comédie Humaine*—the rumors of war on page one, followed, in random succession, by reports of strange crimes, political intrigues, anomalous discoveries in the sciences, the hazard of new fortunes.

21   Just as every nation supposedly gets "the government it deserves," so also it makes of the press whatever it chooses to imagine as its self-portrait. If the covers of all the nation's magazines could be displayed in a gallery, and if the majority of the images reflected dreams of wealth or sexual delight, a wandering Arab might be forgiven for thinking that the United States had confused itself with the Moslem vision of paradise.

22   The newspapers yield only as much as the reader brings to his reading. If the reader doesn't also study foreign affairs, or follow the money markets, or keep up his practice of foreign languages, then what can he expect to learn from the papers?

QUESTIONS AND IDEAS FOR DISCUSSION

1. Lapham offers a spirited defense of journalism, a counterpoint to the criticism of journalism so common elsewhere (including in these pages). Here are some of his assertions; offer your own seconding arguments or refutations. But do as Lapham does: Give examples and draw analogies to support your points.

   Defined as means rather than an end, journalism defends the future against the past. (paragraph 16)

   . . . it isn't the business of the journalist to distinguish between the significant and the worthless. (paragraph 17)

   Just as every nation supposedly gets "the government it deserves," so also it makes of the press whatever it chooses to imagine as its self-portrait. (paragraph 21)

2. This essay was written by a journalist, the editor of *Harper's*, and published in that magazine. Since the essay is a defense of journalism, not only what the journalist-author says but how well he says it must surely figure into his defense of journalism. And, indeed, the argument is offered with grace and style. Discuss Lapham's use of metaphor, parallelism, variation of sentence length, a large and precise vocabulary, and other elements of style. Give examples from the text of the essay.

3. Contrast the style of the first three sentences of Lapham's essay with that of the fourth. What is the effect of the fourth sentence—"This is silly"—in this context?

SUGGESTIONS FOR WRITING AND FURTHER DISCUSSION

1. "I used to rush to the school library and cram the subject, like a python swallowing rabbits; then, still replete as a postprandial python, I would tie myself in clumsy knots to embrace those accursed themes."
   —F. L. Lucas, "What Is Style?"

   Should children, who have experienced so little of education and of life, be required to write essays? Based on your own experience, and directed to the school board or headmaster responsible for your pre-college education, argue your answer to that question. Whether or not you found your early essay-writing experience as agonizing as did F. L. Lucas, try to describe yours vividly and persuasively.

2. Refute Lewis Lapham's defense of journalism, which you may choose to answer point by point. Lapham addresses his argument to the "consumers" of journalism—those who read *Harper's* and newspapers; address your argument to the same audience. Try some persuasive metaphors in your argument, as Lapham does.

3. Lewis Lapham concludes his argument about the value of the press with a challenge for the press's audience: "The newspapers yield only as much as the reader brings to his reading. If the reader doesn't also study foreign affairs, or follow the money markets, or keep up his practice of foreign languages, then what can he expect to learn from the papers?" How much of communication really depends on the participation of the audience? Is it fair to ask of readers and viewers that they be more than passive sponges, soaking up what newspapers, magazines, and television pour forth? Where is the audience supposed to study foreign affairs, anyway, if not in the pages of magazines or of the evening newspaper? Is there something of a Catch-22 in Lapham's challenge to his readers?

   a. Write an essay in which you argue, in support of Lapham's assertion, that news consumers need to educate themselves independently of the newspapers and the television in order to understand and intelligently evaluate both. Give specific examples from recent daily newspapers of information that would be difficult to understand fully without additional, prior knowledge of "foreign affairs, ... money markets, or ... foreign languages"—or some other field.

   b. Write an essay in which you argue against Lapham's assertion as being elitist or impracticable or otherwise flawed. Indicate in your essay how journalism ideally should function for its consumers.

4. "Reason assumes to settle things by weighing them against one another without prejudice, partiality, or excitement; but what affairs in the concrete are settled by is and always will be just prejudices, partialities, cupidities, and excitements."   —William James

Write an essay for which William James's assertion could serve as the thesis statement, centering on a particular incident (or several incidents) that illustrates the absence of reason in settling concrete difficulties.

7

Inductive Reasoning

The shrewd guess, the fertile hypothesis, the courageous leap
to a tentative conclusion—these are the most valuable coin of
the thinker at work.

Jerome Seymour Bruner

PATTERNS OF INDUCTIVE
REASONING

The process of inductive reasoning leads the thinker to a discovery of
relationships between like things (analogies), between causally related
phenomena, and between the assertions of an authority speaking in her
field of expertise and a conclusion having to do with that field of knowledge. *The distinctive feature of inductive reasoning is that the conclusion always stretches beyond the premises; it is never completely assured.* You may ride the same elevator every weekday for eleven years
and, based on that experience, assume that it never will become stuck
between floors. But one dark day, so confident in your inductive conclusion that you are not even aware of your trust, you may get on the
elevator and spend forty-five minutes with a group of strangers between
the fifteenth and sixteenth floors.

Despite the lack of certainty in inductive conclusions, inductive
reasoning is often called the "scientific method" of reasoning, a label
likely to intimidate those of us who would do anything to avoid taking

a chemistry lab class. But even when the people in the white lab coats are employing it, the so-called "scientific method," for all its usefulness, is not rigidly methodical. For example, James Watson, codiscoverer of the double helix structure of DNA, writes in his autobiographical account, *The Double Helix,* that he first became interested in DNA after reading an article written by Linus Pauling, of which he grasped little more than that "it was written with style." Watson was a graduate student at the time, but within two years he played an instrumental role in one of the greatest biochemical discoveries of the twentieth century. Watson's model for DNA resulted not so much from years of plodding labor and lab tests—"scientific induction"—as from an idea that came to him as he was riding a bus to class, an idea "so simple that it had to be right."

Inductive reasoning takes several forms. When two friends of mine, Steve and Scott, were in graduate school, they half-seriously decided to find a minor Olympic event at which they could excel and thereby earn a spot on the Olympic team. Both were in good physical condition; Scott had even been a starting member of the University of Texas football team. In their quest for the perfect Olympic sport for the weekend athlete, they reasoned inductively:

Finding a sport with few U.S. competitors, learning to compete in it, and practicing diligently during our spare time for a year might earn us a place on the U.S. Olympic team.

[CAUSAL ANALYSIS]

Kayaking requires too much shoulder strength.
Sculling, the same.
Sailing requires an expensive investment in equipment.
Bicycling requires expensive equipment and is too popular a sport.
Handball is too popular—too much competition.
Riflery is monotonous, and bad for the ears.
Table tennis is a sport dominated by the Chinese.
Evidently, all minor Olympic sports are inappropriate for our purposes.

[EXAMPLES]

For a couple of weekend athletes to contemplate trying out for the Olympics is like an amateur tennis buff's deciding to take on John McEnroe. Therefore, we would be foolish to attempt to participate in the Olympics.

[LITERAL ANALOGY]

For that matter, for a couple of weekend athletes to contemplate trying out for the Olympics is a lot like a meat butcher's deciding to try a little brain surgery. Therefore, we would be foolish to attempt to participate in the Olympics.

[METAPHORICAL ANALOGY]

All these arguments are inductive, for the simple reason that their conclusions move *beyond* the scope of the premises; each requires an "inductive leap" from premises to conclusion. The conclusions of inductive arguments can be strong and plausible, but they are never certain. Just because none of the sports considered was appropriate to Steve's and Scott's purpose does not mean that another might not be (as of the 1988 Olympics they were able to consider—and quickly reject—yet another sport, tae kwon do). And just because their attempting to become part of the Olympic team was analogous to an amateur tennis player's taking on John McEnroe would not assure their failure in the attempt. Still, failure was inductively probable.

All of us have reasoned similarly, perhaps without realizing it: Kelly has always refused dates with Blake, so she is likely to do so again if he calls her; every native Kansan I have met (and I have met hundreds) has been friendly, so I assume that most Kansans are friendly; you know twelve of the students signed up for Economics 4312, and they are all economics majors, so you assume that the other six students in the class are also economics majors. And you may have read many inductive arguments without realizing that they were inductive, or even that they were arguments. The following defense of the camel is an inductive paragraph that ends with the topic sentence, the conclusion to its argument:

The camel . . . sweats very little; its body temperature can go all the way up to 105 before it begins to sweat at all. Also the camel is very sparing in its urination. It is believed that water which in other animals would be passed off by the body is, by the camel, used over again: in effect recycled, as if the camel had an almost closed air conditioning system. In spite of the old joke that the camel looks as if it had been made by a committee, it is in fact very efficiently designed in terms of its environment.

—Tom Burnam, *Dictionary of Misinformation*

Concrete details noted in this paragraph lead to the conclusion that the camel "is in fact very efficiently designed in terms of its environment."

Induction is centered on the concrete. It involves reasoning from particulars. The concrete and the specific are both attractive and satisfying in a world of shifting standards, a world where reality sometimes seems hard to pin down. Inductive reasoning includes drawing conclusions from analogy, from cause and effect, and from the examination of particulars. The common element among these forms of inductive reasoning is the observation of similar or causally related elements, and the drawing of probable conclusions based on the relationship noted. We will consider each of these three forms of induction in turn. To support inductive arguments, you will sometimes find that your personal knowledge and experience will provide you with all the examples and other evidence you need; for arguments beyond your immediate experience and expertise, refer to Chapter 4's discussion of the kinds of evidence used to support inductive conclusions and deductive premises, and how to find, evaluate, and use that evidence.

ARGUING FROM ANALOGY

Literal Analogy

In an analogy two or more things, people, events, or other phenomena are observed to be alike in several respects; and the conclusion is reached that they are also alike in a further respect that has not yet been observed. Literal analogy involves comparison of things that have fundamental similarities which often are apparent even superficially; metaphorical analogy involves comparison of things that are both apparently and actually different but hold some enlightening, unexpected parallels. Literal analogy may be used—carefully—in argument; metaphorical analogy can provide only illustration, never logical proof. Even literal analogy is at most suggestive, not conclusive, but such is the nature of the inductive process. A literal argument from analogy goes like this:

The climate of Arizona and that of Saudi Arabia are similar, as are their soils and native vegetation. Therefore, the irrigation system which has worked so well in parts of Arizona should prove successful in Saudi Arabia.

Analogical arguments have the form "X and Y share characteristics a, b, c, [and so on]; therefore, they may also share characteristic m." Notice that the conclusion is qualified: X and Y "may" or "are likely to" share, not "will definitely" share, characteristic m. Analogies always break down at some point because the things compared are never completely identical; therefore, we must take care never to push an analogy to that breaking point. We could not, for instance, claim on the basis of climatic and soil similarities between Arizona and Saudi Arabia that the two regions are likely also to have the same number of rivers. Nor could we safely assume that they would be likely to raise identical crops.

The force of the conclusion to an argument from analogy depends on the closeness and the extent of the similarities between the things being compared. To begin with, *the similar features should be pertinent to the conclusion drawn.* In the irrigation argument a further similarity between Arizona and Saudi Arabia might be that each has at least one city with a population over 50,000, but that point of similarity has nothing to do with crop irrigation. To include it would be irrelevant. Second, *the similar characteristics should be several in number, and the greater the number of pertinent similarities, the greater the force of the argument.* Our argument about irrigation systems is reasonably convincing as it stands, since climate, soil, and native vegetation are strong points of appropriate similarity between Arizona and Saudi Arabia. But we would make the analogy even stronger if we could add that both regions contain similar underground water reserves, that both possess the technology and the trained technicians to implement a successful irrigation system, or that the Saudis hope to raise the same kind of crops grown in the irrigated Arizona farmland.

Analogical arguments such as this can carry considerable weight with a reader, although (as in all other inductive arguments) the conclusion is never certain and should not be offered as certain. An inductive leap is required: Just because X and Y are alike in all these respects never assures us beyond all doubt that they also will be alike in any further respect, including the one we have in mind. But the greater the number of pertinent points of similarity, the greater the likelihood of the further similarity we propose. We can argue analogies between World War I and World War II, between the Korean War and the Vietnam War, between Paris fashions and New York fashions, between parents and teachers, between ditch digging and road building, between coal mining and working in an asbestos factory. Where strong, pertinent, and literal correlations are known to exist, the possibility of further correlations is not far-fetched.

Metaphorical Analogy

Analogical argument requires literal analogy—the comparison of things, events, or ideas that are fundamentally similar. Metaphorical analogy, on the other hand, compares things that are fundamentally different in order to create a mental picture that furthers the reader's understanding of the more complex of the entities compared. Sometimes the line between literal and metaphorical analogies is not clearly demarcated; some analogies have both literal and metaphorical elements. But, generally, metaphor is intended to be evocative, to arouse emotional, rather than rational, responses in the reader.

That is not to say that the writer of argument should avoid metaphor—far from it. Metaphorical analogy can clarify and explain concepts (the idea of a "black hole" in space, for example) that would otherwise elude most readers. Although nonlogical—and, if offered as proof, logically fallacious—metaphor may be powerfully persuasive. But whether the comparison is explicit ("My love is like a red, red rose") or suppressed (My love is a red, red rose"), metaphorical analogy draws similarities between things that are fundamentally *unlike.* My love, even if ruddy-faced and sweet-smelling, is not really much like a rose. So I need not—and should not—conclude on the basis of the analogy that he will lose all his hair (as a rose loses its petals) or live a short life. A rose, as Gertrude Stein once observed, is a rose is a rose. A true love is something else altogether.

Evaluating Arguments from Analogy

An argument from analogy always will be fallacious if it purports to guarantee the conclusion, or if it reasons from a metaphorical comparison instead of a literal one. We find such faulty analogies frequently in letters to newspapers, such as the following:

In response to the recent letter from Marvin Crenshaw supporting the *Times Herald*'s views on South Africa and apartheid, I submit both have forgotten how our forefathers created this country.

Our treatment, then and even now, of the original people of America, the Indians, was and is deplorable.

It appears to me that the *Times Herald*, the Crenshaws and the like should start condemning their own failings and butt out of those which don't concern them. Such a "pot calling the kettle black" attitude further alienates the United States in the world today. No wonder no one likes or respects Americans anymore.

—Letter to the *Dallas Times Herald*, 8 Aug. 1983

In this argument the writer argues from a literal analogy—that the white South Africans treat the black South Africans much as the white North Americans treated and continue to treat the Indian North Americans. The analogy is an apt one, but the writer draws a conclusion from it that the premises do not support. He believes that if our government has treated the Indians unfairly, we have no right to condemn the South African government for treating blacks unfairly. In using his analogy to support this conclusion, he commits the fallacy known as **tu quoque** (Latin for "you're another")—that is, you're not entitled to argue a point because you're no better than the people you are criticizing. The pot can call the kettle black if the kettle is indeed black. The pot may be due for a polishing itself, but that is a separate issue logically.

To test the strength of your own or another's argument from analogy, consider the following:

1. Does the argument refrain from claiming that the analogy *guarantees* the conclusion?
2. Is the analogy nonmetaphorical?
3. Are the points of similarity between the entities compared strong, relevant, and numerous?
4. Are the points of dissimilarity (for differences inevitably will exist) minor, irrelevant, and few?
5. Is the inductive leap from the premises to the conclusion a reasonable one, easy to make? That is, is the scope of the conclusion limited according to the limitations of the analogy, and does the conclusion follow logically from the premises?

EXERCISE 7-1

Decide whether or not the following argument from analogy seems reasonable. Is the analogy sufficiently close and literal to support the conclusion inductively? Explain your answer.

In my ignorance, I had always thought that "fresh air" was infinitely available to us. I had imagined that the dirty air around us somehow escaped into the stratosphere, and that new air kept coming in—much as it does when we open a window after a party.

This, of course, is not true, and you would imagine that a grown man with a decent education would know this as a matter of course. What *is* true is that we live in a kind of spaceship called the earth, and only a limited amount of air is *forever* available to use.

The walls of our spaceship enclose what is called the "troposphere," which extends about seven miles up. This is all the air that is available to us. We must use it over and over again for infinity, just as if we were in a sealed room for the lifetime of the earth.

No fresh air comes in, and no polluted air escapes. Moreover, no dirt or poisons are ever "destroyed"—they remain in the air, in different forms, or settle on the earth as "particulates." And the more we burn, the more we replace good air with bad.

Once contaminated, this thin layer of air surrounding the earth cannot be cleansed again. We can clean materials, we can even clean water, but we cannot clean the air. There is nowhere else for the dirt and poisons to go—we cannot open a window in the troposphere and clear out the stale and noxious atmosphere we are creating. . . .

The United States alone is discharging *130 million tons of pollutants a year* into the atmosphere, from factories, heating systems, incinerators, automobiles and airplanes, power plants and public buildings. What is frightening is not so much the death and illness, corrosion and decay they are responsible for—as the fact that this is an *irreversible process*. The air will never be cleaner than it is now.

And this is why *prevention*—immediate, drastic and far-reaching—is our only hope for the future. We cannot undo what we have done. We cannot restore the atmosphere to the purity it had before the Industrial Revolution. But we can, and must, halt the contamination before our spaceship suffocates from its own foul discharges.

—Sydney J. Harris, *For the Time Being*

EXERCISE 7-2

Evaluate the following arguments from analogy according to the above criteria. Identify each as literal or metaphorical. If the analogy is literal, does it hold up as far as the argument takes it? If it seems flawed, explain what the problem is and what might be done to strengthen the inductive value of the analogy.

1. According to *The American Woman 1987–1988* (released by the Congressional Caucus for Women's Issues), female college graduates have a great deal in common with male high school dropouts: Both groups earn about the same amount of money annually.

   —*Time*, 2 Aug. 1987

2. Children should play football, because football is like life. Football teaches teamwork, responsibility, and the ability to pick oneself up after getting knocked down—and life requires mastery of those lessons.

3. Considered little more than hobbyists' toys barely 5 years ago, personal or microcomputers are being produced by some 150 companies today, making the field the biggest growth industry since the automobile. The parallel is not totally auspicious: In its infancy, the U.S. auto industry had hundreds of manufacturers. Today it has four.

   —*Business Week*, 29 August 1983

   (What conclusion is implied by this analogy?)

4. The Student Senate recognized campus organizations for female students, foreign students, students interested in the perceived problem of reverse discrimination, and students belonging to a variety of religious groups. The Gay Students' Organization is, like all of these, a special-interest group and, like some of them, a group interested in political activism. Because of its similarity in kind and purpose to other campus organizations, the GSO deserves recognition, too.

5. Cheating on academic work is like cheating on income taxes. Lots of people do it, it hurts no one, and it makes life a little easier for the cheater. Both kinds of cheating are therefore justifiable.

6. Dr. Huxley ridicules people who "still maintain that the planets are kept in their course by God and not by gravitation." He could equally ridicule those who maintained that London was lit by man and not by electricity.

   —Letter to the London *Times*, quoted in
   E. R. Emmet, *Handbook of Logic*

7. Aspartame has all the desirable qualities that saccharin does. Like saccharin, aspartame is sweet, virtually calorie-free, and combines well with foods. Therefore, aspartame should prove to be an excellent replacement for saccharin in soft drinks and packaged artificial sweeteners.

8. The role of the textbook (or teacher) in a good lab course is like that of a guide in a foreign country. The book should point out what to look (and look out) for, not what the traveler is to see.

   —Miles Pickering, "Are Lab Courses a Waste of Time?",
   from *Chronicle of Higher Education*, 19 February 1980

9. To praise a historian for his accuracy is like praising an architect for using well-seasoned timber or properly mixed concrete in his building. It is a necessary condition of his work, but not his essential function.

—Edward Hallet Carr, *What Is History?*

10. Television, much like marijuana and alcohol, is a kind of addictive buffer. It allows people who have only superficialities in common to be together in a form of peace and seeming contentment.

—Jeffrey Schrank, "There Are No Mass Media—All We Have Is Television," in *Snap, Crackle, and Popular Taste*

ARGUING FROM CAUSE OR EFFECT

A second form of inductive reasoning is used to argue that a given cause or causes lead to a given effect or effects, or that a given effect or effects result from a specific cause or causes. We can argue causally about past, present, or future events. That is, we might argue that the freak behavior of El Niño (a west-to-east Pacific wind current) and the fallout from several volcanic eruptions in the Pacific and in Asia caused the unusually snowy winter in Colorado in 1982–83; or we might argue that an unusually snowy winter this year will result in a late thaw, flooding, and enough mud to hurt the summer tourist trade in the mountain states. In such arguments, like other inductive processes, we again observe particulars and consider the relationship between them. The simplest causal arguments deal with single causes and single effects, and have the conclusion

C is the cause of E;

or

E is caused by C.

Both statements have the same core meaning, and we will treat them as two ways of expressing the same argument. "Infections cause fevers" and "Fevers are caused by infections" are logically equivalent, though grammatically the first statement emphasizes the cause and the second statement emphasizes the effect. More complex causal arguments involve multiple causes and/or multiple effects, such as the following example, in which "A, B, and C" and "E, F, and G" represent any number of causes or effects:

A, B, and C are [or "can be" or "are among"] the causes of E, F, and G.

The following are assertions of causal analysis involving multiple effects or causes:

Poison ivy and wool make me itch.

Imploding the hotel is likely to create a lot of dust and break glass in buildings across the street.

Unemployment, lack of political freedom, and hunger can give rise to despair and revolt.

Our wording of a causal assertion or argument reflects the degree of our certainty about the completeness and sufficiency of the causes or effects we have argued for the phenomena we have noted. "C is the cause of E" indicates certainty that C alone is the necessary and sufficient cause of E; "C is the primary cause of E" acknowledges other contributory causes of E; "C is one of the causes of E" makes a much smaller claim than either of the preceding statements. (In this last case other causes may be equal to or more important than the cause examined.) The same considerations apply when the argument moves backward, from effects to causes.

The first of the three kinds of conclusions to causal arguments, that "C is *the* cause of E," will require more supporting evidence than will "C is *one* of the causes of E" or "C can cause E." But the first conclusion, if it can be supported adequately, is inherently more interesting than the second or third. A strong causal argument supporting the assertion that "U.S. policy in Iran in 1978–79 made the Shah's downfall inevitable" will be read with attention; an argument claiming only that "U.S. policy in Iran may have contributed to the Shah's downfall in 1979," on the other hand, will attract less notice. The extra work involved and the extra evidence required in making a strong claim are often worth the trouble.

In any causal argument, however complex or simple, the writer must demonstrate one of three things:

1. **The cause is both *necessary* to the effect (the effect does not occur without it) and *sufficient* (this cause or these causes are alone enough to make the effect occur).** If the argument demonstrates such a relationship between causes and effects, the conclusion can be a strong one: "Almost certainly C is the cause of E," or "C and D are the causes of E and F." For example, we may argue that high-quality tomato seedlings, soil with good drainage, appropriate temperature conditions, and plenty of rainfall are necessary and sufficient conditions to produce a satisfactory tomato crop.

2. **The cause is *necessary* to the effect but alone may not be sufficient to bring it about.** For example, cold weather is necessary for snow to fall but is not sufficient to make it happen. Moisture in the atmosphere is needed as well, along with other conditions. If an argument demonstrates a partial cause, mention should be made of other contributing causes if they are known, and the conclusion should reflect the partiality of the cause argued: "C is the primary cause of E," for example, or "C is one of the causes of E," or "C, along with D, is one of the causes of E."

3. **The cause is *sufficient* to result in the effect but does not necessarily result in it.** For example, staying out in the midsummer sun all day is sufficient to cause a bad sunburn, but will not necessarily do so. (A person with a dark complexion or a dark tan, or one who frequently applies sunscreen and wears protective clothing, might stay out all day and not burn.) Another example: Smoking is sufficient to cause lung cancer—but not every smoker will develop lung cancer. By the same token, an increase in interest rates is sufficient to cause a drop in the stock market but will not be followed inevitably or automatically by such a drop.

If an argument demonstrates a sufficient but not a necessary relationship between cause and effect, the conclusion may take the form "C *can* cause E." In some arguments of this kind, however, a stronger conclusion can be put forth. Such arguments demonstrate that in the case at hand, the cause did (or probably will) in fact result in the effect claimed. We might justifiably say to a nervous friend, "Of course you will make Mortar Board. You have served on the Honor Council for three years, and you're vice-president of the Student Senate. That's certainly enough to merit your election to membership." In this case the argument from sufficient cause is inductively strong, although the causes cited will not automatically assure election to Mortar Board. The conclusion to such an argument may take the form "C is sufficient to cause E, and in this case has done so" (or "will do so"). Again, multiple sufficient causes or effects may be part of the argument: "C, just like B and D, is sufficient to cause E; but in this case B and D have not occurred (or 'are not likely to occur'), and C has caused (or 'will cause') E."

The Post Hoc Fallacy

The relationship in a causal argument is always chronological (causes must precede effects), but it must be logical as well. If it always rains after I wash my car, I cannot assume that it rains *because* I have washed my car. Along slightly different lines, if my car's finish appears duller after two years of regular washing at the neighborhood automatic carwash, I cannot argue that the abrasive brushes at the carwash have ruined my car's finish, and then sue the owner. Environmental pollution and an inferior finish—in fact, many things over two years—could also contribute to a dull finish. The arguer of causal relationships should eliminate mere coincidence and try to account for all the possible causes or effects of the phenomenon in question.

Despite these twin hazards of coincidence and unaccounted-for multiple causes, causal analysis can produce reasonable inductive conclusions, but only if the arguer bears in mind its limitations and resists the temptation to think that chronology assures a causal relationship. Superstitions arise from this kind of thinking: Two events occur in sequence, and the first is assumed to be the cause of the second. No doubt, somebody once met with misfortune after walking under a ladder, opening an umbrella indoors, or breaking a mirror. And now millions more are apprehensive each time they do the same. Even when we do not rationally believe in a causal relationship, we may act as if we did. If Jim Roberts wears an orange shirt once and finally breaks par, he may wear the shirt every time he plays golf, long after it is faded and frayed.

Then, too, we sometimes oversimplify causal relationships that do exist. If we treat a partial cause or a partial effect as if it were the entire cause or the entire effect, our argument will be unsound. Food and technology embargoes do not assure changes of policy in unfriendly countries, even those that import most of what they consume. The assassination of Archduke Ferdinand was not the only cause of World War I. Practice alone will not make Alicia Pérez the best sprinter on the track team. Sam Elliot's knack for tying complicated knots and whittling will not get him a job as a camp counselor unless those talents are accompanied by other desirable qualifications.

Either of these errors—assuming that chronology implies causal relation or assuming that a partial cause or effect is the entire cause or effect—results in fallacious argument. If every U.S. president elected in years ending with a zero has been the victim of an assassination attempt, I still cannot conclude that years ending with a zero cause bad fortune for presidents. If you reason that, because you have studied more hours than anyone else in your anthropology class, you will make the highest grade in the class on the upcoming exam, you may be disappointed. In both instances we are guilty of the fallacy of reasoning known as **post hoc ergo propter hoc** ("after this, therefore because of this"). The term is frequently called *post hoc* or "false cause." In this case the Latin term is preferable to the English, for the latter can be misleading. The cause ascribed is not always false; it may be, as in the last instance above, merely partial.

Evaluating Arguments from Cause or Effect

To test the strength of your own or another's argument from cause or effect, consider the following:

1. Does the argument refrain from claiming that the conclusion is certain?
2. Does the argument demonstrate that the causal relationship is more than coincidental or chronological?
3. Is the cause (or are the causes) both necessary and sufficient for the effect (or effects)? If necessary but not sufficient, is the partiality of the cause or effect acknowledged? If sufficient but not necessary, have other possible and sufficient causes been ruled out in the case at hand?

EXERCISE 7-3

Evaluate the following arguments from cause or effect according to the above criteria.

1. John bought a new sports car and shortly thereafter was involved in three auto accidents, all of which were technically his fault. Since he had a clean driving record before, the car must have some mechanical malfunction that caused the accidents.
2. John bought a new sports car and shortly thereafter was involved in three auto accidents, all of which were technically his fault. Each accident involved his rear-ending a car ahead of him. Since John had a clean driving record before buying the sports car, and since he is normally a safe and cautious driver, it is possible that the new car has some mechanical malfunction in the braking system that led to the accidents.
3. The increase in World War II-related TV shows during the Vietnam era probably "buttressed administration arguments linking Vietnam with World War II."
   —Erik Barnouw, *Tube of Plenty*
4. People who work all day at green phosphor VDTs (video display terminals) have begun to complain that they see pink auras around everything for several hours each weekday evening. On weekends they have no such complaints. None of the individuals had any such visual problem before beginning to work daily at a VDT. Therefore, it seems likely that the VDTs are causing the workers' visual distortions.
5. This is what explains the attraction of the beach in our society: total physical and mental inertia are highly agreeable, much more so than we allow ourselves to imagine. A beach not only permits such inertia but enforces it, thus neatly eliminating all problems of guilt.
   —John Kenneth Galbraith, preface to Gloria Steinem, *The Beach Book*
6. I know several cabinetmakers who have worked actively into their eighties. There must be something about working with wood that promotes longevity.

7. Katrina made a higher grade in German 4311 than Ellen did because Katrina studied harder.

8. After Mr. Mims eats certain brands of nacho-flavored corn chips, he becomes dizzy and breaks out in a cold sweat. After he eats Chinese food, the same thing happens. Evidently, something in the nacho-flavored corn chips and the Chinese food causes the dizziness and cold sweats. But the only thing the two have in common is the ingredient MSG (monosodium glutamate). Therefore, MSG causes the dizziness and cold sweats.

9. There is more than one reason for the lack of emphasis on foreign languages in the United States, but one word, *Americanization*, explains a major part of it. . . . This Americanization process encouraged Italian, German, Armenian, Japanese, Nigerian, and other immigrants to be "American" in their attitude, culture, and citizenship. A heavily accented English, or strange clothing, or habits that did not fit completely into this new world were "deficiencies" they wanted their children to avoid. . . . The last thing most of these parents wanted their children to learn in school was a foreign language.

—Paul Simon, *The Tongue-Tied Americans*

10. On Friday night, 16 Oct. 1987, a baby was rescued after 58 hours trapped in a well in Midland, Texas. On Monday, 19 Oct., the stock market crashed. Obviously everyone was cashing in stock in order to send money to the trust fund for little Jessica McClure.

ARGUING FROM EXAMPLES

A third form of inductive reasoning involves examining instances, examples, or other bits of data, finding similarities among them, and drawing conclusions about further particular cases or about the entire class of things or events to which all the particulars belong. Suppose, for instance, that it has rained in Cincinnati on each of the eight Tuesdays you have spent there during the last three months. Based on your observations, you may generalize that it nearly always rains on Tuesdays in Cincinnati; or you may conclude that it probably also rained on the four Tuesdays that you did not spend in Cincinnati during the quarter; or you may conclude that it will rain this coming Tuesday in Cincinnati. The last conclusion—that it is likely to rain this coming Tuesday in Cincinnati—concerns an additional particular case, and demonstrates the inaccuracy of the common assertion that inductive argumentation is limited to reasoning from examples to generalizations. We see that inductive reasoning from examples may lead to generalizations or to conclusions about further particular cases. The story of how Ronald Reagan became a Republican illustrates both kinds of conclusions. As actor Bob Cummings recalls it (as quoted in Doug McClelland, *Hollywood on Reagan*), the future Republican president said, "Well, I sat down and made a list of all the people I admired. And they were all Republicans." And on the basis of that generalization from particulars, Reagan reached a decision about a further particular—himself.

Inductive conclusions leading to generalizations are offered as applying to all or most of the members of a particular class and are based on observation of a number of members of the class. Such statements are useful to argument, for they enable us to organize data and make sense of our world, to draw broad conclusions from narrow experience. Although generalizations are based on pertinent data, we do not attempt to examine every instance or every member of a class of things before drawing conclusions about the category of event or class of things observed. We use sampling, instead. High school students visit a college campus and observe the students, then make a generalization about all the students based on those they have seen. A scientist observes the size, shape, and behavior of bacteria when exposed to a particular antibiotic and makes a generalization about the effect of the drug on all bacteria of that type.

Evaluating Arguments from Examples

If the conclusion to an argument based on the examination and enumeration of evidence concerns a further particular case or instance, the arguer has a special problem; individual cases often assert their unique characteristics inconveniently. Tell a rain-weary Scot to visit Phoenix because "it never rains," and the Scot will be drenched in the worst flash flood in ten years. Note that your brother always drops by on Sunday afternoons, and the following week he will show up on Tuesday. Write a letter to the newspaper praising the mayor's politically liberal policy decisions and the next one she makes will be, by your standards, painfully conservative. Buy a collie puppy because your previous five collies were calm, sweet-natured animals, and this one will turn out to be a wild-eyed, howling banshee. The professor who never calls roll will do so the first time you miss class. We can, and must, make conclusions about particular instances, but we rarely can be certain of them.

In making conclusions about additional examples based on observed examples, improve the odds that your conclusion will be borne out by limiting it to individual instances that do not depart in any radical way from those you have observed. For instance, suppose that you have found women in politics to be supportive of women's rights, and so you have made a habit of voting for female political candidates. But in an upcoming election, the lone female candidate announces her opposition to the Equal Rights Amendment. You would not be wise to conclude that this woman will support women's rights once in office. And if winters were mild during your freshman, sophomore, and junior years in the state where you attend college, it would still be wise to pack a coat when you go off to school for your senior year. Weather is not certain; even Florida has an occasional freeze.

Despite the limitations of inductive reasoning about particulars, it is reasonable to expect future instances of a phenomenon to follow the pattern of past instances. If Democrats have almost always won the congressional elections in your district, you expect, inductively, that the Democratic candidate will win the next election, too. But one kind of thinker distrusts inductive regularity, expecting patterns to reverse themselves every so often. This thinker commits the **gambler's fallacy:** Luck, the gambler thinks, is bound to turn. But the laws of probability indicate no such likelihood for any given instance of a phenomenon. For example, my doctor and his wife had a seventh child, and five of the preceding six are girls. The actual probability of the seventh child's being another girl was roughly 50 percent. But the prudent inductive reasoner, observing a trend toward daughters in this family, would have expected another girl. And the gambler would have reasoned that because five out of six are girls, including the last two, the seventh child would certainly be a boy. The prudent inductive reasoner would have been right this time. The couple had a daughter.

It is somewhat safer to draw generalizations from particular cases than to speculate about further particular cases because generalizations allow room for exceptions. And because generalizations permit us to understand many things without having to experience all of them, generalizations are not only useful but necessary: We cannot observe every example of giraffes or of books in order to make statements about either class. However, like most kinds of conclusions, generalizations create problems if they are arrived at erroneously or hastily. First, they may be distorted or simply wrong; second, they fail to account for individual eccentricities; third, they can lead to the kind of misunderstandings exemplified by stereotyping. (Recall the discussion of stereotyping and audience analysis in Chapter 2.) The particulars that constitute our sampling of the entire class should be typical of the class and as numerous as possible. After observing five giraffes in the local zoo, all of whom are sullen and prone to bite, we cannot generalize that giraffes are animals who live in zoos or that giraffes are animals with unpleasant dispositions. We cannot conclude from observing the books in a library, even a large one, that all books have rows of call numbers and letters labeled on their spines. In making generalizations in written arguments, then, we do well to avoid such faulty generalizations as much as possible by testing our samplings and our generalizations—and those of other writers—against the following considerations:

1. Is the evidence *accurate?*
2. Is the evidence *representative?* Is it typical of the class about which the generalization is made?
3. Is the evidence *sufficient* in quantity to warrant the generalization made? What constitutes sufficient evidence depends on the amount of variety in the evidence and in the class from which it is drawn. We could make a fair generalization about the physical characteristics of the tree crab from a small sample; to make a generalization about the political values of Americans would require an enormous or meticulously executed random sampling.
4. Finally, is the *conclusion inductively plausible,* considering the nature and amount of the evidence? That is, does it avoid going improbably far beyond the limits of the evidence?

EXERCISE 7–4

In the following passage X. J. Kennedy claims that King Kong is not so much an ape-monster as he is a courtly lover. Evaluate his argument from examples. Are you convinced? Comment.

In his simian way King Kong is the hopelessly yearning lover of Petrarchan convention. His forced exit from his jungle, in chains, results directly from his single-minded pursuit of Fay. He smashes a Broadway theater when the notion enters his dull brain that the flashbulbs of photographers somehow endanger the lady. His perilous swinging up a skyscraper to pluck Fay from her boudoir is an act of the kindliest of hearts. He's impossible to discourage even though the love of his life can't lay eyes on him without shrieking murder.

—from "Who Killed King Kong?"

Limiting Generalizations

The fourth test—Is the conclusion plausible?—occasionally will make clear that the conclusion you want to make is too broad or requires too great a leap from the evidence. In such cases you must find more evidence to narrow the gap, or else narrow the conclusion itself. The latter, often preferable, enables you to make more accurate statements. Rather than asserting that "blind dates are always miserable experiences," you might narrow that assertion to "Blind dates arranged by relatives are always miserable experiences." Rather than claiming,

"Women are discriminated against in all areas of life," you might narrow that claim to something you could support in a five-page argument: "Women are discriminated against by the life insurance industry," or "Graduates of Schoneman Law School who have child-bearing potential have been discriminated against in the hiring practices of legal firms," or "Female athletes do not receive news coverage on television that is comparable to that accorded male athletes." Generalizations of narrow scope can be more fully developed and supported in a short argument than can such sweeping statements as "Killing can never be justified" or "America's impact on the rest of the world is less today than ever before in the nation's history." Attempting to support inductively such sweeping generalizations in a few pages of argument will inevitably lead to fallacies such as taking for granted things you should be proving (begging the question) and hasty generalizations.

A final word about generalizations: Not all (perhaps not even many) are inductive in origin. We tend to *begin* with a hypothesis—like that which struck James Watson about the structure of DNA—and then test it by accumulating evidence and examples, rather than to collect all kinds of data haphazardly and then suddenly notice a common feature: "Eureka! All the blond males on this campus ride bicycles!" We consider generalizations here because they are established by examples, a means of supporting conclusions that is generally held to be inductive. But we will encounter generalizations again, and frequently, in Chapter 8—Deductive Reasoning.

EXERCISE 7–5

A. Rank the following list of generalizations from 1 (lengthiest argument and greatest amount of evidence likely to be required for support in an essay) to 10 (shortest argument, least amount of evidence likely to be required for support). Assume that your readers would be your rhetoric classmates. Discuss with the rest of the class the differences you find in your rankings. Why are differences likely to occur—what preconceptions and biases do those differences reflect?

B. Reverse the meaning of each generalization (for example, you would change "Women are inferior to men" to "Women are superior to men") and repeat exercise A. What differences do you find in the rankings, and why?

C. Take five generalizations that you numbered 1 through 5 in either set of exercises, and suggest ways of narrowing their scope to a statement that could be adequately supported for the same audience in a paper of five pages or less. List three alternatives for each of the five broad generalizations.

1. The truth is always the strongest argument.

    —Sophocles
2. The Communists intend to destroy the rest of the world.
3. All people should provide for their organs to be donated after their death to needy recipients.
4. All religious cults in this country should be outlawed.
5. Sugar is poison.
6. If we consider democracy not just as a political system, but as a set of institutions which do aim to make everything available to everybody, *it would not be an overstatement to describe advertising as the characteristic rhetoric of democracy.* (emphasis added)

    —Daniel Boorstin, *Democracy and Its Discontents*
7. Computers are bad for children.
8. The electoral college is outmoded and should be abolished.
9. Nothing is more fun than the circus.
10. It is a truth universally acknowledged, that a single man in possession of a good fortune must be in want of a wife.

    —Jane Austen, *Pride and Prejudice*

IS BUSINESS BLUFFING ETHICAL?

Albert Z. Carr

1   A respected businessman with whom I discussed the theme of this article remarked with some heat, "You mean to say you're going to encourage men to bluff? Why, bluffing is nothing more than a form of lying! You're advising them to lie!"

2   I agreed that the basis of private morality is a respect for truth and that the closer a businessman comes to the truth, the more he deserves respect. At the same time, I suggested that most bluffing in business might be regarded simply as game strategy—much like bluffing in poker, which does not reflect on the morality of the bluffer.

3   I quoted Henry Taylor, the British statesman who pointed out that "falsehood ceases to be falsehood when it is understood on all sides that the truth is not expected to be spoken"—an exact description of bluffing in poker, diplomacy, and business. I cited the analogy of the criminal court, where the criminal is not expected to tell the truth when he pleads "not guilty." Everyone from the judge down takes it for granted that the job of the defendant's attorney is to get his client off, not to reveal the truth; and this is considered ethical practice. I mentioned Representative Omar Burleson, the Democrat from Texas, who was quoted as saying, in regard to the ethics of Congress, "Ethics is a barrel of worms"—a pungent summing up of the problem of deciding who is ethical in politics.

4   I reminded my friend that millions of businessmen feel constrained every day to say *yes* to their bosses when they secretly believe *no* and that this is generally accepted as permissible strategy when the alternative might be the loss of a job. The essential point, I said, is that the ethics of business are game ethics, different from the ethics of religion.

5   We can learn a good deal about the nature of business by comparing it with poker. While both have a large element of chance, in the long run the winner is the man who plays with steady skill. In both games ultimate victory requires intimate knowledge of the rules, insight into the psychology of the other players, a bold front, a considerable amount of self-discipline, and the ability to respond swiftly and effectively to opportunities provided by chance.

6   No one expects poker to be played on the ethical principles preached in churches. In poker it is right and proper to bluff a friend out of the rewards of being dealt a good hand. A player feels no more

than a slight twinge of sympathy, if that, when—with nothing better than a single ace in his hand—he strips a heavy loser, who holds a pair, of the rest of his chips. It was up to the other fellow to protect himself. In the words of an excellent poker player, former President Harry Truman, "If you can't stand the heat, stay out of the kitchen." If one shows mercy to a loser in poker, it is a personal gesture, divorced from the rules of the game.

7   Poker has its special ethics, and here I am not referring to rules against cheating. The man who keeps an ace up his sleeve or who marks the cards is more than unethical; he is a crook, and can be punished as such—kicked out of the game or, in the Old West, shot.

8   In contrast to the cheat, the unethical poker player is one who, while abiding by the letter of the rules, finds ways to put the other players at an unfair disadvantage. Perhaps he unnerves them with loud talk. Or he tries to get them drunk. Or he plays in cahoots with someone else at the table. Ethical poker players frown on such tactics.

9   Poker's own brand of ethics is different from the ethical ideals of civilized human relationships. The game calls for distrust of the other fellow. It ignores the claim of friendship. Cunning deception and concealment of one's strength and intentions, not kindness and openheartedness, are vital in poker. No one thinks any the worse of poker on that account. And no one should think any the worse of the game of business because its standards of right and wrong differ from the prevailing traditions of morality in our society. That most businessmen are not indifferent to ethics in their private lives, everyone will agree. My point is that in their office lives they cease to be private citizens; they become game players who must be guided by a somewhat different set of ethical standards.

10   The point was forcefully made to me by a Midwestern executive who has given a good deal of thought to the question: "So long as a businessman complies with the laws of the land and avoids telling malicious lies, he's ethical. If the law as written gives a man a wide-open chance to make a killing, he'd be a fool not to take advantage of it. If he doesn't, somebody else will. There's no obligation on him to stop and consider who is going to get hurt. If the law says he can do it, that's all the justification he needs. There's nothing unethical about that. It's just plain business sense."

11   The illusion that business can afford to be guided by ethics as conceived in private life is often fostered by speeches and articles containing such phrases as, "It pays to be ethical," or "Sound ethics is good business." Actually this is not an ethical position at all; it is a self-serving calculation in disguise. The speaker is really saying that in the long run a company can make more money if it does not

antagonize competitors, suppliers, employees, and customers by squeezing them too hard. He is saying that oversharp policies reduce ultimate gains. That is true, but it has nothing to do with ethics. The underlying attitude is much like that in the familiar story of the shopkeeper who finds an extra $20 bill in the cash register, debates with himself the ethical problem—should he tell his partner?—and finally decides to share the money because the gesture will give him an edge over the s.o.b. the next time they quarrel.

12   I think it is fair to sum up the prevailing attitude of business-men on ethics as follows:

13   We live in what is probably the most competitive of the world's civilized societies. Our customs encourage a high degree of aggres-sion in the individual's striving for success. Business is our main area of competition, and it has been ritualized into a game of strategy. The basic rules of the game have been set by the government, which attempts to detect and punish business frauds. But as long as a com-pany does not transgress the rules of the game set by law, it has the legal right to shape its strategy without reference to anything but its profits. If it takes a long-term view of its profits, it will preserve amicable relations, so far as possible, with those with whom it deals. A wise businessman will not seek advantage to the point where he generates dangerous hostility among employees, competitors, cus-tomers, government, or the public at large. But decisions in this area are, in the final test, decisions of strategy, not of ethics.

14   If a man plans to take a seat in the business game, he owes it to himself to master the principles by which the game is played, including its special ethical outlook. He can then hardly fail to rec-ognize that an occasional bluff may well be justified in terms of the game's ethics and warranted in terms of economic necessity. Once he clears his mind on this point, he is in a good position to match his strategy against that of the other players. He can then determine objectively whether a bluff in a given situation has a good chance of succeeding and can decide when and how to bluff, without a feeling of ethical transgression.

15   To be a winner, a man must play to win. This does not mean that he must be ruthless, cruel, harsh, or treacherous. On the con-trary, the better his reputation for integrity, honesty, and decency, the better his chances of victory will be in the long run. But from time to time every businessman, like every poker player, is offered a choice between certain loss or bluffing within the legal rules of the game. If he is not resigned to losing, if he wants to rise in his com-pany and industry, then in such a crisis he will bluff—and bluff hard.

16   Every now and then one meets a successful businessman who

has conveniently forgotten the small or large deceptions that he practiced on his way to fortune. "God gave me my money," old John D. Rockefeller once piously told a Sunday school class. It would be a rare tycoon in our time who would risk the horse laugh with which such a remark would be greeted.

17   In the last third of the twentieth century even children are aware that if a man has become prosperous in business, he has sometimes departed from the strict truth in order to overcome obstacles or has practiced the more subtle deceptions of the half-truth or the misleading omission. Whatever the form of the bluff, it is an integral part of the game, and the executive who does not master its techniques is not likely to accumulate much money or power.

QUESTIONS AND IDEAS FOR DISCUSSION

1. How, according to Carr, is business like poker? How is it *not* like poker—that is, at what point does the analogy break down?
2. What constitutes lying and cheating depends, says Carr, on the context. Discuss the ways in which he defends and supports this claim in the context of conducting business.
3. If you disagree with Carr's conclusion, how would you go about refuting his thesis to him? How would you go about refuting his thesis to your rhetoric class? Your "Introduction to Marketing" class? Would speaking to the different audiences necessitate making major or minor differences in your own argument?
4. If you agree with Carr's conclusion, what additional examples, analogies, testimony, or other inductive support can you suggest to add to Carr's argument?
5. The audience to whom this essay was initially addressed was businesspeople (business*men*, specifically), readers of the *Harvard Business Review*. Indicate specific details of examples, assumptions, and vocabulary that seem to have been made with that audience in mind. If you work in business now or plan to in the future, do you find yourself able to identify with Carr's stance? If you have no experience in or plans to engage in business as a career, do you find Carr's argument totally alien to your understanding and interests? Explain. Does the way in which businesses are run affect only businesspeople—or all of us?

WHY I WANT A WIFE

Judy Syfers

1   I belong to that classification of people known as wives. I am A Wife. And, not altogether incidentally, I am a mother.

2   Not too long ago a male friend of mine appeared on the scene fresh from a recent divorce. He had one child, who is, of course, with his ex-wife. He is looking for another wife. As I thought about him while I was ironing one evening, it suddenly occurred to me that I, too, would like to have a wife. Why do I want a wife?

3   I would like to go back to school so that I can become economically independent, support myself, and, if need be, support those dependent upon me. I want a wife who will work and send me to school. And while I am going to school I want a wife to take care of my children. I want a wife to keep track of the children's doctor and dentist appointments. And to keep track of mine, too. I want a wife to make sure my children eat properly and are kept clean. I want a wife who will wash the children's clothes and keep them mended. I want a wife who is a good nurturant attendant to my children, who arranges for their schooling, makes sure that they have an adequate social life with their peers, takes them to the park, the zoo, etc. I want a wife who takes care of the children when they are sick, a wife who arranges to be around when the children need special care, because, of course, I cannot miss classes at school. My wife must arrange to lose time at work and not lose the job. It may mean a small cut in my wife's income from time to time, but I guess I can tolerate that. Needless to say, my wife will arrange and pay for the care of the children while my wife is working.

4   I want a wife who will take care of *my* physical needs. I want a wife who will keep my house clean. A wife who will pick up after my children, a wife who will pick up after me. I want a wife who will keep my clothes clean, ironed, mended, replaced when need be, and who will see to it that my personal things are kept in their proper place so that I can find what I need the minute I need it. I want a wife who cooks the meals, a wife who is a *good* cook. I want a wife who will plan the menus, do the necessary grocery shopping, prepare the meals, serve them pleasantly, and then do the cleaning up while I do my studying. I want a wife who will care for me when I am sick and sympathize with my pain and loss of time from school. I want a wife to go along when our family takes a vacation so that someone

can continue to care for me and my children when I need a rest and change of scene.

5   I want a wife who will not bother me with rambling complaints about a wife's duties. But I want a wife who will listen to me when I feel the need to explain a rather difficult point I have come across in my course of studies. And I want a wife who will type my papers for me when I have written them.

6   I want a wife who will take care of the details of my social life. When my wife and I are invited out by my friends, I want a wife who will take care of the babysitting arrangements. When I meet people at school that I like and want to entertain, I want a wife who will have the house clean, will prepare a special meal, serve it to me and my friends, and not interrupt when I talk about things that interest me and my friends. I want a wife who will have arranged that the children are fed and ready for bed before my guests arrive so that the children do not bother us. I want a wife who takes care of the needs of my guests so that they feel comfortable, who makes sure that they have an ashtray, that they are passed the hors d'oeuvres, that they are offered a second helping of the food, that their wine glasses are replenished when necessary, that their coffee is served to them as they like it. And I want a wife who knows that sometimes I need a night out by myself.

7   I want a wife who is sensitive to my sexual needs, a wife who makes love passionately and eagerly when I feel like it, a wife who makes sure that I am satisfied. And, of course, I want a wife who will not demand sexual attention when I am not in the mood for it. I want a wife who assumes the complete responsibility for birth control, because I do not want more children. I want a wife who will remain sexually faithful to me so that I do not have to clutter up my intellectual life with jealousies. And I want a wife who understands that *my* sexual needs may entail more than strict adherence to monogamy. I must, after all, be able to relate to people as fully as possible.

8   If, by chance, I find another person more suitable as a wife than the wife I already have, I want the liberty to replace my present wife with another one. Naturally, I will expect a fresh, new life; my wife will take the children and be solely responsible for them so that I am left free.

9   When I am through with school and have a job, I want my wife to quit working and remain at home so that my wife can more fully and completely take care of a wife's duties.

10   My God, who *wouldn't* want a wife?

QUESTIONS AND IDEAS FOR DISCUSSION

1. This essay was written for the inaugural issue of *Ms.* magazine, Spring 1972. Describe the audience toward which it was probably aimed. Do you fit that description? If not, how does the difference between the initial audience and yourself affect your understanding of and attitude toward Syfers's argument? Must a person be married or have been married in order to be able to judge the argument fairly?

2. Almost two decades have passed since the essay was written. Which of Syfers's inductive points now seem dated, and which still seem apt? Comment specifically.

3. How great or small is the inductive leap between the premises and the conclusion in this essay? Preconceptions and personal biases aside, are we moved to accept Syfers's conclusion on the weight of her examples?

4. How does Syfers analyze her subject and organize her supporting points for the conclusion that "anybody would want a wife"? Is that, by the way, all of her thesis, or is there more to it, implied but not stated?

5. Describe the persona Syfers creates in this essay. How does her use of irony and humorous detail affect her persona? Are we more or less likely to give ear to her serious underlying argument because of the voice with which Syfers speaks? Explain. What seems to be Syfers's persuasive aim?

THE TROUBLE WITH ARCHITECTS

Andrew Ward

1   A woman I know worked for a time in one of those prestigious sweat-shops in which the imposing abodes of America's corporations are designed. A mean woman with an X-Acto knife, she was given the job of constructing the little presentation models with which her firm coaxed its clients even further into the frontiers of modern architecture. But she could stand the subsistence pay, the stiff neck, and the enforced veneration for the firm's presiding genius only long enough to complete a single model: a one-inch-to-one-foot cardboard and Mylar prototype of a huge building slated for construction somewhere in downtown Houston.

2   A few years after she quit the firm she found herself at the Houston airport and decided to kill the two hours she had between planes by taking a cab downtown and finding the building over whose embryo she had labored so long. Though she couldn't remember what company had commissioned it, she figured she had been so intimately acquainted with its design that she could spot it without any trouble.

3   But after an hour's search up and down the city streets, she could not for the life of her find it, and had to assume, as she boarded her plane, that the design had been changed or the project had been canceled just after she had quit. Then, suddenly, looking down at the retreating city as her plane rose in the sky, she saw her building standing right smackdab in the middle of Houston. During her search she must have passed it half a dozen times, but only now, with a bird's-eye view of it on a cardboard and Mylar scale, could she recognize it.

4   I think my friend may have stumbled upon what's wrong with modern architecture: it is best appreciated from a couple of thousand feet off the ground. It is conceived from an aerial point of view, from the Olympian perspective of a god, an angel, a chairman of the board.

5   I visited a firm a while ago whose work is on such a scale and whose aesthetic is so grandiose that I only wish Albert Speer could have tagged along to give me some guidance. Crammed atop fifty waist-high tables in the center of the main studio were thousands of dollars' worth of presentation models representing millions of dollars' worth of buildings. Some were of structures that are already towering over us; others were of headquarters still rising out of the doomed woodlands of suburban Connecticut; still more were of buildings that shall forever remain a gleam in the architect's eye.

6   As I wandered through the studio, my natural perspective was from above. During presentations, executives must have had to stoop pretty far down to get some earthbound notion of what the buildings were going to look like, and stooping does not come naturally to your upper-echelon corporate exec. Getting up close to models can wreck the illusion, anyway; you see a flap of Mylar peeling away, a fleck of rubber cement, the little everyday defects that have no place in a meeting where traffic flow patterns, image, and executive toiletry are up for discussion. No, it is far preferable to maintain one's posture and keep one's distance.

7   What struck me about the models with their breakaway roofs was that they contained some pretty ingenious notions, some intricate and innovative problem-solving, but that none of these could be appreciated by someone trying to walk along a building's barren and wind-whipped facade, or heading for the restroom along one of its dizzying, sloping corridors, or reading back issues in a brass and glass lobby five stories high.

8   That we are but grains of sand on the beach of time, droplets in the ocean of life, is a notion worth considering now and then, but it isn't something sane people want to dwell upon, or in. Nature has been doing a fine job of reminding us of our insignificance without a lot of architects seconding the motion. The hitch, of course, is that the men who commission these buildings don't tend to feel as insignificant as the rest of us (maybe because they aren't as insignificant as the rest of us). And it may even be that they don't really mean to make the rest of us feel insignificant. It's just that the same building that makes a visitor feel puny makes its proprietor, whose experience is charged with the thrill of ownership, feel like a giant.

9   Architecture, especially institutional architecture, may always have been designed and bestowed from above, but since the invention of the airplane the aerial perspective has been given disproportionate validity. Have you ever noticed how exalted our downtown areas appear from the clouds? At some altitudes you could mistake the new convention centers and condo complexes for Utopia. But down on the ground the same places are oppressive, depressing, downright crummy. Part of this effect is a function of distance; from thousands of feet in the air you can't see the litter and the bag ladies. But that can be only part of it, because sometimes the reverse is true.

10   I lived for a while in Cornwall, Connecticut, conceivably the loveliest town in the nation. Most of the houses were built by country carpenters in the eighteenth and nineteenth centuries, and they coexist in absolute harmony (in marked contrast to their occupants). As one walks along the streets, it seems that everyone's lawn

stretches for acres and every grove of trees extends into miles of forest, as if, over time, the town grew organically out of the countryside. But I was once shown some aerial photographs of Cornwall in which the town, stripped of its mystery, looked like a condemned stretch of southern New Jersey. You could see the abandoned cars just beyond the Cotters' back fence, the bald lots gleaned for firewood on the Franklins' hill.

11   An architect would no more have recreated such a scheme and proposed it to a developer than he would serve Kool-Aid to Harold Geneen. He would have tidied up those uneven, impracticably distanced houses into evenly staggered modules, pruned the woodlots, landscaped the pastures, gutted the hardware store to make way for a wok outlet and a quiche parlor, unified the churches, consolidated the schools, and tied the whole thing together with pedestrian walkways and bike paths. Only then could his clients, standing over the one-inch-to-ten-feet mock-up like titans 300 feet tall, come to grips with the theme, the continuity, the concept, at a glance.

12   Maybe the grandiose style is just an outgrowth of the grandiosity of the institutions it services. And perhaps the young turks of modern architecture have already turned their backs on the ostentatious. I don't know. The last young turk I met designed his parents' solar house on the Cape last year; has been reduced to making installation estimates for a carpet warehouse this year; and, if things don't pick up next year, may join his buddy the English major in a cabinetmaking business in Vermont. A look at the major commissions under way just beyond New York's city limits indicates to me that the grandiose is getting grander all the time.

13   I suppose I won't be satisfied until architects return to Asher Benjamin and the golden mean, but if they have any interest in designing buildings to accommodate people, they should at least design structures in the same way they're built: from the ground up.

QUESTIONS AND IDEAS FOR DISCUSSION

1. What effect does Ward's beginning with a narrative illustration have on you as a reader? Does it put you off or entice you to read further? Does the illustration further the essay's argumentative point, or does it, like many a joke beginning many a sermon, merely serve as a warm-up to the *real* topic?

2. What is the writer's thesis in this essay? Where is it stated? What kinds of inductive support does Ward offer for it?

3. Ward makes a serious point, but does so with a light touch. Indicate some of the passages and phrases that show Ward's low-key humor, such as "[the houses] coexist in absolute harmony (in marked contrast to their occupants)." What effect does the humorous note have upon Ward's persuasiveness in the essay?
4. Can you offer examples that would refute Ward's complaints about modern architecture? What are they?

HOW ANNANDALE WENT OUT

Edwin Arlington Robinson

"They called it Annandale—and I was there
To flourish, to find words, and to attend:
Liar, physician, hypocrite, and friend,
I watched him; and the sight was not so fair
As one or two that I have seen elsewhere:
An apparatus not for me to mend—
A wreck, with hell between him and the end,
Remained of Annandale; and I was there.

"I knew the ruin as I knew the man;
So put the two together, if you can,
Remembering the worst you know of me.
Now view yourself as I was, on the spot—
With a slight kind of engine. Do you see?
Like this . . . You wouldn't hang me? I thought not."

QUESTIONS AND IDEAS FOR DISCUSSION

Perhaps we will not do too great an injustice to the poetic merits of "Annandale" to treat it as a mystery to be solved. Some students immediately understand what the poem concerns; others must struggle, clue by clue, bit of evidence by bit, to arrive at a solution. Here is your opportunity to put your inductive skills to the test. From the title and the words of the poem alone, you must determine

1. What is Annandale?
2. Who is the narrator of the poem?
3. What action is the narrator defending?
4. What constitutes the narrator's defense?

Some other questions are incidental to determining the answers to those above:

5. Who is the *him* in line 4?
6. What is the *apparatus* in line 6? How does Robinson mean us to understand the word here, and why do you suppose he has chosen this particular word?

7. What is the "slight kind of engine" in line 13?

8. Sonnets are traditionally love poems, and Robinson has written this poem in the form of a sonnet. How appropriate is the sonnet form to the rhetorical situation here?

For each question indicate the evidence in the poem that supports your answer. You may find that some answers change as you continue to read over the poem. And here is one final question: What large issue does this poem concern?

SUGGESTIONS FOR WRITING AND FURTHER DISCUSSION

1. Albert Carr declares that "the major tests of every move in business, as in all games of strategy, are legality and profit." Not ethics. When Carr's essay on "bluffing" in business was published by the *Harvard Business Review,* the editors solicited additional essays supporting or refuting Carr's argument. Write such an essay, directed to the readers of the *Review.* Use an extended analogy of your own—don't just refute Carr's poker analogy—and examples to support your argument.

2. Write an inductive essay in the spirit of Syfers' "Why I Want a Wife," entitled, "Why I Want an Assistant" or "Why I Want a Computer."

3. Andrew Ward tells us about the experience of seeing things from a new perspective, and about the fresh insights that follow. I am reminded, in this respect, of advice given by etiquette authority and humorist Judith Martin, who assumes in her syndicated etiquette column the persona of "Miss Manners," a woman of acid wit and no-nonsense common sense. Miss Manners advises her readers to set a buffet table "so that it would form an attractive pattern if viewed by a guest hanging from the chandelier." Write an essay in which you look from a new vantage point at something familiar to you and to your audience and attempt to persuade your readers to see it as you do. The new vantage point need not be a physical one; try looking at a political situation or an ethical issue from a new perspective. Your inductive emphasis here will be on examining particulars; that is, on examples.

4. Our imperfect reason often leads us to false conclusions, especially about cause-and-effect relationships. Write an essay in which you speculate about the probable causes or effects of something you have little knowledge about—perhaps what makes a car run, or what makes a camera record photographs and not blank exposures, or what makes a video game work. Your readers you may presume to have little more knowledge of the process than your own. Do not treat the topic face-

tiously; try to construct a reasonable argument based solely on your own observations. (After you have written the essay, look up the topic in an encyclopedia or how-to book, and note the points at which your causal analysis breaks down. Write a brief comment on what sent you astray—and how far—in your original analysis.)

5. Your sister, brother, or friend is a medical student, and writes to you that the "right to die" is a hot issue right now at the medical school. In response, write a letter to the dean of the medical school in which you attack or defend euthanasia. You may choose to limit or qualify either position, perhaps defending euthanasia only when a terminal patient asks for it, or attacking deliberate euthanasia while supporting the right to withhold extraordinary life support. To support your conclusion, cite actual instances of this dilemma from the experiences of your own family and friends or from what you have heard about on the news and in the newspapers.

6. Write an argument from analogy in which you compare a thing, event, process, or person that is familiar to you—but likely to be unfamiliar to your rhetoric classmates—to something else that your classmates should understand readily. For example, "Rappelling down a cliff is not as frightening or as difficult as you might expect; it is very much like—," or "Everyone should experience deep-sea diving at least once in a lifetime. The experience is like—," or "Attending the Olympics is not like attending any other sporting event. The Olympics are more like—," or "My neighbor, Mr. Martino, looks like the retired mechanic that he is, but at heart he is more like—."

8

Deductive Reasoning

One must not always think that feeling is everything. Art is nothing without form.

Gustave Flaubert

DEDUCTION IN FICTION AND FACT

"The identity of the murderer is perfectly obvious," announced the Famous Detective smugly. "He is a left-handed attorney from Kansas City who walks with a limp and was disguised as a ranchhand when he committed the deed."

"But how do you know all this?" gasped the minister and her brother.

"A simple matter of deduction, my friends. The villain wore these cowboy boots (we know this because they still smell of sweaty feet, and are too large for the feet of the deceased). They were intended as part of a disguise, for no real ranchhand would be caught dead—or red-handed—in cowboy boots from Saks, as the label inside indicates these are. The curious wear pattern on the right sole is indicative of a limp, and the dust on the boots is of a kind peculiar to Kansas City. Moreover, the murder weapon was this pair of blood-stained left-handed scissors. You see how obvious it all is!"

"Ah, but you haven't accounted for his being an attorney," said the minister's brother, irritated by the detective's condescension.

"That is the most certain point of all!" the detective exclaimed. "All residents of Kansas City who wear cowboy boots are attorneys."

Whereas in an inductive argument the conclusion moves beyond the premises, in a deductive argument the conclusion is drawn out of the premises. If a deductive argument is logically constructed and its premises are true, its conclusion is certain—with a certainty that induction never presumes. The focus of this chapter will be on how to use deductive reasoning to construct sound and convincing arguments in your essays and other writing.

We associate deductive reasoning with the work of detectives such as Sherlock Holmes and Hercule Poirot and their imitators, like the overconfident fellow above. In the world of fiction, of course, the detective always will be proved right: The killer will indeed turn out to be a murderous, left-handed attorney from Kansas City, who presumably will be caught limping barefooted into his legal offices. But reasoning of this kind strikes us as contrived and unreal; we consequently dismiss deductive reasoning as the concern only of paperback detectives and formal logic textbooks, in which arguments sound nothing like the way people actually talk and write. One of the Famous Detective's arguments, were it to appear in a logic textbook, would look like this:

No real ranchhands are persons who wear cowboy boots from Saks Fifth Avenue.

The murderer is a person who wears cowboy boots from Saks.

Therefore, the murderer is not a real ranchhand.

And, of course, no real person writes arguments this way, neatly and redundantly laid out on separate lines.

But all who reason do so in part deductively. Deductive reasoning is not the province of detective fiction and formal logic only; it is a perfectly natural process of reasoning—so natural, in fact, that we can hardly avoid it for even five minutes of conscious thought. The following examples of deduction look more like the way people really reason than do the Famous Detective's arguments:

"If Carl is angry with me, he won't speak to me at lunch. [Later] He did speak to me at lunch, so evidently he isn't angry after all."

"Marcia must be a music major, because all the women living in Sikes Hall are music majors."

"Mikey won't eat that cereal. He hates all nutritious food."

"Successful actors can't be camera-shy, so Patrick is bound to fail in Hollywood."

We reason along these lines almost any time we do reason. Because deductive reasoning is so much a part of our thinking processes, it makes sense that we should examine the process in order to understand how it works; we may thereby better evaluate the arguments of others and better construct our own. If you have developed thesis statements from enthymemes as discussed in Chapter 2, you are already familiar with deduction. This chapter will help you assess the strength of those—and other—deductive arguments.

INDUCTION AND DEDUCTION

Induction, the subject of the previous chapter, and deduction, the subject of this chapter, are complementary processes of reasoning. Although we are examining them separately for now, most often we will find them used together in written and spoken argument. **The difference between them lies in the relationship between the premises and the conclusion.** In an inductive argument, you will recall, the conclusion moves beyond the premises, and the premises purport only to *offer support* for the conclusion. In a deductive argument, on the other hand, the conclusion is drawn out of the premises, and the premises purport to *guarantee* the conclusion. This difference is illustrated by two arguments, the first inductive and the second deductive:

Ross: "I was paid last Friday and on the two Fridays before that. In fact, I have been paid every Friday since I came to work for the company. I know, then, that I will be paid today, since today is Friday."

Smith: "Since today is Friday, and every Friday is payday, I know I will get a check today."

The conclusion reached in both arguments is that the person speaking will be paid "today." If the premises offered in support of that conclusion are all true (every Friday *is* payday) and related logically to the conclusion, then in the first argument the conclusion is probable but not inevitable. Perhaps the company is having a severe cash-flow problem and will be unable to issue checks today. Perhaps this week a decision has been reached that paychecks will be issued every Monday, or every other Friday, effective immediately. Such will always be the limitation of the inductive "leap of faith" between premises and conclusion, between examples and covering generalization. But in the second argument, if the premises are all true and related logically to the conclusion, the conclusion is inevitable—it is guaranteed.

Of course, you might object, the same calamity that might befall Ross's paycheck might also waylay Smith's. If so, the premise upon which the conclusion is based, "Every Friday is payday," would be shown to be untrue. In a deductive argument, if the premises are true and the argument is structured properly, the conclusion is guaranteed.

A second distinction often made between induction and deduction—that inductive arguments move from particular cases to summarizing generalizations and deductive arguments move from general categories to conclusions about particular cases—is not altogether accurate. For one thing, an inductive argument may conclude with particular cases; you may consider a number of examples and then speculate about another, similar instance, as Ross does in the argument cited above. And a deductive argument may move from generalization to further generalization:

Ice is a factor in poor winter driving conditions, and poor winter driving conditions are a factor in traffic fatalities. Therefore, ice is a factor in traffic fatalities.

As in some examples you have seen, inductive and deductive arguments may even have identical conclusions: "I will be paid today." The difference between deduction and induction lies not in the kinds of conclusions that are drawn but in the ways they are drawn—the relationship of the premises to the conclusion. Both kinds of argument are valuable. Without induction, as logician Wesley Salmon has noted, we could pose no arguments about future events. We could draw no legitimate generalizations. We could not speculate about similarities between phenomena. Without deduction, we could never be completely assured of any conclusion.

VALIDITY, TRUTH, AND SOUNDNESS

The assurance deduction offers is possible only if we create sound arguments. An argument is **sound,** or fully acceptable, if its premises are true and the form of the argument is valid. In order to evaluate the merits of a deductive argument, you must first understand that validity and truth are entirely different qualities in logic. Valid arguments are arguments that are properly structured; **validity** has to do with the *form* of the argument. True statements are actually or theoretically verifiable; **truth** has to do with the *matter* of the argument. How to test for truth and how to locate true statements were major issues in Chapter 4; how to test and how to construct valid deductive arguments will be our concern here. Both truth and validity are necessary components of sound argument, but they must be considered and evaluated separately. Otherwise, you might be tempted to call this argument invalid:

All cats are striped creatures.	(premise)
All striped creatures are mammals.	(premise)
Therefore, all cats are mammals.	(conclusion)

The conclusion is true, but both premises offered as justification for the conclusion are false. The argument, therefore, cannot be sound, but it is valid, as you will see later.

In another argument all the statements may be true, and the form invalid nevertheless:

All lupines are wildflowers.	(premise)
All Texas bluebonnets are wildflowers.	(premise)
Therefore, all Texas bluebonnets are lupines.	(conclusion)

As it happens, all three statements are true, but the premises do not support the conclusion, because just to say that two things are both part of a larger class does not necessarily mean that they overlap within that larger class. The argument is not correctly structured—it is invalid. It just happens here that *Texas bluebonnet* and *lupine* are two names for the same flower.

Clearly, if an argument seems to fall short of being fully acceptable, we must be able to judge both its validity and its truth, for the careless workmanship may be either in the construction or in the materials used.

DISTRIBUTION OF TERMS

What makes an argument valid, its structure "correct"? To answer that question requires a thorough understanding of the words *term* and *distribution*. First, a **term** is a noun, phrase, or clause that constitutes a unit of meaning. Sentences have two terms, a subject term and a predicate term (the latter always says something about the subject term). In the sentence "An unknown assailant gunned down the guerrilla commander," the subject term is "an unknown assailant" and the predicate term is "gunned down the guerrilla commander." In the sentence "Gorillas are shy creatures," "gorillas" is the subject term and "are shy creatures" is the predicate term. A class term, often called simply a **class**, is a grouping of objects (either animate or inanimate) or ideas that share one or more common characteristics. The following are all class terms: *assailants, unknown assailants; people who kill other people, people who kill guerrilla commanders; gorillas, adult gorillas, gorillas living in the wild; creatures, shy creatures, shy but curious creatures.* The class of "gorillas living in the wild" is obviously a smaller class than that of "gorillas," and is a subclass within it, but the two are distinguished from each other by the additional characteristic of "living in the wild" that limits the smaller class.

For an argument to be valid, some of the terms of its statements must be **distributed:** that is, they must be considered in their entirety. If we are saying something about an entire class of things, whether "all gorillas," "all female gorillas living in zoos," or "all gorillas named Chamba," that class is said to be distributed; if we are saying something about less than an entire class of things, whether "some assailants," "many shy creatures," or even "most guerrilla leaders" or "seven hundred assailants" (for *most* does not mean *all,* nor does a specific number, however large), that class is said to be undistributed. Nondistribution of subject terms is indicated by modifiers, as in the examples: *some, most, many,* or *seven hundred.* Distribution of subject terms, on the other hand, may be indicated by modifiers meaning *all* ("every potato chip") or by the absence of any quantitative adjective ("potato chips" we understand to mean "all potato chips").

Distribution of predicate terms is determined by whether the sentence is affirmative ("Unicorns are mythical creatures") or negative ("Some laws are not just"). In the statement "Unicorns are mythical creatures," the entire class of unicorns is included in the subject of the sentence, but the entire class of mythical creatures is not included in the predicate. Dragons are left out, for one thing, and mermaids, for another. Therefore, the subject term in this sentence is said to be distributed; the predicate, undistributed. In the statement "Some laws are not just," part of the class of laws is excluded from all of the class of "things that are just." The subject term in this case is undistributed; the predicate, distributed.

The predicate term of an affirmative sentence, then, is undistributed. The predicate term of a negative sentence is distributed.

Distribution of terms is essential to valid deductive reasoning, because we cannot move arbitrarily from undistributed to distributed terms—that is, we cannot proceed from talking about part of the class of mythical creatures (unicorns) to drawing conclusions about all of the class—and because, despite the wildflower argument above, we cannot assume that if two terms are related to a third, linking term, they must also be related to each other. They cannot be proven to be related to each other unless at some point in our reasoning we consider the entire linking term: *The linking term must be distributed in at least one premise.*

In order to determine whether or not the subject and predicate terms in a sentence are distributed, recast the sentence so that it is expressed as a noun, phrase, or clause plus a copula (a linking verb, any form of *to be*) and another noun, phrase, or clause. Accordingly,

All professors have graduated from college.

would be rephrased as

All professors are persons who have graduated from college.

in order to determine whether the subject and predicate terms are distributed. In this case the subject term, "all professors," is obviously distributed (the entire class of professors is under consideration at the moment), but the predicate term, "persons who have graduated from college," is not distributed. Certainly people other than college professors have graduated from college, but those others are not included here. Thus, the meaning of the sentence is that

All professors are some of the persons who have graduated from college.

We must bear in mind a few further points in order to determine if the subject and predicate terms are distributed:

1. **Distribution can be exclusive as well as inclusive.** If we exclude all of a given class from consideration, our concern is still with all of it. "No professors" excludes the entire class of professors just as "all professors" includes it.
2. **Distribution is not limited to entire species of things.** "All black cats" is just as much a distributed term as "all cats" is; the class under consideration is simply a narrower category.
3. **"All" and "no" need not be explicitly stated if they are clearly implied.** "Cats" implies "all cats," and "cats are not canaries" means that "no cats are canaries."
4. **Individuals and proper names are considered distributed by definition.** When we speak of Socrates, or of a philosopher, we mean all of him or her.
5. **Affirmative statements with distributed subject terms (all A are B) are called *universal affirmative* statements.** The subjects of all universal

affirmative statements are distributed; the predicates are undistributed. "All lotus-eaters are lazy" is a universal affirmative statement.

6. **Affirmative statements with undistributed subject terms (some A are B) are called *particular affirmative* statements.** The subjects of particular affirmative statements are undistributed and so are their predicate terms. "Some travelers are prone to seasickness" is a particular affirmative statement.

7. **Negative statements with distributed subjects terms are called *universal negative* statements.** The subjects of all universal negative statements are distributed, as are their predicate terms. A universal negative statement can take the form *no A are B* or the form *A are not B*. For example, "No Socialists are state governors" and "Scientists are not people who draw hasty conclusions" are both universal negative statements.*

8. **Negative statements with undistributed subject terms (some A are not B) are called *particular negative* statements.** The subjects of all particular negative statements are undistributed; the predicates are distributed. "Some chimpanzees are not fond of bananas," "Many koala bears do not live in Australia," and "Most American buffaloes do not live in large cities" are *all* particular negative statements.

The following sentences are examples of each of the four possible types of statements, and a diagram illustrates each:

Universal Affirmative:

All *successful politicians* are *good speakers.*
    distributed   undistributed

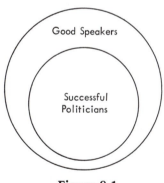

Figure 8-1

*Carefully consider the intended meaning of "All A are not B" statements, however. In some cases such statements actually mean *"Some* A are not B." While "Cats are not canaries" means that *no* cats are canaries, "All engineering majors are not sophomores" or "All pigs are not fat" means *some* are not.

Particular Affirmative:

Some *successful politicians* are *graduates of law school.*
          undistributed   undistributed

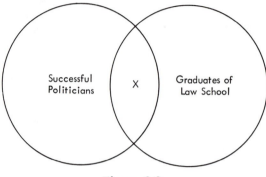

Figure 8-2

Universal Negative:

No *successful politicians* are *persons opposed to civil rights.*
          distributed   distributed

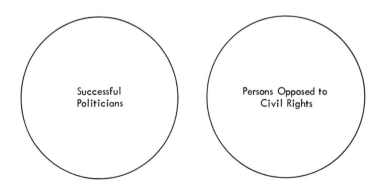

Figure 8-3

Particular Negative:

Some *successful politicians* are not *people fond of kissing babies.*
         undistributed   distributed

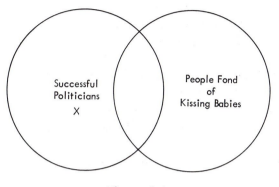

Figure 8-4

An argument links statements of these kinds in order to propose relationships between the terms included in the statements. If you can determine which terms are distributed, you can judge the validity of the
relationships asserted by testing the argument according to applicable
rules. And you can thereby improve the logic of your own prose.

EXERCISE 8–1

Identify all subject terms and all predicate terms in the following statements as either distributed or undistributed. If a statement is not expressed in subject /linking verb/ predicate nominative form, rephrase it
accordingly. For example, you would rephrase "Some sharks eat people"
as "Some sharks are people-eaters," in order to make evident (if it was
not clear already) that both subject and predicate terms in this statement
are undistributed. In a more complex case, "Millions of people inhabit
China" can be restated as "Millions of the living creatures inhabiting
China are people" or "Millions of the people in the world are Chinese,"
depending on the classes you have in mind.

1. Few engineering majors believe they will enjoy English composition.
   ("Few engineering majors are people who believe they will enjoy
   English composition.")

2. All the members of the Spanish honorary fraternity are pleasant people.
3. Some of the members of the Spanish honorary fraternity are not pleasant people.
4. Shakespeare was a great writer.
5. Some of Shakespeare's plays are not great.
6. Smoking should be allowed in all open-air arenas. ("Smoking is an activity that. . . .")
7. Circumstantial evidence has merit in courts of law.
8. Tomatoes are not vegetables.
9. Some varieties of squash are not edible.
10. Most Americans can recite the Pledge of Allegiance.

TESTING VALIDITY: THE SYLLOGISM

If a deductive argument is correctly structured, we say that it is *valid;* that is, it adheres to certain rules governing logical deduction. And indeed it must; but in order to determine whether the rules have been followed, it is sometimes helpful to set out the structure of the argument in explicit and simple terms. An ordinary deductive argument (called an **enthymeme**) makes explicit only part of its structure and implies the rest. "All cats are striped creatures, so they must be mammals" is an enthymeme; and even if we find the missing premise incredible, we have no great difficulty stating what it must be: "All striped creatures are mammals." Our instinctive understanding of logical relationships tells us that much, whether or not we are familiar with syllogisms and enthymemes. In a more complex argument, the implicit premise (or even implicit conclusion) might not be as readily apparent as it is here, or the relationships between ideas as clear. In those cases Aristotle's model for evaluating deductive reasoning, the **syllogism,** can be useful.

The syllogism offers a means of testing validity in arguments—of establishing whether or not the proper structure has been followed. Arguments may look very different from each other, may omit premises, and yet still be valid. The syllogism distills the essence of an argument into a form that may be readily evaluated. In the simplest terms, the structure of a deductive argument is always "If X and Y (the two premises) are both true, and the two statements relate logically to each other and to the conclusion, then Z (the conclusion) is true." A syllogism spells out how statement X is related to statement Y, and how both of them are in turn related to statement Z. A typical syllogism is structured like this:

All A are B.	(statement X)
All B are C.	(statement Y)
Therefore,	
All A are C.	(statement Z)

This is, as it happens, the form of the striped-cat argument we encountered earlier, and of several others along the way.

Formally laid out, a syllogism has exactly three terms (nouns, phrases, or clauses), each used twice, and consists of exactly three statements: two supporting statements (or premises) and a conclusion. This three-term, three-statement formula is not as limiting—or as limited—as it may sound; it is possible to create syllogistic chains of argument (called **sorites**) in which the conclusion of one becomes a premise for the next, and so on, thus allowing a great number of terms and very complex arguments to be evaluated. But for the moment we will discuss only the structure of a simple deductive argument, first by introducing three more terms and setting out the form of a valid categorical syllogism, and then by explaining how to reconstruct a syllogism from an ordinary argument posed elliptically as an enthymeme.

The predicate term of the conclusion to an argument is labeled the **major term;** the subject term of the conclusion is the **minor term;** and the term which links the major and minor terms but does not itself appear in the conclusion is the **middle term.** By the same token, the premise which contains the major term is called the **major premise,** and that which contains the minor term is the **minor premise.** The following syllogism is in standard form:

All <u>Londoners</u> are <u>residents of England</u>.   (major premise)
  middle term   major term

<u>Queen Elizabeth</u> is a <u>Londoner</u>.   (minor premise)
  minor term   middle term

<u>Queen Elizabeth</u> is a <u>resident of England</u>.   (conclusion)
  minor term   major term

To determine whether the syllogism is valid, we need only judge it according to six rules formulated by Aristotle:

1. There must be exactly three terms.
2. The middle term must be distributed at least once.
3. Any term distributed in the conclusion must be distributed in a premise.
4. Only one premise may be negative, or no conclusion is possible.
5. A negative premise requires a negative conclusion.
6. Only one premise may be particular, or no conclusion is possible.

The syllogism we are considering has exactly three terms: *Londoners, Queen Elizabeth,* and *residents of England.* The middle term, *Londoners,* is distributed in the major premise. No term is distributed in the conclusion that was not previously distributed in a premise, for *residents of England* is undistributed in the conclusion, and *Queen Elizabeth,* being a proper noun, is distributed by definition. The syllogism contains no negative premises and no particular premises; so the last three rules do not apply. The syllogism is valid. Its validity also can be shown by a diagram:

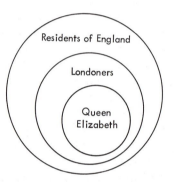

Figure 8-5

EXERCISE 8–2

Test the following syllogisms for *validity only.* Do not be distracted by nonsensical or untrue statements. Identify the three terms in each syllogism and draw diagrams to help you determine which arguments are valid.

1. Rabbits are creatures that multiply rapidly.
   Some creatures that multiply rapidly are household pests.
   Therefore, some rabbits are household pests.
2. Argument is a kind of warfare.
   All warfare is to be avoided.
   Therefore, argument is to be avoided.
3. Professor Higgins's interests are catholic.
   No Catholics are interested in walnut farming.
   Therefore, Professor Higgins's interests do not include walnut farming.

4. No sensible person does things that might endanger life.
   Sky diving might endanger life.
   Therefore, no sensible person goes sky diving.

5. Some frozen yogurt has more calories than ice cream.
   I will not eat anything that has more calories than ice cream.
   Therefore, I will not eat some frozen yogurt.

6. Many voters are Democrats.
   Some Democrats are politically liberal.
   Therefore, some voters are politically liberal.

7. Only the beautiful, the rich, and the brave attend high school reunions. (Rephrase as, "All who attend high school reunions are beautiful, rich, or brave.")
   Snodgrass plans to attend his high school reunion.
   Therefore, Snodgrass is beautiful, rich, or brave.

8. Stiff, mandatory penalties reduce crime.
   Drunk driving is a crime.
   Therefore, stiff, mandatory penalties would reduce the incidence of drunk driving.

9. A are not B.
   B are not C.
   Therefore, A are not C.

10. Elephants are ticklish.
    Ticklish creatures are untrustworthy.
    Therefore, elephants are untrustworthy.

11. Football is like life.
    Chess is like life.
    Therefore, football is like chess.

12. Research into all diseases that threaten a significant number of citizens should be funded heavily by the federal government.
    AIDS is such a disease.
    Therefore, research into AIDS should be funded heavily by the federal government.

13. Elections compromise the impartiality and perhaps the integrity of candidates.
    Judges should not compromise their impartiality or their integrity.
    Therefore, judges should not be candidates for election.

14. All insects are arthropods, and lobsters are arthropods.
    Therefore, lobsters are insects.

15. All who endanger the lives of others should be imprisoned for that offense.
    Drunk drivers endanger the lives of others.
    Therefore, drunk drivers should be imprisoned for that offense.

EXERCISE 8–3

Determine valid conclusions for the following pairs of statements.

1. All A are B.
   No B are C.
   Therefore, ?

2. Some frogs are not handsome princes.
   Only a handsome prince can break the spell.
   (Rephrase as, "All who can break the spell are handsome princes.")
   Therefore, ?

3. All contemptible people are liars.
   Senator Smithers is not a liar.
   Therefore, ?

4. A are not B.
   C are B.
   Therefore, ?

5. All skills that can save lives are skills people should know.
   Cardiopulmonary resuscitation is a skill that can save lives.
   Therefore, ?

6. A student: The best academic major for a person is one that you both like and excel in. I both like and excel in sociology. Therefore, ?

7. Her parents: The best academic major for a person is one that opens the door to high-paying work. Pre-medical majors do that. Therefore, ?

8. All dangerous dogs should be destroyed. Pit bulls are dangerous. Therefore, ?

9. People who work routinely with dangerous chemicals should change their occupation. Chemists work routinely with dangerous chemicals. Therefore, ?

10. Some people feel depressed on holidays. Thanksgiving is a holiday. Therefore, ?

FORMAL FALLACIES

To violate any of the six rules of validity is to commit a **formal fallacy,** so called because of a problem in the structure (form) of the argument— that is, in the kinds of relationships drawn among the terms. A fallacious argument shows carelessness or, less often, deceitfulness; but whatever the reason for the fallacy, such an argument is easily refuted. We will consider the fallacies related to each of the six rules in turn.

There Must Be Exactly Three Terms.   Sometimes an argument will appear to have three terms, but will actually have two or four. If I argue that

All men are mortal beings, and	(major premise)
Margaret is not a man;	(minor premise)
therefore, Margaret is not a mortal being.	(conclusion)

I appear to be using three terms, but the first *men* refers to the entire class of human beings, and the second *man* refers to humans of the male gender. In fact, I have introduced a fourth term, and thereby have committed what is called the fallacy of **equivocation.**

Conversely, sometimes an argument will repeat the same term in different words, so that a premise offered is actually the conclusion in disguised form:

This course is a course that will appeal to you.	(minor premise)
All courses that appeal to you are courses you will like.	(major premise)
Therefore, this course is a course you will like.	(conclusion)

This is the fallacy of **circular reasoning.** The argument goes nowhere; the first premise says, in effect, the same thing as the conclusion. And, as a result, the major premise is a **tautology**; that is, the subject term and the predicate term are synonymous. Circular reasoning is a way of **begging the question**—in other words, taking for granted what you should be proving, or using the conclusion as its own support. To say "You will like this course because it's great" is to beg the question of why the person addressed will like the course: Is the professor witty? Are the textbooks interesting? Does the class never meet on Fridays?

The Middle Term Must Be Distributed at Least Once.   According to rhetorician Richard Weaver, "The fallacy of the undistributed middle is probably responsible for more faulty reasoning than is any other of the formal fallacies." And he is probably right, although begging the question must run the undistributed middle term a close second in frequency. This fallacy is often called the *fallacy of the shared characteristic* (or **guilt by association**), a label which makes clear the fault involved. Consider the following argument:

All Methodists oppose heavy drinking.
All vegetarians oppose heavy drinking.
Therefore,
all Methodists are vegetarians.

We often fall into such lines of reasoning, and we often are wrong, for we have not considered the entire class of people who oppose heavy drinking (a class that includes such otherwise-unrelated groups as Methodists, vegetarians, and members of Alcoholics Anonymous) at any point in the argument: The middle term, or shared characteristic, is undistributed. But if we say,

All Methodists oppose heavy drinking, and
Joe Briggs is a Methodist;
therefore,
Joe Briggs must oppose heavy drinking.

we have reasoned validly.

Any Term Distributed in the Conclusion Must Be Distributed in a Premise. Here again distribution proves crucial to establishing a valid argument. As indicated earlier, we cannot go from considering part of a class to drawing conclusions about all of it, as is done in the following argument:

Some Central American governments are Communist-backed.
All Communist-backed governments are governments ideologically opposed to the United States.
Therefore, all Central American governments are ideologically opposed to the United States.

The problem with this line of reasoning is that it moves from considering some Central American governments to drawing a conclusion about all of them; a term is distributed in the conclusion that was not distributed in the premises. The argument is invalid; it contains the fallacy of **overgeneralization** (also known as the fallacy of composition, or the fallacy of illicit process).

Only One Premise May Be Negative, or No Conclusion Is Possible. Two negative premises leave the reader hanging:

No commodities traders are afraid to take risks.
No people who are afraid to take risks are mountain climbers.

Therefore—what? Commodities traders are likely to be mountain climbers? Not necessarily. We simply cannot draw a conclusion.

A Negative Premise Requires a Negative Conclusion. We cannot exclude a class (or part of it) in the premises and then include it in the conclusion. An affirmative conclusion from a negative premise is logically impossible:

No goldfish are trained circus animals.
Trained circus animals are valuable property.
Therefore, goldfish are also valuable property.

They may be, but not on the basis of these premises. We can conclude only that some valuable property is not goldfish.

Only One Premise May Be Particular, or No Conclusion Is Possible.   Attempting to draw a conclusion from two particular (subject term undistributed) premises results in a muddle like the following.

Some mushrooms are poisonous substances.
Some poisonous substances are man-made.
Therefore,
some mushrooms are man-made.

Not at present. No conclusion about the relationship of mushrooms to man-made substances is possible, because neither class is considered in its entirety.

An argument can be invalid in any of these ways, and a really poor argument may include more than one fallacy at a time. But by far the most common formal fallacies are the fallacies of the *undistributed middle term* and *begging the question*. If you keep an eye out for these two in the arguments you encounter and in your own, you will recognize and avoid most fallacious argument.

EXERCISE 8–4

Identify the following arguments as valid or invalid, and indicate which formal fallacy is committed in the invalid arguments. As in the examples on pages 251–53, 256, use diagrams of the terms and their relationship to each other to help you.

1. Freedom to make political statements is a right protected by law.
   Bumper stickers make political statements.
   Therefore, bumper stickers are protected by law.
2. All addictive substances are harmful to the body.
   Cyanide is harmful to the body.
   Therefore, cyanide is an addictive substance.
3. Some people who take flu shots develop Guillan-Barré Syndrome as a consequence.
   People should not do things that make them develop Guillan-Barré Syndrome as a consequence.
   Therefore, no one should take flu shots.

4. Happiness alters a person's state of mind.
   Altered states of mind make one unfit for driving.
   Therefore, happiness makes one unfit for driving.
5. Americans are uninformed about the dangers of nuclear weapons.
   People who are uninformed about the dangers of nuclear weapons are not able to make informed decisions about them.
   Americans are not able to make informed decisions about nuclear weapons.

THE LIMITATIONS OF LOGIC: TOULMIN'S CORRECTIVE

The relationships drawn in sound deductive argument are attractive in the certainty they offer. You may have underlined or highlighted the statement in an earlier section, "If the premises are true and the argument is structured properly, the conclusion is guaranteed." How comforting that sounds. Life offers few such assurances: We usually look for the fine print and the limitations when we are offered one.

We must do so with argument—even deductive argument—as well. As logicians from Aristotle to Stephen Toulmin and others have pointed out, we rarely find arguments in ordinary prose neatly arranged in formal syllogisms, nor do we find the degree of certainty in ordinary propositions and assertions that we find in logic textbook examples. We are likely to accept arguments on their relative probability, not on their certainty.

In *The Uses of Argument*, Toulmin cites the following as an example of an argument that offers no certainty but rather great probability:

Peterson is a Swede;
Scarcely any Swedes are Roman Catholics;
So, almost certainly, Peterson is not a Roman Catholic.

Notice the qualifiers here: *scarcely any, almost certainly*. Such qualifiers enable us to argue and to accept arguments that we could not grant in unqualified terms. However, the conclusion must not claim a greater degree of certainty than the supporting premises:

Peterson is a Swede;
Fewer than half of all Swedes are Roman Catholics;
So, almost certainly, Peterson is not a Roman Catholic.

In this case we would not be likely to grant the conclusion. *Fewer than half* offers much less certainty in the argument than does *scarcely any*.

In this second version, what would be an acceptable qualifier in the conclusion?

Toulmin's model of argument takes into account some of the special features of rhetorical argument. What we have called the conclusion to an argument, he calls the **claim.** Premises he divides according to their function: Reasons and evidence for the claim are **data** statements; statements that show how the data and claim are related are **warrants,** and are usually implicit rather than explicit. Statements that offer support for the warrants are **backing,** and phrases that limit the scope or degree of probability of any statement are **qualifiers.** The parts of the argument about Peterson could be labeled accordingly:

Peterson is a Swede;
     (data)
Scarcely any Swedes are Roman Catholics;
  (qualifier)   (warrant)
So, almost certainly, Peterson is not a Roman Catholic.
     (qualifier)   (claim)

In form this argument looks a great deal like others in this chapter, and so it is. But while traditional Aristotelian logic centers on the relationships between terms (*Peterson, Swedes,* and *Roman Catholics,* in this example), the Toulmin model centers on the relationships between statements (the claim, the data supporting it, and the warrant linking the two). Toulmin concerns himself with the roles certain kinds of phrases and clauses play in practical argumentation—roles that formal logic ignores. Explanatory and limiting words and sentences, such as qualifiers and backing, are important parts of everyday argument, as Toulmin recognizes. But despite the differences between classical, formal logic and modern, everyday logic, the Aristotelian system and Toulmin's model are more complementary than antagonistic (although the proponents of each have sometimes failed to recognize this). The formal arguments we have examined in this chapter provide a basic framework for analysis of argument; Toulmin's approach and Aristotle's concept of the enthymeme will help us apply those logical principles to everyday reasoning.

THE ENTHYMEME

The **enthymeme,** as you will recall from Chapter 2, is an elliptical argument in which a premise (or sometimes a conclusion) is left unstated. It is left unstated because it seems obvious to the arguer or is clearly implied by the context of the argument. You are already a regular user of enthymemic argument, but you may find it occasionally difficult to analyze and evaluate enthymemes. If they are your own, their truth may seem inescapable; if they are others', their truth or falsity may be obscured by confusing prose. Enthymemes can be reconstructed as syllogisms for analysis, but often such syllogistic arguments appear in disguise. An enthymeme can be a single sentence with apparently too many terms for a syllogism and too few premises:

Jack Snopes: "I'm sure that Psychology 2312 will be an easy course, because Mr. Phillips, the instructor, is a great guy."

This must be an argument: One indicator is that the subordinating conjunction *because* is a verbal indicator (although not an infallible one) that a premise follows and a conclusion precedes it. Certainly the sentence asserts a judgment (that Psychology 2312 will be an easy course) on the basis of another statement (that Mr. Phillips, the instructor, is a great guy). The argument is a deductive one in that the conclusion is drawn out of, and offered as guaranteed by, the premises. But the argument appears to be invalid, with just one premise and as many as six terms: *I, Psychology 2312, easy courses, Mr. Phillips, instructors,* and *great guys.*

To reconstruct a syllogism from such unpromising material, you must work through several steps:

First, identify the conclusion—in this case, "I'm sure that Psychology 2312 will be an easy course." Rephrase the conclusion as a two-term statement linked by a *to be* verb. In our example, the "I'm sure" simply underscores Jack's belief in his conclusion and is not part of the conclusion itself, leaving us with "Psychology 2312 will be an easy course."

Second, having in this way established the major and minor terms ("easy courses" and "Psychology 2312"), look for the linking or "middle" term. If one category is "easy courses," another clearly is "courses taught by great guys." Mr. Phillips's course is a "course taught by a great guy": To mention Mr. Phillips by name is simply and unnecessarily to name the class twice.

Third, reconstruct the premises as two-term statements. In the example argument, one premise is implied but not actually stated: "All courses taught by great guys will be easy courses." The stated premise can be phrased as "Psychology 2312 will be a course taught by a great guy." For simplicity, you may change the form of the verb to present tense, and you may assign letters to designate each term. Here you will have:

All courses taught by great guys are easy courses.	All A are B.
Psychology 2312 is a course taught by a great guy [Mr. Phillips].	[All] C is A.
Therefore, Psychology 2312 is an easy course.	[All] C is B.

Fourth, apply the six rules or draw a diagram to test the syllogism's validity. Our example is valid, but Jack could be headed for trouble, because the truth of his assumption that "all courses taught by great guys will be easy courses" is questionable. When deductive argument is unsound, the fault often lies in what is taken for granted. Sometimes the assumption is factually dubious; sometimes the assumption is just what the arguer should be proving, but the question is begged. In evaluating any enthymeme, be particularly aware of the unstated parts of the argument.

The enthymeme usually centers on possibilities and probabilities rather than on certainties. We speak of "most artistic people" when we know we cannot speak of "all artistic people." We say that "usually employees are promoted on the basis of longevity" when we know that exceptions are sometimes made on the basis of merit or nepotism. Our conclusions are still acceptable and our arguments sound when our deductions are posed in terms of probabilities rather than certainties, *as long as those conclusions reflect exactly the same degree of uncertainty as the premises.* So, if Jordan is a long-term employee and promotions are forthcoming, we can conclude that *probably* she will be promoted. If most artistic people require periods of solitude, and all people who require periods of solitude are people with introspective natures, then we can safely conclude that *most* artistic people are people with introspective natures. The conclusion cannot reflect greater certainty than do the premises.

EXERCISE 8–5

Reconstruct valid syllogisms from the following enthymemes, following the procedure outlined above. Mark the stated premise, implied premise (or implied conclusion), stated conclusion, and the three terms.

1. Since scholarships should be awarded only on the basis of financial need, I don't think Stewart deserves one.
2. Children hate liver, so they shouldn't be forced to eat it.
3. Cynthia is assured of success in life—she just made Phi Beta Kappa.
4. All lying is wrong, so you shouldn't tell your roommate that you like those lavender bedspreads.
5. Chinese is the language spoken by the greatest number of people, so it should be the language of international trade and diplomacy.
6. "But, if virtue is a kind of knowledge, it is clear that it could be taught."　　　—Plato, *Meno* (trans. G. M. A. Grube)

7. All sports are competitive, and competitiveness leads to aggressive behavior in children. Since such behavior in children is to be discouraged, children should not participate in sports.

[Look for a syllogistic chain, or sorites, here: The conclusion of the first argument is a premise of the second.]

EXERCISE 8-6

Test the degree of probability in the conclusions of the following arguments (some of which are enthymemes) against the degree of probability in the premises. Change the qualifiers in the conclusions that seem overgeneralized or unnecessarily narrow.

1. Robert is probably a graduate of Purdue, since his car has a Purdue sticker on the rear window.
2. Because several of the children asked to see the movie again, I know that at least some of them enjoyed it.
3. High humidity, heavy cloud cover, and low barometric pressure often precede rain. Today we have all three conditions, so I know it will rain.
4. Studying hard makes passing the philosophy exam likely. I have studied hard, so there is a slim chance I will pass the philosophy exam.
5. People without jobs always vote against the current administration in a presidential election. Therefore, it is likely that the current administration will be defeated in the next election.
6. Because Mexico City is suffering from severe and ever-increasing pollution and overpopulation, the city is doomed to become an uninhabitable ghost town by the twenty-first century.
7. Since Jimmy Hoffa has been missing since 1975, he may be dead.

EXERCISE 8-7

Locate as many enthymemes as you can in the following paragraph from Clarence Darrow's *Crime and Criminals*. Reduce or expand each to a syllogism, and then evaluate each argument for soundness.

The only way in the world to abolish crime and criminals is to abolish the big ones and the little ones together. Make fair conditions of life. Give men a chance to live. Abolish the right of private ownership of land, abolish monopoly, make the world partners in production, partners in the good things of life. Nobody would steal if he could get something of his own some easier way. Nobody will commit burglary when he has a house full. No girl will go out on the streets when she has a comfortable place at home. The man who owns a sweatshop or a department store may not be to blame himself for the condition of his girls, but when he pays them five dollars, three dollars, and two dollars a week, I wonder where he thinks they will get the rest of their money to live. The only way to cure these conditions is by equality. There should be no jails. They do not accomplish what they pretend to accomplish. If you would wipe them out there would be no more criminals than now. They terrorize nobody. They are a blot upon any civilization, and a jail is an evidence of the lack of charity of the people on the outside who make the jails and fill them with the victims of their greed.

HYPOTHETICAL AND
ALTERNATIVE ARGUMENTS

The syllogisms and enthymemes we have looked at so far have all been **categorical** deductive arguments, that is, arguments concerned with establishing relationships among different classes of things. Two other common forms of deductive reasoning are **hypothetical** and **alternative** (or *disjunctive*) arguments. The former argues the outcome of hypothetical (If . . . then . . .) propositions; the latter argues for one alternative among two or more (Either . . . or . . .). The rules for hypothetical and alternative arguments are different from those governing categorical arguments, but even fewer in number.

A valid hypothetical syllogism takes one of two forms:

If A, then B.	If A, then B.
A.	Not B.
Therefore, B.	Therefore, not A.

In hypothetical propositions, the "if" clause is called the **antecedent,** and the "then" clause is called the **consequent.** Put into ordinary English, such arguments look something like this:

If today is Wednesday, [then] I must go to class.   (hypothesis)
    (antecedent)   (consequent)
Today is Wednesday.   (antecedent confirmed)
Therefore, I must go to class.   (consequent confirmed)

or

If today is Wednesday, [then] I must go to class.	(hypothesis)
(antecedent) (consequent)	
I do not have to go to class.	(consequent denied)
Therefore, today is not Wednesday.	(antecedent denied)

The argument that runs through your head after the alarm goes off may go something like the above, though it is more likely to resemble the first line of reasoning than the second. The two other possible versions of the argument are invalid and take one of these forms:

If A, then B.	If A, then B.
B.	Not A.
Therefore, A.	Therefore, not B.

Using the same hypothesis, "If today is Wednesday, I must go to class," the invalidity of these forms becomes evident:

If today is Wednesday, [then] I must go to class.	(hypothesis)
(antecedent) (consequent)	
I must go to class.	(consequent affirmed)
Therefore, today is Wednesday.	(antecedent affirmed)

or

If today is Wednesday, [then] I must go to class.	(hypothesis)
(antecedent) (consequent)	
Today is not Wednesday.	(antecedent denied)
Therefore, I need not go to class today.	(consequent denied)

The problem in the first argument is apparent: Just because the arguer must go to class does not necessarily imply that today is Wednesday, unless Wednesday is the only day the speaker's classes meet (and the hypothesis tells us nothing on that score). This illogical line of reasoning goes by the appropriate, if unimaginative, name of **fallacy of affirming the consequent.** It is in the second premise, which does affirm the consequent, that the argument goes astray. If we grant the truth of the hypothesis and of the consequent, we still cannot grant the truth of the antecedent on the basis of this argument.

The problem with the second argument is equally evident. It offers a hypothesis, denies the antecedent, and on that basis attempts to deny the consequent. But just because the antecedent is not true or does not happen does not necessarily prevent the consequent's being true or taking place. This line of reasoning succumbs to the **fallacy of denying the antecedent,** as you probably guessed.

Evaluating hypothetical arguments is relatively simple, then: There are but two terms to understand (antecedent and consequent) and but four ways to construct arguments from hypotheses, two valid and two invalid.

Alternative arguments are nearly as simple. They are "either . . . or . . ." arguments in which the arguer explores two or more alternatives and rejects all the possible alternatives but one:

Either A or B.	Either A or B.
Not A.	Not B.
Therefore, B.	Therefore, A.

Either A, B, or C.	Either A, B, C, or D.
Not A.	Not A.
Not B.	Not C.
Therefore, C.	Not D.
	Therefore, B.

All these examples, and any number of others, are valid. They share the characteristic that every given alternative but one is denied. They share as well a necessary assumption: At least one of the alternatives must be true. But they also share an assumption that may not seem necessary at first: More than one of the alternatives may be true; in fact, all the alternatives may be true. Therefore, when a friend says, "I will either move to Boston or go to graduate school," she is saying that she will definitely do one of the two—but she also may do both, if she enrolls at a graduate school in the Boston area.

Bear in mind that second logical possibility—that more than one alternative may turn out to be true—is the most difficult part of evaluating and creating disjunctive arguments. In ordinary conversation we tend to act as if all alternatives are mutually exclusive: Either your friend will move to Boston or she will go to graduate school, but not both. Unless mutual exclusivity is explicitly stated, a writer or speaker runs the risk of committing the **fallacy of affirming an alternative** (or disjunct):

Either A or B.		Either A or B.
A.	or	B.
Therefore, not B.		Therefore, not A.

You can repair the reasoning in such arguments by arguing between obviously contrary alternatives—alternatives that cannot both be true at the same time, as in "Either it is the day for the board meeting or it is not"—or by stating explicitly, "but not both": Either A or B, but not both. A. Therefore, not B. However, you must be positive that the alternatives *are* mutually exclusive, as in the following cases:

Either I will take my car to the carwash, or I will wash it here at home (but not both).
I am taking my car to the carwash.
Therefore, I have decided not to wash it at home.

Either I will wash my car or I will not wash my car.
I will wash my car.
(Therefore, I am not going to let it remain dirty.)

The problem in creating mutually exclusive and complete alternatives is, of course, the very real difficulty in making sure that you have considered all the possible alternatives. Sometimes disjunctive arguments oversimplify; they seem to imply that complex issues can be reduced to simple and limited alternatives. Arguments of this sort commit the fallacy of regarding issues as cut and dried, black and white. The people who make them forget about all the shades of gray—all the other possibilities. For example:

Either we increase defense spending or we surrender to the Russians.
We can't surrender to the Russians.
Therefore, we must increase defense spending.
[Are these our only options?]

Either Bill, Fred, or Lee should be the next editor of *The Daily Campus*.
Bill can't do the job next year, and Lee also has other commitments.
Therefore, Fred should be the next editor.
[But what about Meg, or Phil, or Charlotte? Other students besides those named might also be qualified.]

This is the **black or white** fallacy. Study "either . . . or . . ." arguments carefully. Do they consider all the possible alternatives?

EXERCISE 8–8

Are the following hypothetical and alternative arguments valid or invalid? If they are invalid, explain why.

1. Remember last year, when I said, "If we elect Marvin Vottler as mayor, we will overcome our city's fiscal difficulties"? Well, we didn't elect Vottler, and, sure enough, we haven't resolved our fiscal problems.
2. Either we have the party catered, we fix all the food ourselves, or we ask all the guests to bring covered dishes. We can't afford to have the party catered, and we don't have time or energy to fix all the

food ourselves. So, we'd better ask all the guests to bring covered dishes.

3. If Elizabeth is a spy, she will have a miniaturized camera.
   She is not a spy.
   Therefore, she does not have a miniaturized camera.

4. Either we move to a larger apartment or we get a smaller dog.
   We are getting a smaller dog.
   Therefore, we are not moving to a larger apartment.

5. If a student has freshly pressed clothes, freshly cut hair, and a poorly concealed look of panic, he or she must be a new freshman. You don't have the clothes, the haircut, or the look of panic—so you must not be a new freshman. Right?

6. The numbers of police officers will increase if the pay and working conditions are improved. The numbers have not increased, so we must conclude that the pay and working conditions have not improved.

7. As I see it, people who go into medicine either are anxious to make a lot of money or are concerned about people. My neighbor Dr. Georgia Bloom is anxious to make a lot of money, so I know she is not concerned about people.

8. If a newspaper prints something, it must be true. The newspaper did not print your story, so it must not be true.

9. Either Jesus is what he said he is or he was the biggest con man and liar of all time. He was not the biggest con man and liar of all time, so he must be what he said he is—the son of God.

10. If schizophrenia . . . turns out to have a biochemical cause and cure, schizophrenia would no longer be one of the diseases for which a person would be involuntarily committed.
    —Thomas Szasz, "The Crime of Commitment"
    (Supply a minor premise and conclusion drawn from this hypothesis.)

11. If the report is late, the deal is off. So the deal is off.

12. Either we remodel the office or we hire two additional employees. The remodeling can wait, but the need for more help won't. Therefore, we will hire two additional employees.

13. If you preserve both the body and a sculptured image of it, immortality is assured.
    —ancient Egyptian belief
    (Supply a minor premise and conclusion drawn from this hypothesis.)

14. "The [Lyndon] Johnson competence was not, of course, confined to domestic matters. If his own intelligence and experience were involved, he was equally good on foreign policy," as in the case of his decision to send grain to India.
    —John Kenneth Galbraith, from a review of Lyndon Johnson's *The Vantage Point*

15. In the late 1980s the federal government had to decide either to grant amnesty to illegal farm workers or to reduce agricultural acreage— or yield—significantly. No one wanted to reduce agricultural acreage or yield. So amnesty was granted to large numbers of illegal farm workers.

I have called deduction "a perfectly natural process of reasoning," but at this point it may seem to you to be anything but natural: a process involving unfamiliar terms and rules, and too many ways to go wrong. However, by the same token, if you have been playing tennis for many years, and a tennis-pro friend suddenly comments on your particular style of service, you may become so self-conscious for a short time that you double-fault every serve. But after you get over the initial awkwardness at having something pointed out to you that you were accustomed to doing without reflection, you will return to a successful and quite possibly improved serve. Your improvement will be all the more marked if your serve was poor to begin with, and no one had ever before told you what you were doing wrong.

As with tennis, so with argument? Not in all respects, of course, but you may be surprised to find that, if you have grasped the rules and relationships set out here, you will recognize similar processes of reasoning in the reading selections that follow. More, you will be able to judge in a specific and conscious way the readings and the arguments they contain, and to refute invalid arguments. Read the following selections first for enjoyment, and then you will enjoy all the more seeing how they use deductive reasoning to amuse you or to challenge your own opinions. If you agree with the arguments presented, you will now be able to say why; if you disagree, you will now have the tools with which to refute invalid arguments.

SHOULD WE ABOLISH THE PRESIDENCY?

Barbara Tuchman

1   Owing to the steady accretion of power in the executive over the last forty years, the institution of the Presidency is not now functioning as the Constitution intended, and this malfunction has become perilous to the state. What needs to be abolished, or fundamentally modified, I believe, is not the executive power as such but the executive power as exercised by a single individual.

2   We could substitute true Cabinet government by a directorate of six, to be nominated as a slate by each party and elected as a slate for a single six-year term with a rotating chairman, each to serve for a year as in the Swiss system. The Chairman's vote would carry the weight of two to avoid a tie. (Although a five-man Cabinet originally seemed preferable when I first proposed the plan in 1968, I find that the main departments of government, one for each member of the Cabinet to administer, cannot be rationally arranged under fewer than six headings—see below.)

3   Expansion of the Presidency in the twentieth century has dangerously altered the careful tripartite balance of governing powers established by the Constitution. The office has become too complex and its reach too extended to be trusted to the fallible judgment of any one individual. In today's world no one man is adequate for the reliable disposal of power that can affect the lives of millions—which may be one reason lately for the notable non-emergence of great men. Russia no longer entrusts policy-making to one man. In China governing power resides, technically at least, in the party's central executive committee, and when Mao goes the inheritors are likely to be more collective than otherwise.

4   In the United States the problem of one-man rule has become acute for two reasons. First, Congress has failed to perform its envisioned role as safeguard against the natural tendency of an executive to become dictatorial, and equally failed to maintain or even exercise its own rights through the power of the purse.

5   It is clear, moreover, that we have not succeeded in developing in this country an organ of representative democracy that can match the Presidency in positive action or prestige. A Congress that can abdicate its right to ratify the act of war, that can obediently pass an enabling resolution on false information and remain helpless to remedy the situation afterward, is likewise not functioning as the Con-

stitution intended. Since the failure traces to the lower house—the body most directly representing the citizenry and holding the power of the purse—responsibility must be put where it belongs: in the voter. The failure of Congress is a failure of the people.

6   The second reason, stemming perhaps from the age of television, is the growing tendency of the Chief Executive to form policy as a reflection of his personality and ego needs. Because his image can be projected before fifty or sixty or a hundred million people, the image takes over; it becomes an obsession. He must appear firm, he must appear dominant, he must never on any account appear "soft," and by some magic transformation which he has come to believe in, he *must* make history's list of "great" Presidents.

7   While I have no pretensions to being a psychohistorian, even an ordinary citizen can see the symptoms of this disease in the White House since 1960, and its latest example in the Christmas bombing of North Vietnam. That disproportionate use of lethal force becomes less puzzling if it is seen as a gesture to exhibit the Commander-in-Chief ending the war with a bang, not a whimper.

8   Personal government can get beyond control in the U.S. because the President is subject to no advisers who hold office independently of him. Cabinet ministers and agency chiefs and national-security advisers can be and are—as we have lately seen—hired and fired at whim, which means that they are without constitutional power. The result is that too much power and therefore too much risk has become subject to the idiosyncrasies of a single individual at the top, whoever he may be.

9   Spreading the executive power among six eliminates dangerous challenges to the ego. Each of the six would be designated from the time of nomination as secretary of a specific department of government affairs, viz:

1. Foreign, including military and CIA. (Military affairs should not, as at present, have a Cabinet-level office because the military ought to be solely an instrument of policy, never a policy-making body.)
2. Financial, including Treasury, taxes, budget, and tariffs.
3. Judicial, covering much the same as at present.
4. Business (or Production and Trade), including Commerce, Transportation, and Agriculture.
5. Physical Resources, including Interior, Parks, Forests, Conservation, and Environment Protection.
6. Human Affairs, including HEW, Labor, and the cultural endowments.

10   It is imperative that the various executive agencies be incorporated under the authority of one or another of these departments.

11   Cabinet government is a perfectly feasible operation. While this column was being written, the Australian Cabinet, which governs like the British by collective responsibility, overrode its Prime Minister on the issue of exporting sheep to China, and the West German Cabinet took emergency action on foreign-exchange control.

12   The usual objection one hears in this country that a war emergency requires quick decision by one man seems to me invalid. Even in that case, no President acts without consultation. If he can summon the Joint Chiefs, so can a Chairman summon his Cabinet. Nor need the final decision be unilateral. Any belligerent action not clearly enough in the national interest to evoke unanimous or strong majority decision by the Cabinet ought not to be undertaken.

13   How the slate would be chosen in the primaries is a complication yet to be resolved. And there is the drawback that Cabinet government could not satisfy the American craving for a father-image or hero or superstar. The only solution I can see to that problem would be to install a dynastic family in the White House for ceremonial purposes, or focus the craving entirely upon the entertainment world, or else to grow up.

Analysis of Barbara Tuchman, "Should We Abolish the Presidency?"

In this essay Barbara Tuchman argues for the replacement of the office and functions of president of the United States with a six-person cabinet in which all the former executive functions would be vested. Her thesis, carefully qualified, is stated in the first paragraph: "What needs to be abolished, or fundamentally modified, is . . . the executive power as exercised by a single individual." Her argument centers on the reasons for this proposal, reasons that are grounded first in the practicability and justness of a cabinet government in contrast to the abuses of power inevitable in an individual chief executive. Tuchman is not concerned with proving the existence of these abuses; she anticipates that her readers will agree with her basic assumptions.

To evaluate the argument properly, we must ferret out its specific assumptions and examine them. Two enthymemes are buried in the first sentence of Tuchman's essay. Working backward from the major conclusion, the thesis, and looking for the premises, both implicit and explicit, we can reconstruct the deductive arguments that form the foundation of Tuchman's essay:

The presidency was intended by the Constitution to be one of three *equal* branches of government.   (Implicit Premise)

The presidency is not now one of three *equal* branches of government.
                                                                        (Implicit Premise)

[Therefore,] the presidency is not now functioning as the Constitution intended.
                            (Stated Conclusion and Premise to Second Argument)

What does not function as the Constitution intended is perilous to the State and should be abolished or fundamentally modified.   (Implicit Premise)

[Therefore,] the presidency should be abolished or fundamentally modified.
                                    (Stated Conclusion and Thesis of Essay)

Some of the implicit statements, as is often the case, comprise the heart of the argument. The first implicit premise, that the executive was intended to be a branch of government equal in power to the Congress and the Supreme Court, is not controversial. Tuchman accordingly offers no lengthy support for this premise; but her "first justification" for abolishing the one-person presidency loosely supports the premise by advancing the argument that one person cannot well fulfill the Constitution's aims of equality for the executive branch. The second implicit premise—that the presidency is not equal to, but rather stronger than, the Congress— is subject to debate. Tuchman supports that premise with her "second justification," showing just how the president's power has come to be so disproportionately great. She may, however, beg the question of whether or not the power *is* disproportionately great. She offers but a single specific example of excessive power: President Nixon's authorization of the Christmas 1972 bombing of North Vietnam. And the decision to drop those bombs was made collectively with members of the cabinet and the military.

We might also have some trouble with the third implicit premise, forming part of the second argument in the chain: that what does not function as the Constitution intended is perilous to the State. The framers of the Constitution would marvel at half the functions of American government as we know it today. For example, the two-party political system, which emerged after the Constitution was adopted, is now integral to our governmental structure. Governments can and must mature and evolve as the world changes. Tuchman cannot assume that we will automatically grant this implicit part of her argument, on which much of the rest of it hangs.

If we do grant Tuchman's implicit premises and her conclusions, we must grant that her argument is sound (true premises logically linked); all that remains is to ask, "But replace the president with what?" The second paragraph provides Tuchman's answer to that question, and the balance of the essay offers her reasons. Except for its lack of a formal conclusion, the essay follows the divisions of a classical argument: The first two paragraphs introduce the writer's thesis; the third gives background and preparatory information; paragraphs 4 through 11 develop the points of the main argument (divided between attention to the problem, in paragraphs 4 through 8, and the solution, in paragraphs 9 through 11); and the last two paragraphs offer a refutation of the opposing viewpoints.

Loosely related to the first premise of the thesis argument, as noted above, is Tuchman's "first justification" that one-man rule is uncommon and unwise in the world today: "No one man is adequate for the reliable disposal of power that can affect millions." Tuchman illustrates her point with an analogy comparing the government of the United States to those of other countries, using as examples the governments of Russia and China. Since Russia and China are perceived by Americans as being more authoritarian than our own country, the analogy has an ironic force. We have more power vested in a single individual than do either of these countries, for Tuchman has been proven correct in her post-Mao prediction for China. Paragraphs 4 and 5 argue causally that the presidency got into trouble because the Congress became weak (no longer counterbalancing the presidency), and the Congress became weak because the citizens elected weak and unqualified representatives, and that therefore "the failure of [the presidency] is a failure of the people."

As a second justification for replacing the presidency with a six-member cabinet, Tuchman offers a second causal analysis: Television has inspired an obsession with "image" on the part of the chief executive; and the obsession with image has led in turn to policy making based on the image that policy projects, rather than its inherent worth or usefulness. Paragraph 7 argues what Tuchman sees as a consequence of this image-consciousness and focus on the individual character of the president. This single individual has no peers to assist him, no one who may not be fired at the president's whim. Stated as syllogisms, the problem is that

The U.S. president has no independent advisors.   (Stated Premise)

A president with no independent advisors is a president who has too much power.
                                                            (Implicit Premise)
The U.S. president has too much power.
                    (Stated Conclusion of First Argument; Premise of Second)
A president who has too much power presents too great a risk to the country.
                                                            (Stated Premise)

Therefore, the U.S. president [as the office now exists] presents too great a risk to the country.
                                                            (Implicit Conclusion)

The argument is valid. If it has any weakness, it is likely to lie in the implicit premise—is a president with no independent advisors automatically a president who has too much power? Surely his power must depend more directly on what has been granted by the provisions of the Constitution, and on the strength of Congress and the Supreme Court. If we find the premises to be true, however, we must grant the conclusion. The one-person presidency is dangerous.

A specific solution to the "dangerous challenges to the ego" inherent in a one-person executive is spelled out in paragraphs 9 and 10, in which Tuchman proposes six cabinet positions and indicates their respective responsibilities. In paragraph 11 she offers analogical support for leadership-by-committee by citing the successful cabinets of Australia and West Germany, which are empowered to overrule their respective prime ministers. Then, in paragraphs 12 and 13, Tuchman anticipates key objections to her plan and defends it against those objections. She offers no formal conclusion, but ends with a disjunctive enthymeme tinged with sarcasm: "The only solution I can see to that problem [the 'American craving for a father-image or hero or superstar'] would be to install a dynastic family in the White House for ceremonial purposes, or focus the craving entirely upon the entertainment world, or else to grow up." We need no prompting to see which of the three alternatives Tuchman regards as the only acceptable one.

QUESTIONS AND IDEAS FOR DISCUSSION

1. This essay was written (during the political upheaval that has been known almost from the beginning as "Watergate") in an attempt to offer a constructive solution to the problems created by the power vested in the presidency. How does Tuchman use definition to restrict her thesis?

2. Tuchman's solution to the problem of the presidency can be expressed as an alternative argument:

   The presidency must be administered either by an individual or by a group. It should not be administered by an individual. Therefore, it should be administered by a group.

   Based on the argument Tuchman gives, create a categorical syllogism that supports (and concludes with) the minor premise of the argument just given: "The presidency should not be administered by an individual."

3. "The problem of one-man rule has become acute for two reasons." What are those reasons? Is this a deductive argument? Explain.

4. "The usual objection one hears in this country that a war emergency requires quick decision by one man seems to me invalid." Examine Tuchman's argument refuting that objection. How does she use the word *invalid* here?

WE'LL NEVER CONQUER SPACE

Arthur C. Clarke

1   Man will never conquer space. Such a statement may sound ludicrous, now that our rockets are already 100 million miles beyond the
moon and the first human travelers are preparing to leave the atmosphere. Yet it expresses a truth which our forefathers knew, one we
have forgotten—and our descendants must learn again, in heartbreak
and loneliness.

2   Our age is in many ways unique, full of events and phenomena
which never occurred before and can never happen again. They distort our thinking, making us believe that what is true now will be
true forever, though perhaps on a larger scale. Because we have an-
nihilated distance on this planet, we imagine that we can do it once
again. The facts are far otherwise, and we will see them more clearly
if we forget the present and turn our minds towards the past.

3   To our ancestors, the vastness of the earth was a dominant fact
controlling their thoughts and lives. In all earlier ages than ours, the
world was wide indeed, and no man could ever see more than a tiny
fraction of its immensity. A few hundred miles—a thousand, at the
most—was infinity. Only a lifetime ago, parents waved farewell to
their emigrating children in the virtual certainty that they would
never meet again.

4   And now, within one incredible generation, all this has changed.
Over the seas where Odysseus wandered for a decade, the Rome-
Beirut Comet whispers its way within the hour. And above that, the
closer satellites span the distance between Troy and Ithaca in less
than a minute.

5   Psychologically as well as physically, there are no longer any
remote places on earth. When a friend leaves for what was once a far
country, even if he has no intention of returning, we cannot feel that
same sense of irrevocable separation that saddened our forefathers.
We know that he is only hours away by jet liner, and that we have
merely to reach for the telephone to hear his voice.

6   In a very few years, when the satellite communication network
is established, we will be able to see friends on the far side of the
earth as easily as we talk to them on the other side of the town.
Then the world will shrink no more, for it will have become a di-
mensionless point.

7   But the new stage that is opening up for the human drama will
never shrink as the old one has done. We have abolished space here
on the little earth; we can never abolish the space that yawns between the stars. Once again we are face to face with immensity and

must accept its grandeur and terror, its inspiring possibilities and its dreadful restraints. From a world that has become too small, we are moving out into one that will be forever too large, whose frontiers will recede from us always more swiftly than we can reach out towards them.

8   Consider first the fairly modest solar, or planetary, distances which we are now preparing to assault. The very first Lunik made a substantial impression upon them, traveling more than 200 million miles from the earth—six times the distance to Mars. When we have harnessed nuclear energy for spaceflight, the solar system will contract until it is little larger than the earth today. The remotest of the planets will be perhaps no more than a week's travel from the earth, while Mars and Venus will be only a few hours away.

9   This achievement, which will be witnessed within a century, might appear to make even the solar system a comfortable, homely place, with such giant planets as Saturn and Jupiter playing much the same role in our thoughts as do Africa or Asia today. (Their qualitative differences of climate, atmosphere and gravity, fundamental though they are, do not concern us at the moment.) To some extent this may be true, yet as soon as we pass beyond the orbit of the moon, a mere quarter-million miles away, we will meet the first of the barriers that will separate the earth from her scattered children.

10   The marvelous telephone and television network that will soon enmesh the whole world, making all men neighbors, cannot be extended into space. It will never be possible to converse with anyone on another planet.

11   Do not misunderstand this statement. Even with today's radio equipment, the problem of sending speech to the other planets is almost trivial. But the messages will take minutes—sometimes hours—on their journey, because radio and light waves travel at the same limited speed of 186,000 miles a second.

12   Twenty years from now you will be able to listen to a friend on Mars, but the words you hear will have left his mouth at least three minutes earlier, and your reply will take a corresponding time to reach him. In such circumstances, an exchange of verbal messages is possible—but not a conversation.

13   Even in the case of the nearby moon, the 2-½ second time-lag will be annoying. At distances of more than a million miles, it will be intolerable.

14   To a culture which has come to take instantaneous communication for granted, as part of the very structure of civilized life, this "time barrier" may have a profound psychological impact. It will be a perpetual reminder of universal laws and limitations against which

not all our technology can ever prevail. For it seems as certain as anything can be that no signal—still less any material—can ever travel faster than light.

15   The velocity of light is the ultimate speed limit, being part of the very structure of space and time. Within the narrow confines of the solar system, it will not handicap us too severely, once we have accepted the delays in communication which it involves. At the worst, these will amount to 20 hours—the time it takes a radio signal to span the orbit of Pluto, the outermost planet.

16   Between the three inner worlds of the earth, Mars, and Venus, it will never be more than 20 minutes—not enough to interfere seriously with commerce or administration, but more than sufficient to shatter those personal links of sound or vision that can give us a sense of direct contact with friends on earth, wherever they may be.

17   It is when we move out beyond the confines of the solar system that we come face to face with an altogether new order of cosmic reality. Even today, many otherwise educated men—like those savages who can count to three but lump together all numbers beyond four—cannot grasp the profound distinction between solar and stellar space. The first is the space enclosing our neighboring worlds, the planets; the second is that which embraces those distant suns, the stars, and it is literally millions of times greater.

18   There is no such abrupt change of scale in terrestrial affairs. To obtain a mental picture of the distance to the nearest star, as compared with the distance to the nearest planet, you must imagine a world in which the closest object to you is only five feet away—and then there is nothing else to see until you have traveled a thousand miles.

19   Many conservative scientists, appalled by these cosmic gulfs, have denied that they can ever be crossed. Some people never learn; those who 60 years ago scoffed at the possibility of flight, and ten (even five!) years ago laughed at the idea of travel to the planets, are now quite sure that the stars will always be beyond our reach. And again they are wrong, for they have failed to grasp the great lesson of our age—that if something is possible in theory, and no fundamental scientific laws oppose its realization, then sooner or later it will be achieved.

20   One day, it may be in this century, or it may be a thousand years from now, we shall discover a really efficient means of propelling our space vehicles. Every technical device is always developed to its limit (unless it is superseded by something better), and the ultimate speed for spaceships is the velocity of light. They will never reach that goal, but they will get very close to it. And then the nearest star will be less than five years' voyaging from the earth.

21   Our exploring ships will spread outwards from their home over an ever-expanding sphere of space. It is a sphere which will grow at almost—but never quite—the speed of light. Five years to the triple system of Alpha Centauri, 10 to the strangely-matched doublet Sirius A and B, 11 to the tantalizing enigma of 61 Cygni, the first star suspected to possess a planet. These journeys are long, but they are not impossible. Man has always accepted whatever price was necessary for his explorations and discoveries, *and the price of Space is Time.*

22   Even voyages which may last for centuries or millennia will one day be attempted. Suspended animation has already been achieved in the laboratory, and may be the key to interstellar travel. Self-contained cosmic arks which will be tiny traveling worlds in their own right may be another solution, for they would make possible journeys of unlimited extent, lasting generation after generation.

23   The famous Time Dilation effect predicted by the Theory of Relativity, whereby time appears to pass more slowly for a traveler moving at almost the speed of light, may be yet a third. And there are others.

24   Looking far into the future, therefore, we must picture a slow (little more than half a billion miles an hour!) expansion of human activities outwards from the solar system, among the suns scattered across the region of the galaxy in which we now find ourselves. These suns are on the average five light-years apart; in other words, we can never get from one to the next in less than five years.

25   To bring home what this means, let us use a down-to-earth analogy. Imagine a vast ocean, sprinkled with islands—some desert, others perhaps inhabited. On one of these islands an energetic race has just discovered the art of building ships. It is preparing to explore the ocean, but must face the fact that the very nearest island is five years' voyaging away, and that no possible improvement in the techniques of shipbuilding will ever reduce this time.

26   In these circumstances (which are those in which we will soon find ourselves) what could the islanders achieve? After a few centuries, they might have established colonies on many of the nearby islands and have briefly explored many others. The daughter colonies might themselves have sent out further pioneers, and so a kind of chain reaction would spread the original culture over a steadily expanding area of the ocean.

27   But now consider the effects of the inevitable, unavoidable time-lag. There could be only the most tenuous contact between the home island and its offspring. Returning messengers could report what had happened on the nearest colony—five years ago. They could never

bring information more up to date than that, and dispatches from the more distant parts of the ocean would be from still further in the past—perhaps centuries behind the times. There would never be news from the other islands, but only history.

28   All the star-borne colonies of the future will be independent, whether they wish it or not. Their liberty will be inviolably protected by Time as well as Space. They must go their own way and achieve their own destiny, with no help or hindrance from Mother Earth.

29   At this point, we will move the discussion on to a new level and deal with an obvious objection. Can we be sure that the velocity of light is indeed a limiting factor? So many "impassible" barriers have been shattered in the past; perhaps this one may go the way of all the others.

30   We will not argue the point, or give the reasons why scientists believe that light can never be outraced by any form of radiation or any material object. Instead, let us assume the contrary and see just where it gets us. We will even take the most optimistic possible case and imagine that the speed of transportation may eventually become infinite.

31   Picture a time when, by the development of techniques as far beyond our present engineering as a transistor is beyond a stone axe, we can reach anywhere we please instantaneously, with no more effort than by dialing a number. This would indeed cut the universe down to size and reduce its physical immensity to nothingness. What would be left?

32   Everything that really matters. For the universe has two aspects—its scale, and its overwhelming, mind-numbing complexity. Having abolished the first, we are now face-to-face with the second.

33   What we must now try to visualize is not size, but quantity. Most people today are familiar with the simple notation which scientists use to describe large numbers; it consists merely of counting zeroes, so that a hundred becomes 10^2, a million, 10^6, a billion, 10^9 and so on. This useful trick enables us to work with quantities of any magnitude, and even defense budget totals look modest when expressed as $\$5.76 \times 10^9$ instead of $\$5,760,000,000$.

34   The number of other suns in our own galaxy (that is, the whirlpool of stars and cosmic dust of which our sun is an out-of-town member, lying in one of the remoter spiral arms) is estimated at about 10^{11}—or written in full, 100,000,000,000. Our present telescopes can observe something like 10^9 other galaxies, and they show no sign of thinning out even at the extreme limit of vision.

35   There are probably at least as many galaxies in the whole of creation as there are stars in our own galaxy, but let us confine ourselves to those we can see. They must contain a total of about 10^{11}

times 10^9 stars, or 10^{20} stars altogether. 1 followed by 20 other digits is, of course, a number beyond all understanding.

36   Before such numbers, even spirits brave enough to face the challenge of the light-years must quail. The detailed examination of all the grains of sand on all the beaches of the world is a far smaller task than the exploration of the universe.

37   And so we return to our opening statement. Space can be mapped and crossed and occupied without definable limit; but it can never be conquered. When our race has reached its ultimate achievements, and the stars themselves are scattered no more widely than the seed of Adam, even then we shall still be like ants crawling on the face of the earth. The ants have covered the world, but have they conquered it—for what do their countless colonies know of it, or of each other?

38   So it will be with us as we spread outwards from Mother Earth, loosening the bonds of kinship and understanding, hearing faint and belated rumours at second—or third—or thousandth-hand of an ever-dwindling fraction of the entire human race.

39   Though Earth will try to keep in touch with her children, in the end all the efforts of her archivists and historians will be defeated by time and distance, and the sheer bulk of material. For the number of distinct societies or nations, when our race is twice its present age, may be far greater than the total number of all the men who have ever lived up to the present time.

40   We have left the realm of human comprehension in our vain effort to grasp the scale of the universe: so it must always be, sooner rather than later.

41   When you are next outdoors on a summer night, turn your head towards the zenith. Almost vertically above you will be shining the brightest star of the northern skies—Vega of the Lyre, 26 years away at the speed of light, near enough the point-of-no-return for us short-lived creatures. Past this blue-white beacon, 50 times as brilliant as our sun, we may send our minds and bodies, but never our hearts.

42   For no man will ever turn homewards from beyond Vega, to greet again those he knew and loved on the earth.

QUESTIONS AND IDEAS FOR DISCUSSION

1. Express Clarke's main argument as a syllogism with the conclusion, "Man will never conquer space." Is the argument sound?
2. Clarke acknowledges the probability of future space travel but para-

doxically denies the possibility of conquering space. The paradox is resolved by his restricted definition of *conquer*. Much of his argument hinges on the definitions of this and other key terms. What other words does Clarke restrict in meaning in order to prove his points?

3. Do you agree with Clarke's assertion that "if something is possible in theory, and no fundamental scientific laws oppose its realization, then sooner or later it will be achieved"? Evaluate his reasoning.

THE TELL-TALE HAT

Arthur Conan Doyle

1   I had called upon my friend Sherlock Holmes upon the second morning after Christmas, with the intention of wishing him the compliments of the season. He was lounging upon the sofa in a purple dressing-gown, a pipe-rack within his reach upon the right, and a pile of crumpled morning papers, evidently newly studied, near at hand. Beside the couch was a wooden chair, and on the angle of the back hung a very seedy and disreputable hard-felt hat, much the worse for wear, and cracked in several places. A lens and a forceps lying upon the seat of the chair suggested that the hat had been suspended in this manner for the purpose of examination.

2   "You are engaged," said I; "perhaps I interrupt you."

3   "Not at all. I am glad to have a friend with whom I can discuss my results. The matter is a perfectly trivial one" (he jerked his thumb in the direction of the old hat), "but there are points in connection with it which are not entirely devoid of interest and even of instruction."

4   I seated myself in his arm-chair and warmed my hands before the crackling fire, for a sharp frost had set in, and the windows were thick with the ice crystals. "I suppose," I remarked, "that, homely as it looks, this thing has some deadly story linked on to it—that it is the clew which will guide you in the solution of some mystery and the punishment of some crime."

5   "No, no. No crime," said Sherlock Holmes, laughing. "Only one of those whimsical little incidents which will happen when you have four million human beings all jostling each other within the space of a few square miles. Amid the action and reaction of so dense a swarm of humanity, every possible combination of events may be expected to take place, and many a little problem will be presented which may be striking and bizarre without being criminal. We have already had experience of such."

6   "So much so," I remarked, "that of the last six cases which I have added to my notes, three have been entirely free of any legal crime."

7   "Precisely. You allude to my attempt to recover the Irene Adler papers, to the singular case of Miss Mary Sutherland, and to the adventure of the man with the twisted lip. Well, I have no doubt that this small matter will fall into the same innocent category. You know Peterson, the commissionaire?"

8   "Yes."

9   "It is to him that this trophy belongs."

10   "It is his hat."

11   "No, no; he found it. Its owner is unknown. I beg that you will look upon it, not as a battered billycock, but as an intellectual problem. And, first, as to how it came here. It arrived upon Christmas morning, in company with a good fat goose, which is, I have no doubt, roasting at this moment in front of Peterson's fire. The facts are these: about four o'clock on Christmas morning, Peterson, who, as you know, is a very honest fellow, was returning from some small jollification, and was making his way homeward down Tottenham Court Road. In front of him he saw, in the gaslight, a tallish man, walking with a slight stagger, and carrying a white goose slung over his shoulder. As he reached the corner of Goodge Street, a row broke out between this stranger and a little knot of roughs. One of the latter knocked off the man's hat, on which he raised his stick to defend himself, and, swinging it over his head, smashed the shop window behind him. Peterson had rushed forward to protect the stranger from his assailants; but the man, shocked at having broken the window, and seeing an official-looking person in uniform rushing towards him, dropped his goose, took to his heels, and vanished amid the labyrinth of small streets which lie at the back of Tottenham Court Road. The roughs had also fled at the appearance of Peterson, so that he was left in possession of the field of battle, and also of the spoils of victory in the shape of this battered hat and a most unimpeachable Christmas goose."

12   "Which surely he restored to their owner?"

13   "My dear fellow, there lies the problem. It is true that 'For Mrs. Henry Baker' was printed upon a small card which was tied to the bird's left leg, and it is also true that the initials 'H. B.' are legible upon the lining of this hat; but as there are some thousands of Bakers, and some hundreds of Henry Bakers in this city of ours, it is not easy to restore lost property to any one of them."

14   "What, then, did Peterson do?"

15   "He brought round both hat and goose to me on Christmas morning, knowing that even the smallest problems are of interest to me. The goose was retained until this morning, when there were signs that, in spite of the slight frost, it would be well that it should be eaten without unnecessary delay. Its finder has carried it off, therefore, to fulfil the ultimate destiny of a goose, while I continue to retain the hat of the unknown gentleman who lost his Christmas dinner."

16   "Did he not advertise?"

17   "No."

18   "Then, what clew could you have as to his identity?"

19   "Only as much as we can deduce."

20   "From his hat?"

21   "Precisely."

22   "But you are joking. What can you gather from this old battered felt?"

23   "Here is my lens. You know my methods. What can you gather yourself as to the individuality of the man who has worn this article?"

24   I took the tattered object in my hands and turned it over rather ruefully. It was a very ordinary black hat of the usual round shape, hard, and much the worse for wear. The lining had been of red silk, but was a good deal discolored. There was no maker's name; but, as Holmes just remarked, the initials "H.B." were scrawled upon one side. It was pierced in the brim for a hat-securer, but the elastic was missing. For the rest, it was cracked, exceedingly dusty, and spotted in several places, although there seemed to have been some attempt to hide the discolored patches by smearing them with ink.

25   "I can see nothing," said I, handing it back to my friend.

26   "On the contrary, Watson, you can see everything. You fail, however, to reason from what you see. You are too timid in drawing your inferences."

27   "Then, pray tell me what it is that you can infer from this hat?"

28   He picked it up and gazed at it in the peculiar introspective fashion which was characteristic of him. "It is perhaps less suggestive than it might have been," he remarked, "and yet there are a few inferences which are very distinct, and a few others which represent at least a strong balance of probability. That the man was highly intellectual is of course obvious upon the face of it, and also that he was fairly well-to-do within the last three years, although he has now fallen upon evil days. He had foresight, but has less now than formerly, pointing to a moral retrogression, which, when taken with the decline of his fortunes, seems to indicate some evil influence, probably drink, at work upon him. This may account also for the obvious fact that his wife has ceased to love him."

29   "My dear Holmes!"

30   "He has, however, retained some degree of self-respect," he continued, disregarding my remonstrance. "He is a man who leads a sedentary life, goes out little, is out of training entirely, is middle-aged, has grizzled hair which he has had cut within the last few days, and which he anoints with lime-cream. These are the more patent facts which are to be deduced from his hat. Also, by-the-way, that it is extremely improbable that he has gas laid on in his house."

31   "You are certainly joking, Holmes."

32   "Not in the least. It is possible that even now, when I give you these results, you are unable to see how they are attained?"

33   "I have no doubt that I am very stupid; but I must confess that I am unable to follow you. For example, how did you deduce that this man was intellectual?"

34   For answer Holmes clapped the hat upon his head. It came right over the forehead and settled upon the bridge of his nose. "It is a question of cubic capacity," said he; "a man with so large a brain must have something in it."

35   "The decline of his fortunes, then?"

36   "This hat is three years old. These flat brims curled at the edge came in then. It is a hat of the very best quality. Look at the band of ribbed silk and the excellent lining. If this man could afford to buy so expensive a hat three years ago, and has had no hat since, then he has assuredly gone down in the world."

37   "Well, that is clear enough, certainly. But how about the foresight and the moral retrogression?"

38   Sherlock Holmes laughed. "Here is the foresight," said he, putting his finger upon the little disk and loop of the hat-securer. "They are never sold upon hats. If this man ordered one, it is a sign of a certain amount of foresight, since he went out of his way to take this precaution against the wind. But since we see that he has broken the elastic, and has not troubled to replace it, it is obvious that he has less foresight now than formerly, which is a distinct proof of a weakening nature. On the other hand, he has endeavored to conceal some of these stains upon the felt by daubing them with ink, which is a sign that he has not entirely lost his self-respect."

39   "Your reasoning is certainly plausible."

40   "The further points, that he is middle-aged, that his hair is grizzled, that it has been recently cut, and that he uses lime-cream, are all to be gathered from a close examination of the lower part of the lining. The lens discloses a large number of hair-ends, clean cut by the scissors of the barber. They all appear to be adhesive, and there is a distinct odor of lime-cream. This dust, you will observe, is not the gritty, gray dust of the street, but the fluffy brown dust of the house, showing that it has been hung up in-doors most of the time; while the marks of moisture upon the inside are proof positive that the wearer perspired very freely, and could, therefore, hardly be in the best of training."

41   "But his wife—you said that she had ceased to love him."

42   "This hat has not been brushed for weeks. When I see you, my

dear Watson, with a week's accumulation of dust upon your hat, and when your wife allows you to go out in such a state, I shall fear that you also have been unfortunate enough to lose your wife's affection."

43   "But he might be a bachelor."

44   "Nay, he was bringing home the goose as a peace-offering to his wife. Remember the card upon the bird's leg."

45   "You have an answer for everything. But how on earth do you deduce that the gas is not laid on in his house?"

46   "One tallow stain, or even two, might come by chance; but when I see no less than five, I think that there can be little doubt that the individual must be brought into frequent contact with burning tallow—walks up-stairs at night probably with his hat in one hand and a guttering candle in the other. Anyhow, he never got tallow-stains from a gas-jet. Are you satisfied?"

47   "Well, it is very ingenious," said I, laughing; "but since, as you said just now, there has been no crime committed, and no harm done, save the loss of a goose, all this seems to be rather a waste of energy."

48   Sherlock Holmes had opened his mouth to reply, when the door flew open, and Peterson, the commissionaire, rushed into the apartment with flushed cheeks and the face of a man who is dazed with astonishment.*

QUESTIONS AND IDEAS FOR DISCUSSION

1. Express the following argument as a syllogism, and evaluate its soundness.

   "But his wife—you said that she had ceased to love him." "This hat has not been brushed for weeks. When I see you, my dear Watson, with a week's accumulation of dust upon your hat, and when your wife allows you to go out in such a state, I shall fear that you also have been unfortunate enough to lose your wife's affection."

2. Pose another three of Holmes's arguments as syllogisms and evaluate them. Is the reasoning consistently deductive? Is it consistently sound? If not, is there any pattern to the kind of error in reasoning committed? Discuss Holmes's reasoning.

3. At one point Holmes rebukes Watson: "On the contrary, Watson, you can see everything. You fail, however, to reason from what you see. You are too timid in drawing your inferences." Can we agree with Holmes's judgment here? Explain.

*But to find out just *why* Peterson is dazed with astonishment, you must read the rest of "The Blue Carbuncle" in *The Sign of Four.*

THE LOGIC LESSON, OR MY CAT SOCRATES

Eugene Ionesco

In this scene from Act I of Ionesco's play *Rhinoceros*, two conversations are in progress simultaneously at terrace tables outside a cafe on the square in a small French town. One, between the fastidiously attired Jean and his disheveled, hung-over friend Berenger, concerns the nature of existence; the other, between an elegant old gentleman and a man "with a little grey moustache, an eyeglass, and wearing a straw hat," who has introduced himself as a logician, concerns the nature of reason. The two separate conversations, heard in tandem, offer telling and frequently hilarious comments on each other. Here we see logic at its most illogical.

LOGICIAN: [*to the* OLD GENTLEMAN] Here is an example of a syllogism. The cat has four paws. Isidore and Fricot both have four paws. Therefore Isidore and Fricot are cats.

OLD GENTLEMAN: [*to the* LOGICIAN] My dog has got four paws.

LOGICIAN: [*to the* OLD GENTLEMAN] Then it's a cat.

BERENGER: [*to* JEAN] I've barely got the strength to go on living. Maybe I don't even want to.

OLD GENTLEMAN: [*to the* LOGICIAN, *after deep reflection*] So then logically speaking, my dog must be a cat?

LOGICIAN: [*to the* OLD GENTLEMAN] Logically, yes. But the contrary is also true.

BERENGER: [*to* JEAN] Solitude seems to oppress me. And so does the company of other people.

JEAN: [*to* BERENGER] You contradict yourself. What oppresses you—solitude, or the company of others? You consider yourself a thinker, yet you're devoid of logic.

OLD GENTLEMAN: [*to the* LOGICIAN] Logic is a very beautiful thing.

LOGICIAN: [*to the* OLD GENTLEMAN] As long as it is not abused.

BERENGER: [*to* JEAN] Life is an abnormal business.

JEAN: On the contrary. Nothing could be more natural, and the proof is that people go on living.

BERENGER: There are more dead people than living. And their numbers are increasing. The living are getting rarer.

JEAN: The dead don't exist, there's no getting away from that!. . . . Ah! Ah. . . . ! [*He gives a huge laugh.*] Yet you're oppressed by them, too? How can you be oppressed by something that doesn't exist?

BERENGER: I sometimes wonder if I exist myself.

JEAN: You don't exist, my dear Berenger, because you don't think. Start thinking, then you will.

LOGICIAN: [*to the* OLD GENTLEMAN] Another syllogism. All cats die. Socrates is dead. Therefore Socrates is a cat.

OLD GENTLEMAN: And he's got four paws. That's true. I've got a cat named Socrates.

LOGICIAN: There you are, you see . . .

JEAN: [*to* BERENGER] Fundamentally, you're just a bluffer. And a liar. You say that life doesn't interest you. And yet there's somebody who does.

BERENGER: Who?

JEAN: Your little friend from the office who just went past. You're very fond of her!

OLD GENTLEMAN: [*to the* LOGICIAN] So Socrates was a cat, was he?

LOGICIAN: Logic has just revealed the fact to us.

JEAN: [*to* BERENGER] You didn't want her to see you in your present state. [BERENGER *makes a gesture.*] That proves you're not indifferent to everything. But how can you expect Daisy to be attracted to a drunkard?

LOGICIAN: [*to the* OLD GENTLEMAN] Let's get back to our cats.

OLD GENTLEMAN: [*to the* LOGICIAN] I'm all ears.

BERENGER: [*to* JEAN] In any case, I think she's already got her eye on someone.

JEAN: Oh, who?

BERENGER: Dudard. An office colleague, qualified in law, with a big future in the firm—and in Daisy's affections. I can't hope to compete with him.

LOGICIAN: [*to the* OLD GENTLEMAN] The cat Isidore has four paws.

OLD GENTLEMAN: How do you know?

LOGICIAN: It's stated in the hypothesis.

BERENGER: [*to* JEAN] The Chief thinks a lot of him. Whereas I've no future, I've no qualifications. I don't stand a chance.

OLD GENTLEMAN: [*to the* LOGICIAN] Ah! In the hypothesis.

JEAN: [*to* BERENGER] So you're giving up, just like that . . .?

BERENGER: What else can I do?

LOGICIAN: [*to the* OLD GENTLEMAN] Fricot also has four paws. So how many paws have Fricot and Isidore?

OLD GENTLEMAN: Separately or together?

JEAN: [*to* BERENGER] Life is a struggle, it's cowardly not to put up a fight!

LOGICIAN: [*to the* OLD GENTLEMAN] Separately or together, it all depends.

BERENGER: [*to* JEAN] What can I do? I've nothing to put up a fight with.

JEAN: Then find yourself some weapons, my friend.

OLD GENTLEMAN: [*to the* LOGICIAN, *after painful reflection*] Eight, eight paws.

LOGICIAN: Logic involves mental arithmetic, you see.

OLD GENTLEMAN: It certainly has many aspects!

BERENGER: [*to* JEAN] Where can I find the weapons?

LOGICIAN: [*to the* OLD GENTLEMAN] There are no limits to logic.

JEAN: Within yourself. Through your own will.

QUESTIONS AND IDEAS FOR DISCUSSION

1. What is the flaw in the Logician's syllogisms?

   The cat has four paws.   All cats die.
   Isidore and Fricot both have four   Socrates is dead.
   paws.   Therefore, Socrates is a cat.
   Therefore, Isidore and Fricot are cats.

2. Reconstruct Jean's enthymeme, below, as a syllogism.

   "You don't exist, my dear Berenger, because you don't think. Start thinking, then you will."

3. Evaluate and comment on Jean's argument that "nothing could be more natural [than life], and the proof is that people go on living."

SONNET FOR A PHILOSOPHER

Anonymous

"In categorical syllogisms," my logic professor said,
"Universal affirmatives distribute their subject terms only;
Thus," he said, "If 'All men are mortal,' the statement
Applies to all men but does not encompass mortality.
Or take another case: Sherman said 'War is Hell.'
The statement applies to all wars, but does not exhaust
The possibilities of Hell. Thus, Hell is not War."
He may be right. But I wanted to ask how many
Wars he's been to and how many other possibilities
Of Hell he could conceive. I didn't ask.
It would have been something less than
A universal affirmative. "All men are
Mortal" is a safe example, well distributed.
Only the logical mind escapes mortality and the
predicated Hell that is War.

QUESTIONS AND IDEAS FOR DISCUSSION

1. The anonymous author of this poem argues the limitations of logic. Are his or her objections well-founded? Can you answer them?
2. Does the logic professor's statement—"Thus, Hell is not War"—follow inevitably from the rules for distribution of terms? Think about the statement in light of the discussion of predication in Chapter 5.

SUGGESTIONS FOR WRITING AND
FURTHER DISCUSSION

1.   But I wanted to ask how many
Wars he'd been to and how many other possibilities
Of Hell he could conceive.   —"Sonnet for a Philosopher"
Write an essay that "conceives other possibilities of Hell" than that proposed by the author of "Sonnet for a Philosopher"—an essay that argues that Hell can take another form as well. Focus on a kind of experience, with particular examples, that was or can be hellish.

2. Here is the situation: You have found a down ski jacket in the front seat of your unlocked car. It is navy, size 42, and is marked with the insignia of a famous line of expensive ski wear, but the label has been removed from the back of the neckline and carefully resewn along the front waist seam. The lining of one sleeve is almost ripped out, and the jacket, although otherwise showing little wear, is filthy. Take these details, add whatever else you might "observe," and deduce the identity of the owner, after the manner of Sherlock Holmes.

3. "On the contrary, Watson, you can see everything. You fail, however, to reason from what you see. You are too timid in drawing your inferences."   —Sherlock Holmes

   Write an essay in which you describe something or someone you have seen (perhaps an old man who sits on a bench at your bus stop every day, or a package abandoned under a tree near the library, or a letter left unopened on your roommate's dresser) and "reason from what you see."

4. Listen to the generalizations you and the people around you use in a day. Write an essay, addressed to an audience of your peers, in which you oppose the use or defend the necessity of broad generalizations. Consider this the question: Can we function without generalization? You may find it helpful to review the discussion of stereotyping in Chapter 2 and the discussion of generalizing from particulars in Chapter 7.

5. "Logic is a very beautiful thing. . . . There are no limits to logic."
                                                        —Ionesco, *Rhinoceros*

   Write an essay, either supporting or opposing the Logician's claim, for an audience of your rhetoric classmates that holds the opposite viewpoint. Your observations and writing so far in the course should provide you with examples to back up your contentions.

6. ". . . the great lesson of our age [is] that if something is possible in theory, and no fundamental scientific laws oppose its realization, then sooner or later it will be achieved."   —Arthur Clarke

   Construct an essay with a conditional deductive framework in which Arthur Clarke's hypothesis, above, is the major premise. The "something" that he argues eventually will be achieved is travel to the stars. Your "something" might be the cloning of human life, a worldwide international government, robot housekeepers, the elimination of cancer, the three-minute mile, or some other theoretical possibility. Any source material you use to support your case must be documented appropriately.

7. Write an essay, addressed to Barbara Tuchman, in which you refute her argument in "Should We Abolish the Presidency?" or offer a solution to the problems of the presidency that is different from hers.

9

Fallacies

"Will you walk into my parlor?" said the spider to the fly;
'Tis the prettiest little parlor that ever you did spy."

Mary Howitt, "The Spider and the Fly"

WHY STUDY FALLACIES?

Fallacies are arguments gone awry. Most of the time we think of fallacious arguments as intentionally deceptive, but that view is oversimplified. Not every user of fallacies intends to ensnare the unwary in a sticky web of lies. Many fallacious arguments result from carelessness or mistakes on the arguer's part; so to say that fallacies are "lies" is not always fair. On the other hand, to call fallacies "errors in reasoning" connotes lack of intention, and fallacies can be deliberate, as the fly in the poem learns to her sorrow. No matter what their genesis, however, our primary consideration in evaluating arguments containing fallacies is not the degree of intention or innocence in the arguer but rather the logical effect the fallacies have on the argument and the emotional effect they have on us, the audience.

Were we exclusively creators of arguments, and not also receivers of them, there might be little need to discuss fallacies. We could concentrate only on the positive aspects of how to develop an argument, and not worry about the negative aspects of how arguments fall apart or mislead us or try to gain our assent by playing on our emotions. But we are audience as well as author; and even as well-intentioned authors of argument we are susceptible to mistakes in reasoning.

All the same, won't identifying and studying fallacies permit the unscrupulous to use them more effectively, or tempt the scrupulous to do likewise? Perhaps, but if enough people become aware of fallacies and how they persuade, fewer people will be able to get away with using fallacies to deceive. We will never be completely invulnerable to fallacious appeals, of course; we are susceptible on an emotional level even to appeals that we regard skeptically. Jeffrey Schrank's essay "The Language of Advertising Claims" (included in the readings for this chapter) has this caution for the overconfident:

> Although few people admit to being greatly influenced by ads, surveys and sales figures show that a well-designed advertising campaign . . . works below the level of conscious awareness and it works even on those who claim immunity to its message. Ads are designed to have an effect while being laughed at, belittled, and all but ignored.

In examining fallacies and their role in persuasion, we will look particularly at fallacies in advertising and in political rhetoric, for those two arenas provide many examples of fallacious argument. But we will examine, too, the role of fallacies in everyday life and everyday conversation. Max Shulman's "Love Is a Fallacy" offers a tongue-in-cheek look at the fallacy of trying to apply logic to love. And magazine advertisements illustrate the use of fallacious emotional appeals in place of reason to sell products.

KINDS OF FALLACIES

Fallacies are of two basic kinds. The first kind we have examined in Chapters 7 and 8: **formal fallacies**. Formal fallacies are errors in the *form* of the argument, the relationships drawn among premise statements and between premises and conclusion. Post hoc reasoning is an inductive formal fallacy, for example, and guilt by association is a deductive formal fallacy. Most formal fallacies are **non sequiturs** (in Latin, "does not follow"), because their conclusions do not logically follow from the premises. Where a more precise problem can be identified, however, it is best to identify it as such in order that it might be precisely remedied.

FORMAL FALLACIES

The fallacies identified and discussed in Chapters 7 and 8 are listed below, with page references.

INDUCTIVE FALLACIES

False Analogy	comparison offered as proof	p. 216
Post Hoc	false or partial cause	p. 221
Hasty Generalization	inadequate sampling	p. 226
Gambler's Fallacy	assumes trends reverse themselves	p. 226

DEDUCTIVE FALLACIES

Equivocation	two terms masquerading as one	p. 259
Tautology	one term masquerading as two	p. 259
Guilt by Association	undistributed middle term	p. 259
Overgeneralization	generalization from particular premise	p. 260
Affirming Consequent	*then* true, therefore *if* true	p. 268
Denying Antecedent	*if* false, therefore *then* false	p. 268
Affirming an Alternative	forgets that *or* can imply *and*	p. 269
Black or White	no possibility of multiple options	p. 270

The second basic kind of fallacy results from problems of accuracy or relevance in the statements themselves. Since such fallacies have to do more with the content or "matter" of the argument than with the formal relationships among statements, such fallacies are called **material fallacies**. Many material fallacies are, either deliberately or inadvertently, **red herrings**. That is, the statements and arguments offered are irrelevant to the issue at hand and draw the arguers, like bloodhounds distracted by a smelly fish, off the scent.

Fallacies, like both fish and garden plants, sometimes go by several names. The black-or-white fallacy and the false dilemma, for example, are two names for the same problem, just as vinca and periwinkle are the same plant—and in both the logical and botanical realms we fall back on Latin nomenclature when the common English names proliferate too rapidly. The important thing is not so much to memorize a list of names for fallacies but rather to understand the underlying problem that a given fallacy demonstrates. The name provides only a verbal shorthand for reference.

The common fallacies we will examine in this chapter have been grouped together as fallacious assumptions, appeals, attacks, distortions, and dodges. Most of these fallacies (except for the fallacious assumptions) are material fallacies. Therefore, we will be particularly on guard against irrelevant arguments and inaccurate premises and conclusions.

ASSUMPTIONS

Fallacious assumptions are at the core of many fallacious arguments. When we make unwarranted assumptions, taking for granted what really needs to be supported with evidence and arguments, we **beg the question**. As we discussed briefly in Chapter 8, to beg the question is to assume what we should be proving, or to take for granted what our audience may not be ready to grant us. If a political candidate declares, "You can count on me to work to increase our nation's military strength," some listeners may be thinking, "Does our military strength *need* to be increased?" The candidate has begged that question, treating it as settled when to the audience the question is anything but settled. In so doing, the candidate creates a fallacious argument, one based on possibly unsound premises.

Begged questions frequently are hidden in the unwritten premises of enthymemic arguments. For example, someone wrote in a letter to our local morning paper, "Because he is a Democrat, Ted Kennedy would be a president concerned about the needs of the people." The unstated premise here is "All Democrats are concerned about the needs of the people." Some readers may question that assumption, and the letter writer has begged the question. Young Democrats might not be bothered; John Birchers would be. We have to make some assumptions in argument, but we much consider both our subject and our audience in order to avoid assuming too much and so begging important questions.

Fallacious assumptions take several forms. Most basic of all is the unsupported and unwarranted assertion, such as that made by the politician promising to increase military strength. "Of course, we all love tapioca" is another such assertion, as is "All property owners are responsible citizens." Other fallacious, question-begging assumptions are made in statements of circular reasoning and in loaded phrases and complex questions.

Circular Reasoning

A circular argument literally goes nowhere; it uses the conclusion as a premise, often in different words. "I can't lose weight because I'm too fat to exercise" is a circular argument; it claims, "I'm too fat because I'm too fat," although not in so many words. Or take the argument, "We can't justify paying public school teachers more because we can't get good teachers." Higher pay might *attract* better teachers and enable the school systems to keep their good teachers. Spelled out more explicitly, the argument says, "We can't pay public school teachers more [in order to attract good teachers] because we can't attract good teachers [without more pay]." Here we go 'round the mulberry bush.

Loaded Phrases

The adjective and noun phrases used to describe the subject of an argument can be telling. When a person is identified as a thief, a liar, a child snatcher, or a bum, we are expected to accept the judgment implicit in that label as well as whatever action is predicated. For example, if citizen Jones says, "That lying socialist Wanda Morgan wants to bankrupt our country," how do we reply? If we say, "Really? How do you know she wants to bankrupt the country?" we have tacitly granted the truth of the loaded phrase "lying socialist." Jones has begged the question of Morgan's membership in the Socialist party and just how and when and about what she told lies.

The following contain loaded phrases:

A caring mother loves her children enough to stay home with them, to provide the full-time nurture that is essential to a defenseless child's well-being.

That idiot Thompson thinks that if he plants his vegetable garden in February, he'll have that many more months to enjoy homegrown vegetables.

Of course, those deluded liberals who advocate a welfare state will support the candidacy of Shannon Maguire.

Complex Questions

The complex, or loaded, question combines at least two questions, with the answer to at least one of them assumed by the questioner to be true. The classic example of the loaded question is "Have you stopped beating your wife?" To answer either yes or no validates the assumption that "you have beaten your wife in the past." The question is really two questions—"Have you beaten your wife?" and "If so, have you now stopped beating her?"—with the first question begged. Here are other loaded questions:

What is Barry's problem, anyway?

What kind of car do you want to buy for me, Dad?

What dessert are we having tonight?

APPEALS

Fallacious appeals are directed to our sentiments, our sympathies, our snobberies, and our respect for famous or authoritative names. The appeals we will examine here are the appeal to popular sentiments, snob appeal, the bandwagon fallacy, the fallacious appeal to pity, and the fallacious appeal to authority. Bear in mind that the appeals to pity and to authority have legitimate uses in argument as well as the fallacious uses on which we will center our attention here. The appeal to pity can stir people to help war orphans and flood victims, for instance, and the appeal to legitimate authorities speaking within their fields of expertise provides useful inductive support for an argument.

Appeal to Popular Sentiments

The *ad populum* appeal, the appeal to popular sentiments, uses emotional and noncontroversial topics to win assent from an audience without having to confront substantive issues. It consists of verbal flag waving—celebrations of motherhood, apple pie, education, freedom, independence, and the Common Man (and, presumably, Woman)—and it is a favorite of some politicians and preachers. Patriotism is a desirable quality, certainly, but it is vulnerable to abuse: "Patriotism and pride are what make our country great. Vote for Matt Edwards and continue that great tradition." This fallacy is structurally a red herring, distracting the reader or listener from the realization that no argument has been advanced to justify the claim. Just what are Matt Edwards's qualifications, and what makes voting for him such a patriotic act? Or take appeals to buy "the all-American widget, Pro-Ace" or "Grandma's Cookies." What makes a product "all-American," anyway, and how does being American-made assure its quality and desirability? One suspects that no real grandmother oversees the cooking of "Grandma's Cookies," any more than elves bake a competing brand. Anything "natural" sells these days, but just what does "natural" mean when the ingredients include ethoxylated mono- and di-glycerides, calcium sulfate, and potassium bromate?

A quick look through political and charitable solicitations adds many ad populum appeals (to *American* values) to this small sampling. Some examples:

Making decent, affordable health care available to all Americans is the Gray Panthers' highest priority.
—Gray Panthers Project Fund solicitation

The people at HALT [Help Abolish Legal Tyranny] . . . have served notice on the legal profession. It is time to bring the legal system closer to the people, HALT members say.
—California lawyer quoted in HALT solicitation

If you have any doubts about becoming a member, just remember that every day that passes means 4,400 more American babies are killed by abortion.
—National Right to Life Committee, Inc., solicitation

Your immediate tax-deductible contribution will help us defend and preserve reproductive freedoms on *many fronts* while continuing our national programs of service and education.
—Planned Parenthood Federation of America, Inc., solicitation

Snob Appeal

If the ad populum appeal is the fallacious appeal to the biases of Average People, the appeal to snobbery is, in the words of Professor Hugh Rank, the appeal to the "Best" People. (In turn, the next fallacy we will discuss, the Bandwagon, Rank calls the appeal to the Most People.) Snob appeal always involves premises irrelevant to the conclusion, but the appeal is strong: Use this product and you, too, can be Successful, Elegant, and Rich Beyond Your Dreams—or at least pretend to be! Now, purchasing a particular brand of sherry or dress shirt in no way leads to success unless the people we want to impress are buying the fallacy as well. A rash of "Dress for Success" books has capitalized on the fact that many people believe that appearance *is* reality—so much so that looking successful and having all the right snobbish accoutrements can inspire the confidence of other people and in turn lead to real "success" as defined by possessions and income. The emotional appeal of this fallacy cannot be overestimated—it sells a tremendous amount of imported carbonated water at $1.00 or so a bottle to otherwise sensible people.

Although in advertising much snob appeal is based on material possessions, the fallacy occurs in intellectual appeals as well. And then there is the curious case of the reverse snob—"I'm just a plain and simple person"—but he or she is really appealing to the popular attitudes of the Average Person, and committing an ad populum fallacy.

Bandwagon Fallacy

If everybody's doing it, that's reason enough: Jump on the bandwagon. Simmons can cheat on his income tax because "everybody does." Businesspeople wear long-sleeved shirts in Atlanta in the broiling hot summer because "everybody does." Some people go to college only because "everybody does." Or buy products because so many have been sold: Seven million people can't be wrong, right? If all these people have bought video cassette recorders, I'd better buy one, too.

There is a converse to this fallacy: "Nobody does" or "it just isn't done." Perhaps it is time they should! At least, they should consider the possibility. To say that beginning instructors at one university can't be paid a living wage because "nobody does" [pay that wage] is to offer no reason at all. If we require precedents for everything, we advocate inertia.

The bandwagon fallacy, or appeal to what "most people" think, is a question-begging fallacy in that it affects the form as well as the substance of an argument—as is evident from a tired student's attempt to avoid too much mental strain in developing an essay rebutting another's argument: "Let us begin by assuming that the third premise is correct, seeing that it is most commonly believed to be true." And the fallacy has unshakable hold on politicians, as professional poll taker George Gallup noted in 1944. His words apply just as well today:

> The bandwagon theory is one of the oldest delusions of politics. It is a time-honored custom for candidates in an election to announce that they are going to win. The misconception under which these politicians labor is that a good many people will vote for a man regardless of their convictions just to be able to say that they voted for the winner.
> —Quoted in Charles W. Roll and Albert H. Cantril,
> *Polls: Their Use and Misuse in Politics*

Gallup's experience was that in voting matters the bandwagon appeal has relatively little effect. But no politician will ever believe that claim.

Fallacious Appeal to Pity

The appeal to pity, which also goes by the lofty Latin name of *ad misericordiam*, is an evasive tactic. Arguers appealing to their readers' or listeners' pity do not present an argument to justify their assertions; they instead offer a hard-luck story designed to make the readers feel sorry for them. Of all fallacies, the appeal to pity may be the hardest to resist, particularly when the problems are indeed touching and the difficulties real. And, as noted earlier, the appeal to pity has its legitimate uses. Why else but for pity would anyone become a blood or organ donor or do volunteer work? The appeal to pity is unacceptable, however, when the premises function as excuse or self-justification and are really irrelevant to the conclusion.

I hope you will forgive my pointing out that *ad misericordiam* is a favorite fallacy of students who have done poorly on papers or exams. You know the litany: "I couldn't concentrate on the test because my dog died last week and my girlfriend just walked out on me." Or, "If I don't pass this course, I'll lose my scholarship and have to dig ditches for the rest of my life." Of course, the fallacious appeal to pity is hardly restricted to the academic sphere. Here are some examples from other fields:

> "I have spent all my adult life working for you in the State Senate. I have not gotten rich at the taxpayers' expense. Be loyal to one who has been loyal to you; vote for me once again."

"Don't yell at me for not getting the report out on time. My cat ran away last week and I've been too brokenhearted to concentrate on my work."

"Give me the job—I need it more than do the other applicants."

Fallacious Appeal to Authority

As discussed in Chapter 4, authorities speaking in their fields of expertise are useful sources to the writers of argument; we can call out the big guns to support our theses. But however venerable an authority Julia Child may be on the matter of how to poach salmon in a light broth, we will not call upon her to support our arguments on the illegal poaching of baby seals. Nor ought we to rely on the authority of people who play the roles of doctors on daytime television to help us decide which brand of aspirin to buy. Be wary of any appeals to the authority of individuals referred to simply as "Dr. So-and-so." That degree might be a Ph.D. in mechanical engineering, education, medicine—or it might have been purchased from a diploma mill. Dr. Blank, the mechanical engineer, can provide authoritative testimony about the strength of a dam or a bridge; Dr. Bland, the professor of education, may have expertise in early childhood cognitive skills; and Dr. Black, the M.D., may be able to support our argument about bacteria. But we will not cite Dr. Blank on cures for the common cold, Dr. Bland on the ability of a building to resist hurricane-force winds, or Dr. Black on the best methods for teaching children to read. And we will not cite Dr. Blarney, the graduate of the diploma mill, in support of any argument whatsoever.

ATTACKS

If an appeal won't do the trick, many an unscrupulous arguer will try an attack instead. The two most common forms of verbal attack are the *ad hominem* and *tu quoque* personal attacks and the appeal to force—the threat.

Personal Attack

If you can't think of a good response to an argument, you may be tempted to undermine the credible persona of the arguer with a personal attack. Reasonable people attempt not to attack the arguer instead of the argument, of course, but we all have our weak moments. Luckily for those with a sense of fair play, intelligent audiences are rarely sidetracked for long by an attack on the opposing team, and most find such attacks offensive even when they are not themselves the targets. Unfortunately, however, the more emotional the subject, the less likely that reason will figure in the discussion of it. Abortion is such an issue, about which both sides are prone to attack the character of the proponents of the other side, rather than to attempt to offer reasoned arguments. Gun control is another issue concerning which personal attacks often replace reason. Politicians who are caught in close races or who are trailing in the polls also tend to shift from a discussion of issues to a discussion of the opponent's bad character and dubious friends. Rhetoricians still call the fallacy by its Latin name, *ad hominem* ("against the man"), and the personal counterattack by its Latin name, *tu quoque* ("you're another").

Some examples of personal attacks and counterattacks:

The chief executive officer of the largest company with which we compete was thrown out of college for cheating on a Spanish exam. I wouldn't buy his product if I were you.

How can you speak so smugly in favor of gun control? I know for a fact that you didn't report some of your income last year. You should clean up your own affairs before you involve yourself in other people's.

Dr. Cohen's family counseling can't be worth much. He's been divorced.

Threats

The threat, whether veiled or direct, is antithetical to logical argument. It is the verbal equivalent of a fist to the jaw or a gun jammed against the ribs. The writer who resorts to threats strays about as far from reason as it is possible to go. Reasonable writers resort to threats only when appeals to reason have proven fruitless; they may then write, "I'll see you in court." Unreasonable writers resort to threats much more readily. Such a person might write, "The note I'm holding on your last venture comes due this month, doesn't it? Heard you are having a little cash flow problem at the moment. Hope we can work something out. By the way, my nephew Sylvester would like to talk to you about a job with your company. I'm confident you can find a good place for him." A less subtle individual might tape a note to a neighbor's door: "If you want to stay healthy, you'll keep your dog out of my yard." Taken to extremes, threats occur in such particularly ugly forms as blackmail or extortion.

DISTORTIONS

Distortions or exaggerations do to arguments what those wavy mirrors at carnivals do to your appearance. The mirrors can make your head appear long and misshapen, much too large for your body. Your arms seem to hang down to your ankles. You become, in the mirror's contorted reflection, ridiculous. Distortions of arguments work in just this way to refute caricatured versions of assertions and arguments while claiming to refute the assertions and arguments themselves.

Exaggeration

Often called the *straw man* fallacy, exaggerations of premises and conclusions readily make even a sound and sensible argument appear ridiculous. The metaphor of the straw man is apt: A man of straw, however big, is much easier to knock down than is a real flesh-and-blood human being. But some will dress up the man of straw to masquerade as a real person, then knock down the straw man, and finally declare the real man—not the straw surrogate—to be vanquished.

For example, consider this argument against the Equal Rights Amendment:

The advocates of the E.R.A. want their children brought up by strangers because they believe all women should work outside the home. They want their daughters to fight on the front lines in military action and be forced to use co-ed public restrooms. They want to emasculate men. Surely we must oppose this irrational amendment.

The writer of this argument has exaggerated the potential effects of the E.R.A. beyond what is either intended or likely to happen as a result of the amendment's adoption. By making the issue appear ridiculous through exaggeration, the writer makes the straw version of the E.R.A. argument easy to refute.

Oversimplification

Instead of building up an exaggerated man of straw, oversimplification reduces the straw man to a limp skeletal structure that can be leveled with a puff. Oversimplifying an argument can make it appear silly or unsubstantial; in either event oversimplification constitutes fallacious distortion of the real argument. Typically, crucial premises or crucial qualifications are omitted. Instead of identifying all the reasons why many people advocate generating nuclear energy for fuel, an oversimplified argument ignores all but one or two reasons: "The proponents of nuclear energy development just want to save money. That's all that concerns them." Another such argument might run along these lines: "Organizations that enable dying children to fulfill their last wish, perhaps to go to Disneyland or to meet Michael Jackson, can help only a handful of the terminally ill children in this country. Since they reach so few, they should not be supported." True, these organizations can help only a small proportion of children directly, but this argument oversimplifies the good achieved through creating public awareness of killing

and crippling diseases (an awareness often followed by increased donations for research) and inspiring hope in many more children and their
families than just those few who go to Disneyland. The realization that
people care is powerful medicine.

Trivial Objections

A third form of distortion singles out poorly chosen examples or
minor premises, challenges them, and then claims that the entire argument has been refuted. Consider the following trivial objections:

This textbook can't be any good. It has a chartreuse cover, and what student is
going to take seriously a book with a chartreuse cover?

I have decided not to marry Vince. I just don't like that beard.

We are canceling the subscription to your magazine that our nephew gave us for
Christmas. For a science-oriented magazine to send out gift cards illustrated
with eight-pointed snowflakes (when real snowflakes are hexagonal) is a sure
sign that it cannot be relied upon for accuracy.

A cover does not make a textbook, a beard does not make a man, and an
eight-pointed snowflake on a Christmas card does not prove that a magazine is not to be trusted for scientific accuracy!

DODGES

Like distortions, dodges are ways of refusing to deal with the real issue.
Dodges shift responsibility for logical proof away from the writer. We
will look at three kinds of dodges: (1) If nothing or no one shows that I
am wrong, then I am right. (2) I have stated my position; so if I am wrong,
it is up to you to prove it. (3) If you are challenging my position logically
and successfully, then what I first said has been misinterpreted. When I
said X, actually I meant Y. The first dodge is the refuge of the lazy as
well as the disreputable: the lack of contrary evidence. Rather than offer
proof, the arguer claims the absence of disproof. The second dodge similarly challenges reader or audience by shifting the burden of proof. And
the third is a verbal weasel, shifting ground in the argument, modifying
what has been claimed while pretending that the argument remains un-
changed and has been merely misinterpreted.

Lack of Contrary Evidence

Logically, flawed or inadequate evidence set forth to support one
conclusion is not bolstered by the inadequacy or absence of evidence to

the contrary. Examples of fallacious reasoning that overlook this simple truth abound:

Of course we should go ahead with the McClusky Project; nobody has voiced any objections to it.

It is going to rain tomorrow, because the sky is overcast and none of the tele-vision weather forecasters has said it will not rain.

Shifting Burden of Proof

"Here is my assertion. If it is wrong, you prove it." This kind of dodge, if the writer gets away with it, allows the writer to avoid the real work of reasoning. The best kind of response to this fallacy is to challenge the hypothesis—"if it is wrong, you prove it"—by demanding that the person making the assertion offer reasoning and evidence in its support. If the hypothesis itself is not challenged, the writer can offer a valid conditional argument as "proof" of the contention:

If the assertion is wrong, you show me how.	If A, then B.
You cannot show me how the assertion is wrong.	Not B.
Therefore, the assertion is right.	Therefore, not A.

The form of this argument is valid, but the hypothesis is unsound. Here are some unsound hypotheses that attempt to shift the burden of proof:

I'm going to hire Ben. Why shouldn't I?

Imprisonment turns amateurs into professional, hardened criminals. Anyone who disagrees has some work to do in order to prove that incarceration does not have this effect.

The theory of natural selection is unsound, and it is doubtful that anyone can make a convincing case for it.

Shifting Ground

Shifting ground is a deliberate evasive tactic to which some writers and speakers resort when they realize their argument has been success-fully challenged or even refuted. They simply declare that they never made quite the claim that has been challenged, and then modify their position to something less shaky: "I never actually claimed X; I meant Y." "I didn't say I couldn't help you on the project; I just can't help you *at this time.*"

This fallacy is not committed only in response to challenges, for occasionally writers who are either careless or unsure of the strength of their position will shift ground in the middle of their argument. This kind of shift occurs most often when writers really have not thought through what they intend to advocate. In this way a writer might begin to argue in favor of adding a plus or minus designation (with corresponding numerical values) to each letter grade at Alta College, and then decide in midargument that such a system might well lower most students' grade point averages. It would be tempting to alter the essay's controlling idea at that point, shifting ground to the position that "really, plusses and minuses should appear on the transcript but should not be figured into the numerical grade point equivalents." If compelled to make such a change, the writer is also compelled to revise the thesis stated earlier and any inconsistencies in the argument that develops the thesis.

DETECTING FALLACIES

Fallacious arguments often bother us even before we know exactly why, or what label to assign them. When asked, "Have you stopped trying to annoy Professor Wiggins?" we respond huffily, "Who ever said I *was* trying to annoy her?" The reply goes right to the heart of the fallacy, a complex question. We are not taken in by the argument, "Don't take Professor Slocum's class; he's gay. Or Mr. Schneider's; he's Jewish." Sometimes, however, the fallacy is so subtle or complex that we accept it, perhaps reluctantly, not quite sure that the reasoning makes sense, yet not quite sure that it is wrong. It is in this dusky area that the study of fallacies proves most enlightening, in order that we need not puzzle too long over the arguments by a master of fallacy as well as of logic:

"In boxing and other kinds of fighting, skill in attack goes with skill in defence, does it not?"
"Of course."
"So, too, the ability to save from disease implies the ability to produce it undetected, while ability to bring an army safely through a campaign goes with ability to rob the enemy of his secrets and steal a march on him in action."
"I certainly think so."
"So a man who's good at keeping a thing will be good at stealing it."
"I suppose so."
"So if the just man is good at keeping money safe, he will be good at stealing it too."
"That at any rate is the conclusion the argument leads to."
"So the just man turns out to be a kind of thief."
—Plato, *The Republic*, trans. H. D. P. Lee

At one time this line of reasoning might have left us scratching our heads, aware that the argument goes awry but not quite sure how or where, but no more: The faulty analogy, non sequitur, shift in ground, and overgeneralization are obvious. A just man is not like a doctor, a soldier, or a banker in every respect, although the class of just people may contain members of the other three classes. A man who is good at keeping a thing is not always good at stealing it; the latter ability does not follow necessarily from the former. Nor is "a man who is good at keeping a thing" synonymous with "a just man." And the conclusion overgeneralizes from the preceding assertion that the just man "will be good at stealing" to a conclusion that he necessarily *will* steal. The argument sounds logical but is completely fallacious.

Stalking fallacies can be challenging and even entertaining. Many fallacies, once you are able to recognize them confidently, will strike you as absurdly funny. The hunt can even become an armchair sport; you can fill a bulletin board with your trophies without the taxidermy expense big game hunters face. Here are a few specimens from my own collection:

In civilized society, personal merit will not serve you so much as money will. Sir, you may make the experiment. Go into the street and give one man a lecture on morality, and another a shilling, and see which will respect you most.
—Samuel Johnson

We evolved because of change.
—Student Essay

I have given my answer; if it is wrong, it is your job to refute it.
—Socrates

Discussion in class . . . means letting twenty young blockheads and two cocky neurotics discuss something that neither their teacher nor they know.
—Vladimir Nabokov

For if life has no meaning, then we would have no vision of life and life would have no purpose, because life would be void.
—Student Essay

Even if you do not know the names of the fallacies demonstrated by these statements, you should now recognize their logical shortcomings. What problems do you see?

EXERCISE 9–1

Most of the following sentences and passages contain fallacies described in Chapters 7, 8, or 9. Identify the primary fallacy in each. Which assertions and arguments, if any, are *not* fallacious?*

*I am indebted to my colleagues, Tony Howard, of Collin County College, and Virginia Oram, of Richland College, for suggesting several of these examples.

1. South Africa has been charged with human rights violations, yet the only rights its communist neighbors offer are the right to be shot and the right to starve.
   —Student Essay

2. Ladies and gentlemen of the jury, you have convicted Snake Mason on five counts of murdering kindergarten children. But before you decide to send him to the electric chair, consider his poor mother, who is dependent solely on him, and his wife, who at this moment is in labor with twins at the county hospital. How can you leave them bereft of his support and comfort?

3. The governor's speech was filled with political rhetoric, sheer empty promises. And to think that at this university instructors actually teach a course in rhetoric! It's disgraceful.

4. After spending one semester in Reed College, Alison Smith dropped out and joined a bizarre religious cult. Obviously Reed exerts a poor influence on young people.

5. Final examinations should be eliminated because they are not worth taking.

6. Our church does not use the Nicene Creed because at one point it states that "we believe in one holy, catholic, and Apostolic Church." And we're not Catholic; we're Protestant.

7. To the editors: The attempt to blame the Middle East conflict on the PLO in your editorial of April 14 lacks perception and understanding. The PLO is recognized by over 110 nations in the world as the legitimate representative of the Palestinians—Israel is recognized by maybe 50 nations at best.

   Israel has perpetrated terror, disenfranchised the Palestinians from their land, and has capriciously [sic] taken U.S. taxpayer dollars to promote its racist policies.
   —Letter to Editor, *Dallas Morning News*, 26 Apr. 1983

8. You can drown on a tablespoon of water, so it follows that you should not drink the stuff.

9. Russell lives across the street from his uncle. Consequently the two have developed a warm relationship.
   —Student Essay

10. He is a genius because, without an education, he can cope well in society.
    —Student Essay

11. In your opinion, which of the following will be the biggest threat to the country in the future—big business, big labor, or big government?
    —*Gallup Poll of Public Opinion, 1981,*
    Scholarly Resources, Inc.

12. Babies are like puppies in many respects. Both are small and cute and apparently helpless. But babies, like puppies, are more capable than we realize. If you toss a puppy in the water, it will dogpaddle

instinctively; by the same token, the best way to teach a baby to swim is simply to toss him or her in the water.

13. According to Jane Fonda, the current U.S. policy regarding nuclear weapons is unsound. Therefore, we should change it.

14. If truth is on our side, the task should not be too formidable. If truth is not on our side, then our critics are right and we are wrong, advertising is wrong, business is wrong, and America is wrong. I, for one, am convinced that America is right.

> —Roy E. Larson, of Time, Inc., in a speech to the Association of National Advertisers, 1961; in *Speaking of Advertising*, ed. John S. Wright and Daniel S. Warner

15. I see no difference between a man killing a chicken and a man killing a human being, by overwork and forcing ghetto conditions upon him, both so that he can eat a little better. If you can justify killing to eat meat, you can justify the conditions of the ghetto. I cannot justify either one.   —Dick Gregory, *The Shadow That Scares Me*

16. You claim that everybody wants to adopt, escort, or be [singer] Whitney Houston. I hope not. This lady is no role model for today's youth. She is a smoker, dresses in skintight clothes in her videos, and, on the cover of her new record, appears in unbuttoned jeans.

> —Letter to *Time*, 3 Aug. 1987

17. There is no reason why women should not be drafted. Therefore, they should be.

18. One of the past U.S. Presidents was a pipe-puffer who picked several other pipe-puffers to sit in his cabinet. It was not surprising when his administration made a shambles of the economy.

> —Rhoda Nichter, *Yes, I Do Mind if You Smoke*

19. "All men are created equal" does not mean that all men are the same. What it does mean is that each should be accorded full respect and full rights for his humanity *and* for his differences from other people.

> —Margaret Mead and Rhoda Metreux, *A Way of Seeing*

20. To the editor: I was appalled to read in the 1983 Statistical Abstracts of the United States that 98 percent of American households own at least one TV set, 88 percent of which are color. Since 12 percent of American households live below the poverty level, 8 percent of the people we consider to be living in poverty have TV sets. Isn't it time we redefine the word "poverty"? Thirty years ago, only the rich had TVs; now we owe everyone a set.

Even worse is that the average daily viewing time is 6.7 hours. I resent working 8–10 hours a day to finance the social programs that pay for these items of idle entertainment. While these people waste seven hours a day vegetating in front of the tube, they could be doing constructive labor. And don't give me the "no jobs" argument. Any boss will gladly pay the same as a TV does for seven hours of your time.   —Letter to the Editor, *Dallas Morning News*, 26 Apr. 1983

21. How can the federal government expect to make any significant headway in reducing the demand for illegal drugs when the drug addiction that kills more U.S. citizens annually than all the illegal drugs combined is legal, socially accepted, and subsidized by federal tax dollars? I am referring, of course, to tobacco addiction. Mr. President, if you are serious about fighting dangerous drugs, I would suggest that you start at the top of the list.

—Letter to *USA Today,* 11 Aug. 1986

22. Parents who allow others to care for their children do so in order to be free of their responsibility.

—Student Essay

23. St. Louis—A man who supports his family by scavenging for food and cans to sell says passage of a bill banning people from rummaging through garbage bins will force him into crime. . . . "If you don't let us go through trash, what are we going to do for an honest living?" Swanigan, 43, said.

—UPI report, 25 March 1984

24. If male-only or female-only clubs were harmful, they would have been banned already.

—Student Essay

25. The insurance industry wants your money—and your rights [through getting legislatures to limit the amount of jury awards in lawsuits]. . . . These are the choices our legislators face: protect insurance profits—or protect our jury system and the rights of victims to be compensated for the harm done them.

—"Hands Up!" brochure from the Texas Trial Lawyers Association

---

EXERCISE 9-2

Read the following newspaper columns, looking for reasonable arguments and fallacies in both. Identify the fallacies you find. Which contains more fallacious claims? Then, in a paragraph or two, discuss ways of making one of the two positions more reasonable: What would you take out or rephrase? What points would you add?

In 1968, I was an organizer of the first protest against the Miss America Pageant. We were angry that women were being judged for how they looked, not who they were—and that their bodies were being commercialized.

Nothing has changed. This pageant, like all the others, is still exploiting women as much as ever. It is a silly, irrelevant, destructive anachronism.

What do women walking down a runway in bathing suits have to do with the real way women are living their lives? Bloody little.

Most people know that. When I travel around the country, I don't find any huge sentimental attachment to the pageant. It's like the hoop skirt—people don't take it seriously. Among younger women, it's an incredibly corny joke.

But in a sense, we'd be better off if people did take it seriously. Other pageants are more blatant, but they all send the same message: Men are judged by who they are and what they do; women are judged by what they look like. Women are sexual objects; their bodies are all that's of interest.

That is the message of pornography, and beauty pageants are simply the flip side of the pornographic coin.

The Miss America Pageant and *Penthouse* are the same in their basic sexism. And they need each other to survive: The pornographic sensibility needs a virginal image to violate. The pageant needs pornographers to sell the fresh-cheeked, wholesome image of American womanhood as a sexual fantasy.

It is also a fundamentally conservative fantasy. As a myth of sexual purity and prudery, of wholesome family values, the pageant becomes a kind of super-patriotism. Winners travel around the world to visit the troops and give pep talks to American boys to fight and die for the fatherland.

That's why some people got so upset about Vanessa Williams: She violated the American Legion fantasy of purity.

But these fantasies have no relevance to the lives of ordinary women, who are concerned with child care, equal opportunity, economic survival, and not being raped in the streets. Discrimination in education, jobs, and income is still rampant. That's why some young women enter beauty pageants in the first place; they tend to come from lower-middle-class backgrounds and need the scholarship money.

We'd all be better off if these pageants didn't exist. Creating the plastic woman and then selling her on television is a ridiculous waste of time.

But I have to admit mild amusement at the latest Miss America-*Penthouse* "scandal." Pageant officials are wringing their hands in public, but they're probably delighted at the publicity. *Penthouse* and the pageant—they're a marriage made in heaven, and they deserve each other.

—Robin Morgan, "Pageants are sexist, silly and destructive,"
USA Today, Sept. 14, 1984

The Miss America Pageant exploits women? That's a ridiculous statement on the face of it.

Any organization that provides $4.25 million annually in scholarship money, the largest source of scholarship money for women in the world—and that provides opportunity for some 80,000 young women a year—can hardly be called exploitive.

It's been said by some that if one were to use the word "exploit," the shoe would be on the other foot. It is the young women who exploit the Miss America Pageant, and we solicit that.

Is the swimsuit competition sexist? No. If young women in swimsuits are sexist, then thousands of women on America's beaches are sexist. If the critics had their way, we'd have to close every beach in America.

Physical fitness, poise under trying conditions—I would hardly regard those things as sexist. Sexism, just as in pornography, is just in the eye of the beholder.

And to say that we judge only on beauty shows gross ignorance of what actually happens at the Miss America Pageant. The judges are fully instructed that what we seek is not an ideal—not the girl next door or even a role model.

The judges, all of whom are experts in a variety of fields, are asked to judge a young woman not only in beauty, which is only one facet of a human being, but in intelligence, articulation [sic], poise, and grace.

Our contestants are no different from other young women. We carefully explain that we're not trying to present Miss America as someone unattainable, on top of Mt. Olympus, but as someone within the reach of anyone—a goal anyone can aspire to.

And we don't, as some critics charge, insist on outdated standards of virtue. In fact, we don't insist on any whatsoever, except some very obvious things. For example, you must never have been married, and you must never have been convicted of a crime. In any job interview, you'd be asked questions like that and far worse.

People sometimes misunderstand us because they see only the two-hour telecast. That is merely the climax showcase, and you can't convey our philosophical message fully in such a short time.

We provide opportunities for tens of thousands of young women. In my 33 years of experience, I've found that when you have been Miss Whatever, the doors open for you. There's not a job, a profession, or an occupation that is not ably filled by young women who have competed at some time.

Other pageants do exploit young women—through entrance fees, charges for franchises, and so forth. If people understand this, they wouldn't lump us together under one generic term: beauty pageants.

—Albert Marks, Jr., "Our pageant sexist? Don't be ridiculous,"
USA Today, Sept. 14, 1984

EXERCISE 9-3

Read the letters to the editor of your local or campus newspaper for several days. Analyze the frequency of different patterns of reasoning: analogy, examining particulars, enthymemes, and so on. Which kinds of reasoning occur most often? Give examples. Then look for fallacies. Which kinds occur most often? Again, give examples.

EXERCISE 9-4

Rewrite one logically flawed letter to the editor of your local or campus newspaper, attempting to eliminate the fallacies while preserving the point of view and conclusion reached by the original letter writer. Comment on any special problems you encounter in making the improvements.

THE CHECKERS SPEECH

Richard M. Nixon

1   My Fellow Americans: I come before you tonight as a candidate for the Vice Presidency and as a man whose honesty and integrity have been questioned.

2   The usual political thing to do when charges are made against you is to either ignore them or to deny them without giving details.

3   I believe we've had enough of that in the United States, particularly with the present Administration in Washington, D. C. To me the office of the Vice Presidency of the United States is a great office, and I feel that the people have got to have confidence in the integrity of the men who run for that office and who might obtain it.

4   I have a theory, too, that the best and only answer to a smear or to an honest misunderstanding of the facts is to tell the truth. And that's why I'm here tonight. I want to tell you my side of the case.

5   I am sure that you have read the charge and you've heard that I, Senator Nixon, took $18,000 from a group of my supporters.

6   Now, was that wrong? And let me say that it was wrong—I'm saying, incidentally, that it was wrong and not just illegal. Because it isn't a question of whether it was legal or illegal, that isn't enough. The question is, was it morally wrong?

7   I say that it was morally wrong if any of that $18,000 went to Senator Nixon for my personal use. I say that it was morally wrong if it was secretly given and secretly handled. And I say that it was morally wrong if any of the contributors got special favors for the contributions that they made.

8   And now to answer those questions let me say this:

9   Not one cent of the $18,000 or any other money of that type ever went to me for my personal use. Every penny of it was used to pay for political expenses that I did not think should be charged to the taxpayers of the United States.

10   It was not a secret fund. As a matter of fact, when I was on "Meet the Press," some of you may have seen it last Sunday—Peter Edson came up to me after the program and he said, "Dick, what about this fund we hear about?" And I said, Well, there's no secret about it. Go out and see Dana Smith, who was the administrator of the fund. And I gave him his address, and I said that you will find

that the purpose of the fund simply was to defray political expenses that I did not feel should be charged to the Government.

11   And third, let me point out, and I want to make this particularly clear, that no contributor to this fund, no contributor to any of my campaigns, has ever received any consideration that he would not have received as an ordinary constituent.

12   I just don't believe in that and I can say that never, while I have been in the Senate of the United States, as far as the people that contributed to this fund are concerned, have I made a telephone call for them to an agency, or have I gone down to an agency in their behalf. And the record will show that, the records which are in the hands of the Administration. . . .

13   And so now what I am going to do—and incidentally this is unprecedented in the history of American politics—I am going at this time to give to this television and radio audience a complete financial history; everything I've earned; everything I've spent; everything I owe. And I want you to know the facts. I'll have to start early.

14   I was born in 1913. Our family was one of modest circumstances and most of my early life was spent in a store out in East Whittier. It was a grocery store—one of those family enterprises. The only reason we were able to make it go was because my mother and dad had five boys and we all worked in the store.

15   I worked my way through college and to a great extent through law school. And then, in 1940, probably the best thing that ever happened to me happened, I married Pat—sitting over here. We had a rather difficult time after we were married, like so many of the young couples who may be listening to us. I practiced law; she continued to teach school. I went into the service.

16   Let me say that my service record was not a particularly unusual one. I went to the South Pacific. I guess I'm entitled to a couple of battle stars. I got a couple of letters of commendation but I was just there when the bombs were falling and then I returned. I returned to the United States and in 1946 I ran for the Congress.

17   When we came out of the war, Pat and I—Pat during the war had worked as a stenographer and in a bank and as an economist for a Government agency—and when we came out the total of our savings from both my law practice, her teaching and all the time that I was in the war—the total for that entire period was just a little less than $10,000. Every cent of that, incidentally, was in Government bonds.

18   Well, that's where we start when I go into politics. Now what have I earned since I went into politics? Well, here it is—I jotted it down, let me read the notes. First of all I've had my salary as a Congressman and as a Senator. Second, I have received a total in this

past six years of $1,600 from estates which were in my law firm at the time that I severed my connection with it.

19   And, incidentally, as I said before, I have not engaged in any legal practice and have not accepted any fees from business that came into the firm after I went into politics. I have made an average of approximately $1,500 a year from nonpolitical speaking engagements and lectures. And then, fortunately, we've inherited a little money. Pat sold her interest in her father's estate for $3,000 and I inherited $1,500 from my grandfather.

20   We live rather modestly. For four years we lived in an apartment in Park Fairfax, in Alexandria, Va. The rent was $80 a month. And we saved for the time that we could buy a house.

21   Now, that was what we took in. What did we do with this money? What do we have today to show for it? This will surprise you, because it is so little, I suppose, as standards generally go, of people in public life. First of all, we've got a house in Washington which cost $41,000 and on which we owe $20,000.

22   We have a house in Whittier, Calif., which cost $13,000 and on which we owe $10,000. My folks are living there are the present time.

23   I have just $4,000 in life insurance, plus my G. I. policy which I've never been able to convert and which will run out in two years. I have no life insurance whatever on Pat. I have no life insurance on our two youngsters, Patricia and Julie. I own a 1950 Oldsmobile car. We have our furniture. We have no stocks and bonds of any type. We have no interest of any kind, direct or indirect, in any business.

24   Now, that's what we have. What do we owe? Well, in addition to the mortgage, the $20,000 mortgage on the house in Washington, the $10,000 one on the house in Whittier, I owe $4,500 to the Riggs Bank in Washington, D.C. with interest 4½ per cent.

25   I owe $3,500 to my parents and the interest on that loan which I pay regularly, because it's part of the savings they made through the years they were working so hard, I pay regularly 4 per cent interest. And then I have a $500 loan which I have on my life insurance.

26   Well, that's about it. That's what we have and that's what we owe. It isn't very much but Pat and I have the satisfaction that every dime we've got is honestly ours. I should say this—that Pat doesn't have a mink coat. But she does have a respectable Republican cloth coat. And I always tell her that she'd look good in anything.

27   One other thing I probably should tell you because if I don't they'll probably be saying this about me too, we did get something—a gift—after the election. A man down in Texas heard Pat on the radio mention the fact that our two youngsters would like to have a dog. And, believe it or not, the day before we left on this campaign trip we got a message from Union Station in Baltimore saying they

had a package for us. We went down to get it. You know what it was.

28   It was a little cocker spaniel dog in a crate that he sent all the way from Texas. Black and white spotted. And our little girl—Trisha, the 6-year-old—named it Checkers. And you know, the kids love the dog and I just want to say this right now, that regardless of what they say about it, we're gonna keep it. . . .

29   Now, let me say this: I know that this is not the last of the smears. In spite of my explanation tonight other smears will be made; others have been made in the past. And the purpose of the smears, I know, is this—to silence me, to make me let up.

30   Well, they just don't know who they're dealing with. . . . I intend to continue the fight. . . .

31   And I want to tell you why. Because, you see, I love my country. And I think my country is in danger. And I think that the only man that can save America at this time is the man that's running for President on my ticket—Dwight Eisenhower. . . .

32   And I say that the only man who can lead us in this fight to rid the Government of both those who are Communists and those who have corrupted this Government is Eisenhower, because Eisenhower, you can be sure, recognizes the problem and he knows how to deal with it. . . .

33   And just let me say this. We hear a lot about prosperity these days but I say, why can't we have prosperity built on peace rather than prosperity built on war? Why can't we have prosperity and an honest government in Washington, D.C., at the same time? Believe me, we can. And Eisenhower is the man that can lead this crusade to bring us that kind of prosperity.

34   And, now, finally, I know that you wonder whether or not I am going to stay on the Republican ticket or resign.

35   Let me say this: I don't believe that I ought to quit because I'm not a quitter. And, incidentally, Pat's not a quitter. After all, her name was Patricia Ryan and she was born on St. Patrick's Day, and you know the Irish never quit.

36   But the decision, my friends, is not mine. I would do nothing that would harm the possibilities of Dwight Eisenhower to become President of the United States. And for that reason I am submitting to the Republican National Committee tonight through this television broadcast the decision which it is theirs to make.

37   Let them decide whether my position on the ticket will help or hurt. And I am going to ask you to help them decide. Wire and write the Republican National Committee whether you think I should stay on or whether I should get off. And whatever their decision is, I will abide by it.

38   But just let me say this last word. Regardless of what happens I'm going to continue this fight. I'm going to campaign up and down America until we drive the crooks and the Communists and those that defend them out of Washington. And remember, folks, Eisenhower is a great man. Believe me. He's a great man. And a vote for Eisenhower is a vote for what's good in America.

QUESTIONS AND IDEAS FOR DISCUSSION

1. Under similar circumstances today, would a speech like this one prove equally successful? Explain the reasons for your answer. Then, by consulting *The New York Times Index* or *Vital Speeches of the Day*, locate a recent speech in which a public figure offers a defense of a statement, position, or action. Assuming that Nixon's appeals are typical of a 1950s defensive political speech, comment on the similarities and the differences between defensive political speeches of the 1950s and those today. Which seem greater, the points of resemblance or the differences?
2. Pat Nixon later did acquire a mink coat. According to Nixon's line of reasoning in paragraph 28, what conclusions may we draw?
3. In a short passage of what has come to be known as the "Checkers" speech, not excerpted above, Nixon says the following:

   "Mr. Mitchell, the chairman of the Democratic National Committee, made the statement that if a man couldn't afford to be in the United States Senate he shouldn't run for the Senate. . . . I don't agree with Mr. Mitchell when he says that only a rich man should serve his Government in the United States Senate or in the Congress."

   What fallacy does Nixon commit here?
4. The latter part of Nixon's speech centers on the theme "Regardless of what happens I'm going to continue this fight." What fight does he mean? Has he shifted ground? Comment.

LIES, FALLACIES, AND SANTA CLAUS

T. J. Stone
(Student Essay)

1   As a child approaches her second or third Christmas, her parents may begin telling her about the wonderful old elf, Santa Claus, who brings presents to good little girls and boys on the night of December 24 in the United States, but as late as January 6 in some countries, and not at all in others. In Spain, for instance, the Magi take over the gift-giving responsibilities. After all, the logistics involved for a single old man in a sleigh to deliver so many gifts in a single night are nearly overwhelming. But the child is not burdened with all these complications: She is assured categorically that Santa Claus is coming to her house on Christmas Eve after she falls asleep, and she may leave milk and cookies for him if she likes.

2   The whole thing is a terrific deal for the child who early learns not to question too closely. For the inquisitive child, however, the troubles begin early:

3   "Well, Mom, but what about Todd? He gets presents, too, but he doesn't have a chimney like us."

4   "And you say this man is fat? How does he fit down the chimney without getting stuck?"

5   "How does Santa Claus keep track of which kids get which presents?"

6   "What about Sally? She's so nice, but she gets hardly any presents. Does Santa just not like some kids?"

7   Never let it be said that a child cannot reason. She wants to believe (and is afraid that if she doesn't believe, the presents will stop coming!), but she can't help but see the gaping holes in the story Mom and Dad present. And Mom and Dad staunchly insist on the sleigh and the eight reindeer and, generally, the whole program. Oh, if there is no chimney, they are willing to admit that Santa will use a window, but nothing so prosaic as the front door. And they cough and mumble something indistinct when pressed about the little children who get no presents, or very few. So the child, knowing what is good for her, either keeps her questions to herself or suspends her disbelief.

8   Is either of these alternatives really a healthy one? What is the virtue of telling lies to a small child, assuring her all the while that they are the gospel truth? The Santa Claus lie may be small, and relatively harmless in the long run, but it requires, for the sake of tradition, that parents tell their children things that are not true, and

that children suppress their developing powers of reasoning. Some tradition!

9   A more sensible alternative is possible. Do not do away with Santa Claus or presents or Christmas trees—simply do away with the lies and evasions. Like little Virginia, many years ago, children today will find the truth just as enchanting as the fibs and fallacies. The spirit of sharing and giving at Christmastime is represented by a "pretend" figure known as Santa Claus. Real people do the giving, and children can be part of that giving: Those with more toys than they need can select one or more that they might have received to take to the Salvation Army or another charitable organization so that little Sally can have some toys at Christmas, too. No enjoyment is lost to the child who learns about Santa as a symbol and who reads "The Night Before Christmas" for what it is—a delightful fairy tale. And no loss of innocence occurs at age seven or eight in children who have known the truth all along. Santa is just too wonderful a part of Christmas to be put in the position of being exposed as a lie.

QUESTIONS AND IDEAS FOR DISCUSSION

1. Does Stone's last sentence contradict the rest of her essay? Explain.
2. What defense can you offer for the usual presentation of Santa Claus to children? Is there any virtue in telling children lies, however well-intentioned?
3. Think of other Western traditions that are based on "lies," such as the tooth fairy, the stork that brings babies, or the Easter bunny. Are these deceptions justified? Comment.

THE LANGUAGE OF ADVERTISING CLAIMS

Jeffrey Schrank

1   High school students, and many teachers, are notorious believers in their immunity to advertising. These naive inhabitants of consumerland believe that advertising is childish, dumb, a bunch of lies, and influences only the vast hordes of the less sophisticated. Their own purchases are made purely on the basis of value and desire, with advertising playing only a minor supporting role. They know about Vance Packard and his "hidden persuaders" and the adwriter's psychosell and bag of persuasive magic. They are not impressed.

2   Advertisers know better. Although few people admit to being greatly influenced by ads, surveys and sales figures show that a well-designed advertising campaign has dramatic effects. A logical conclusion is that advertising works below the level of conscious awareness and it works even on those who claim immunity to its message. Ads are designed to have an effect while being laughed at, belittled, and all but ignored.

3   A person unaware of advertising's claim on him or her is precisely the one most defenseless against the adwriter's attack. Advertisers delight in an audience which believes ads to be harmless nonsense, for such an audience is rendered defenseless by its belief that there is no attack taking place. The purpose of a classroom study of advertising is to raise the level of awareness about the persuasive techniques used in ads. One way to do this is to analyze ads in microscopic detail. Ads can be studied to detect their psychological hooks, they can be used to gauge values and hidden desires of the common person, they can be studied for their use of symbols, color, and imagery. But perhaps the simplest and most direct way to study ads is through an analysis of the language of the advertising claim. The "claim" is the verbal or print part of an ad that makes some claim of superiority for the product being advertised. After studying claims, students should be able to recognize those that are misleading and accept as useful information those that are true. A few of these claims are downright lies, some are honest statements about a truly superior product, but most fit into the category of neither bold lies nor helpful consumer information. They balance on the narrow line between truth and falsehood by a careful choice of words.

4   The reason so many ad claims fall into this category of pseudo-information is that they are applied to parity products, products in which all or most of the brands available are nearly identical. Since no one superior product exists, advertising is used to create the il-

lusion of superiority. The largest advertising budgets are devoted to parity products such as gasoline, cigarettes, beer and soft drinks, soaps, and various headache and cold remedies.

5   The first rule of parity involves the Alice in Wonderlandish use of the words "better" and "best." In parity claims, "better" means "best" and "best" means "equal to." If all the brands are identical, they must all be equally good, the legal minds have decided. So "best" means that the product is as good as the other superior products in its category. When Bing Crosby declares Minute Maid Orange Juice "the best there is" he means it is as good as the other orange juices you can buy.

6   The word "better" has been legally interpreted to be a comparative and therefore becomes a clear claim of superiority. Bing could not have said that Minute Maid is "better than any other orange juice." "Better" is a claim of superiority. The only time "better" can be used is when a product does indeed have superiority over other products in its category or when the better is used to compare the product with something other than competing brands. An orange juice could therefore claim to be "better than a vitamin pill," or even "the better breakfast drink."

7   The second rule of advertising claim analysis is simply that if any product is truly superior, the ad will say so very clearly and will offer some kind of convincing evidence of the superiority. If an ad hedges the least bit about a product's advantage over the competition you can strongly suspect it is not superior—maybe equal to but not better. You will never hear a gasoline company say "we will give you four miles per gallon more in your car than any other brand." They would love to make such a claim, but it would not be true. Gasoline is a parity product, and, in spite of some very clever and deceptive ads of a few years ago, no one has yet claimed one brand of gasoline better than any other brand.

8   To create the necessary illusion of superiority, advertisers usually resort to one or more of the following ten basic techniques. Each is common and easy to identify.

1 The Weasel Claim

9 A weasel word is a modifier that practically negates the claim that follows. The expression "weasel word" is aptly named after the egg-eating habits of weasels. A weasel will suck out the inside of an egg, leaving it appear intact to the casual observer. Upon examination, the egg is discovered to be hollow. Words or claims that appear substantial upon first look but disintegrate into hollow meaninglessness on analysis are weasels. Commonly used weasel words include "helps" (the champion weasel); "like" (used in a comparative sense);

"virtual" or "virtually"; "acts" or "works"; "can be"; "up to"; "as much as"; "refreshes"; "comforts"; "tackles"; "fights"; "come on"; "the feel of"; "the look of"; "looks like"; "fortified"; "enriched"; and "strengthened."

Samples of Weasel Claims

"*Helps control* dandruff *symptoms* with *regular use.*" The weasels include "helps control," and possibly even "symptoms" and "regular use." The claim is not "stops dandruff."

"Leaves dishes *virtually* spotless." We have seen so many ad claims that we have learned to tune out weasels. You are supposed to think "spotless," rather than "virtually" spotless.

"Only half the price of *many* color sets." "Many" is the weasel. The claim is supposed to give the impression that the set is inexpensive.

"Tests confirm one mouthwash *best* against mouth odor."

"Hot Nestlés' cocoa is the very *best.*" Remember the "best" and "better" routine.

"Listerine *fights* bad breath." "Fights" not "stops."

"Lots of things have changed, but Hershey's *goodness* hasn't." This claim does not say that Hershey's chocolate hasn't changed. "Bacos, the crispy garnish that tastes just *like* its name."

2 The Unfinished Claim

10 The unfinished claim is one in which the ad claims the product is better, or has more of something, but does not finish the comparison.

Samples of Unfinished Claims

"Magnavox gives you more." More what?

"Anacin: Twice as much of the pain reliever doctors recommend most." This claim fits in a number of categories but it does not say twice as much of what pain reliever.

"Supergloss does it with more color, more shine, more sizzle, more!"

"Coffee-mate gives coffee more body, more flavor." Also note that "body" and "flavor" are weasels.

"You can be sure if it's Westinghouse." Sure of what?

"Scott makes it better for you."
"Ford LTD—700% quieter."

When the FTC asked Ford to substantiate this claim, Ford revealed that they meant the inside of the Ford was 700% quieter than the outside.

3 The "We're Different and Unique" Claim

11   This kind of claim states that there is nothing else quite like the product advertised. For example, if Schlitz would add pink food coloring to its beer they could say, "There's nothing like new pink Schlitz." The uniqueness claim is supposed to be interpreted by readers as a claim to superiority.

Samples of "We're Different and Unique" Claims
"There's no other mascara like it."

"Only Doral has this unique filter system."

"Cougar is like nobody else's car."

"Either way, liquid or spray, there's nothing else like it."

"If it doesn't say Goodyear, it can't be polyglas." "Polyglas" is a trade name copyrighted by Goodyear. Goodrich or Firestone could make a tire exactly identical to the Goodyear one and yet couldn't call it "polyglas"—a name for fiberglass belts.

"Only Zenith has chromacolor." Same as the "polyglas" gambit. Admiral has solarcolor and RCA has accucolor.

4 The "Water is Wet" Claim

12   "Water is wet" claims say something about the product that is true for any brand in that product category (e.g., "Schrank's water is really wet"). The claim is usually a statement of fact, but not a real advantage over the competition.

Samples of "Water is Wet" Claim
"Mobil: the Detergent Gasoline." Any gasoline acts as a cleaning agent.

"Great Lash greatly increases the diameter of every lash."

"Rheingold, the natural beer." Made from grains and water as are other beers.

"SKIN smells different on everyone." As do many perfumes.

5 The "So What" Claim

13   This is the kind of claim to which the careful reader will react by saying, "So what?" A claim is made which is true but which gives no real advantage to the product. This is similar to the "water is wet" claim except that it claims an advantage which is not shared by most of the other brands in the product category.

Samples of the "So What" Claim

"Geritol has more than twice the iron of ordinary supplements." But is twice as much beneficial to the body?

"Campbell's gives you tasty pieces of chicken and not one but two chicken stocks." Does the presence of two stocks improve the taste?

"Strong enough for man but made for a woman." This deodorant claim says only that the product is aimed at the female market.

6 The Vague Claim

14   The vague claim is simply not clear. This category often overlaps with others. The key to the vague claim is the use of words that are colorful but meaningless, as well as the use of subjective and emotional opinions that defy verification. Most contain weasels.

Samples of the Vague Claim

"Lips have never looked so luscious." Can you imagine trying to either prove or disprove such a claim?

"Lipsavers are fun—they taste good, smell good and feel good."

"Its deep rich lather makes hair feel good again."

"For skin like peaches and cream."

"The end of meatloaf boredom."

"Take a bite and you'll think you're eating on the Champs Elysées."

"Winston tastes good like a cigarette should."

"The perfect little portable for all-around viewing with all the features of higher priced sets."

"Fleishman's makes sensible eating delicious."

7 The Endorsement or Testimonial

15   A celebrity or authority appears in an ad to lend his or her stellar qualities to the product. Sometimes the people will actually claim to use the product, but very often they don't. There are agencies surviving on providing products with testimonials.

Samples of Endorsements or Testimonials

"Joan Fontaine throws a shot-in-the-dark party and her friends learn a thing or two."

"Darling, have you discovered Masterpiece? The most exciting men I know are smoking it." (Eva Gabor)

"Vega is the best handling car in the U.S." This claim was challenged by the FTC, but GM answered that the claim is only a direct quote from *Road and Track* magazine.

8 The Scientific or Statistical Claim

16   This kind of ad uses some sort of scientific proof or experiment, very specific numbers, or an impressive sounding mystery ingredient.

Samples of Scientific or Statistical Claims

"Wonder Bread helps build strong bodies 12 ways." Even the weasel "helps" did not prevent the FTC from demanding this ad be withdrawn. But note that the use of the number 12 makes the claim far more believable than if it were taken out.

"Easy-Off has 33% more cleaning power than another popular brand."

"Another popular brand" often translates as some other kind of oven cleaner sold somewhere. Also the claim does not say Easy-Off works 33% better.

"Special Morning—33% more nutrition." Also an unfinished claim.

"Certs contains a sparkling drop of Retsyn."

"ESSO with HTA."

"Sinarest. Created by a research scientist who actually gets sinus headaches."

9 The "Compliment the Consumer" Claim

17   This kind of claim butters up the consumer by some form of flattery.

Samples of "Compliment the Consumer" Claim

"We think a cigar smoker is someone special."

"If what you do is right for you, no matter what others do, then RC Cola is right for you."

"You pride yourself on your good home cooking. . . ."

"The lady has taste."

"You've come a long way, baby."

10 The Rhetorical Question

18   This technique demands a response from the audience. A question is asked and the viewer or listener is supposed to answer in such a way as to affirm the product's goodness.

Samples of the Rhetorical Question

"Plymouth—isn't that the kind of car America wants?"

"Shouldn't your family be drinking Hawaiian Punch?"

"What do you want most from coffee? That's what you get most from Hills."

"Touch of Sweden: could your hands use a small miracle?"

QUESTIONS AND IDEAS FOR DISCUSSION

1. Schrank claims that "a logical conclusion is that advertising works below the level of conscious awareness and it works even on those who claim immunity to its message." Does Schrank convince you of his claim? With what premises does he support it?
2. Why, according to Schrank, are advertising claims so often empty or fallacious? Give an example of a specific parity product being advertised today for which superiority is claimed.
3. Some of the fallacious claims Schrank points to correspond to fallacies identified elsewhere in this chapter. One is the question-begging rhetorical question, in which the consumer's answer is already implied. What are others? What kinds of fallacious claims does Schrank identify that we have not discussed up to this point?
4. Give additional examples from current print and television advertising for each of Schrank's ten fallacies. Do you find any fallacies he has not discussed? Comment.

True Cracks Taste Barrier!

© Lorillard, U.S.A., 1984

New True Laser-Cut "Flavor Chamber" Filter Improves Flavor...*Without Increasing Tar!*

Laser technology breakthrough challenges taste of higher tar brands.

True Exclusive. A unique filtration system that delivers a flavor-rich tobacco experience at a mere 5 mg. tar. A taste satisfaction we believe challenges cigarettes containing up to twice the tar.

More Good News!
New True is packed with extra tobacco so you can enjoy it longer. Noticeably longer.

New Breakthrough True. *Why not test it against the only taste that counts? Yours!*

It tastes too good to be True.

New BREAKTHROUGH True

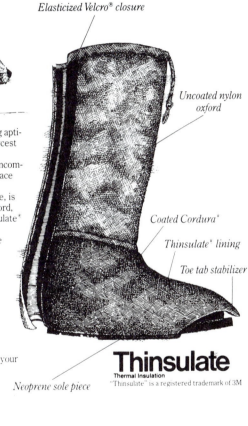

QUESTIONS AND IDEAS FOR DISCUSSION

1. Discuss the kinds of appeals, fallacious or otherwise, in the preceding advertisements. (Bear in mind that not all advertising appeals are fallacious.) Describe the audience to which each appears to be addressed. Which advertisement do you find most appealing personally? Which least appealing? Why? Do you believe you are part of the intended audience for each of the advertisements?

2. Read the advertisements in a current magazine for either general or specialized audiences. What kinds of products predominate? What kinds of appeals are made? What fallacies do you find? (Give examples.) Try to find at least one advertisement that contains no fallacies. Bring examples to class for comment and discussion.

3. If you have recently received requests for donations from nonprofit agencies, political action groups, or politicians, examine them for appropriate and fallacious emotional appeals. What kinds of appeals do you find yourself responding to favorably? What kinds of appeals put you off? Why? Bring an example of a solicitation to class for comment and discussion.

4. Read the classified ads in your local newspapers that describe houses or condominiums for sale. Pick out one that you find persuasive, in which the property sounds like a particularly good buy and for which an open house is advertised. Go to the open house, and comment in a paragraph on any differences you find between the rhetoric and the reality. Note any factual errors or misleading emotional appeals.

LOVE IS A FALLACY

Max Shulman

Cool was I and logical. Keen, calculating, perspicacious, acute and astute—I was all of these. My brain was as powerful as a dynamo, as precise as a chemist's scales, as penetrating as a scalpel. And—think of it!—I was only eighteen.

It is not often that one so young has such a giant intellect. Take, for example, Petey Bellows, my roommate at the university. Same age, same background, but dumb as an ox. A nice enough fellow, you understand, but nothing upstairs. Emotional type. Unstable. Impressionable. Worst of all, a faddist. Fads, I submit, are the very negation of reason. To be swept up in every new craze that comes along, to surrender yourself to idiocy just because everybody else is doing it—this, to me, is the acme of mindlessness. Not, however, to Petey.

One afternoon I found Petey lying on his bed with an expression of such distress on his face that I immediately diagnosed appendicitis. "Don't move," I said. "Don't take a laxative. I'll get a doctor."

"Raccoon," he mumbled thickly.

"Raccoon?" I said, pausing in my flight.

"I want a raccoon coat," he wailed.

I perceived that his trouble was not physical, but mental. "Why do you want a raccoon coat?"

"I should have known it," he cried, pounding his temples. "I should have known they'd come back when the Charleston came back. Like a fool I spent all my money for textbooks, and now I can't get a raccoon coat."

"Can you mean," I said incredulously, "that people are actually wearing raccoon coats again?"

"All the Big Men on Campus are wearing them. Where've you been?"

"In the library," I said, naming a place not frequented by Big Men on Campus.

He leaped from the bed and paced the room. "I've got to have a raccoon coat," he said passionately. "I've got to!"

"Petey, why? Look at it rationally. Raccoon coats are unsanitary. They shed. They smell bad. They weigh too much. They're unsightly. They——"

"You don't understand," he interrupted impatiently. "It's the thing to do. Don't you want to be in the swim?"

"No," I said truthfully.

"Well, I do," he declared. "I'd give anything for a raccoon coat. Anything!"

My brain, that precision instrument, slipped into high gear. Anything?" I asked, looking at him narrowly.

"Anything," he affirmed in ringing tones.

I stroked my chin thoughtfully. It so happened that I knew where to get my hands on a raccoon coat. My father had had one in his undergraduate days; it lay now in a trunk in the attic back home. It also happened that Petey had something I wanted. He didn't *have* it exactly, but at least he had first rights on it. I refer to his girl, Polly Espy.

I had long coveted Polly Espy. Let me emphasize that my desire for this young woman was not emotional in nature. She was, to be sure, a girl who excited the emotions, but I was not one to let my heart rule my head. I wanted Polly for a shrewdly calculated, entirely cerebral reason.

I was a freshman in law school. In a few years I would be out in practice. I was well aware of the importance of the right kind of wife in furthering a lawyer's career. The successful lawyers I had observed were, almost without exception, married to beautiful, gracious, intelligent women. With one omission, Polly fitted these specifications perfectly.

Beautiful she was. She was not yet of pin-up proportions, but I felt sure that time would supply the lack. She already had the makings.

Gracious she was. By gracious I mean full of graces. She had an erectness of carriage, an ease of bearing, a poise that clearly indicated the best of breeding. At table her manners were exquisite. I had seen her at the Kozy Kampus Korner eating the specialty of the house—a sandwich that contained scraps of pot roast, gravy, chopped nuts, and a dipper of sauerkraut—without even getting her fingers moist.

Intelligent she was not. In fact, she veered in the opposite direction. But I believed that under my guidance she would smarten up. At any rate, it was worth a try. It is, after all, easier to make a beautiful dumb girl smart than to make an ugly smart girl beautiful.

"Petey," I said, "are you in love with Polly Espy?"

"I think she's a keen kid," he replied, "but I don't know if you'd call it love. Why?"

"Do you," I asked, "have any kind of formal arrangement with her? I mean are you going steady or anything like that?"

"No. We see each other quite a bit, but we both have other dates. Why?"

"Is there," I asked, "any other man for whom she has a particular fondness?"

"Not that I know of. Why?"

I nodded with satisfaction. "In other words, if you were out of the picture, the field would be open. Is that right?"

"I guess so. What are you getting at?"

"Nothing, nothing," I said innocently, and took my suitcase out of the closet.

"Where you going?" asked Petey.

"Home for the week end." I threw a few things into the bag.

"Listen," he said, clutching my arm eagerly, "while you're home, you couldn't get some money from your old man, could you, and lend it to me so I can buy a raccoon coat?"

"I may do better than that," I said with a mysterious wink and closed my bag and left.

"Look," I said to Petey when I got back Monday morning. I threw open the suitcase and revealed the huge, hairy, gamy object that my father had worn in his Stutz Bearcat in 1925.

"Holy Toledo!" said Petey reverently. He plunged his hands into the raccoon coat and then his face. "Holy Toledo!" he repeated fifteen or twenty times.

"Would you like it?" I asked.

"Oh yes!" he cried, clutching the greasy pelt to him. Then a canny look came into his eyes. "What do you want for it?"

"Your girl," I said, mincing no words.

"Polly?" he said in a horrified whisper. "You want Polly?"

"That's right."

He flung the coat from him. "Never," he said stoutly.

I shrugged. "Okay. If you don't want to be in the swim, I guess it's your business."

I sat down in a chair and pretended to read a book, but out of the corner of my eye I kept watching Petey. He was a torn man. First he looked at the coat with the expression of a waif at a bakery window. Then he turned away and set his jaw resolutely. Then he looked back at the coat, with even more longing in his face. Then he turned away, but with not so much resolution this time. Back and forth his head swiveled, desire waxing, resolution waning. Finally he didn't turn away at all; he just stood and stared with mad lust at the coat.

"It isn't as though I was in love with Polly," he said thickly. "Or going steady or anything like that."

"That's right," I murmured.

"What's Polly to me, or me to Polly?"

"Not a thing," said I.

"It's just been a casual kick—just a few laughs, that's all."

"Try on the coat," said I.

He complied. The coat bunched high over his ears and dropped all the way down to his shoe tops. He looked like a mound of dead raccoons. "Fits fine," he said happily.

I rose from my chair. "Is it a deal?" I asked, extending my hand.

He swallowed. "It's a deal," he said and shook my hand.

I had my first date with Polly the following evening. This was in the nature of a survey; I wanted to find out just how much work I had to do to get her mind up to the standard I required. I took her first to dinner. "Gee, that was a delish dinner," she said as we left the restaurant. Then I took her to a movie. "Gee, that was a marvy movie," she said as we left the theater. And then I took her home. "Gee, I had a sensaysh time," she said as she bade me good night.

I went back to my room with a heavy heart. I had gravely underestimated the size of my task. This girl's lack of information was terrifying. Nor would it be enough merely to supply her with information. First she had to be taught to *think*. This loomed as a project of no small dimensions, and at first I was tempted to give her back to Petey. But then I got to thinking about her abundant physical charms and about the way she entered a room and the way she handled a knife and fork, and I decided to make an effort.

I went about it, as in all things, systematically. I gave her a course in logic. It happened that I, as a law student, was taking a course in logic myself, so I had all the facts at my finger tips. "Polly," I said to her when I picked her up on our next date, "tonight we are going over to the Knoll and talk."

"Oo, terrif," she replied. One thing I will say for this girl: you would go far to find another so agreeable.

We went to the Knoll, the campus trysting place, and we sat down under an old oak, and she looked at me expectantly. "What are we going to talk about?" she asked.

"Logic."

She thought this over for a minute and decided she liked it. "Magnif," she said.

"Logic," I said, clearing my throat, "is the science of thinking. Before we can think correctly, we must first learn to recognize the common fallacies of logic. These we will take up tonight."

"Wow-dow!" she cried, clapping her hands delightedly.

I winced, but went bravely on. "First let us examine the fallacy called Dicto Simpliciter."

"By all means," she urged, batting her lashes eagerly.

"Dicto Simpliciter means an argument based on an unqualified generalization. For example: Exercise is good. Therefore everybody should exercise."

"I agree," said Polly earnestly. "I mean exercise is wonderful. I mean it builds the body and everything."

"Polly," I said gently, "the argument is a fallacy. *Exercise is good* *is* an unqualified generalization. For instance, if you have heart disease, exercise is bad, not good. Many people are ordered by their doctors *not* to exercise. You must *qualify* the generalization. You must say exercise is *usually* good, or exercise is good *for most people*. Otherwise you have committed a Dicto Simpliciter. Do you see?"

"No," she confessed. "But this is marvy. Do more! Do more!"

"It will be better if you stop tugging at my sleeve," I told her, and when she desisted, I continued. "Next we take up a fallacy called Hasty Generalization. Listen carefully: You can't speak French. I can't speak French. Petey Bellows can't speak French. I must therefore conclude that nobody at the University of Minnesota can speak French."

"Really?" said Polly, amazed. *"Nobody?"*

I hid my exasperation. "Polly, it's a fallacy. The generalization is reached too hastily. There are too few instances to support such a conclusion."

"Know any more fallacies?" she asked breathlessly. "This is more fun than dancing even."

I fought off a wave of despair. I was getting nowhere with this girl, absolutely nowhere. Still, I am nothing if not persistent. I continued. "Next comes Post Hoc. Listen to this: Let's not take Bill on our picnic. Every time we take him out with us, it rains."

"I know somebody just like that," she exclaimed. "A girl back home—Eula Becker, her name is. It never fails. Every single time we take her on a picnic——"

"Polly," I said sharply, "it's a fallacy. Eula Becker doesn't *cause* the rain. She has no connection with the rain. You are guilty of Post Hoc if you blame Eula Becker."

"I'll never do it again," she promised contritely, "Are you mad at me?"

I sighed. "No, Polly, I'm not mad."

"Then tell me some more fallacies."

"All right. Let's try Contradictory Premises."

"Yes, let's," she chirped, blinking her eyes happily.

I frowned, but plunged ahead. "Here's an example of Contradictory Premises: If God can do anything, can He make a stone so heavy that He won't be able to lift it?"

"Of course," she replied promptly.

"But if He can do anything, He can lift the stone," I pointed out.

"Yeah," she said thoughtfully. "Well, then I guess He can't make the stone."

"But He can do anything," I reminded her.

She scratched her pretty, empty head. "I'm all confused," she admitted.

"Of course you are. Because when the premises of an argument contradict each other, there can be no argument. If there is an irresistible force, there can be no immovable object. If there is an immovable object, there can be no irresistible force. Get it?"

"Tell me some more of this keen stuff," she said eagerly.

I consulted my watch. "I think we'd better call it a night. I'll take you home now, and you go over all the things you've learned. We'll have another session tomorrow night."

I deposited her at the girls' dormitory, where she assured me that she had had a perfectly terrif evening, and I went glumly home to my room. Petey lay snoring in his bed, the raccoon coat huddled like a great hairy beast at his feet. For a moment I considered waking him and telling him that he could have his girl back. It seemed clear that my project was doomed to failure. The girl simply had a logic-proof head.

But then I reconsidered. I had wasted one evening; I might as well waste another. Who knew? Maybe somewhere in the extinct crater of her mind a few embers still smoldered. Maybe somehow I could fan them into flame. Admittedly it was not a prospect fraught with hope, but I decided to give it one more try.

Seated under the oak the next evening I said, "Our first fallacy tonight is called Ad Misericordiam."

She quivered with delight.

"Listen closely," I said. "A man applies for a job. When the boss asks him what his qualifications are, he replies that he has a wife and six children at home, the wife is a helpless cripple, the children have nothing to eat, no clothes to wear, no shoes on their feet, there are no beds in the house, no coal in the cellar, and winter is coming."

A tear rolled down each of Polly's pink cheeks. "Oh, this is awful, awful," she sobbed.

"Yes, it's awful," I agreed, "but it's no argument. The man never answered the boss's question about his qualifications. Instead he appealed to the boss's sympathy. He committed the fallacy of Ad Misericordiam. Do you understand?"

"Have you got a handkerchief?" she blubbered.

I handed her a handkerchief and tried to keep from screaming while she wiped her eyes. "Next," I said in a carefully controlled tone, "we will discuss False Analogy. Here is an example: Students should be allowed to look at their textbooks during examinations. After all, surgeons have X rays to guide them during an operation, lawyers have briefs to guide them during a trial, carpenters have blueprints to guide them when they are building a house. Why, then, shouldn't students be allowed to look at their textbooks during an examination?"

"There now," she said enthusiastically, "is the most marvy idea I've heard in years."

"Polly," I said testily, "the argument is all wrong. Doctors, lawyers, and carpenters aren't taking a test to see how much they have learned, but students are. The situations are altogether different, and you can't make an analogy between them."

"I still think it's a good idea," said Polly.

"Nuts," I muttered. Doggedly I pressed on. "Next we'll try Hypothesis Contrary to Fact."

"Sounds yummy," was Polly's reaction.

"Listen: If Madame Curie had not happened to leave a photographic plate in a drawer with a chunk of pitchblende, the world today would not know about radium."

"True, true," said Polly, nodding her head. "Did you see the movie? Oh, it just knocked me out. That Walter Pidgeon is so dreamy. I mean he fractures me."

"If you can forget Mr. Pidgeon for a moment," I said coldly, "I would like to point out that the statement is a fallacy. Maybe Madame Curie would have discovered radium at some later date. Maybe somebody else would have discovered it. Maybe any number of things would have happened. You can't start with a hypothesis that is not true and then draw any supportable conclusions from it."

"They ought to put Walter Pidgeon in more pictures," said Polly. "I hardly ever see him any more."

One more chance, I decided. But just one more. There is a limit to what flesh and blood can bear. "The next fallacy is called Poisoning the Well."

"How cute!" she gurgled.

"Two men are having a debate. The first one gets up and says, 'My opponent is a notorious liar. You can't believe a word that he is going to say.' . . . Now, Polly, think. Think hard. What's wrong?"

I watched her closely as she knit her creamy brow in concentration. Suddenly a glimmer of intelligence—the first I had seen—came into her eyes. "It's not fair," she said with indignation. "It's not a bit fair. What chance has the second man got if the first man calls him a liar before he even begins talking?"

"Right!" I cried exultantly. "One hundred per cent right. It's not fair. The first man has *poisoned the well* before anybody could drink from it. He has hamstrung his opponent before he could even start. . . . Polly, I'm proud of you."

"Pshaw," she murmured, blushing with pleasure.

"You see, my dear, these things aren't so hard. All you have to do is concentrate. Think—examine—evaluate. Come now, let's review everything we have learned."

"Fire away," she said with an airy wave of her hand.

Heartened by the knowledge that Polly was not altogether a cretin, I began a long, patient review of all I had told her. Over and over and over again I cited instances, pointed out flaws, kept hammering away without letup. It was like digging a tunnel. At first everything was work, sweat, and darkness. I had no idea when I would reach the light, or even *if* I would. But I persisted. I pounded and clawed and scraped, and finally I was rewarded. I saw a chink of light. And then the chink got bigger and the sun came pouring in and all was bright.

Five grueling nights this took, but it was worth it. I had made a logician out of Polly; I had taught her to think. My job was done. She was worthy of me at last. She was a fit wife for me, a proper hostess for my many mansions, a suitable mother for my well-heeled children.

It must not be thought that I was without love for this girl. Quite the contrary. Just as Pygmalion loved the perfect woman he had fashioned, so I loved mine. I decided to acquaint her with my feelings at our very next meeting. The time had come to change our relationship from academic to romantic.

"Polly," I said when we next sat beneath our oak, "tonight we will not discuss fallacies."

"Aw, gee," she said, disappointed.

"My dear," I said, favoring her with a smile, "we have now spent five evenings together. We have gotten along splendidly. It is clear that we are well matched."

"Hasty Generalization," said Polly brightly.

"I beg your pardon," said I.

"Hasty Generalization," she repeated. "How can you say that we are well matched on the basis of only five dates?"

I chuckled with amusement. The dear child had learned her lessons well. "My dear," I said, patting her hand in a tolerant manner, "five dates is plenty. After all, you don't have to eat a whole cake to know that it's good."

"False Analogy," said Polly promptly. "I'm not a cake. I'm a girl."

I chuckled with somewhat less amusement. The dear child had learned her lessons perhaps too well. I decided to change tactics. Obviously the best approach was a simple, strong, direct declaration of love. I paused for a moment while my massive brain chose the proper words. Then I began:

"Polly, I love you. You are the whole world to me, and the moon and the stars and the constellations of outer space. Please, my darling, say that you will go steady with me, for if you will not, life will be meaningless. I will languish. I will refuse my meals. I will wander the face of the earth, a shambling, hollow-eyed hulk."

There, I thought, folding my arms, that ought to do it.

"Ad Misericordiam," said Polly.

I ground my teeth. I was not Pygmalion; I was Frankenstein, and my monster had me by the throat. Frantically I fought back the tide of panic surging through me. At all costs I had to keep cool.

"Well, Polly," I said, forcing a smile, "you certainly have learned your fallacies."

"You're darn right," she said with a vigorous nod.

"And who taught them to you, Polly?"

"You did."

"That's right. So you do owe me something, don't you, my dear? If I hadn't come along you never would have learned about fallacies."

"Hypothesis Contrary to Fact," she said instantly.

I dashed perspiration from my brow. "Polly," I croaked, "you mustn't take all these things so literally. I mean this is just classroom stuff. You know that the things you learn in school don't have anything to do with life."

"Dicto Simpliciter," she said, wagging her finger at me playfully.

That did it. I leaped to my feet, bellowing like a bull. "Will you or will you not go steady with me?"

"I will not," she replied.

"Why not?" I demanded.

"Because this afternoon I promised Petey Bellows that I would go steady with him."

I reeled back, overcome with the infamy of it. After he promised, after he made a deal, after he shook my hand! "The rat!" I shrieked, kicking up great chunks of turf. "You can't go with him, Polly. He's a liar. He's a cheat. He's a rat."

"Poisoning the Well," said Polly, "and stop shouting. I think shouting must be a fallacy too."

With an immense effort of will, I modulated my voice. "All right," I said. "You're a logician. Let's look at this thing logically. How could you choose Petey Bellows over me? Look at me—a brilliant student, a tremendous intellectual, a man with an assured future. Look at Petey— a knothead, a jitterbug, a guy who'll never know where his next meal is coming from. Can you give me one logical reason why you should go steady with Petey Bellows?"

"I certainly can," declared Polly. "He's got a raccoon coat."

QUESTIONS AND IDEAS FOR DISCUSSION

1. In a prefatory note to "Love Is a Fallacy," Max Shulman shares with us the following tidbit:

> Charles Lamb, as merry and enterprising a fellow as you will meet in a month of Sundays, unfettered the informal essay with his memorable *Old China* and *Dream Children*. There follows an informal essay that ventures even beyond Lamb's frontier. Indeed, "informal" may not be quite the right word to describe this essay; "limp" or "flaccid" or possibly "spongy" are perhaps more appropriate.

Vague though its category, it is without doubt an essay. It develops an argument; it cites instances; it reaches a conclusion. Could Carlyle do more? Could Ruskin?

Read, then, the following essay which undertakes to demonstrate that logic, far from being a dry, pedantic discipline, is a living, breathing thing, full of beauty, passion, and trauma.

Describe Shulman's tone in this introduction. Is "Love Is a Fallacy" an essay? Put Shulman's claim that it is into the form of a categorical syllogism and evaluate it.

2. Is love a fallacy? Why or why not? Why does Shulman indicate that it is a fallacy?

3. Dobie Gillis (the narrator) teaches Polly Espy some fallacies we have discussed, occasionally under different names. What, for example, is the fallacy of dicto simpliciter? What is poisoning the well? Dobie also lectures Polly on some fallacies we have not discussed. Name these and give your own examples of them to back up Dobie's.

4. Polly asserts that "shouting must be a fallacy, too." Do you agree? Explain.

5. Many of my students have told me that they remember the fallacies described in "Love Is a Fallacy" more vividly than any others. How does Shulman make his "lesson" memorable? Point to specific features of the text to support your judgment.

SUGGESTIONS FOR WRITING AND FURTHER DISCUSSION

1. Defend advertising against its many critics. Show Jeffrey Schrank and the rest of us that advertising can be clever, illuminating, and helpful—or any other combination of qualities you believe you can support concretely. Defend, if you can, even the use of what Schrank considers to be deception in advertising messages.

2. Schrank claims that "ads are designed to have an effect while being laughed at, belittled, and all but ignored." However, his argument centers not on this claim but on the nature of the messages themselves. Write an essay for which this claim could serve as the thesis. Use examples of current television, billboard, and print media advertising to support your conclusions about how ads achieve their effect with or without our conscious cooperation.

3. Following a suggestion of Schrank's (not reprinted here with the essay), write copy for honest advertisements to correct what you regard as distorted or misleading claims and inferences in three specific ads. Then write an essay on the problems and difficulties you encountered, if any, or on the ease of the undertaking, if that was the case. Conclude

by claiming either that honest ads are not hard to create and that therefore dishonest advertisers have no excuse; or that honest ads are nearly impossible to create and that the only recourse for the consumer must be *caveat emptor*—let the buyer beware.

4. . . . [T]he historians and archaeologists will one day discover that the ads of our time are the richest and most faithful reflections that any society ever made of its entire range of activities.

—Marshall McLuhan

You are a historian of the mid-twenty-fourth century, researching the lives of ordinary people in the latter twentieth century. You have available to you a wealth of print advertisements. Studying the ads alone, what hypotheses can you draw about life in the 1980s? Support your claim with reference to specific ads.

5. Write an essay, based on your own experiences, that substantiates the claim in Shulman's title, "Love Is a Fallacy."

6. Read a recent political speech by the president or another leading politician (as reprinted in *Vital Speeches* or *The New York Times*) and write an analysis of it in terms of style and logic. Does it commit any of the fallacies most prevalent in the "Checkers" speech? Any new ones? Or does it speak truth, directly and specifically? Be careful that your conclusions, based on a single speech, are not too sweeping.

7. Compare the "Checkers" speech with some of the speeches Richard Nixon made in the 1960 and 1968 presidential campaigns (consult the appropriate volumes of *Vital Speeches of the Day*), with his inaugural addresses as governor of California and as president, and with his resignation speech in 1973. What similarities and what differences do you find? Develop a thesis that argues either that the kinds of appeals Nixon used remained constant throughout his political career (and therefore that the public should have gotten the idea long before Watergate), or that his use of emotional appeals changed over the years. If the latter, show in what ways and to what extent the appeals changed. Write an argumentative essay putting forward your conclusions.

8. Since teaching people about effective means of persuasion and about fallacies may enable them to mislead others, should students be required to pass a course in ethics or to demonstrate good moral character before being allowed to enroll in a course in persuasion and argumentation? Write an essay—addressed to the dean, the president, and the provost of the university or college in which you are enrolled—arguing your answer to this question.

10
Readings for Further Discussion

The test of a first-rate intelligence is the ability to hold two opposed ideas in the mind at the same time and still retain the ability to function.

F. Scott Fitzgerald

When we all think alike, no one thinks very much.

Walter Lippmann

The following selections address a variety of issues, from language to laws to human behavior, from matters of great scope to others of more modest dimensions; and they speak in a variety of voices, from that of a great leader addressing his countrymen and women to that of the person sitting next to you on the bus, smoking a cigarette. It is an unruly assemblage; some of the authors speak to each other as well as to us, and all of them attempt to persuade us of their often conflicting conclusions. Ours is to compare, evaluate, agree, disagree, or (despite the fact that these readings are paired as if every subject had but two sides to it) find a middle ground. If Lippmann's statement is true, there is little danger of little thinking for the reader of these pages. There remains only Fitzgerald's challenge to give us pause.

WHEN SMOKE GETS IN YOUR EYES . . . SHUT THEM

Fran Lebowitz

1 As a practicing member of several oppressed minority groups, I feel that I have on the whole conducted myself with the utmost decorum. I have, without exception, refrained from marching, chanting, appearing on *The David Susskind Show* or in any other way making anything that could even vaguely be construed as a fuss. I call attention to this exemplary behavior not merely to cast myself in a favorable light but also to emphasize the seriousness of the present situation. The present situation that I speak of is the present situation that makes it virtually impossible to smoke a cigarette in public without the risk of fine, imprisonment or having to argue with someone not of my class.

2 Should the last part of that statement disturb the more egalitarian among you, I hasten to add that I use the word "class" in its narrower sense to refer to that group more commonly thought of as "my kind of people." And while there are a great many requirements for inclusion in my kind of people, chief among them is an absolute hands-off policy when it comes to the subject of smoking.

3 Smoking is, if not my life, then at least my hobby. I love to smoke. Smoking is fun. Smoking is cool. Smoking is, as far as I am concerned, the entire point of being an adult. It makes growing up genuinely worthwhile. I am quite well aware of the hazards of smoking. Smoking is not a healthful pastime, it is true. Smoking is indeed no bracing dip in the ocean, no strenuous series of calisthenics, no two laps around the reservoir. On the other hand, smoking has to its advantage the fact that it is a quiet pursuit. Smoking is, in effect, a dignified sport. Not for the smoker the undue fanfare associated with downhill skiing, professional football or race-car driving. And yet, smoking is—as I have stated previously—hazardous. Very hazardous. Smoking, in fact, is downright dangerous. Most people who smoke will eventually contract a fatal disease and die. But they don't brag about it, do they? Most people who ski, play professional football or drive race cars, will not die—at least not in the act—and yet they are the ones with the glamorous images, the expensive equipment and the mythic proportions. Why this should be I cannot say, unless it is simply that the average American does not know a daredevil when he sees one. And it is the average American to whom I address this discourse because it is the average American who is responsible

for the recent spate of no-smoking laws and antismoking sentiment. That it is the average American who must take the blame I have no doubt, for unquestionably the *above*-average American has better things to do.

4   I understand, of course, that many people find smoking objectionable. That is their right. I would, I assure you, be the very last to criticize the annoyed. I myself find many—even most—things objectionable. Being offended is the natural consequence of leaving one's home. I do not like aftershave lotion, adults who roller-skate, children who speak French, or anyone who is unduly tan. I do not, however, go around enacting legislation and putting up signs. In private I avoid such people; in public they have the run of the place. I stay at home as much as possible, and so should they. When it is necessary, however, to go out of the house, they must be prepared, as am I, to deal with the unpleasant personal habits of others. That is what "public" means. If you can't stand the heat, get back in the kitchen.

5   As many of you may be unaware of the full extent of this private interference in the public sector, I offer the following report:

HOSPITALS

6   Hospitals are, when it comes to the restriction of smoking, perhaps the worst offenders of all. Not only because the innocent visitor must invariably walk miles to reach a smoking area, but also because a hospital is the singularly most illogical place in the world to ban smoking. A hospital is, after all, just the sort of unsavory and nerve-racking environment that makes smoking really pay off. Not to mention that in a hospital, the most frequent objection of the nonsmoker (that *your* smoke endangers *his* health) is rendered entirely meaningless by the fact that everyone there is already sick. Except the visitor—who is not allowed to smoke.

RESTAURANTS

7   By and large the sort of restaurant that has "no-smoking tables" is just the sort of restaurant that would most benefit from the dulling of its patrons' palates. At the time of this writing, New York City restaurants are still free of this divisive legislation. Perhaps those in power are aware that if the New Yorker was compelled to deal with just one more factor in deciding on a restaurant, there would be a mass return to home cooking. For there is, without question, at least in my particular circle, not a single person stalwart enough, after a forty-minute phone conversation, when everyone has finally and at long last agreed on Thai food, downtown, at 9:30, to then bear up

under the pressures inherent in the very idea of smoking and no-smoking tables.

MINNESOTA

8 Due to something called the Minnesota Clean Air Act, it is illegal to smoke in the baggage-claim area of the Minneapolis Airport. This particular bit of news is surprising, since it has been my personal observation that even nonsmokers tend to light up while waiting to see if their baggage has accompanied them to their final destination. As I imagine that this law has provoked a rather strong response, I was initially quite puzzled as to why Minnesota would risk alienating what few visitors it had been able to attract. This mystery was cleared up when, after having spent but a single day there, I realized that in Minnesota the Clean Air Act is a tourist attraction. It may not be the Beaubourg, but it's all their own. I found this to be an interesting, subtle concept, and have suggested to state officials that they might further exploit its commercial possibilities by offering for sale plain blue postcards emblazoned with the legend: Downtown Minneapolis.

AIRPLANES

9 Far be it from me to incite the general public by rashly suggesting that people who smoke are smarter than people who don't. But I should like to point out that I number among my acquaintances not a single nicotine buff who would entertain, for even the briefest moment, the notion that sitting six inches in front of a smoker is in any way healthier than sitting six inches behind him.

TAXICABS

10 Perhaps one of the most chilling features of New York life is hearing the meter click in a taxicab before one has noticed the sign stating: PLEASE DO NOT SMOKE. DRIVER ALLERGIC. One can, of course, exercise the option of disembarking immediately should one not mind being out a whole dollar, or one can, more thriftily, occupy oneself instead by attempting to figure out just how it is that a man who cannot find his way from the Pierre Hotel to East Seventy-eighth Street has somehow managed to learn the English word for allergic.

A QUESTION OF RIGHTS

Rhoda Nichter

1   "I have a right to smoke! You are infringing on my rights!" is one fairly typical response by a smoker who is asked to refrain.

2   Let us examine this question of rights. True, the smoker has a right to smoke. It is a legal addiction. He has the right to commit slow suicide. But he does not have the right to take the bystanding nonsmoker along with him on his mad trip.

3   Actually, if the smoker smokes where it affects the bystanding nonsmoker, *he* is infringing on the nonsmoker's right to breathe God's clean air. When a nonsmoker is in an enclosed smoke-infested place, he becomes an *involuntary* smoker, forced to smoke against his will. The smoker inflicts an unwanted condition on others if he claims the right to smoke anywhere he wishes.

4   It is not a question of whether the smoker has a right to smoke. It is a question of whether he has a right to pollute the nonsmoker's breathing space. It is a question of whether he has a right to alter the air so that it is unfit for others to breathe.

5   English philosopher John Stuart Mill stated, "A right ceases to be a right when it infringes on the right of another."

6   Just as the smoker's right to swing his fist ends where my nose begins, his right to smoke also ends where my nose begins.

VOTING

LET'S NOT GET OUT THE VOTE

Robert E. Coulson

1   Three years ago anyone who failed to vote had to face the combined scorn of both political parties, the schoolteachers, boy scouts, war veterans, chambers of commerce, and leagues of women voters. Last year bar associations, girl scouts, tavern keepers, President Eisenhower, radio and TV stations, and junior chambers of commerce joined the crusade. There is every prospect that in future elections, nonvoters will face jail sentences or fines, or be called to testify before investigating committees.

2   Before this happens, someone should come to their defense. Nonvoters are often more intelligent, more fair-minded, and just as loyal as voters. The right not to vote is as basic as the right to. If voting is made a duty, it ceases to be a privilege.

3   Let's look at the voting behavior of Mr. and Mrs. Whipcord and Mrs. Whipcord's brother Harold, on the day of the local school-board election. Mrs. Whipcord says, "I have studied the candidates and have made up my mind. I will vote for Jones." Mr. Whipcord says, "I know nothing about the candidates or the issues. I will stay home, and allow the election to be decided by the votes of those who have made a study and formed an opinion." Harold says, "I don't know anything about the candidates or the problems, but by golly, I'm going to vote. It's my duty. I'll pick the fellows with the shortest names."

4   If there is a bad citizen among these three, which one is it? Whose procedure is least likely to bring good government to the school district?

5   Non-voting, multiplied by the thousands, is said to mean voter apathy, and this is supposed to be a sin. Have we lost our sacred American right to be apathetic? Suppose Mr. Whipcord studied the candidates carefully and concluded that Candidate Jones was a boob and Candidate Smith was a thief. Is it un-American to refuse to choose between them? Or suppose he is satisfied that Jones and Smith are equally qualified, equally able, and that the school's problems are in good hands no matter which man wins. He is not apathetic; he is satisfied. Why should he be forced to choose between candidates on some esoteric basis?

6   The notion that "getting out the vote" makes for better election

results is neither non-partisan, patriotic, nor logical. It is a device to favor the machines of both parties. It handicaps independent candidates, unfairly burdens the party in power, makes elections more expensive to conduct, greatly slows the tallying, and—worst of all—places the emphasis on the ritual of voting rather than the thought behind the vote.

7   If you fill in all the blank spaces on the ballot, the political machines will steal three-fourths of your vote. Let's see how this works, in a typical primary election.

8   Here are seven offices to be filled by nomination, with two or three candidates for each office. Citizen Stringfellow is interested in seeing Jones win for Auditor. He has no information about the candidates for Attorney General, Treasurer, Superintendent of Schools, or the others. He votes for Jones and then looks on down the list. He has been persuaded that it is his duty to vote for *somebody* for each office. So for six of the seven names, he marks an X opposite the name best known to him, or the name on top, or the name suggested by his committeeman. These are machine candidates, and Citizen Stringfellow has given away six-sevenths of his vote.

9   After him, comes Citizen Stalwart, who knows the candidates for two of the seven offices. He also fills in all the blanks, letting the machine steal five-sevenths of his vote. One of his blind votes cancels out the intelligent vote cast by Citizen Stringfellow. At this rate, during a day's balloting, the candidates backed by the strongest machines with the biggest publicity budgets will win, even though not a single voter had an intelligent preference for them.

10   Is this what Thomas Jefferson had in mind?

11   "Getting out the vote" is always partisan. A calm and dignified effort benefits the party in power. An excited or hysterical effort benefits the party out of power. The Republicans were very happy to use the pressure of "neutral" groups in the 1952 elections. But they had better learn that this is a two-edged sword. Next time, the girl scouts, veterans' groups, radio stations, newspapers, and community funds may be out needling the Republicans with propaganda.

12   "Vote this time or your vote may be gone forever." "This may be your last chance." "Vote now or never." Anyone who is led to the polls by such arguments is going to vote against whoever brought us to the edge of this crevasse. As the pressure on the public increases, the party out of power is most likely to benefit in direct proportion to it.

13   All public-opinion surveys show that a certain proportion of the electorate has no opinion about many vital issues, does not know who is running for office, and does not care. A gentle campaign to bring a submissive one-third of the apathetic sheep to the polls gets

out a voting majority for the candidates who have had the greatest amount of publicity—who usually belong to the party in power. A rip-snorting effort to get out all the ignoramuses tends to turn them into the rebel column, and thus benefits the outs.

14   In either event, the girl scouts should wash their hands of it. The job of getting out the vote is a partisan effort which belongs to the professionals.

15   The silliest idea of all is the notion that it is un-American or unpatriotic not to vote. "A plague on both your houses" is a fair American attitude—all too often a logical one. Stupidity does not become wisdom by being multiplied.

16   In every election not more than one-third of the people care very much how it comes out. A certain percentage may have some sort of belief or opinion without feeling very strongly about it; another percentage may have studied the matter a little without forming an opinion; another percentage may not even have studied it; and so on, until we come to the people who are not even aware that an election is being held. The more we urge these people to clutter up the polling place, the more delay there is in voting, the more the cost of ballots and clerks, and the closer the returns.

17   If Candidate Jones would normally have won by 3,000 votes to 1,000, and we corral 10,000 more people into the polling places, won't Candidate Jones still win, by 8,000 to 6,000? Mathematically the last-minute coin flippers may make the election look close, but what patriotic purpose is accomplished?

18   And if the coin-flippers should happen to defeat the will of the informed majority, the cause of good government would emphatically not have been served.

19   Our city had a referendum recently in which the people voted for a tax increase to build an incinerator and against a tax increase to operate it. Every one of your communities has probably known referendums where the voters approved the bonds for a school but disapproved the sites, or voted for the site and against the bonds. All those voters who marked in opposite directions on the same afternoon were unwisely pressured into voting.

20   You have also seen primary elections where the boob with the catchy name ran away from the able man whose publicity was colorless. You have seen final elections where the straight party voters and the blank fillers smothered any discriminating choices which the thoughtful voters had made. You may have noticed with distress some of the undignified didos, cruel epithets, pompous verbosities, and Shakespearean gestures with which even good men become burdened early in their campaigns. All of these are caused in large mea-

sure by "get out the vote" efforts which emphasize putting a cross in half the squares.

21   Instead of urging people to vote, we ought to be urging them to study and form opinions. If thought and inspection of the candidates do not create a real desire to vote, then the citizen should be encouraged to stay at home on election day. A low vote is part of the public record and itself a significant voter reaction which ought to be preserved. Maybe neither of the candidates was worth voting for.

22   Certainly the right to vote is important and should not be curtailed. A fool who is willing to walk all the way to the polling place should be given every freedom to record every stupid impulse he feels, for these will tend to cancel each other out. But no one should pretend that marking X in a square is any proof of patriotism or even intelligence. It is not your duty to vote, but, if you choose to, then it should be your duty to be intelligent about it.

FOR COMPULSORY VOTING

Alan Wertheimer

1   As the Presidential election approaches we will no doubt be asked to recall that it was, in part, the demand for the "right to vote" that led to independence. Editorial writers throughout America will predictably bemoan the low level of participation and implore us to feel doubly guilty for failing to vote in this Bicentennial and Presidential election year.

2   Rather than conduct these ritual "get-out-the-vote" dances, why not simply make voting compulsory?

3   That we even seem compelled to urge citizens to exercise a right (what other *rights* do we need to urge citizens to exercise?) indicates that we may err in thinking of voting as a *right* at all. If citizens have a duty to vote, we should penalize those who fail to do their duty.

4   My argument for compulsory voting makes several (I think uncontroversial) assumptions: Competitive elections are desirable—for all their problems and deficiencies they are preferable to alternative methods of obtaining political leaders; it is technically possible to administer a compulsory-voting program (nonvoters would pay a tax or fine as in Belgium, the Netherlands, and Australia); compulsory voting works—it *does* increase the percentage of eligible voters who actually vote.

5   Elections can be understood as "public goods." A public good is any good that if made available to *any* member of a community must be made available to *all* members, generally because there is no feasible way to exclude noncontributors from enjoying the good. Public highways, national defense and police protection are examples of public good.

6   Now if the benefit of a public good is available to all, it is irrational for one to *voluntarily* contribute to its provision, in terms of money, time or energy. The rational citizen will attempt to "free ride," to enjoy the benefits while minimizing or avoiding the cost, as when we attempt to pay the lowest tax possible (or none at all).

7   All Americans benefit from the peaceful change of leadership and the fact that elections keep all elected officials (even those we do not support) at least somewhat responsive to our preferences. Voters and nonvoters alike receive these benefits and receive additional benefits if their preferred candidate wins. It follows that the rational citizen will not vote but will ride by avoiding the costs (including information cost) involved in voting.

8   I am not suggesting that we should not vote, merely that it is

not in one's *individual interest* to vote, because no single vote will affect the outcome of the election and the electoral system will not crumble if any one of us fails to vote. We get the same benefits regardless of what we do.

9   It is not surprising that many citizens fail to vote. Rather, why do so many act irrationally (if altruistically) and vote?

10   First, some people are simply willing to sacrifice their interest for the public good.

11   Second, many people overestimate the importance of their vote. Third, many vote to assuage their sense of guilt. But this hardly happens spontaneously. We systematically encourage citizens to overestimate the importance of their vote and to feel guilty when they do not vote—and it works.

12   What would compulsory voting do? First we would be spared the ritual propaganda campaigns in which we lie to ourselves about the significance of our individual votes and drum up our feelings of guilt. Second, we could be allowed to abstain, and thus citizens could specifically indicate that no candidate was satisfactory. Third, because it is largely the poor who tend not to vote, compulsory voting would increase their political power, as candidates would be forced to become more responsive to their interests. Fourth, since those who prefer candidates who are unlikely to win often do not vote, elections would provide a more accurate description of the nation's political preferences.

REPRODUCTIVE SURROGACY

THE RATIONALE FOR SURROGATE MOTHERHOOD

Ethics Committee of the American Fertility Society

1   A surrogate mother is a woman who is artificially inseminated with the sperm of a man who is not her husband; she carries the pregnancy and then turns the resulting child over to the man to rear. In almost all instances, the man has chosen to use a surrogate mother because his wife is infertile. After the birth, the wife will adopt the child.

2   Unlike surrogate gestational motherhood, which involves an embryo transfer after in vivo or in vitro fertilization (IVF), surrogate motherhood depends only on the technology of artificial insemination. The primary reason for the use of surrogate motherhood as a reproductive option is to produce a child with a genetic link to the husband.

3   The use of the term "surrogate" for the woman who is the genetic and gestational mother of the child appears a misnomer to some people, who argue that the adoptive mother is actually the "surrogate" for the biologic mother, who has given up the child. Nevertheless, a contrary position can be articulated, because the adoptive woman will be performing the major mothering role by rearing the child, with the biologic mother serving as a surrogate for her in providing the component for reproduction that she lacks. Although the term "surrogate mother" is, in any case, ambiguous and not a medical term, it has nevertheless received widespread public recognition and will be used in this report to mean a woman who conceives and gestates a child to be reared by the biologic father and his wife. The use of a surrogate mother, who provides the egg and the womb for the child, is currently much more common than the use of a surrogate gestational mother, who provides only the womb. . . .

4   Surrogate motherhood has received scant attention in the medical literature. . . .

5   One reason for the lack of scientific attention to the medical aspects of surrogate motherhood is that it has developed in an entrepreneurial setting, generally apart from medical institutions. Although the founders of some surrogate mother programs are physicians, the majority are lawyers, social workers, or persons with no professional training. However, most programs do use the services of a physician to perform a physical examination of the surrogate mother and to perform the artificial insemination. The extent to which these programs undertake an independent assessment of the infertility of the wife is unclear. Some couples who

have infertility problems that could be helped by drugs, surgery, IVF, or other alternatives may be employing a surrogate at a substantial fee because they do not undergo medical screening as part of the surrogate program and thus do not realize that they have other options. Existing surrogate mother programs generally perform medical screening on the surrogate, and some perform a physical on the man who will provide the sperm.

6   Some women serve as surrogate mothers for an infertile friend or relative and charge no fee. In other instances, the surrogate mother is a stranger who receives compensation for her services.

7   The demographic studies of surrogate mothers, which deal mainly with potential paid surrogates, have found that their average age is 25. Over one-half of the women are married, one-fifth divorced, and about one-fourth single. Over one-half (57%) are Protestant and 42% are Catholic. Over one-half are high school graduates and over one-fourth have schooling beyond high school.

8   Polls show that the public is less favorably disposed toward surrogate motherhood as an infertility solution than it is toward IVF, artificial insemination-donor (AID), embryo donation, or adoption. However, surveys of the public and of child welfare professionals regarding how the law should handle surrogate motherhood indicate that most people feel that the procedure should not be banned but rather should be regulated.

9   When a woman is infertile, she and her husband may need the assistance of a surrogate mother to conceive and carry a child for her. Sperm from the husband of the infertile woman is used to inseminate the surrogate mother, who will carry the pregnancy and then turn the resulting child over to the couple.

10   The primary medical indication for use of a surrogate mother is the inability of a woman to provide either the genetic or the gestational component for childbearing, for example, a woman who has had a hysterectomy combined with removal of the ovaries. This is the only situation in which surrogate motherhood provides the sole medical solution. For other indications, other medical options are possible, although they may not be readily available.

11   A second indication for surrogate motherhood is the inability to provide the genetic component, for example, because of premature menopause or the desire not to risk passing on a genetic defect. Under these circumstances, the woman could alternatively have the genetic component provided through egg or embryo donation, but donors might be more difficult to find than surrogate mothers.

12   A third indication for the use of a surrogate mother is the inability to gestate. A woman with severe hypertension, a uterine malformation, or the absence of a uterus after hysterectomy may use the services of a surrogate mother. If that woman wanted to provide the genetic compo-

nent for her child, she and her husband could create an embryo either in vitro or in vivo, then have it transferred to a surrogate gestational mother.

13   The use of a surrogate mother is also available as a secondary approach for women with any other type of infertility; essentially, it eliminates the need for the social mother to play any biologic role in reproduction. . . .

14   For some couples, of whom the wife has no uterus or ovaries, the use of a surrogate mother is the only means to have a child genetically related to one of them. In all of its applications, the use of a surrogate mother allows the infertile woman who wishes to rear a child the opportunity to adopt an infant more rapidly than by waiting several years for a traditional adoption. In addition, it allows her to rear her husband's genetic child.

15   For the husband of an infertile woman, the use of a surrogate may be the only way in which he can conceive and rear a child with a biologic tie to himself, short of divorcing his wife and remarrying only for that reason or of having an adulterous union. Certainly, the use of a surrogate mother under the auspices of a medical practitioner seems far less destructive of the institution of the family than the latter two options.

16   For the child, the use of a surrogate mother gives him or her an opportunity that would not otherwise be available: the opportunity to exist. Furthermore, the child would be reared by a couple who so wanted him or her that they were willing to participate in a novel process with potential legal and other risks.

17   The process offers potential benefits for the surrogates as well. As in the case of organ transplantation, it offers them the chance to be altruistic. In addition, some surrogate mothers enjoy being pregnant. Moreover, one preliminary study found that about one-third of surrogate mothers may be using the process to help themselves psychologically. These are women who in the past have voluntarily aborted or given up a child through adoption and have then become surrogate mothers in order to relive the experience of pregnancy in a psychologically satisfactory way. Those women who become surrogate mothers for a fee are benefited by having another income option. For example, some divorced women with young children have chosen to be surrogates in order to support their children and to remain at home to care for them.

18   Although there are potential risks to surrogacy, those risks can be understood by the prospective participants. Thus informed, they can engage in competent decision making about whether or not to pursue this reproductive option. Initial data indicate that the couples and surrogates can understand in advance how they will react to the procedure. "Preliminary evidence indicates that only a few surrogates and the parental couple felt surprised by their own psychological responses after the relinquishment or by the other party's response." . . .

19   As to potential psychological harm to the child, there is concern that the child's self-identity might be confused because of his or her blurred genealogy. The use of a surrogate mother does not have to have a "blurring" effect on the child's genealogy. Situations in which full disclosures are made to the child about the personal history of the surrogate (and perhaps even her identity) might provide clear knowledge of genealogy. However, it is true that any use of a third party may make the genealogy more complex and perhaps bothersome to the child. Even if there are psychological risks, most infertile couples who go through with a reproduction arrangement that involves a third party do so as a last resort. In some cases, their willingness to make sacrifices to have a child may testify to their worthiness as loving parents. A child conceived through surrogate motherhood may be born into a much healthier climate than a child whose birth was unplanned. For this reason, some of the risks caused by confused genealogy may be outweighed by possible benefits to the child of having parents who want him or her.

20   Concerns are also raised by payment to a surrogate. Some people may approve of voluntary surrogate motherhood but disapprove of surrogate motherhood for a fee. The ramifications of prohibiting payment are widespread, however, because there are not enough voluntary surrogates to meet the needs of infertile couples. Because a surrogate mother has a much greater involvement in reproduction than does a donor of sperm, eggs, or embryos, she usually requires remuneration. On the couple's side, spending money for childbearing does not in itself seem unethical. Even without the involvement of a surrogate, couples spend substantial sums to investigate and treat their infertility. This financial outlay does not seem to create unusually high expectations about the child that might lead to psychological problems for him or her.

21   Commercialization in connection with giving up a child for adoption has traditionally been banned on the grounds that it might force biologic mothers to give up children whom they do not wish to give up and that the mere willingness to pay for a child does not guarantee that the potential parent will treat the child well. Because the sperm donor is merely turning over a gamete, whereas the surrogate mother is turning over a child, the latter action may seem to fit more closely into traditional concerns about baby selling. Nevertheless, paying the surrogate a fee is readily distinguishable from paying an already pregnant woman for her child. The payment to a surrogate is made in exchange for her help in creating a child, not in exchange for possession of the child. Because the decision is made before the pregnancy ensues and the arrangement is entered into with the specific intention of relinquishing the child, the woman is less likely than an already-pregnant woman to be coerced into giving up a child whom she wishes to keep. Because the child will be reared by the genetic father and his wife, it may be more likely that the

rearing father will have a greater sense of responsibility for the child than if the child were turned over to a stranger. Because the surrogate's responsibilities are set out in a contract before the conception occurs, she is more likely to understand and abide by them and less likely later to harass the couple with a change of heart.

22   A psychiatrist who has interviewed over 500 potential surrogates and who has followed several dozen surrogates through their pregnancies and beyond has written about surrogates' financial motivation, "There is no evidence that such a motivating factor results in more adverse psychological, medical, or legal consequences." . . .

23   The Committee finds that surrogate motherhood is a matter that requires intense scrutiny. The Committee does not recommend the use of a surrogate mother for a nonmedical reason, such as the convenience of the rearing mother, because nonmedical reasons seem inadequate to justify using a surrogate to undertake the risks of pregnancy and delivery. As for surrogate motherhood for medical reasons, the Committee is dismayed by the scarcity of empiric evidence about how the surrogacy process works and how it affects those involved. Nevertheless, this process offers promise as the only medical solution to infertility in a couple of whom the woman has no uterus and who does not produce eggs or does not want to risk passing on a genetic defect that she carries.

24   There may be individual practitioners or medical groups asked to aid a surrogate mother arrangement who find that the reservations about the procedure outweigh the benefits, i.e., that the procedure is not in the best interests of the persons integrally and adequately considered. In that circumstance, the practitioner or group could ethically decline to participate in the arrangement. . . .

25   The Committee recommends that if surrogate motherhood is pursued, it should be pursued as a clinical experiment. Among the issues to be addressed in the research on surrogate mothers are the following:

   a. the psychological effects of the procedure on the surrogates, the couples, and the resulting children
   b. the effects, if any, of bonding between the surrogate and the fetus in utero
   c. the appropriate screening of the surrogate and the man who provides the sperm
   d. the likelihood that the surrogate will exercise appropriate care during the pregnancy
   e. the effects of having the couple and the surrogate meet or not meet
   f. the effects on the surrogate's own family of her participation in the process
   g. the effects of disclosing or not disclosing the use of a surrogate mother or her identity to the child

h. other issues that shed light on the effects of surrogacy on the welfare of the various persons involved and on society.

26   In the course of the clinical experiments on surrogate motherhood, special attention should be paid to whether the surrogate and the couple have given voluntary, informed consent. Both the surrogate and the man providing the sperm should be screened for infectious diseases, and the surrogate should be screened for genetic defects. . . .

27   So that potential conflicts of interest or exploitation by professionals can be avoided, the Committee recommends that professionals receive only their customary fees for services and receive no finder's fees for participation in surrogate motherhood. Although it would be preferable that surrogates not receive payment beyond compensation for expenses and their inconvenience, the Committee recognizes that in some cases payment will be necessary for surrogacy to occur. If surrogate motherhood turns out to be useful, a change in the law would be appropriate for assurance that the couple who contract with a surrogate mother are viewed as the legal parents.

SURROGATE MOTHERHOOD: AN ETHICAL DILEMMA

William E. May

1   Surrogate mothering. Several news stories have focused on the ethical and legal problems posed by the use of "surrogate mothers." One widely reported story dealt with the plight of Mary Beth Whitehead and the Sterns. Mary Beth, a married woman, had agreed to bear a child for William and Elizabeth Stern, and to relinquish all rights to the child as soon as it was born. Accordingly, she was artificially inseminated with the sperm of William Stern. Nonetheless, when the baby was born, she decided she was too emotionally attached to the child to give it up. A fierce legal battle over custody of the child ensued.

2   Other news stories have called attention to a new kind of commercial enterprise, surrogate parenting agencies, which seek to put infertile married women anxious for "a child of their own" in touch with women willing to serve as surrogates. For a commission—of course—these agencies will draw up a contract between the couple and the willing woman. The owner of one such agency recently declared that he wanted "to see [his company] become the Coca-Cola of the surrogate parenting industry."

3   Obviously, a surrogate mother is a woman who agrees to bear a child for another woman, who—in theory—will act as the child's mother after birth. Usually the surrogate arrangement is made to help a couple, otherwise childless, to have a child "of their own." The surrogate can become pregnant in two ways. The first, which is at present the more common procedure, is to inseminate the surrogate artificially with sperm "provided" by the infertile woman's husband. In this case, the child is genetically the offspring of the surrogate and of the infertile woman's husband.

4   The second method, more infrequently used, is through *in vitro* fertilization and embryo transfer. In this case ova are removed from the ovaries of the infertile wife—who may be unable to conceive because of a missing uterus. Sperm taken from the husband are then used to fertilize these ova in the laboratory, and one (or more) of the developing embryos is selected for implantation into the womb of the surrogate. In this case the child is genetically the offspring of the married couple, with the surrogate acting as a "host" during pregnancy.

5   Several permutations and combinations of the surrogate arrangement are possible. One is to resort to it in order to prevent the transmission of a genetic malady. If, for example, both husband and wife are carriers of a recessive genetic defect (for example, Tay-Sachs disease), or if the wife, because of her age, runs the risk of having a child crippled

by Down's Syndrome, they can make a surrogate arrangement with a woman known to be free of the recessive genetic defect or in an age group not at high risk of conceiving a Down's Syndrome child. This woman can then be inseminated artificially with the husband's sperm, then bear the child, then turn it over to the husband and wife. Still another possible customer for surrogate mothering is a single woman who wants to raise a child but does not want to be bothered with pregnancy. By somehow obtaining the sperm of a man she deemed a suitable father and then finding a woman agreeable to being a surrogate, she could have a child without the fuss and commitment of marriage.

6   Ordinarily, the woman who agrees to be the surrogate does so for a fee (the going rate is approximately $10,000 plus expenses), but this is not a necessary condition; a woman could consent simply out of the kindness of her heart, particularly if she is a relative or close friend of a couple wanting a child.

7   Justification of surrogate mothering customarily involves the following considerations. The first argument is that use of this procedure involves no injustice, because all the parties to the arrangement give free and informed consent to it; hence, no one's rights are violated. While some might object that the surrogate "sells" her body and thus does something akin to prostitution, surrogation proponents say one ought to remember that the surrogate freely chooses to give her body for this purpose, and the purpose is not, as in prostitution, primarily selfish or involuntary; rather the purpose is good, voluntary—even sometimes selfless: namely, to help an otherwise childless couple to have a healthy child "of their own." Moreover, these supporters might say, "sale" of the body may not even be required—a woman can consent to be a surrogate with no consideration of financial gain. While supporters acknowledge that widespread acceptance of surrogation might tempt financially strapped women to "sell" their bodies, and might lead to the exploitation of the poor and ignorant, they say these evils are not inherent and can be avoided. Legal measures can be taken, these proponents say, to prevent the exploitation of the economically or emotionally crippled, to protect the rights of both surrogates and married couples, and to prevent abuse of this procedure by unmarried individuals seeking to have children.

8   A second justification used to support surrogate mothering is the great good it can bring about. The desire of a married couple to have a "child of their own," the argument goes, is surely a natural and legitimate one. Although it may be impossible, because of the wife's infertility, to have a child that is genetically the offspring of husband and wife, artificial insemination by the husband will at least enable them to have a child who is in truth the husband's flesh and blood—and the surrogate, in her kindness, merely cooperates with them in realizing this desire. The wife, although not the child's biological mother, can still give it a

mother's love and care, say these supporters. In fact, they say, a biblical precedent for surrogate mothering seems to exist in the case of Rachel: Was she not helped in mothering the children of Jacob through the ministry of her handmaids?

9   Surrogation supporters similarly argue that the desire of a couple to have a "normal" child and not one crippled by a genetic disease is natural and legitimate. In fact, they argue, would not a man and wife be acting irresponsibly if they knowingly took the chance of passing on to their children some dread disease, when they could avoid this terrible evil by resorting to artificial insemination of a surrogate?

10   In short, these supporters say, use of surrogate mothers is morally justifiable insofar as it does not inherently involve any injustice, either to the surrogate or to the consenting couple, and because it helps to fulfill legitimate desires, avoid serious evils, and bring about great goods.

11   But serious objections—in my opinion even devastating objections—can be raised against the use of surrogate mothers. First of all, in marrying, a man and woman are to give themselves irrevocably to one another, and they are to give themselves completely.

12   This means that they give to one another their power to generate human life, their procreativity. Just as it is wrong for a married person to "give" himself or herself in sexual union to a non-spouse, that is, to commit adultery, so it is wrong for a married person to "give" himself or herself to another procreatively, that is, to share with someone other than his or her spouse the power to generate human life. The reason is simply that in getting married one gives to one's spouse irrevocably and exclusively one's whole person, including one's power to give life. In short, one major reason it is wrong to use surrogate mothers by artificially inseminating them with the husband's sperm is that this entails an attack on marriage itself.

13   But, some may ask, what if the surrogate is not inseminated artificially but rather becomes pregnant after an embryo, conceived in a petri dish by inseminating the wife's ova with her own husband's sperm, is implanted in the surrogate's womb? This surely involves no attack upon the marriage, they might say.

14   To answer this question adequately, it would be necessary to undertake a full scale examination of *in vitro* fertilization. Although this is not possible here, I believe that such generation of human life is immoral. The child comes to exist not through the one-flesh loving union of husband and wife, but in the laboratory, as the end product of a series of nonmarital acts. The participation of husband and wife in this procedure is not rooted in their marital relationship; rather, it is rooted simply in the fact that they are producers of gametic materials, sperm and ova. The life generated is not "begotten" in their act of marital love; rather it is "produced" by others, the technicians who manipulate the sperm

and ova. This way of generating human life removes it from the marital embrace and transfers it to the laboratory. By doing so, it tears apart the bonds uniting marriage, the marital act, and the loving generation of new human life through the personal act of the spouses. . . .

15   In sum, use of surrogate mothers constitutes an attack on marriage and *human* parenthood. Artificial insemination of the surrogate violates the marriage because the husband freely chooses to share with someone other than his wife his power to give life, a power that he has, by marrying, irrevocably and exclusively committed to his spouse. Surrogate mothering after *in vitro* fertilization of the wife's ova by her husband's sperm violates the meaning of human parenthood because it generates new human life, a new human person, not by "begetting" it through the one-flesh marital union of husband and wife, but rather by "making" it in the laboratory.

16   The woman who consents to be a surrogate willingly cooperates in these violations of the sanctity of marriage and the dignity of human life in its generation. She may do so for altruistic reasons; she may do it "out of love," and in a desire to help a married couple fulfill their desires—the chief argument for surrogate mothering is based on the thesis that a good end justifies the means. This thesis, though, is false and terribly misleading. Our actions indeed "get things done," that is, they have results, both good and bad. But more importantly, they "get things said," that is, they tell us something; actions speak louder than words. Through our actions we "say" something; we reveal who we are: liars or cheaters or adulterers or masturbators; or faithful, chaste, and upright persons. At the heart of our actions is a self-determined choice that abides within us and gives to us our "character," our moral identity. Thus a truly authentic ethic is as much concerned with means as it is with ends, with the actions we freely choose to do as well as with the ends for the sake of which we choose to perform these actions. If we are to act rightly, both means and ends must be good. We cannot justify immoral means by the goods they are intended to achieve nor by the evils they are designed to avoid. Just as one can rationalize being a surrogate because it was done "for love's sake," so too can one rationalize killing someone "for love's sake," as in mercy killing. But the good one hopes to achieve does not justify the evil one chooses to do.

17   The surrogate, moreover, freely chooses, if she is artificially inseminated, to become the mother of the child she then conceives; yet at the same time she refuses to accept responsibility for its care. She refuses to accept the responsibilities of a mother. She is like a husband who abandons his wife and child after birth, or like a man who gives life to a child through fornication and then refuses to care for the child to whom he has given life.

18   Women who consent to being surrogates may be well motivated;

their purpose is to "help" others realize their desires. But good motives are not sufficient to make what they choose to do morally good. Their choice is, in truth, internally inconsistent, for they choose both to be and not to be mothers. Moreover, they cooperate in a procedure that, as has been seen, violates the meaning of marriage and of human parenthood.

19   Much more could be said to show that surrogate mothering is wrong and terribly foolish: it ordinarily requires the husband to masturbate; it could lead to terrible exploitation of the poor and unreflective; it can lead to terrible conflicts between the surrogate and those she seeks to "help" if, as is natural, she becomes emotionally attached to the child she carries; and so on. But the main reason this procedure is wrong, in my opinion, is the violence it does to marriage and to the God-given bonds uniting marriage, the marital act, and the loving begetting of new human persons.

CENSORSHIP

PORNOGRAPHY, OBSCENITY, AND THE CASE FOR CENSORSHIP

Irving Kristol

1   Being frustrated is disagreeable, but the real disasters in life begin when you get what you want. For almost a century now, a great many intelligent, well-meaning and articulate people have argued eloquently against any kind of censorship of art and entertainment. Within the past ten years, courts and legislatures have found these arguments so persuasive that censorship is now a relative rarity in most states.

2   Is there triumphant exhilaration in the land? Hardly. Somehow, things have not worked out as they were supposed to, and many civil-libertarians have said this was not what they meant. They wanted a world in which Eugene O'Neill's *Desire Under the Elms* could be produced, or James Joyce's *Ulysses* published, without interference. They got that, of course; but they also got a world in which homosexual rape is simulated on the stage, in which the public flocks to witness professional fornication, in which New York's Times Square has become a hideous marketplace for printed filth.

3   But does this really matter? Might not our disquiet be merely a cultural hangover? Was anyone ever corrupted by a book?

4   This last question, oddly enough, is asked by the same people who seem convinced that advertisements in magazines or displays of violence on television *do* have the power to corrupt. It is also asked, incredibly enough and in all sincerity, by university professors and teachers whose very lives provide the answer. After all, if you believe that no one was ever corrupted by a book, you have also to believe that no one was ever improved by a book. You have to believe, in other words, that art is morally trivial and that education is morally irrelevant.

5   To be sure, it is extremely difficult to trace the effects of any single book (or play or movie) on any reader. But we all know that the ways in which we use our minds and imaginations do shape our characters and help define us as persons. That those who certainly know this are moved to deny it merely indicates how a dogmatic resistance to the idea of censorship can result in a mindless insistence on the absurd.

6   For the plain fact is that we all believe that there is a point at which the public authorities ought to step in to limit the "self-expres-

sion" of an individual or a group. A theatrical director might find someone willing to commit suicide on the stage. We would not allow that. And I know of no one who argues that we ought to permit public gladiatorial contests, even between consenting adults.

7   No society can be utterly indifferent to the ways its citizens publicly entertain themselves. Bearbaiting and cockfighting are prohibited only in part out of compassion for the animals; the main reason is that such spectacles were felt to debase and brutalize the citizenry who flocked to witness them. The question with regard to pornography and obscenity is whether they will brutalize and debase our citizenry. We are, after all, not dealing with one book or one movie. We are dealing with a general tendency that is suffusing our entire culture.

8   Pornography's whole purpose, it seems to me, is to treat human beings obscenely, to deprive them of their specifically human dimension. Imagine a well-known man in a hospital ward, dying an agonizing death. His bladder and bowels empty themselves of their own accord. His consciousness is overwhelmed by pain, so that he cannot communicate with us, nor we with him. Now, it would be technically easy to put a television camera in his room and let the whole world witness this spectacle. We don't do it—at least not yet—because we regard this as an obscene invasion of privacy. And what would make the spectacle obscene is that we would be witnessing the extinguishing of humanity in a human animal.

9   Sex—like death—is an activity that is both animal and human. There are human sentiments and human ideals involved in this animal activity. But when sex is public, I do not believe the viewer can see the sentiments and the ideals, but sees only the animal coupling. And that is why when most men and women make love, they prefer to be alone—because it is only when you are alone that you can make love, as distinct from merely copulating. When sex is a public spectacle, a human relationship has been debased into a mere animal connection.

10   But even if all this is granted, it doubtless will be said that we ought not to be unduly concerned. Free competition in the cultural marketplace, it is argued by those who have never otherwise had a kind word to say for laissez-faire, will dispose of the problem; in the course of time, people will get bored with pornography and obscenity.

11   I would like to be able to go along with this reasoning, but I think it is false, and for two reasons. The first reason is psychological; the second, political.

12   In my opinion, pornography and obscenity appeal to and provoke a kind of sexual regression. The pleasure one gets from pornography and obscenity is infantile and autoerotic; put bluntly, it is a

masturbatory exercise of the imagination. Now, people who masturbate do not get bored with masturbation, just as sadists don't get bored with sadism, and voyeurs don't get bored with voyeurism. In other words, like all infantile sexuality, it can quite easily become a permanent self-reinforcing neurosis. And such a neurosis, on a mass scale, is a threat to our civilization and humanity, nothing less.

13   I am already touching upon a political aspect of pornography when I suggest that it is inherently subversive of civilization. But there is another political aspect, which has to do with the relationship of pornography and obscenity to democracy, and especially to the quality of public life on which democratic government ultimately rests.

14   Today a "managerial" conception of democracy prevails—wherein democracy is seen as a set of rules and procedures, and *nothing but* a set of rules and procedures, by which majority rule and minority rights are reconciled into a state of equilibrium. Thus, the political system can be fully reduced to its mechanical arrangements.

15   There is, however, an older idea of democracy—fairly common until about the beginning of this century—for which the conception of the quality of public life is absolutely crucial. This idea starts from the proposition that democracy is a form of self-government, and that you are entitled to it only if that "self" is worthy of governing. Because the desirability of self-government depends on the character of the people who govern, the older idea of democracy was very solicitous of the condition of this character. This older democracy had no problem in principle with pornography and obscenity; it censored them; it was not about to permit people to corrupt themselves.

16   But can a liberal—today—be for censorship? Yes, but he ought to favor a liberal form of censorship.

17   I don't think this is a contradiction in terms. We have no problem contrasting *repressive* laws governing alcohol, drugs and tobacco with laws *regulating* (that is, discouraging the sale of) alcohol, drugs and tobacco. We have not made smoking a criminal offense. We have, however, and with good liberal conscience, prohibited cigarette advertising on television. The idea of restricting individual freedom, in a liberal way, is not at all unfamiliar to us.

18   I therefore see no reason why we should not be able to distinguish repressive censorship from liberal censorship of the written and spoken word. In Britain, until a few years ago, you could perform almost any play you wished—but certain plays, judged to be obscene, had to be performed in private theatrical clubs. In the United States, all of us who grew up using public libraries are familiar with the circumstances under which certain books could be circulated only to adults, while still other books had to be read in the library. In

both cases, a small minority that was willing to make a serious effort to see an obscene play or book could do so. But the impact of obscenity was circumscribed, and the quality of public life was only marginally affected.

19   It is a distressing fact that any system of censorship is bound, upon occasion, to treat unjustly a particular work of art—to find pornography where there is only gentle eroticism, to find obscenity where none really exists, or to find both where the work's existence ought to be tolerated because it serves a larger moral purpose. That is the price one has to be prepared to pay for censorship—even liberal censorship.

20   But if you look at the history of American or English literature, there is precious little damage you can point to as a consequence of the censorship that prevailed throughout most of that history. I doubt that many works of real literary merit ever were suppressed. Nor did I notice that hitherto suppressed masterpieces flooded the market when censorship was eased.

21   I should say, to the contrary, that literature has lost quite a bit now that so much is permitted. It seems to me that the cultural market in the United States today is awash in dirty books, dirty movies, dirty theater. Our cultural condition has not improved as a result of the new freedom.

22   I'll put it bluntly: if you care for the quality of life in our American democracy, then you have to be for censorship.

DEFENDING INTELLECTUAL FREEDOM

Eli M. Oboler

1   The Henry Luce Professor of Urban Values at New York University, Irving Kristol, was rather less than urbane in his strictures against pornography and obscenity—or what he defines as such—in his March 23, 1971 article, "Pornography, Obscenity, and the Case for Censorship," which first appeared in the *New York Times* magazine and was recently reprinted in two issues of this *Newsletter* (September and November, 1971). He has exhumed a great many of the tired old pro-censorship arguments, but added a new dimension; he has coined a new phrase, "liberal censorship," which, despite all protestations to the contrary, is clearly a contradiction in terms.

2   Indeed, his whole essay is on the hyperbolic, exaggerated level illustrated by his undocumented statement that ". . . pornography . . . is inherently and purposefully subversive of civilization and its institutions." He is even more specific and direct in this: ". . . if you care for the quality of life in our American democracy, then you have to be for censorship." Blithely, he sells creative art down the river: "There are . . . some few works of art that are in the special category of the comic-ironic 'bawdy' (Boccaccio, Rabelais). It is such works of art that are likely to suffer at the hands of the censor. *That is the price* [my italics] one has to be prepared to pay for censorship—even liberal censorship." Snick-snack! Off with Boccaccio's head! Snip-snip! Eliminate Rabelais! And Joyce and Swift and Henry Miller and— but Kristol, contrary to all factual evidence, says, "If you look at the history of American or English literature, there is precious little damage you can point to as a consequence of the censorship that prevailed throughout most of that history."

3   Let alone the gross inexactitude of this dogmatic opinion, Kristol really ought to do a little study of the hundreds of years and thousands of literary creations between the writing of *Beowulf* and the first English legal censorship, that of Edmund Curll's *Venus in the Cloister*, in 1727. During those centuries after centuries, "most" of the history of English literature occurred. The quoted statement is only one of many examples of Kristollian *obiter dicta* which have a nice, ringing sound—but are actually quite hollow of solid fact, when closely examined.

4   It is really almost incredible that he would seriously make such a statement as "very few works of literature—of real literary merit, I mean—ever were suppressed; and those that were, were not suppressed for long." The long, long list of Anne Haight's well-known

Banned Books is a simple answer to the first claim; and it is certainly a specious, unsound argument to say that "those that were, were not suppressed for long." *Any* length of time is contrary to the fundamental tenets of freedom of speech and expression in which, presumably, "liberal" Kristol believes.

5   Incidentally, near the end of his article, he admits that "We had censorship of pornography and obscenity for 150 years," which in simple mathematical process would indicate that censorship began in 1821. This is a most interesting date, just about 93 years after it historically began! Kristol, as I said, needs at least a capsule course in the facts of the story of censorship.

6   *If* Kristol's facts were right, one might be willing to consider the logic of his argumentation, which, on the whole, is rather persuasive. But if "liberal" censorship has to be based on misinformation and exaggeration, then it is no more worth the consideration of reasonable men and women than *il*liberal censorship.

7   Admittedly, this brief reply to Kristol is itself a polemic, rather than in a reasonable vein. The reader is referred to my forthcoming book for a lengthy, historically based, positive set of facts and arguments concerning the merits and demerits of censorship of writings about sex.* Suffice it here, in a necessarily limited space, to say that Kristol has clearly failed to consider the most basic of all issues in the censorship/noncensorship dispute.

8   In a long perspective, the fear of the word is really the fear of the human. Like reverse Terences, those who censor and favor censorship are really saying, "I am human, but everything human is alien to me."† Men and women are men and women *because* of their sexual drives, and denial of this fact by even a never-ending line of censors—liberal *or* illiberal!—will not eliminate maleness and femaleness and the male-female relationship. The censor will never outlast biology.

**Defending Intellectual Freedom* (Westport, CT: Greenwood Press, 1980).

†Terence, a Roman playwright (185–159 B.C.), wrote in his *Heauton Timorumenos:* "I am a man, I count nothing human indifferent to me."

AIDS TESTING

WE NEED ROUTINE TESTING FOR AIDS

William J. Bennett

1   The AIDS epidemic may be the most serious health threat of this century. How best to deal with it has been the subject of a vigorous national debate. And out of this debate is emerging a growing and welcome consensus on a number of issues.

2   We can all agree, for example, on the need to care for those afflicted with AIDS, by helping to ensure that families, states, localities, hospitals and others have the resources to provide adequate medical care for those suffering from this disease. We can all agree that we must prevent violations of the civil rights of those who are carriers of the AIDS virus. And we can all agree on the need to educate all of our citizens, including young people, about how the AIDS virus is transmitted and how to guard against it. Moreover, there is now nearly universal agreement on a further point: the need for more widespread AIDS testing.

3   We need more testing for several reasons:

- Testing provides important epidemiological information, allowing us to determine just how widespread the virus is.
- Testing informs individuals if they have contracted AIDS so they can seek proper medical treatment.
- If an individual tests positive, he will know that he must refrain from activities that would endanger the life of another person.
- If an individual tests positive, he or the public health authorities can alert others who may be at risk.

4   While there is general agreement on the need for more widespread AIDS testing, some balk at going about this in the most effective way. They call for more testing, but only voluntary testing. They reject out of hand proposals for routine testing of individuals upon certain occasions: for example, for some or all of those admitted to hospitals, for those being treated at clinics serving "high-risk" populations, for couples seeking marriage licenses, and for prison inmates. Some individuals are so concerned about guaranteeing privacy that they will not allow even the confidential notification of other individuals possibly infected, or at risk of being infected, by someone found to be an AIDS carrier.

5   What has emerged, then, is a troubling paradox: Confronted with this grave public health threat, with a disease that is expected to claim more American lives by 1991 than did the Vietnam and Korean wars

combined, we have failed to employ routine testing and contact notifi-cation—commonly accepted public health measures for other similarly transmitted diseases.

6   An extraordinary gap has developed, between the recognition of the magnitude of the threat of AIDS and the failure to adopt eminently rea-sonable and useful public health measures to respond to it, measures for which there is long precedent.

7   Opponents of routine testing offer several arguments against it. None is convincing.

8   One argument is that routine testing would drive the principal classes of AIDS victims (homosexuals and intravenous drug users) "un-derground," because some individuals would be so fearful of discrimi-nation as a result of testing positive.

9   First of all, even if a few individuals did go "underground," we would have to balance this fact with the crucial information more wide-spread routine testing would produce for individuals, and for society. This information would save lives.

10   Second, the possibility that some individuals may avoid testing can be minimized by strong guarantees of appropriate confidentiality and nondiscrimination.

11   Third, we would not, of course, eliminate voluntary AIDS testing sites even as we adopt a policy of select, routine testing. Routine testing would serve in conjunction with, and not in lieu of, voluntary and even voluntary anonymous testing. And states and localities could, in certain circumstances, allow exceptions to routine testing.

12   It is precisely by making testing routine, by dealing with it just as we treat other similar communicable diseases, that we will go a long way toward lessening the stigma that now surrounds AIDS tests.

13   Above all, I would point out that most estimates are that the great majority of AIDS carriers are currently unaware that they are infected. Routine testing at appropriate occasions—along with much more readily available voluntary testing—would surely decrease the number of indi-viduals who might be unwittingly spreading the disease.

14   A second argument against routine testing is that it could lead to violations of confidentiality, particularly as it relates to the notification of past sexual partners.

15   A number of precautions can be taken to guard against this. For example, in many states today, if a person tests positive for syphilis, health authorities will ask the names of people with whom that person has been intimate. Then, without mentioning the name of the syphilis carrier, health authorities will confidentially notify those people who may have contracted the disease and recommend that they come in and be tested. This has long been standard public health practice. It can be done for AIDS as well. To protect others, it certainly should be done.

16   The American Medical Association's Principles of Medical Ethics recognize that a physician may reveal otherwise confidential information if this is necessary to protect the welfare of another individual or the community. There has long been recognition of the need in some instances to balance a patient's right to confidentiality and a physician's obligation to protect lives. In the case of AIDS, confidentiality would be superseded only in certain circumstances, such as to inform public health officials or to inform a wife that her husband has AIDS.

17   A third argument made against routine testing is that the AIDS test is costly and unreliable.

18   In fact, experience at the Department of Defense shows that testing can be done for less than $5 a person. The additional cost of counseling those who test positive is well worth the money.

19   The AIDS tests are reliable and have been used successfully. Moreover, a proper testing program includes provisions for double-checking positive test results.

20   There is no denying that a program of routine testing and contact notification presents some challenges. Few decisions on AIDS are easy. But the difficulty of the task cannot discourage us from facing up to our responsibilities. For what is the alternative? To go on as we have been? We cannot do that.

21   By now, the facts are clear: Business as usual is not enough. If we are to contain the spread of this deadly epidemic, routine testing must play a part. The real question we face is whether we will adopt aggressive public health measures now when time is still on our side and the spread of the virus can be curbed. Objections noted, cautions observed, civil liberties protected: We must now do what is essential to save lives.

AIDS: THE LEGAL EPIDEMIC

Arthur S. Leonard

1   At the very heart of the AIDS legal epidemic is "the Test," its uses, and abuses. The test is actually a set of laboratory procedures to detect antibodies to Human Immunodeficiency Virus (HIV, also known as LAV and HTLV-III). This virus, believed by most researchers to play a central role in AIDS and related medical disorders, stimulates the lymphatic system to produce detectable antibodies, usually within a few months of the virus being introduced into the body.

2   The test currently licensed by the Food and Drug Administration (FDA) for screening blood donations, called ELISA, is a highly sensitive test for these antibodies. If they are in the blood, the test will almost always be positive. However, in order to obtain this high degree of reactivity, the test had to be designed to react positively in doubtful cases as well, and the ELISA test is known for having a significant rate of false-positive results when used for screening donations at blood banks.

3   In addition to ELISA, there is a nonstandardized test called Western blot, which is a much more specific test for HIV antibodies. Because Western blot is more expensive and difficult to perform accurately, it is normally used only as a confirmatory test. If a blood sample repeatedly tests positive on ELISA testing, a Western blot is supposed to be used to be sure the ELISA positive is not false.

4   Newer tests are under development but not yet licensed for routine use. These tests are designed to detect the presence of HIV itself, rather than antibodies, and would presumably be more accurate than an antibody test because they would detect the viral presence, regardless of whether antibodies have been formed. The shortcomings of ELISA in this regard are illustrated by some recent cases of infection where transfused blood tested negative because infection was too recent for antibodies to have formed.

5   When the FDA licensed ELISA in March, 1985, lesbian and gay rights organizations expressed great concern about potential misuses of the test, as well as its shortcomings. Intense lobbying by the National Gay & Lesbian Task Force, with legal advice and assistance from Lambda Legal Defense and Education Fund, resulted in an agreement with the FDA to label the test kits with an unequivocal statement that ELISA was *solely* for the purpose of blood screening, and was neither a diagnostic test for AIDS nor an appropriate test for screening *people.*

6   After the test became available, however, various government agencies took actions inconsistent with this labeling restriction. The military began to use the test to screen recruits and active personnel, the State

Department has announced plans to test foreign service personnel and their dependents, and the Labor Department has announced it will test Job Corps employees and program participants. Despite statements that ELISA is not a diagnostic test for AIDS, the federal Centers for Disease Control (CDC) has added a positive test result to the surveillance definition, when present in conjunction with other physical symptoms.

7   Employers, insurance companies, schools, and prisons have all been implicated in test misuse, or proposals to use the test for screening people improperly. There have been legislative proposals to use the test for marriage licensing, to justify detention of prostitutes, and to monitor individual behavior.

8   Because of reports that the test had a high false-positive rate and, as a antibody test, a significant false-negative rate (because the test will be negative for an infected person whose system has not started producing antibodies), Lambda seriously considered back in 1985 bringing a legal challenge against licensing the test. But a careful review of the law governing FDA licensing procedures, the traditional deference courts pay to decisions made by "expert" administrative agencies, and scientific data Lambda obtained from the government through filing of an information request, persuaded Lambda that a legal challenge would be a waste of scarce resources, since a successful outcome was unlikely.

9   Instead, Lambda, as well as National Gay Right Advocates (NGRA, based in San Francisco), Gay & Lesbian Advocates & Defenders (GLAD, based in Boston), and scores of lesbian and gay attorneys and American Civil Liberties Union (ACLU) cooperating attorneys in other parts of the country, have spent considerable time since March 1985 battling individual instances of misuse of the tests and advocating against large-scale misuse proposed by the insurance industry and some federal and state officials.

10   Is the test legal? Can someone be *required* to take it? The answers to these questions depend upon the context in which the test is demanded, and the uses to which the results would be put. There are some federal and state laws, as well as constitutional principles, that might restrict the use of the test under certain circumstances, and it is important that gay people in particular, as members of a so-called "high-risk group," be aware of them.

11   As a matter of constitutional law, it may be that personal privacy rights guaranteed by the 14th and 4th Amendments of the Constitution would preclude the government from requiring you to take an antibody test unless there was a good reason for the government to suspect that the test would reveal evidence of unlawful conduct or was necessary to achieve some important benefit for society. The Supreme Court has held, for example, that law enforcement officials can subject persons suspected of drunk driving to tests to detect alcohol in their blood under certain

circumstances. The police, however, cannot randomly stop cars and subject drivers to blood alcohol testing in the absence of any other evidence indicating they might be driving under the influence.

12   Can police authorities routinely subject persons arrested for prostitution to ELISA testing? This is being done in some parts of the country, and legal challenges to such practices would present an interesting new twist on the drunk driving cases. Certainly, if an infected prostitute continued to engage in unprotected sex with customers, the prostitute would be in violation of laws forbidding the knowing transmission of sexually transmitted diseases, but we should remember that prostitution itself is illegal in every state except Nevada.

13   Could government routinely test all "risk group" members as part of a program designed to prevent the spread of HIV? The answer to this is uncertain, and at some point the question may have to be posed to the courts. There are already cases pending in which government officials are trying to require antibody testing of individuals arrested under various circumstances. For example, a member of a gay marching band who allegedly bit a police officer during a scuffle on Gay Pride Day in California is contesting a court ruling that he undergo antibody testing.

14   What about the use of the test [for] a marriage license? In many states, applicants for marriage licenses are already tested for venereal diseases. Why not AIDS? Isn't there a good argument that a prospective spouse should know about the danger to him- or herself of infection by HIV? Should a positive test result preclude marriage, or merely result in counseling of the prospective spouses about "safe sex" practices? No state has yet legislated in this area, but there are a host of proposals pending in legislatures around the country. If the test is presented as a public health measure, the courts may well defer to the "expertise" of health officials who insist that testing is necessary.

15   The test has already popped up in several lawsuits involving the rights of parents to visit their children. A nurse who works with AIDS patients was required to undergo antibody testing before her ex-husband would permit her to see her kids. Gay parents are routinely demanded to take antibody tests as part of custody and visitation litigation, although not all courts agree to go along with such demands. It is hard to discern a general legal principle to control this sort of situation, other than that courts in such cases have broad discretion to take actions deemed to be "in the best interest of the child."

16   The military, prison, foreign services, and Job Corps testing programs that have been adopted or discussed raise serious constitutional and statutory issues.

17   The military tests have already been unsuccessfully challenged in federal court. Judges usually defer to statements by the military that a particular procedure is necessary for national security purposes, even

though that procedure may be restrictive of rights protected in civilian life. Concern that the military was using HIV antibody testing as a way to detect gays and IV-drug users, who would then be subjected to less-than-honorable discharges, led to Congressional adoption of an amendment to a recent appropriations bill, forbidding the military from using the tests for that purpose. Recent military pronouncements, however, indicate that attempts will be made to get around the legislative ban, and lawsuits will surely result.

18   Testing in prisons presents special concerns, due to the unusual nature of the prison environment, in which there is likely to be forcible sex under circumstances where "safer sex" practices are unlikely to be observed. Prison officials have rejected suggestions that condoms be provided for prisoners (with some exceptions being reported for conjugal visits). In a recent case, a labor arbitrator ruled that prison guards had a right, under their collective bargaining agreement, to know whether prisoners were infected, and in effect ordered the prison to require antibody testing and reveal the results to the guard union. (The collective bargaining agreement stated that guards had a right to know about dangerous infectious diseases among prisoners they were guarding.) The prison is appealing the arbitrator's decision to a court, claiming that HIV infection presents no danger to guards and that this testing thus should not be required. In some prisons, inmates with AIDS, or those who test positive, are routinely segregated from other prisoners, ostensibly to protect them from violence, rather than to protect the other prisoners from infection.

19   The foreign service and Job Corps testing programs may come under attack not only on constitutional grounds, but also based on sections 501 and 504 of the federal Rehabilitation Act, which forbid handicap discrimination in federal employment and under federal programs. Regulations interpreting this law forbid the use of medical tests to screen out "otherwise qualified handicapped persons."

20   The State Department argues that certain countries are demanding that American personnel be tested, and that postings to some parts of the world with inadequate medical facilities would be dangerous for persons likely to develop AIDS. The former argument could be seriously challenged by analogy to religious discrimination claims brought by Jewish employees against companies which exclude them from job assignments in Moslem countries on the ground that those countries would not want American Jews to work there. Several courts have upheld such lawsuits. The latter argument seems incredible, since it seems likely that American foreign service personnel who might develop symptoms indicative of AIDS or AIDS-Related Complex could be transported relatively quickly to appropriate medical facilities. While there may be some justification for the State Department wanting to know which overseas personnel might need special attention, justification for excluding anti-

body-positive individuals from the foreign service, as the department proposes, seems slim.

21   The Job Corps testing seems less defensible than the military or foreign service testing. Job Corps officials claim that sexual activities and IV-drug use may take place in dormitories, where the virus could be spread. Such a rationale would justify testing in every communal living setting, including college dormitories, lumber camps, and other isolated worksites but would seem directly contrary to the Rehabilitation Act and, in private employment, state laws forbidding disability discrimination. I suspect that, as in many uses of the test, the Job Corps testing program is designed to rid the corps of sexually active gays or participants who would incur serious medical costs. There is a growing body of precedent forbidding governmental programs from discriminating on the basis of sexual orientation, and the cost-avoidance rationale would violate the Rehabilitation Act.

22   Finally, under the heading of "closing the barn door after the horses are gone," there is the emergency regulation adopted by the Immigration Service to use the test in excluding persons from entry into the country. HIV is here, and it seems unlikely that an occasional infected immigrant is going to contribute greatly to spreading the epidemic; but, once again, the regulation seems unlikely to fall to legal attack, since many of the constitutional protections which apply to persons resident in the country have been held by the federal courts not to apply to aliens seeking entry.

23   Legal ramifications of so-called "AIDS testing" will continue to play a significant role in the unfolding legal epidemic around AIDS.

CHRISTIANITY

WHY I AM AN AGNOSTIC

Clarence Darrow

1   An agnostic is a doubter. The word is generally applied to those who doubt the verity of accepted religious creeds or faiths. Everyone is an agnostic as to the beliefs or creeds they do not accept. Catholics are agnostic to the Protestant creeds, and the Protestants are agnostic to the Catholic creed. Anyone who thinks is an agnostic about something, otherwise he must believe that he is possessed of all knowledge. And the proper place for such a person is in the madhouse or the home for the feeble-minded. In a popular way, in the western world, an agnostic is one who doubts or disbelieves the main tenets of the Christian faith.

2   I would say that belief in at least three tenets is necessary to the faith of a Christian: a belief in God, a belief in immortality, and a belief in a supernatural book. Various Christian sects require much more, but it is difficult to imagine that one could be a Christian, under any intelligent meaning of the word, with less. Yet there are some people who claim to be Christians who do not accept the literal interpretation of all the Bible, and who give more credence to some portions of the book than to others.

3   I am an agnostic as to the question of God. I think that it is impossible for the human mind to believe in an object or thing unless it can form a mental picture of such object or thing. Since man ceased to worship openly an anthropomorphic God and talked vaguely and not intelligently about some force in the universe, higher than man, that is responsible for the existence of man and the universe, he cannot be said to believe in God. One cannot believe in a force excepting as a force that pervades matter and is not an individual entity. To believe in a thing, an image of the thing must be stamped on the mind. If one is asked if he believes in such an animal as a camel, there immediately arises in his mind an image of the camel. This image has come from experience or knowledge of the animal gathered in some way or other. No such image comes, or can come, with the idea of a God who is described as a force.

4   Man has always speculated upon the origin of the universe, including himself. I feel, with Herbert Spencer, that whether the universe had an origin—and if it had—what the origin is will never be known by man. The Christian says that the universe could not

make itself; that there must have been some higher power to call it into being. Christians have been obsessed for many years by Paley's argument that if a person passing through a desert should find a watch and examine its spring, its hands, its case and its crystal, he would at once be satisfied that some intelligent being capable of design had made the watch. No doubt this is true. No civilized man would question that someone made the watch. The reason he would not doubt it is because he is familiar with watches and other appliances made by man. The savage was once unfamiliar with a watch and would have had no idea upon the subject. There are plenty of crystals and rocks of natural formation that are as intricate as a watch, but even to intelligent man they carry no implication that some intelligent power must have made them. They carry no such implication because no one has any knowledge or experience of someone having made these natural objects which everywhere abound.

5   To say that God made the universe gives us no explanation of the beginning of things. If we are told that God made the universe, the question immediately arises: Who made God? Did he always exist, or was there some power back of that? Did he create matter out of nothing, or is his existence co-extensive with matter? The problem is still there. What is the origin of it all? If, on the other hand, one says that the universe was not made by God, that it always existed, he has the same difficulty to confront. To say that the universe was here last year, or millions of years ago, does not explain its origin. This is still a mystery. As to the question of the origin of things, man can only wonder and doubt and guess.

6   As to the existence of the soul, all people may either believe or disbelieve. Everyone knows the origin of the human being. They know that it came from a single cell in the body of the mother, and that the cell was one out of ten thousand in the mother's body. Before gestation the cell must have been fertilized by a spermatozoön from the body of the father. This was one out of perhaps a billion spermatozoa that was the capacity of the father. When the cell is fertilized a chemical process begins. The cell divides and multiplies and increases into millions of cells, and finally a child is born. Cells die and are born during the life of the individual until they finally drop apart, and this is death.

7   If there is a soul, what is it, and where did it come from, and where does it go? Can anyone who is guided by his reason possibly imagine a soul independent of a body, or the place of its residence, or the character of it, or anything concerning it? If man is justified in any belief or disbelief on any subject, he is warranted in the disbelief in a soul. Not one scrap of evidence exists to prove any such impossible thing.

8   Many Christians base the belief of a soul and God upon the Bible. Strictly speaking, there is no such book. To make the Bible, sixty-six books are bound into one volume. These books were written by many people at different times, and no one knows the time or the identity of any author. Some of the books were written by several authors at various times. These books contain all sorts of contradictory concepts of life and morals and the origin of things. Between the first and the last nearly a thousand years intervened, a longer time than has passed since the discovery of America by Columbus.

9   When I was a boy the theologians used to assert that the proof of the divine inspiration of the Bible rested on miracles and prophecies. But a miracle means a violation of a natural law, and there can be no proof imagined that could be sufficient to show the violation of a natural law; even though proof seemed to show violation, it would only show that we were not acquainted with all natural laws. One believes in the truthfulness of a man because of his long experience with the man, and because the man has always told a consistent story. But no man has told so consistent a story as nature.

10   If one should say that the sun did not rise, to use the ordinary expression, on the day before, his hearer would not believe it, even though he had slept all day and knew that his informant was a man of the strictest veracity. He would not believe it because the story is inconsistent with the conduct of the sun in all the ages past.

11   Primitive and even civilized people have grown so accustomed to believing in miracles that they often attribute the simplest manifestations of nature to agencies of which they know nothing. They do this when the belief is utterly inconsistent with knowledge and logic. They believe in old miracles and new ones. Preachers pray for rain, knowing full well that no such prayer was ever answered. When a politician is sick, they pray for God to cure him, and the politician almost invariably dies. The modern clergyman who prays for rain and for the health of the politician is no more intelligent in this matter than the primitive man who saw a separate miracle in the rising and setting of the sun, in the birth of an individual, in the growth of a plant, in the stroke of lightning, in the flood, in every manifestation of nature and life.

12   As to prophecies, intelligent writers gave them up long ago. In all prophecies facts are made to suit the prophecy, or the prophecy was made after the facts, or the events have no relation to the prophecy. Weird and strange and unreasonable interpretations are used to explain simple statements, that a prophecy may be claimed.

13   Can any rational person believe that the Bible is anything but a human document? We now know pretty well where the various books came from, and about when they were written. We know that

they were written by human beings who had no knowledge of science, little knowledge of life, and were influenced by the barbarous morality of primitive times, and were grossly ignorant of most things that men know today. For instance, Genesis says that God made the earth, and he made the sun to light the day and the moon to light the night, and in one clause disposes of the stars by saying that "he made the stars also." This was plainly written by someone who had no conception of the stars. Man, by the aid of his telescope, has looked out into the heavens and found stars whose diameter is as great as the distance between the earth and the sun. We now know that the universe is filled with stars and suns and planets and systems. Every new telescope looking further into the heavens only discovers more and more worlds and suns and systems in the endless reaches of space. The men who wrote Genesis believed, of course, that this tiny speck of mud that we call the earth was the center of the universe, the only world in space, and made for man, who was the only being worth considering. These men believed that the stars were only a little way above the earth, and were set in the firmament for man to look at, and for nothing else. Everyone today knows that this conception is not true.

14   This origin of the human race is not as blind a subject as it once was. Let alone God creating Adam out of hand, from the dust of the earth, does anyone believe that Eve was made from Adam's rib—that the snake walked and spoke in the Garden of Eden—that he tempted Eve to persuade Adam to eat an apple, and that it is on that account that the whole human race was doomed to hell—that for four thousand years there was no chance for any human to be saved, though none of them had anything whatever to do with the temptation; and that finally men were saved only through God's son dying for them, and that unless human beings believed this silly, impossible and wicked story they were doomed to hell? Can anyone with intelligence really believe that a child born today should be doomed because the snake tempted Eve and Eve tempted Adam? To believe that is not God-worship; it is devil-worship.

15   Can anyone call this scheme of creation and damnation moral? It defies every principle of morality, as man conceives morality. Can anyone believe today that the whole world was destroyed by flood, save only Noah and his family and a male and female of each species of animal that entered the Ark? There are almost a million species of insects alone. How did Noah match these up and make sure of getting male and female to reproduce life in the world after the flood had spent its force? And why should all the lower animals have been destroyed? Were they included in the sinning of man? This is a story which could not beguile a fairly bright child of five years of age today.

16   Do intelligent people believe that the various languages spoken by man on earth came from the confusion of tongues at the Tower of Babel, some four thousand years ago? Human languages were dispersed all over the face of the earth long before that time. Evidences of civilizations are in existence now that were old long before the date that romancers fix for the building of the Tower, and even before the date claimed for the flood.

17   Do Christians believe that Joshua made the sun stand still, so that the day could be lengthened, that a battle might be finished? What kind of person wrote that story, and what did he know about astronomy? It is perfectly plain that the author thought that the earth was the center of the universe and stood still in the heavens, and that the sun either went around it or was pulled across its path each day, and that the stopping of the sun would lengthen the day. We know now that had the sun stopped when Joshua commanded it, and had it stood still until now, it would not have lengthened the day. We know that the day is determined by the rotation of the earth upon its axis, and not by the movement of the sun. Everyone knows that this story simply is not true, and not many even pretend to believe the childish fable.

18   What of the tale of Balaam's ass speaking to him, probably in Hebrew? Is it true, or is it a fable? Many asses have spoken, and doubtless some in Hebrew, but they have not been that breed of asses. Is salvation to depend on a belief in a monstrosity like this?

19   Above all the rest, would any human being today believe that a child was born without a father? Yet this story was not at all unreasonable in the ancient world; at least three or four miraculous births are recorded in the Bible, including John the Baptist and Samson. Immaculate conceptions were common in the Roman world at the time and at the place where Christianity really had its nativity. Women were taken to the temples to be inoculated of God so that their sons might be heroes, which meant, generally, wholesale butchers. Julius Caesar was a miraculous conception—indeed, they were common all over the world. How many miraculous-birth stories is a Christian now expected to believe?

20   In the days of the formation of the Christian religion, disease meant the possession of human beings by devils. Christ cured a sick man by casting out the devils, who ran into the swine, and the swine ran into the sea. Is there any question but what that was simply the attitude and belief of a primitive people? Does anyone believe that sickness means the possession of the body by devils, and that the devils must be cast out of the human being that he may be cured? Does anyone believe that a dead person can come to life? The miracles recorded in the Bible are not the only instances of dead men

coming to life. All over the world one finds testimony of such miracles; miracles which no person is expected to believe, unless it is his kind of a miracle. Still at Lourdes today, and all over the present world, from New York to Los Angeles and up and down the lands, people believe in miraculous occurrences, and even in the return of the dead. Superstition is everywhere prevalent in the world. It has been so from the beginning, and most likely will be so unto the end.

21   The reasons for agnosticism and skepticism are abundant and compelling. Fantastic and foolish and impossible consequences are freely claimed for the belief in religion. All the civilization of any period is put down as a result of religion. All the cruelty and error and ignorance of the period has no relation to religion. The truth is that the origin of what we call civilization is not due to religion but to skepticism. So long as men accepted miracles without question, so long as they believed in original sin and the road to salvation, so long as they believed in a hell where man would be kept for eternity on account of Eve, there was no reason whatever for civilization: life was short, and eternity was long, and the business of life was preparation for eternity.

22   When every event was a miracle, when there was no order or system or law, there was no occasion for studying any subject, or being interested in anything excepting a religion which took care of the soul. As man doubted the primitive conceptions about religion, and no longer accepted the literal, miraculous teachings of ancient books, he set himself to understand nature. We no longer cure disease by casting out devils. Since that time, men have studied the human body, have built hospitals and treated illness in a scientific way. Science is responsible for the building of railroads and bridges, of steamships, of telegraph lines, of cities, towns, large buildings and small, plumbing and sanitation, of the food supply, and the countless thousands of useful things that we now deem necessary to life. Without skepticism and doubt, none of these things could have been given to the world.

23   The fear of God is not the beginning of wisdom. The fear of God is the death of wisdom. Skepticism and doubt lead to study and investigation, and investigation is the beginning of wisdom.

24   The modern world is the child of doubt and inquiry, as the ancient world was the child of fear and faith.

WHAT ARE WE TO MAKE OF JESUS CHRIST?

C. S. Lewis

1   What are we to make of Jesus Christ? This is a question which has, in a sense, a frantically comic side. For the real question is not what are we to make of Christ, but what is He to make of us? The picture of a fly sitting deciding what it is going to make of an elephant has comic elements about it. But perhaps the questioner meant what are we to make of Him in the sense of 'How are we to solve the historical problem set us by the recorded sayings and acts of this Man?' This problem is to reconcile two things. On the one hand you have got the almost generally admitted depth and sanity of His moral teaching, which is not very seriously questioned, even by those who are opposed to Christianity. In fact, I find when I am arguing with very anti-God people that they rather make a point of saying, 'I am entirely in favour of the moral teaching of Christianity'—and there seems to be a general agreement that in the teaching of this Man and of His immediate followers, moral truth is exhibited at its purest and best. It is not sloppy idealism, it is full of wisdom and shrewdness. The whole thing is realistic, fresh to the highest degree, the product of a sane mind. That is one phenomenon.

2   The other phenomenon is the quite appalling nature of this Man's theological remarks. You all know what I mean, and I want rather to stress the point that the appalling claim which this Man seems to be making is not merely made at one moment of His career. There is, of course, the one moment which led to His execution. The moment at which the High Priest said to Him, 'Who are you?' 'I am the Anointed, the Son of the uncreated God, and you shall see Me appearing at the end of all history as the judge of the Universe.' But that claim, in fact, does not rest on this one dramatic moment. When you look into His conversation you will find this sort of claim running through the whole thing. For instance, He went about saying to people, 'I forgive your sins.' Now it is quite natural for a man to forgive something you do to *him*. Thus if somebody cheats *me* out of £5 it is quite possible and reasonable for me to say, 'Well, I forgive him, we will say no more about it.' What on earth would you say if somebody had done *you* out of £5 and *I* said, 'That is all right, I forgive him'? Then there is a curious thing which seems to slip out almost by accident. On one occasion this Man is sitting looking down on Jerusalem from the hill above it and suddenly in comes an extraordinary remark—'I keep on sending you prophets and wise men.' Nobody comments on it. And yet, quite suddenly, almost in-

cidentally, He is claiming to be the power that all through the centuries is sending wise men and leaders into the world. Here is another
curious remark: in almost every religion there are unpleasant ob-
servances like fasting. This Man suddenly remarks one day, 'No one
need fast while I am here.' Who is this Man who remarks that His
mere presence suspends all normal rules? Who is the person who can
suddenly tell the School they can have a half-holiday? Sometimes
the statements put forward the assumption that He, the Speaker, is
completely without sin or fault. This is always the attitude. 'You, to
whom I am talking, are all sinners,' and He never remotely suggests
that this same reproach can be brought against Him. He says again,
'I am begotten of the One God, before Abraham was, I am,' and
remember what the words 'I am' were in Hebrew. They were the
name of God, which must not be spoken by any human being, the
name which it was death to utter.

3   Well, that is the other side. On the one side clear, definite moral
teaching. On the other, claims which, if not true, are those of a
megalomaniac, compared with whom Hitler was the most sane and
humble of men. There is no half-way house and there is no parallel
in other religions. If you had gone to Buddha and asked him 'Are you
the son of Brahma?' he would have said, 'My son, you are still in the
vale of illusion.' If you had gone to Socrates and asked, 'Are you
Zeus?' he would have laughed at you. If you had gone to Mohammed
and asked, 'Are you Allah?' he would first have rent his clothes and
then cut your head off. If you had asked Confucius, 'Are you Heaven?',
I think he would have probably replied, 'Remarks which are not in
accordance with nature are in bad taste.' The idea of a great moral
teacher saying what Christ said is out of the question. In my opinion,
the only person who can say that sort of thing is either God or a
complete lunatic suffering from that form of delusion which undermines the whole mind of man. If you think you are a poached egg,
when you are looking for a piece of toast to suit you, you may be
sane, but if you think you are God, there is no chance for you. We
may note in passing that He was never regarded as a mere moral
teacher. He did not produce that effect on any of the people who
actually met Him. He produced mainly three effects—Hatred—Terror—Adoration. There was no trace of people expressing mild approval.

4   What are we to do about reconciling the two contradictory phenomena? One attempt consists in saying that the Man did not really
say these things, but that His followers exaggerated the story, and so
the legend grew up that He had said them. This is difficult because
His followers were all Jews; that is, they belonged to that Nation
which of all others was most convinced that there was only one

God—that there could not possibly be another. It is very odd that this horrible invention about a religious leader should grow up among the one people in the whole earth least likely to make such a mistake. On the contrary we get the impression that none of His immediate followers or even of the New Testament writers embraced the doctrine at all easily.

5   Another point is that on that view you would have to regard the accounts of the Man as being *legends*. Now, as a literary historian, I am perfectly convinced that whatever else the Gospels are they are not legends. I have read a great deal of legend and I am quite clear that they are not the same sort of thing. They are not artistic enough to be legends. From an imaginative point of view they are clumsy, they don't work up to things properly. Most of the life of Jesus is totally unknown to us, as is the life of anyone else who lived at that time, and no people building up a legend would allow that to be so. Apart from bits of the Platonic dialogues, there are no conversations that I know of in ancient literature like the Fourth Gospel. There is nothing, even in modern literature, until about a hundred years ago when the realistic novel came into existence. In the story of the woman taken in adultery we are told Christ bent down and scribbled in the dust with His finger. Nothing comes of this. No one has ever based any doctrine on it. And the art of *inventing* little irrelevant details to make an imaginary scene more convincing is a purely modern art. Surely the only explanation of this passage is that the thing really happened? The author put it in simply because he had *seen* it.

6   Then we come to the strangest story of all, the story of the Resurrection. It is very necessary to get the story clear. I heard a man say, 'The importance of the Resurrection is that it gives evidence of survival, evidence that the human personality survives death.' On that view what happened to Christ would be what had always happened to all men, the difference being that in Christ's case we were privileged to see it happening. This is certainly not what the earliest Christian writers thought. Something perfectly new in the history of the Universe had happened. Christ had defeated death. The door which had always been locked had for the very first time been forced open. This is something quite distinct from mere ghost-survival. I don't mean that they disbelieved in ghost-survival. On the contrary, they believed in it so firmly that, on more than one occasion, Christ had had to assure them that He was *not* a ghost. The point is that while believing in survival they yet regarded the Resurrection as something totally different and new. The Resurrection narratives are not a picture of survival after death; they record how a totally new mode of being has arisen in the Universe. Something new had ap-

peared in the Universe: as new as the first coming of organic life. This Man, after death, does not get divided into 'ghost' and 'corpse.' A new mode of being has arisen. That is the story. What are we going to make of it?

7   The question is, I suppose, whether any hypothesis covers the facts so well as the Christian hypothesis. That hypothesis is that God has come down into the created universe, down to manhood— and come up again, pulling it up with Him. The alternative hypothesis is not legend, nor exaggeration, nor the apparitions of a ghost. It is either lunacy or lies. Unless one can take the second alternative (and I can't), one turns to the Christian theory.

8   'What are we to make of Christ?' There is no question of what we can make of Him, it is entirely a question of what He intends to make of us. You must accept or reject the story.

9   The things He says are very different from what any other teacher has said. Others say, 'This is the truth about the Universe. This is the way you ought to go,' but He says, '*I* am the Truth, and the Way, and the Life.' He says, 'No man can reach absolute reality, except through Me. Try to retain your own life and you will be inevitably ruined. Give yourself away and you will be saved.' He says, 'If you are ashamed of Me, if, when you hear this call, you turn the other way, I also will look the other way when I come again as God without disguise. If anything whatever is keeping you from God and from Me, whatever it is, throw it away. If it is your eye, pull it out. If it is your hand, cut it off. If you put yourself first you will be last. Come to Me everyone who is carrying a heavy load; I will set that right. Your sins, all of them, are wiped out; I can do that. I am Rebirth, I am Life. Eat Me, drink Me, I am your Food. And finally, do not be afraid, I have overcome the whole Universe.' This is the issue.

WOMEN'S RIGHTS

THE CASE FOR EQUALITY

Caroline Bird

1 Is it a good idea to treat men and women exactly alike?

2   What would happen if we tried it?

3   Is it even possible?

4   "After all, men and women are different," people argue. "You can't treat them alike!"

5   Just as we formerly had laws that said that noblemen had certain privileges because of their names, so we now have laws that say that men and women have certain privileges because of their sex. If we think we can't treat men and women alike, it may only be because the law hasn't done it.

6   But it can be done. In a provocative article in *The George Washington Law Review* of December 1965, Pauli Murray and Mary Eastwood reviewed the laws affecting men and women as separate sexes and reported that all such laws would be either clearer or fairer if rewritten in terms of situations, as all other laws are written. It wouldn't be necessary, they pointed out, to say that the crime of rape could be committed only by men or that maternity benefits could be claimed only by women. By definition, these situations apply to one sex only. A woman can't commit rape. A man can't have a baby. The conditions that seem to require special treatment for men or women can all be defined without mentioning sex. If all persons were liable for military or jury service, for instance, men and women could both claim exemption because they had dependents. Women able to serve would relieve the men for whom the draft is now a real hardship.

7   There is no reason why women should not be drafted. The crack Israeli Army drafts all boys and single girls at the age of 18. Girls who marry during their draft terms, as three out of ten do, go into the reserves. Pregnant women and mothers are excused, but women officers in the regular army get four months of fully paid leave beginning with the ninth month of pregnancy. Israeli women soldiers have fought in bloody battles in the past, but they are now assigned to handle paperwork, communications, and medical services in units with men.

8   It isn't necessary to require that husbands support wives in order to protect children. Both partners to a marriage could simply be

required to support each other and their children in case of need. There is nothing morally repugnant about requiring money or services from the partner best able to give them, regardless of sex. . . .

9   All these legal inequalities could be remedied, but the real question is: Do we want to do it? Do we really want to treat men and women alike? The only way to find out is to examine, as best we can, what the change would do. The most radical effects would be felt in the field of employment. If access, pay, promotion, and conditions of work for every job were open equally to men and women, as Title VII plainly requires, there would be no legal or moral basis for what Pauli Murray and Mary Eastwood call ". . . the assumption that financial support of a family by the husband-father is a gift from the male sex to the female sex, and, in return, the male is entitled to preference in the outside world."

10   Supposing individuals were hired in all occupations without regard to sex. Women would compete with men in areas now closed to them, but they would not compete with each other as much as they now do for "women's jobs." Women who stayed in "women's jobs" would win higher wages. As the wages rose, men would be attracted to these fields. Since the lowest-paying jobs are those dominated by women, equal opportunity would have the same effect as raising the minimum wage. . . .

11   If, along with sex equality, we expect all adults to work, women who could not show that they were earning their keep at home would have to find jobs. According to one estimate, full utilization of "womanpower" would add ten million workers to the labor force. If these women could work wherever they were needed, they would free men from the obligation to earn that injures and limits some of them as grievously as the obligation to do housework now injures and limits some women. This is no idle supposition. As we have noticed earlier, under full employment many families find it makes more sense for women to work and support their menfolk.

12   If women were freer to choose where they worked, they would take a good hard look at some of the chores that now keep them at home. What, for instance, is the actual money value of staying at home all day long to do two hours of cleaning? Of hauling groceries from the supermarket? Of waiting in the pediatrician's office for an hour? In 1968, mothers expect all sorts of people to waste their time. The waste is not necessary, and it is not motherhood.

13   A woman we know solved the problem of the doctor's waiting room by arranging for a baby-sitter to take her son to the appointment. She found that she could continue working in her office for an hour or more while they waited for his turn. She could earn more at her own trade than she could have saved in cab fare and baby-

sitting fees, even though the expense was not deductible. A working woman has to operate a home in a world that assumes that a home-maker's time is worth less than the wages of the lowest-paid worker for money. Deliveries are arranged on the assumption that she can sit home all day long and wait. No one calculates the time cost of shopping, either, especially in crowded discount houses and super-markets, where women on budgets are forced to shop. No one counts the time cost of toting shoes to and from the repairman, or exchang-ing goods that may have been ordered by telephone to save time, but weren't right on arrival. Purchasing departments count the cost of the time that clerks use when they check prices and quality before buying, but housewives don't add the cost of their time to the price paid for family purchases.

14   If all adults were required to work, and free to choose the kind of work they wanted, many women would leave their homes and thereby create more paying jobs. Baby-sitters and service workers, many of them now considered unemployable because of age or lack of education, would be drawn out of their isolation and into the labor force. But all of these newcomers would not necessarily find them-selves doing what housewives used to do at home. Many would find jobs in services especially organized to do housework efficiently.

15   More women could afford housekeeping services that now exist for the very rich alone. More charge-and-deliver grocers would be needed to serve the growing number of housewives who would not mind paying more to save the time they now spend shopping in self-service supermarkets. Cleaning services could contract to keep a house in shape by sending in teams of machine-equipped profession-als to tidy for an hour or so every day; maintenance services em-ploying salaried mechanics could keep all household gear operating for a flat annual fee; yard services like those run by teams of Japanese gardeners in Los Angeles could contract to keep lawns mowed and garden beds weeded. Food take-out services and caterers proliferating around the country would increase to serve the growing number of women who like to entertain but don't have time to cook.

16   These new services would be cheaper in real economic terms, because specialists working at what they enjoy are more efficient than amateurs doing chores they may detest. But the big gain would be a better use of talent. If the born cooks, cleaners, and children's nurses were paid well enough so that they could make careers out of their talents, domestic services would attract women who now enjoy household arts but hesitate to practice them professionally because they don't want to be treated as "servants." Women who have never worked often have trouble with servants because they have never learned how to hold employees to objective standards. If

most women worked, domestic service could become more attractive, since, hopefully, domestic workers would begin to be treated more like office workers. . . .

17   Billions of words and hours of thought have been expanded on the complexities of race relations. Progress, said the sophisticated, will have to be slow. You cannot change a way of life overnight. Yet today it is clear that however agonizing the changes have been, the problem has never been all that complicated. What we did to the blacks was just plain wrong, and everybody knew it.

18   So with the employment of women. Relations between the sexes are complicated, and change is hard, but the way women are treated is just plain wrong.

19   It is wrong to make aspiring women prove they are twice as good as men.

20   It is wrong to pay women less than men for the same work just because they will work for less.

21   It is wrong to exclude women from work they can do so that they have to work for less in the jobs open to them.

22   It is wrong to make aspiring women pay the penalty of women who are content to be used as a labor reserve.

23   It is wrong to assume that because some women can't do mathematics, *this* woman can't do mathematics.

24   It is wrong to expect women to work for their families or the nation and then to step aside when their families or the nation wants them out of the way.

25   It is wrong to deny individuals born female the right to inconvenience their families to pursue art, science, power, prestige, money, or even self-expression, in the way that men in pursuit of these goals inconvenience their families as a matter of course.

26   It is wrong to impute motives to women instead of letting them speak for themselves.

27   It is wrong to ridicule, sneer, frighten, or brainwash anyone unable to fight back.

28   It is wrong, as well as wasteful and dangerous, to discourage talent.

29   All these things are wrong, and everybody knows it. And just as "separate but equal" schools limited white children as well as black, so the doctrine that women are different but equal limits men. Mary Wollstonecraft, John Stuart Mill, George Bernard Shaw, and President Goheen of Princeton were all concerned about sex inequality in part at least because of the damage it does to men. David Riesman points out that every boundary we impose on women we impose on men also.

30   Equity speaks softly and wins in the end. But it is expedience,

with its loud voice, that sets the time of victory. The cotton gin did not make slavery wrong, but it helped a lot of Southerners to *see* that slavery was wrong. The immigrant vote did not make woman suffrage right, but it frightened politicians into enfranchising women on the theory that the educated women of politically conservative old American stock would vote more readily than the submissive women of politically unpredictable ethnic groups.

31   So with equal opportunity for women. Conditions conspire to help people see the inequity and the advantages of ending it. First the pill gives women control over their fate so that they can be as responsible as men. Then modern medicine prolongs the lives of women so that all now have decades of potential working life, beyond child-rearing age, during which none of the limitations imposed on women make sense. Next, modern technology takes their work out of the home and invites them to do it elsewhere, and for pay. It frees more mothers of the work of bringing up children, and gives it to schools. Meanwhile, the new technology is less and less a respecter of old-fashioned sex differences. It eliminated the need for physical strength very rapidly and is now eliminating the need for "detail work."

32   What the new technology needs is educated manpower that can learn new skills. What it doesn't need is more ordinary people without skills. Both needs strengthen the case for equal opportunity for the underprivileged majority of Americans who were born female.

PAID HOMEMAKING: AN IDEA IN SEARCH OF A POLICY

William J. Byron, S.J.

1   Parents in the U.S. have no economic incentive to care for their children at home. If that strikes no one as strange, it is only because our nation takes it for granted that economic incentives belong in the marketplace and other motives explain behavior at home. So, full-time care for a "priceless" child by that child's natural parent in a supportive home environment is unrewarded economically.

2   Those who know the price of everything and the value of nothing are, as Oscar Wilde said so well, cynics. What can be said of a nation that regards its children as priceless, but attaches no economic value to child-care by the person best qualified to provide it? Shortsighted will do for the moment. Further reflection might prompt us to label as both unwise and dangerous the absence of national support for parents who want to be full-time homemakers.

3   The issue is complicated. Children are our nation's greatest treasure, our most precious resource. In the vast majority of cases, children develop best in a stable family unit, in an environment of love—of parents for each other and of both for the child. Moreover, children need to experience parental love expressed in the form of presence. An attentive, affirming presence seems to work best.

4   Yet, we know that parents are often left without partners. We also know that economic necessity frequently drives both parents into the labor market. Sometimes, a desire to give full stretch to one's talents encourages mothers for whom employment is not an economic necessity to step into the job market. (Our cultural presumption that fathers can enjoy that same full stretch only in employment other than homemaking remains unchallenged, even unexamined.) Then there are those mothers who go to work only for the sake of their offspring, to supplement the family income so that the youngsters can have more—more material things, more and better education, more developmental opportunities, but less parental presence. Presence (or absence, depending on your point of view) is the coin in which the parent-child relationship pays the price for two-paycheck marriages, or for one-parent households where the parent is employed outside the home.

5   Should homemakers be paid for their services? Not housekeepers, babysitters, or day-care providers, but homemakers—parents who choose to devote full time to the task of rearing children.

6   On Nov. 24, 1983, the Vatican published a "Charter on the Rights of the Family." It is the product of worldwide consultation and a formal process of reflection and research that began in 1980. The charter speaks principally to governments. Article 10 declares:

Families have a right to social and economic order in which the organization of work permits the members to live together and does not hinder the unity, well-being, health and the stability of the family, while offering also the possibility of wholesome recreation.

a) Remuneration for work must be sufficient for establishing and maintaining a family with dignity, either through a suitable salary, called a "family wage," or through other social measures such as family allowances or the remuneration of the work in the home of one of the parents; it should be such that mothers will not be obliged to work outside the home to the detriment of family life and especially of the education of the children.

b) The work of the mother in the home must be recognized and respected because of its value for the family and for society.

7   Those "other social measures" lie, for the most part, undesigned and hidden in the imaginations of academics and social theorists. Government should be encouraging their development. Although the Vatican statement targets no specific purse from which homemakers' pay could be drawn, the only likely source is government. Neil Gilbert, in *Capitalism and the Welfare State* (Yale University Press, 1983), proposes that the full-time homemaker receive a "social credit" for each year spent at home with children who are under 17 years of age. According to this plan, accumulated credits would either pay for higher education or entitle the homemaker to preferred hiring status in the Civil Service once the youngsters are raised and the parent is ready to enter or reenter the labor market. Gilbert specifies the Federal government as the provider of this benefit which, like a veteran's benefit, would compensate the homemaker for time spent out of the workforce, but in service to the nation.

8   In Gilbert's scheme, each unit of social credit (one child per year of full-time care) could be exchanged for either "(a) tuition for four units of undergraduate academic training, (b) tuition for three units of technical school training, (c) tuition for two units of graduate education, or (d) an award of one-fourth of a preference point on federal civil service examinations." The parent is the implied beneficiary of the tuition grant in this G.I. Bill-type scenario. The policy would surely be more attractive and effective if an option to designate the homemaker's child as the educational beneficiary were made explicit.

9   The social credit idea bars no parent, male or female, from opting for paid employment or professional activity outside the home. It doesn't even discourage outside work. It simply provides an incentive to parents who might prefer homemaking to labor market activity. It also answers the need of those parents who bring home the second paycheck just "to put the kids through college." Under this plan, they would stay home,

accumulate the social credits, and eventually redeem them in tuition payments.

10   When the legislative imagination takes up this idea, as I hope will be the case before long, some constraints will have to be set. The first would be an appropriate family income limit above which neither parent would be eligible. Those who do qualify could, if the policy so directs, be required to treat as taxable income the cash value of the credits exchanged for tuition. By keeping the benefit tax-free, however, legislators would preserve for the beneficiary freedom of choice between independent and state-supported higher education. Spending the credits for tuition at the higher priced independent colleges would mean a higher cash value and thus more taxable income. It is better to keep the benefit tax-free.

11   It is conceivable that the eligible person who decides to be a full-time homemaking parent would soon become economically active at home. "Worksteading" is the new word for this. With the arrival of the "information economy" and the installation of computers and word processors in the home, the probability of more at-home paid employment rises sharply. Protection for the integrity of the social credit program could come from the Internal Revenue Service and would have to be written into the law. It would be easy to come up with an IRS device that would decertify from social credit eligibility the homemaker who reports earnings above a relatively low limit specified in the law. Again, the economic incentive. In this case, the threatened loss of the credit would serve as encouragement to hold firm on the homemaking commitment in the face of attractive remunerative at-home business opportunities.

12   The credits would, of course, be nontransferable from family to family. Some might argue for a limit on the number of credits one homemaker could earn (Gilbert suggests a three-child maximum), but sensitivity to parental freedom with respect to family size would be an important consideration in any public policy relating to the family.

13   The program would be more flexible, and thus more practical and attractive, if parents could alternate on the full-time homemaker responsibility. In effect, the parents would commit themselves, as a couple, to the provision of one full-time homemaker's services each year from the birth of a child until that child reaches his or her 17th birthday. This would open up the possibility for a mother (more often than not, the mother will be the parent with full-time homemaking responsibilities) to work outside the home. There would be no loss of credit so long as the father personally provides the child care. It is worth noting that a shared responsibility for earning social credits through homemaking could

promote cooperation over career competition between spouses in the
modern marriage.

14　　　The value of the credit would best be expressed as a percentage of
the cost of higher education—100% of the cost of tuition, fees, and books,
regardless of the college chosen. The inclusion of other expenses that
complete the so-called "cost of attending" (room and board, transportation, spending money) would be a matter of legislative choice. The point
of specifying the percentage, rather than an absolute sum, is to relieve
the parent of anxiety concerning the erosion of the credit by inflation
and the consequent inability—17 years later—to convert the credits into
payment for tuition, fees, and books. It seems to me that one year's credit
should be worth one-17th of the price, at the point of consumption, of
tuition, fees, and books. The total cost of tuition, fees, and books ("costs
of education," as distinguished from "cost of attendance") would be completely covered in those cases where a child received full-time parental
home care for the first 17 years of life.

15　　　The proposal is clearly intended to reinforce the nuclear family unit
by rewarding a parent for remaining at home. As a policy idea, it will go
nowhere unless there is widespread conviction that society needs the
services of full-time homemakers.

16　　　Such persons need not be confined to quarters all day long. They
would be free to be with their youngsters in a variety of at-home and
out-of-home ways and at times not possible for the busy parent burdened
with a work schedule. The homemaker's schedule would focus on the
child. It would promote parental presence—to the child. When one considers how such time might be spent, expressions like "creative leisure"
and "shared learning" come to mind, as do thoughts of joint participation
in arts, crafts, games, museum visits, sightseeing "voyages of discovery,"
and similar engagements. School plays and athletic contests would attract more spectators. The schools themselves would be able to draw on
a larger supply of volunteer service. As the nation deplores the condition
of its schools, it should notice the promise this policy holds for the
promotion of life of the mind *at home,* a development which would be
nothing but good for the schools.

17　　　This policy proposal is open to the criticism that it envisions a
middle-class program that would be unavailable to the working poor who,
credits or not, could not afford not to work. The criticism is quite fair.
This proposal would not meet the needs of those who absolutely have
to work. They demonstrate the power of economic incentives; many—
by no means all—would prefer to be homemakers. To meet their needs
(and to assist others who are less pressed for funds, but most anxious to
combine careers and parental responsibilities), it is important to consider

for inclusion in a national family policy measures that would encourage flexible work schedules, make day-care facilities more widely available, and make child-care expenses more readily deductible.

18   In addition, Gilbert deals with an issue that will certainly be raised by many voices in this policy debate:

> For women who want a balanced family life and a full-time career, a family credit scheme would open a successive route along which both are possible. Because this route encompasses a 25-to-30-year period of employment, it may close off a few career options which require early training and many years of preparation. There must be some price for enjoying the choice of two callings in life. This is a different path from the continuous paid career line that men typically follow. It may be better.

19   I have tested the social credit idea in the op-ed forum and in conversations with friends. The strongest negative reaction chided me for trying to "bribe" people into child-care, "to shoehorn women back into the kitchen and/or the nursery."

20   On the other hand, the mother of two disabled sons applauded the idea: "The need for social reform to strengthen the family is so great that one would imagine that America as a nation and as a culture depends on the policy you advocate. It is indeed puzzling how an issue that is so fundamental—and so simply obvious—could have been overlooked for so long." The policy, by the way, might well allow for extra credits for homemakers serving handicapped children.

21   Endorsement of the idea also came from a middle-aged male who described himself as a "well traveled parent who longs for more time in the home."

22   A public affairs director in a Federal agency offered a reflective comment which touches upon the crucial question of who will guide the formation of values in one's children:

> As a career women who has been on both sides of the fence (I stayed home until the children were 10 and 14 and then joined the work force 10 years ago), I think your plan has merit. It seems to me that I have been extremely lucky—I was able to start a career later in life because of extremely hard work and fortunate circumstances. Not everyone is so positioned. I would not have wanted someone else "raising" my children and giving them different views on morality and philosophy from my own. Each parent wants to pass on his basic beliefs to his children, and it is impossible for young women today to do that if they see their child for one or two hectic hours a day.

23   R. Sargent Shriver, Democratic candidate for Vice President in 1972, called my attention to a speech he gave on "The Family" during that campaign. He repeated the maxim: What is good for families is good for nations; what hurts families, hurts nations. He further remarked that "the institution that has served human beings best and disappointed them least is the family."

24   A retired obstetrician, himself a father of eight, found the proposal to be "on target." In his medical practice, he said, he "was always well aware of the importance of a mother or parent in a home at all times with growing children; there can be no substitute."

25   Recently, I talked with a 36-year-old man whose educational credentials include a doctorate and a law degree. He has worked as a college professor, as well as a lawyer. His *curriculum vitae* notes his full-time service as a "homemaker" for the past three years. His wife, also a lawyer, has been in the labor market while he cares for two young children at home. Another child was expected soon. With the birth of their third child, the lawyer-mother planned to remain at home as the professor-lawyer-father returned to paid employment in the market economy. This is easy enough for well-educated professionals, but it only happens when parents regard it as important that their children have the full-time attention of one or the other throughout childhood.

26   Less well-educated parents are no less concerned about child development, just less able, for economic reasons, to consider full-time homemaking as a real option. If the option were available, it would be just that—an option, not an enforced condition. People would be free to take it or leave it, as their values and preferences direct.

27   We have no such option in the U.S. today because of the presence of economic pressure and the absence of a national family policy. The social credit idea addresses a policy vacuum. It surely deserves some discussion and debate.

MINORITIES' RIGHTS

A CALL FOR UNITY

Members of the Birmingham Clergy

April 12, 1963

1   We the undersigned clergymen are among those who, in January, issued "An Appeal for Law and Order and Common Sense," in dealing with racial problems in Alabama. We expressed understanding that honest convictions in racial matters could properly be pursued in the courts, but urged that decisions of those courts should in the meantime be peacefully obeyed.

2   Since that time there had been some evidence of increased forebearance and a willingness to face facts. Responsible citizens have undertaken to work on various problems which cause racial friction and unrest. In Birmingham, recent public events have given indication that we all have opportunity for a new constructive and realistic approach to racial problems.

3   However, we are now confronted by a series of demonstrations by some of our Negro citizens, directed and led in part by outsiders. We recognize the natural impatience of people who feel that their hopes are slow in being realized. But we are convinced that these demonstrations are unwise and untimely.

4   We agree rather with certain local Negro leadership which has called for honest and open negotiation of racial issues in our area. And we believe this kind of facing of issues can best be accomplished by citizens of our own metropolitan area, white and Negro, meeting with their knowledge and experience of the local situation. All of us need to face that responsibility and find proper channels for its accomplishment.

5   Just as we formerly pointed out that "hatred and violence have no sanction in our religious and political traditions," we also point out that such actions as incite to hatred and violence, however technically peaceful those actions may be, have not contributed to the resolution of our local problems. We do not believe that these days of new hope are days when extreme measures are justified in Birmingham.

6   We commend the community as a whole, and the local news media and law enforcement officials in particular, on the calm manner in which these demonstrations have been handled. We urge the

public to continue to show restraint should the demonstrations continue, and the law enforcement officials to remain calm and continue to protect our city from violence.

7   We further strongly urge our own Negro community to withdraw support from these demonstrations, and to unite locally in working peacefully for a better Birmingham. When rights are consistently denied, a cause should be pressed in the courts and in negotiations among local leaders, and not in the streets. We appeal to both our white and Negro citizenry to observe the principles of law and order and common sense.

C.C.J. CARPENTER, D.D., L.L.D., Bishop of Alabama; JOSEPH A. DURICK, D.D., Auxiliary Bishop, Diocese of Mobile-Birmingham; RABBI MILTON L. GRAFMAN, Temple Emanu-El, Birmingham, Alabama; BISHOP PAUL HARDIN, Bishop of the Alabama-West Florida Conference of the Methodist Church; BISHOP NOLAN B. HARMON, Bishop of the North Alabama Conference of the Methodist Church; GEORGE M. MURRAY, D.D., L.L.D., Bishop Coadjutor, Episcopal Diocese of Alabama; EDWARD V. RAMAGE, Moderator, Synod of the Alabama Presbyterian Church in the United States; EARL STALLINGS, Pastor, First Baptist Church, Birmingham, Alabama.

LETTER FROM BIRMINGHAM JAIL

Martin Luther King, Jr.

April 16, 1963

MY DEAR FELLOW CLERGYMEN:

1   While confined here in the Birmingham city jail, I came across your recent statement calling my present activities "unwise and untimely." Seldom do I pause to answer criticism of my work and ideas. If I sought to answer all the criticisms that cross my desk, my secretaries would have little time for anything other than such correspondence in the course of the day, and I would have no time for constructive work. But since I feel that you are men of genuine good will and that your criticisms are sincerely set forth, I want to try to answer your statement in what I hope will be patient and reasonable terms.

2   I think I should indicate why I am here in Birmingham, since you have been influenced by the view which argues against "outsiders coming in." I have the honor of serving as president of the Southern Christian Leadership Conference, an organization operating in every southern state, with headquarters in Atlanta, Georgia. We have some eighty-five affiliated organizations across the South, and one of them is the Alabama Christian Movement for Human Rights. Frequently we share staff, educational and financial resources with our affiliates. Several months ago the affiliate here in Birmingham asked us to be on call to engage in a nonviolent direct-action program if such were deemed necessary. We readily consented, and when the hour came we lived up to our promise. So I, along with several members of my staff, am here because I was invited here. I am here because I have organizational ties here.

3   But more basically, I am in Birmingham because injustice is here. Just as the prophets of the eighth century B.C. left their villages and carried their "thus saith the Lord" far beyond the boundaries of their home towns, and just as the Apostle Paul left his village of Tarsus and carried the gospel of Jesus Christ to the far corners of the Greco-Roman world, so am I compelled to carry the gospel of freedom beyond my own home town. Like Paul, I must constantly respond to the Macedonian call for aid.

4   Moreover, I am cognizant of the interrelatedness of all communities and states. I cannot sit idly by in Atlanta and not be concerned about what happens in Birmingham. Injustice anywhere is a

threat to justice everywhere. We are caught in an inescapable network of mutuality, tied in a single garment of destiny. Whatever affects one directly, affects all indirectly. Never again can we afford to live with the narrow, provincial "outside agitator" idea. Anyone who lives inside the United States can never be considered an outsider anywhere within its bounds.

5   You deplore the demonstrations taking place in Birmingham. But your statement, I am sorry to say, fails to express a similar concern for the conditions that brought about the demonstrations. I am sure that none of you would want to rest content with the superficial kind of social analysis that deals merely with effects and does not grapple with underlying causes. It is unfortunate that demonstrations are taking place in Birmingham, but it is even more unfortunate that the city's white power structure left the Negro community with no alternative.

6   In any nonviolent campaign there are four basic steps: collection of the facts to determine whether injustices exist; negotiation; self-purification; and direct action. We have gone through all these steps in Birmingham. There can be no gainsaying the fact that racial injustice engulfs this community. Birmingham is probably the most thoroughly segregated city in the United States. Its ugly record of brutality is widely known. Negroes have experienced grossly unjust treatment in the courts. There have been more unsolved bombings of Negro homes and churches in Birmingham than in any other city in the nation. These are the hard, brutal facts of the case. On the basis of these conditions, Negro leaders sought to negotiate with the city fathers. But the latter consistently refused to engage in good-faith negotiation. . . .

7   You may well ask: "Why direct action? Why sit-ins, marches and so forth? Isn't negotiation a better path?" You are quite right in calling for negotiation. Indeed, this is the very purpose of direct action. Nonviolent direct action seeks to create such a crisis and foster such a tension that a community which has constantly refused to negotiate is forced to confront the issue. It seeks so to dramatize the issue that it can no longer be ignored. My citing the creation of tension as part of the work of the nonviolent-resister may sound rather shocking. But I must confess that I am not afraid of the word "tension." I have earnestly opposed violent tension, but there is a type of constructive, nonviolent tension which is necessary for growth. Just as Socrates felt that it was necessary to create a tension in the mind so that individuals could rise from the bondage of myths and half-truths to the unfettered realm of creative analysis and objective appraisal, so must we see the need for nonviolent gadflies to create the

kind of tension in society that will help men rise from the dark depths of prejudice and racism to the majestic heights of understanding and brotherhood.

8   The purpose of our direct-action program is to create a situation so crisis-packed that it will inevitably open the door to negotiation. I therefore concur with you in your call for negotiation. Too long has our beloved Southland been bogged down in a tragic effort to live in monologue rather than dialogue.

9   One of the basic points in your statement is that the action that I and my associates have taken in Birmingham is untimely. . . . My friends, I must say to you that we have not made a single gain in civil rights without determined legal and nonviolent pressure. Lamentably, it is an historical fact that privileged groups seldom give up their privileges voluntarily. Individuals may see the moral light and voluntarily give up their unjust posture; but, as Reinhold Niebuhr has reminded us, groups tend to be more immoral than individuals.

10   We know through painful experience that freedom is never voluntarily given by the oppressor; it must be demanded by the oppressed. Frankly, I have yet to engage in a direct-action campaign that was "well timed" in the view of those who have not suffered unduly from the disease of segregation. For years now I have heard the word "Wait!" It rings in the ears of every Negro with piercing familiarity. This "Wait" has almost always meant "Never." We must come to see, with one of our distinguished jurists, that "justice too long delayed is justice denied."

11   We have waited for more than 340 years for our constitutional and God-given rights. The nations of Asia and Africa are moving with jetlike speed toward gaining political independence, but we still creep at horse-and-buggy pace toward gaining a cup of coffee at a lunch counter. Perhaps it is easy for those who have never felt the stinging darts of segregation to say, "Wait." But when you have seen vicious mobs lynch your mothers and fathers at will and drown your sisters and brothers at whim; when you have seen hate-filled policemen curse, kick and even kill your black brothers and sisters; when you see the vast majority of your twenty million Negro brothers smothering in an airtight cage of poverty in the midst of an affluent society; when you suddenly find your tongue twisted and your speech stammering as you seek to explain to your six-year-old daughter why she can't go to the public amusement park that has just been advertised on television, and see tears welling up in her eyes when she is told that Funtown is closed to colored children, and see ominous clouds of inferiority beginning to form in her little mental sky, and see her beginning to distort her personality by developing an unconscious

bitterness toward white people; when you have to concoct an answer for a five-year-old son who is asking: "Daddy, why do white people treat colored people so mean?"; when you take a cross-country drive and find it necessary to sleep night after night in the uncomfortable corners of your automobile because no motel will accept you; when you are humiliated day in and day out by nagging signs reading "white" and "colored"; when your first name becomes "nigger," your middle name becomes "boy" (however old you are) and your last name becomes "John," and your wife and mother are never given the respected title "Mrs."; when you are harried by day and haunted by night by the fact that you are a Negro, living constantly at tiptoe stance, never quite knowing what to expect next, and are plagued with inner fears and outer resentments; when you are forever fighting a degenerating sense of "nobodiness"—then you will understand why we find it difficult to wait. There comes a time when the cup of endurance runs over, and men are no longer willing to be plunged into the abyss of despair. I hope, sirs, you can understand our legitimate and unavoidable impatience.

12   You express a great deal of anxiety over our willingness to break laws. This is certainly a legitimate concern. Since we so diligently urge people to obey the Supreme Court's decision of 1954 outlawing segregation in the public schools, at first glance it may seem rather paradoxical for us consciously to break laws. One may well ask: "How can you advocate breaking some laws and obeying others?" The answer lies in the fact that there are two types of laws; just and unjust. I would be the first to advocate obeying just laws. One has not only a legal but a moral responsibility to obey just laws. Conversely, one has a moral responsibility to disobey unjust laws. I would agree with St. Augustine that "an unjust law is no law at all."

13   Now, what is the difference between the two? How does one determine whether a law is just or unjust? A just law is a man-made code that squares with the moral law or the law of God. An unjust law is a code that is out of harmony with the moral law. To put it in the terms of St. Thomas Aquinas: An unjust law is a human law that is not rooted in eternal law and natural law. Any law that uplifts human personality is just. Any law that degrades human personality is unjust. All segregation statutes are unjust because segregation distorts the soul and damages the personality. It gives the segregator a false sense of superiority and the segregated a false sense of inferiority. Segregation, to use the terminology of the Jewish philosopher Martin Buber, substitutes an "I-it" relationship for an "I-thou" relationship and ends up relegating persons to the status of things. Hence segregation is not only politically, economically and sociologically unsound, it is morally wrong and sinful. Paul Tillich has said that

sin is separation. Is not segregation an existential expression of man's tragic separation, his awful estrangement, his terrible sinfulness? Thus it is that I can urge men to obey the 1954 decision of the Supreme Court, for it is morally right; and I can urge them to disobey segregation ordinances, for they are morally wrong.

14   Let us consider a more concrete example of just and unjust laws. An unjust law is a code that a numerical or power majority group compels a minority group to obey but does not make binding on itself. This is *difference* made legal. By the same token, a just law is a code that a majority compels a minority to follow and that it is willing to follow itself. This is *sameness* made legal.

15   Let me give another explanation. A law is unjust if it is inflicted on a minority that, as a result of being denied the right to vote, had no part in enacting or devising the law. Who can say that the legislature of Alabama which set up that state's segregation laws was democratically elected? Throughout Alabama all sorts of devious methods are used to prevent Negroes from becoming registered voters, and there are some counties in which, even though Negroes constitute a majority of the population, not a single Negro is registered. Can any law enacted under such circumstances be considered democratically structured?

16   Sometimes a law is just on its face and unjust in its application. For instance, I have been arrested on a charge of parading without a permit. Now, there is nothing wrong in having an ordinance which requires a permit for a parade. But such an ordinance becomes unjust when it is used to maintain segregation and to deny citizens the First-Amendment privilege of peaceful assembly and protest.

17   I hope you are able to see the distinction I am trying to point out. In no sense do I advocate evading or defying the law, as would the rabid segregationist. That would lead to anarchy. One who breaks an unjust law must do so openly, lovingly, and with a willingness to accept the penalty. I submit that an individual who breaks a law that conscience tells him is unjust, and who willingly accepts the penalty of imprisonment in order to arouse the conscience of the community over its injustice, is in reality expressing the highest respect for law.

18   Of course, there is nothing new about this kind of civil disobedience. It has evidenced sublimely in the refusal of Shadrach, Meshach and Abednego to obey the laws of Nebuchadnezzar, on the ground that a higher moral law was at stake. It was practiced superbly by the early Christians, who were willing to face hungry lions and the excruciating pain of chopping blocks rather than submit to certain unjust laws of the Roman Empire. To a degree, academic freedom is a reality today because Socrates practiced civil disobedience.

In our own nation, the Boston Tea Party represented a massive act of civil disobedience.

19   We should never forget that everything Adolf Hitler did in Germany was "legal" and everything the Hungarian freedom fighters did in Hungary was "illegal." It was "illegal" to aid and comfort a Jew in Hitler's Germany. Even so, I am sure that, had I lived in Germany at the time, I would have aided and comforted my Jewish brothers. If today I lived in a Communist country where certain principles dear to the Christian faith are suppressed, I would openly advocate disobeying that country's anti-religious laws.

20   I must make two honest confessions to you, my Christian and Jewish brothers. First, I must confess that over the past few years I have been gravely disappointed with the white moderate. I have almost reached the regrettable conclusion that the Negro's great stumbling block in his stride toward freedom is not the White Citizen's Counciler or the Ku Klux Klanner, but the white moderate, who is more devoted to "order" than to justice; who prefers a negative peace which is the absence of tension to a positive peace which is the presence of justice; who constantly says: "I agree with you in the goal you seek, but I cannot agree with your methods of direct action"; who paternalistically believes he can set the timetable for another man's freedom; who lives by a mythical concept of time and who constantly advises the Negro to wait for a "more convenient season." Shallow understanding from people of good will is more frustrating than absolute misunderstanding from people of ill will. Lukewarm acceptance is much more bewildering than outright rejection.

21   I had hoped that the white moderate would understand that law and order exist for the purpose of establishing justice and that when they fail in this purpose they become the dangerously structured dams that block the flow of social progress. I had hoped that the white moderate would understand that the present tension in the South is a necessary phase of the transition from an obnoxious negative peace, in which the Negro passively accepted his unjust plight, to a substantive and positive peace, in which all men will respect the dignity and worth of human personality. Actually, we who engage in nonviolent direct action are not the creators of tension. We merely bring to the surface the hidden tension that is already alive. We bring it out in the open, where it can be seen and dealt with. Like a boil that can never be cured so long as it is covered up but must be opened with all its ugliness to the natural medicines of air and light, injustice must be exposed, with all the tension its exposure creates, to the light of human conscience and the air of national opinion before it can be cured.

22   In your statement you assert that our actions, even though peaceful, must be condemned because they precipitate violence. But is this a logical assertion? Isn't this like condemning a robbed man because his possession of money precipitated the evil act of robbery? Isn't this like condemning Socrates because his unswerving commitment to truth and his philosophical inquiries precipitated the act by the misguided populace in which they made him drink hemlock? Isn't this like condemning Jesus because his unique God-consciousness and never-ceasing devotion to God's will precipitated the evil act of crucifixion? We must come to see that, as the federal courts have consistently affirmed, it is wrong to urge an individual to cease his efforts to gain his basic constitutional rights because the quest may precipitate violence. Society must protect the robbed and punish the robber. . . .

23   You speak of our activity in Birmingham as extreme. At first I was rather disappointed that fellow clergymen would see my non-violent efforts as those of an extremist. I began thinking about the fact that I stand in the middle of two opposing forces in the Negro community. One is a force of complacency, made up in part of Negroes who, as a result of long years of oppression, are so drained of self-respect and a sense of "somebodiness" that they have adjusted to segregation; and in part of a few middle-class Negroes who, because of a degree of academic and economic security and because in some ways they profit by segregation, have become insensitive to the problems of the masses. The other force is one of bitterness and hatred, and it comes perilously close to advocating violence. It is expressed in the various black nationalist groups that are springing up across the nation, the largest and best-known being Elijah Muhammad's Muslim movement. Nourished by the Negro's frustration over the continued existence of racial discrimination, this movement is made up of people who have lost faith in America, who have absolutely repudiated Christianity, and who have concluded that the white man is an incorrigible "devil."

24   I have tried to stand between these two forces, saying that we need emulate neither the "do-nothingism" of the complacent nor the hatred and despair of the black nationalist. For there is the more excellent way of love and nonviolent protest. I am grateful to God that, through the influence of the Negro church, the way of non-violence became an integral part of our struggle.

25   If this philosophy had not emerged, by now many streets of the South would, I am convinced, be flowing with blood. And I am further convinced that if our white brothers dismiss as "rabble-rousers" and "outside agitators" those of us who employ nonviolent direct action, and if they refuse to support our nonviolent efforts, millions

of Negroes will, out of frustration and despair, seek solace and security in black-nationalist ideologies—a development that would inevitably lead to a frightening racial nightmare.

26   Oppressed people cannot remain oppressed forever. The yearning for freedom eventually manifests itself, and that is what has happened to the American Negro. Something within has reminded him of his birthright of freedom, and something without has reminded him that it can be gained. Consciously or unconsciously, he has been caught up by the *Zeitgeist*, and with his black brothers of Africa and his brown and yellow brothers of Asia, South America and the Caribbean, the United States Negro is moving with a sense of great urgency toward the promised land of racial justice. If one recognizes this vital urge that has engulfed the Negro community, one should readily understand why public demonstrations are taking place. The Negro has many pent-up resentments and latent frustrations, and he must release them. So let him march; let him make prayer pilgrimages to the city hall; let him go on freedom rides—and try to understand why he must do so. If his repressed emotions are not released in nonviolent ways, they will seek expression through violence; this is not a threat but a fact of history. So I have not said to my people: "Get rid of your discontent." Rather, I have tried to say that this normal and healthy discontent can be channeled into the creative outlet of nonviolent direct action. And now this approach is being termed extremist.

27   But though I was initially disappointed at being categorized as an extremist, as I continued to think about the matter I gradually gained a measure of satisfaction from the label. Was not Jesus an extremist for love: "Love your enemies, bless them that curse you, do good for them that hate you, and pray for them which despitefully use you, and persecute you." Was not Amos an extremist for justice: "Let justice roll down like waters and righteousness like an everflowing stream." Was not Paul an extremist for the Christian gospel: "I bear in my body the marks of the Lord Jesus." Was not Martin Luther an extremist: "Here I stand; I cannot do otherwise, so help me God." And John Bunyan: "I will stay in jail to the end of my days before I make a butchery of my conscience." And Abraham Lincoln: "This nation cannot survive half slave and half free." And Thomas Jefferson: "We hold these truths to be self-evident, that all men are created equal . . ." So the question is not whether we will be extremists, but what kind of extremists we will be. Will we be extremists for hate or for love? Will we be extremists for the preservation of injustice or for the extension of justice? In that dramatic scene on Calvary's hill three men were crucified. We must never forget that all three were crucified for the same crime—the crime of extremism.

Two were extremists for immorality, and thus fell below their environment. The other, Jesus Christ, was an extremist for love, truth and goodness, and thereby rose above his environment. Perhaps the South, the nation and the world are in dire need of creative extremists.

28   I had hoped that the white moderate would see this need. Perhaps I was too optimistic; perhaps I expected too much. I suppose I should have realized that few members of the oppressor race can understand the deep groans and passionate yearnings of the oppressed race, and still fewer have the vision to see that injustice must be rooted out by strong, persistent and determined action. I am thankful, however, that some of our white brothers in the South have grasped the meaning of this social revolution and committed themselves to it. They are still too few in quantity, but they are big in quality. Some—such as Ralph McGill, Lillian Smith, Harry Golden, James McBride Dabbs, Ann Braden and Sarah Patton Boyle—have written about our struggle in eloquent and prophetic terms. Others have marched with us down nameless streets of the South. They have languished in filthy, roach-infested jails, suffering the abuse and brutality of policemen who view them as "dirty nigger-lovers." Unlike so many of their moderate brothers and sisters, they have recognized the urgency of the moment and sensed the need for powerful "action" antidotes to combat the disease of segregation. . . .

29   I hope the church as a whole will meet the challenge of this decisive hour. But even if the church does not come to the aid of justice, I have no despair about the future. I have no fear about the outcome of our struggle in Birmingham, even if our motives are at present misunderstood. We will reach the goal of freedom in Birmingham and all over the nation, because the goal of America is freedom. Abused and scorned though we may be, our destiny is tied up with America's destiny. Before the pilgrims landed at Plymouth, we were here. Before the pen of Jefferson etched the majestic words of the Declaration of Independence across the pages of history, we were here. For more than two centuries our forebears labored in this country without wages; they made cotton king; they built the homes of their masters while suffering gross injustice and shameful humiliation—and yet out of a bottomless vitality they continued to thrive and develop. If the inexpressible cruelties of slavery could not stop us, the opposition we now face will surely fail. We will win our freedom because the sacred heritage of our nation and the eternal will of God are embodied in our echoing demands.

30   Before closing I feel impelled to mention one other point in your statement that has troubled me profoundly. You warmly commended the Birmingham police force for keeping "order" and "preventing

violence." I doubt that you would have so warmly commended the police force if you had seen its dogs sinking their teeth into unarmed, nonviolent Negroes. I doubt that you would so quickly commend the policemen if you were to observe their ugly and inhumane treatment of Negroes here in the city jail; if you were to watch them push and curse old Negro women and young Negro girls; if you were to see them slap and kick old Negro men and young boys; if you were to observe them, as they did on two occasions, refuse to give us food because we wanted to sing our grace together. I cannot join you in your praise of the Birmingham police department.

31   It is true that the police have exercised a degree of discipline in handling the demonstrators. In this sense they have conducted themselves rather "nonviolently" in public. But for what purpose? To preserve the evil system of segregation. Over the past few years I have consistently preached that nonviolence demands that the means we use must be as pure as the ends we seek. I have tried to make clear that it is wrong to use immoral means to attain moral ends. But now I must affirm that it is just as wrong, or perhaps even more so, to use moral means to preserve immoral ends. Perhaps Mr. Connor and his policemen have been rather nonviolent in public, as was Chief Pritchett in Albany, Georgia, but they have used the moral means of nonviolence to maintain the immoral end of racial injustice. As T. S. Eliot has said: "The last temptation is the greatest treason: To do the right deed for the wrong reason."

32   I wish you had commended the Negro sit-inners and demonstrators of Birmingham for their sublime courage, their willingness to suffer and their amazing discipline in the midst of great provocation. One day the South will recognize its real heroes. They will be the James Merediths, with the noble sense of purpose that enables them to face jeering and hostile mobs, and with the agonizing loneliness that characterizes the life of the pioneer. They will be old, oppressed, battered Negro women, symbolized in a seventy-two-year-old woman in Montgomery, Alabama, who rose up with a sense of dignity and with her people decided not to ride segregated buses, and who responded with ungrammatical profundity to one who inquired about her weariness: "My feets is tired, but my soul is at rest." They will be the young high school and college students, the young ministers of the gospel and a host of their elders, courageously and nonviolently sitting in at lunch counters and willingly going to jail for conscience' sake. One day the South will know that when these disinherited children of God sat down at lunch counters, they were in reality standing up for what is best in the American dream and for the most sacred values in our Judaeo-Christian heritage, thereby bringing our nation back to those great wells of democracy which

were dug deep by the founding fathers in their formulation of the Constitution and the Declaration of Independence.

33   Never before have I written so long a letter. I'm afraid it is much too long to take your precious time. I can assure you that it would have been much shorter if I had been writing from a comfortable desk, but what else can one do when he is alone in a narrow jail cell, other than write long letters, think long thoughts and pray long prayers?

34   If I have said anything in this letter that overstates the truth and indicates an unreasonable impatience, I beg you to forgive me. If I have said anything that understates the truth and indicates my having a patience that allows me to settle for anything less than brotherhood, I beg God to forgive me.

35   I hope this letter finds you strong in the faith. I also hope that circumstances will soon make it possible for me to meet each of you, not as an integrationist or a civil-rights leader but as a fellow clergyman and a Christian brother. Let us all hope that the dark clouds of racial prejudice will soon pass away and the deep fog of misunderstanding will be lifted from our fear-drenched communities, and in some not too distant tomorrow the radiant stars of love and brotherhood will shine over our great nation with all their scintillating beauty.

Yours for the cause of Peace and Brotherhood,
MARTIN LUTHER KING, JR.

THE MIDDLE EAST

SHARING THE LAND AND THE LEGACY

Rami Khouri

1   When the state of Israel was created in 1948, the Jewish people realized a dream they had carried in their hearts since the destruction of the Second Temple, some 2,000 years ago. Their years of wandering, persecution and struggle had come to an end. Or so it was thought to be.

2   The reality is rather different, for since the establishment of Israel in 1948 Israel and the Arabs have fought five major wars. Israel has not had genuine peace and security. It has, thanks to massive American aid and the fervor of its own people, only enjoyed a military advantage. It has been able to defend itself, but not to find a place among the nation-states of the Middle East.

3   For the four million Palestinian people, the establishment of Israel as a Jewish state in 1948 marked the start of the Palestinian diaspora, of Palestinian homelessness and political disenfranchisement.

4   Let us forget, for the moment, the rights and wrongs of the past, and apportion neither guilt, nor righteousness, in the history of Arab-Israeli warfare.

5   The challenge before the people of the Middle East today is not how to ascribe blame for the horrors of the past, but rather how to reconcile conflicting Arab and Israeli claims in order that we may all share the land of Palestine—and the promise of the future.

6   On the surface, political circumstances in the Middle East and further afield suggest that Arab-Israeli reconciliation is a distant and naive dream. But beneath the surface, things may be slightly less discouraging.

7   Consider the following:

1. In 1967, the Arab summit at Khartoum rejected negotiations, recognition or coexistence with Israel. In the 1982 Arab summit at Fez, the Arab world proposed a peace plan based on negotiations with Israel, leading to ultimate coexistence on the basis of an Israeli state living side-by-side with a Palestinian state. The shift in the Arab peace posture since 1967 has been dramatic, but insufficiently appreciated in the West.

8   2. In Israel, public opinion polls since 1967 have shown a consistent trend toward more and more Israelis who are willing to make peace with the Palestinians and the other Arab states on the basis of an Israeli withdrawal from parts or all of the occupied West Bank and Gaza. A small but growing number of Israeli politicians and peace groups have accepted

the principle of the mutual and simultaneous self-determination of Israelis and Palestinians. The Israelis have realized most recently in Lebanon that military force can never resolve political disputes.

9   3. In the United States, the traditional concern for Israel's security has been increasingly matched by an appreciation of Palestinian rights. The Reagan initiative of September 1982 was a step forward in this respect, though it was immediately rejected by the Israeli government, and also failed to satisfy the Arab demand for Palestinian self-determination.

10   Efforts now taking place in the Middle East again aim to reinvigorate the forces of peace on both sides. Jordan and the Palestine Liberation Organization (PLO) reached agreement on February 11, [1985] on a joint position that envisages a peaceful settlement of the Arab-Israeli conflict, based on Israeli statehood and security, and Palestinian self-determination. Egypt has made some specific proposals. Israel's response has left the door open for direct talks with a Jordanian-Palestinian team. The United States has tried to keep the momentum for peace alive.

11   The prospects for direct negotiations between Arabs and Israelis are distant, as always, but perhaps less distant than they were a few years ago. The opportunity that now challenges us all is nothing less than peace among all the children of Abraham—Christians, Moslems and Jews.

12   The Jewish people have secured their state, and fortified it militarily. But they have not secured that which should be more dear to them than anything else in this world—the acceptance of their Arab brothers and sisters, their Semitic cousins, their Abrahamic family.

13   History has taught us all that genuine security does not come from the strength of guns, but rather from the mercy, forgiveness and acceptance of one's adversary. There are increasing numbers of Israelis and Arabs who have become convinced that warfare cannot resolve the Arab-Israeli conflict. It can only be resolved by assuring the rights of both Israelis and Palestinians, in the historical land of Palestine they both covet. . . .

14   An international consensus has emerged in recent years that envisages the resolution of the Arab-Israeli conflict through the satisfaction of Israeli demands for recognition and security, and of Palestinian demands for self-determination and security. In the Fez peace plan and the Jordan-PLO accord, the Arab world has outlined its vision of a Middle East at peace, with security guaranteed for Israel, a Palestinian state confederated with Jordan, and all the other Arab states.

15   The people of Israel and their many supporters in the West must soon decide: Is their objective the false security that comes from occupying Arab lands and denying Palestinian rights? Or is their objective the genuine security that can only emanate from a peace that satisfies Palestinian as well as Israeli demands?

16   For the first time since 1948, the Arab world is talking in terms of a negotiated, peaceful and permanent resolution of the conflict with Israel. We are talking about international guarantees for the security of all states in the region, including an Israeli and a Palestinian state.

17   The opportunity before us today will not remain on the table for very long. The history of the Arab-Israeli conflict is one of short-lived opportunities that have been missed because of inflexible political attitudes, and invariably replaced by a resurgent extremism on both sides.

18   A new opportunity now presents itself: An opportunity to satisfy Palestinian demands for the promise of national self-determination that Woodrow Wilson articulated for all the people of the free world in 1918. An opportunity for Israel and the Jewish people to enjoy the kind of genuine security they have sought unsuccessfully for two millennia. An opportunity for the Arab states to get on with the challenges of nation-building and fulfilling the vast potential of their people.

19   If this opportunity is to be seized, reasonable people on all sides will have to reinforce the conviction that peace, security and the right of self-determination, like liberty, are indivisible, and must be granted to both Israelis and Palestinians. If balance and reciprocity are our guidelines, the dream of a just peace can be attained. And the legacy of Abraham can be realized at last.

MAPS OF REVENGE

Meron Benvenisti

1 A little while ago, just before the Passover vacation, my son Yuval came home with the itinerary for his school outing. My father, who was there at the time, asked to see it. Glancing through it, I could see something was making him angry. "Why are all the place names in Arabic?" he demanded. "Don't they know in the Scouts that these places have Hebrew names?" His reaction was not surprising. My father, eighty-seven, a teacher and a geographer, has devoted his whole life to one thing: creating a new Hebrew map of Eretz Israel and instilling in young people a love of country. For years he has been a member of the official "naming committees" whose task it was to Hebraize all the names on the ordinance map of Eretz Israel and to name new Jewish settlements. His maps can be seen on the walls of classrooms throughout Israel. In fact the huge blue-brown-and-green wall map he drew is imprinted in the visual memory of hundreds of thousands of Israelis. . . .

2 Changing place names in order to arrive at a Hebrew map of Eretz Israel was considered by my father a sacred task. He was one of Israel's first geographers—awarded the Israel Prize for his life's work. And now, after sixty years, that his own grandson should come to him with Arab names instead of Hebrew ones seemed to him tantamount to sacrilege. Like all immigrant societies, we attempted to erase all alien names, but here the analogy becomes complicated because we were not simply an immigrant society or an army of conquerors. At our coming, we reestablished contact with those same landscapes and places from which we had been physically removed for two thousand years but whose names we had always preserved. We carried around with us for centuries our *geographia sacra*, not only biblical names but all the mishnaic and talmudic names. Wherever we were dispersed—in France, Germany, Egypt, Persia—we would study texts and learn about the rosters of priestly duty in the Temple enumerating by turn their home villages in the Galilee. People who knew nothing about the physical reality of those villages knew their names by heart. So when we returned to the land it was the most natural thing to seek out those ancient places and identify them. . . .

3 From a very early age, perhaps four or five, I and my brother would accompany my father on his Sabbath expeditions. And so it was that the Arab names of villages and mountains, groves and springs became those of my childhood. I remember the names perfectly—they became second nature to me—and when I travel around the country I unfailingly recall the previous names. The Arab names. I have a friend who lives in a Jewish

village in the Jerusalem corridor. When he mentions the Hebrew name
Shoevah, I immediately think of it as Saris, the Arab name. . . .

4   The Hebrew map of Israel constitutes one stratum in my consciousness, underlaid by another stratum of the previous Arab map. Those
names turn me and anyone who was born into them into sons of the
same homeland—but also into mortal enemies. I can't help but reflect
on the irony that my father, by taking me on his trips and hoping to
instill in me the love of our Hebrew homeland, imprinted in my memory,
along with the new names, the names he wished to eradicate.

5   This brings me, strangely enough, to the Lebanon war. I was aware
for quite some time that Palestinian research institutes in Beirut were
compiling files on each Palestinian village in Israel. Since the beginning
of the war I wondered about the fate of those files. I was fairly sure that
General Sharon and General Eitan would search them out, seize them,
and destroy them in order to complete the eradication of Arab Palestine.
This is what eventually happened when the Israeli Army entered West
Beirut. I knew that some of the information in those files was purely
imaginary and was used as propaganda against my country. Every refugee,
even the lowliest, is convinced that he used to own at least a hundred
acres of orchards and a large house in Israel. It is an understandable
tendency to magnify the scale of what they lost. But the point is—and
there lies the irony and the tragedy—that they have created their own
geographia sacra, just as we did in our Diaspora. Their map-making is
the answer to our Hebrew, Israeli map. They are trying by an act of will
to recreate and preserve the old reality, the one we erased in order to
create our own. Their map-making is as far removed from reality as our
memorizing the list of villages of the priestly roster.

6   Not only are the refugee camps organized by sections according to
the villages in Palestine from which the refugees originated, their children are taught exclusively with reference to the pre-1948 map of Palestine. On their maps hundreds of Palestinian villages, long since destroyed, are shown, but the Jewish cities, settlements, roads, and ports
are omitted. Everything that happened subsequent to their departure is
perceived as an aberration. Their refusal to cope with the stark and cruel
reality causes them to believe that what the Jews print on their maps is
sheer fiction. . . .

7   At this point in our conflict, maps cease being geographical and
turn into an act of faith, a call for action, for revenge. I'll destroy your
map as you have destroyed mine. A zero-sum game that is played out
not only in words and symbols, but in concrete deeds of destruction.

8   There is no point in asking who started. It is true that my father
had started his Hebrew map to gain symbolic possession of his ancestral
land. But he believed that he was doing so peaceably, not disinheriting
anybody. Indeed he and most of his generation genuinely believed that

there was enough room in the country for everybody. The Palestinians did not take him seriously. For them he was a romantic Westerner, just like the British and German explorers who came before him and left, with their strange compasses, sextants, and theodolites. They did not realize that his map-making was of a different sort, that he intended to settle down and teach his children the names he invented, and by so doing, to perpetuate them and thus transform symbolic possession into actual possession. When the Arabs realized the danger, it was too late. They tried to destroy my father physically, but they failed. He offered them compromises, but they rejected them. Finally an all-out war decided the issue; they were driven out, and his map triumphed. Then we set out to transform the land, to construct our own edifices, to plan our own orchards. But we also deliberately destroyed the remnants our enemies left lest they come back and attempt to lay claim to it. We knew that had they won they would have destroyed our work. But we won, so we became the destroyers. Who is the victim? Who is the culprit? Who is the judge? . . .

9   Almost two million Palestinians still live on their land, cherish it, and are determined to preserve their own map and physical forms. It is impossible to erase their contribution to the landscape of our shared homeland, no matter how hard people try. Someone, someday, will raise the question and will demand an answer. Are we ready to merge the two maps? Are we ready to stop eradicating each other's names? When such questions can be asked, perhaps the dissonance and conflict that plague so many Israelis will be resolved.

10   When at a certain stage I left my own immediate surroundings to seek out a more universal dimension to my experiences, I found myself in the Grand Opera House of Belfast. The first performance of Brian Friel's *Translations* was given in the Opera House—rebuilt after twenty-four bombing incidents—to an all-Catholic audience. The play dealt with the substitution of an English map of Ireland for the original, the ultimate symbolic expression of possession. When the play ended, I said to my friend, a Catholic, "You know what? We've been doing the same thing all along—translating, changing names, creating a new reality." My friend regarded me for a moment with an expression of the utmost sadness and said at last, "Well, if that's the case, may God have mercy on you all!"

Selected References

CHAPTER 1

Aristotle. *The Rhetoric of Aristotle.* Trans. Lane Cooper. Englewood Cliffs, NJ: Prentice-Hall, 1960.

Booth, Wayne C. *Now Don't Try to Reason with Me.* Chicago: The University of Chicago Press, 1970.

Brooks, Cleanth, and Robert Penn Warren. *Modern Rhetoric.* New York: Harcourt, Brace & World, 1970.

Corbett, Edward P. J. *Classical Rhetoric for the Modern Student.* 2nd ed. New York: Oxford University Press, 1971.

Jordan, John E., ed. *Questions of Rhetoric.* New York: Holt, Rinehart, & Winston, Inc., 1971.

Mannes, Marya. "How Do You Know It's Good?" In *But Will It Sell?* Philadelphia: J. B. Lippincott Co., 1964.

Plato. *Apology, Crito,* and *Phaedrus.* Trans. Jowett. *Dialogues of Plato,* Ed. Justin D. Kaplan. New York: Washington Square Press, 1950. (And various other editions.)

Pospesel, Howard. *Arguments: Deductive Logic Exercises.* Englewood Cliffs, NJ: Prentice-Hall, 1971.

Robinson, James Harvey. "On Various Kinds of Thinking." *The Mind in the Making.* New York: Harper & Bros., 1921.

Weaver, Richard M. *Language Is Sermonic.* Baton Rouge, LA: Louisiana State University Press, 1970.

CHAPTER 2

Baker, Sheridan. *The Complete Stylist and Handbook.* New York: Crowell, 1976. 6–9, 11.

Booth, Wayne C. "The Rhetorical Stance." *Now Don't Try to Reason With Me: Essays and Ironies for a Credulous Age.* Chicago: The University of Chicago Press, 1970.

Burke, Kenneth. *A Rhetoric of Motives.* Berkeley and Los Angeles, CA: University of California Press, 1969. 43–65.

Enos, Richard Leo. "Ciceronian *Disposito* as an Architecture for Creativity in Composition: A Note for the Affirmative." *Rhetoric Review* 4.1 (September 1985): 108–110.

Green, Lawrence D. "Enthymemic Invention and Structural Prediction." *College English* 41 (February 1980): 623–34.

Larson, Richard L. "Discovery Through Questioning: A Plan for Teaching Rhetorical Invention," *College English* 30 (November 1968): 132–33.

Long, Russell C. "Writer-Audience Relationships: Analysis or Invention?" *College Composition and Communication* 31 (May 1980): 221–26.

Lucas, F. L. "Party of One" ("What Is Style?"), *Holiday*, March 1960: 11, 14–16, 18–21.

Ong, Walter J. "The Writer's Audience Is Always a Fiction," *PMLA* 90 (1975): 9–21.

Park, Douglas B. "The Meaning of 'Audience,'" *College English* 44 (March 1982): 247–57.

CHAPTER 3

Charlton, James, ed. *The Writer's Quotation Book.* Yonkers, NY: The Pushcart Press, 1980.

Copi, Irving. *Introduction to Logic,* 6th ed. New York: Macmillan, 1982. 127 ff. 138–73.

Langer, Susanne K. "The Lord of Creation," *Fortune,* Jan. 1944.

Munson, Ronald. *The Way of Words: An Informal Logic.* Boston: Houghton Mifflin, 1976. 98–140.

Runkle, Gerald. *Good Thinking: An Introduction to Logic.* New York: Holt, Rinehart & Winston, 1978. 41–55.

Sindler, Allan P. *Bakke, DeFunis, and Minority Admissions.* New York: Longman, 1978.

Stevens, Wallace: "The Noble Rider and the Sound of Words." In *The Necessary Angel: Essays on Reality and the Imagination.* New York: Random House-Vintage, 1951.

Szasz, Thomas. *The Second Sin.* Garden City, NY: Anchor Press, 1973.

CHAPTER 4

Barzun, Jacques, and Henry Graff. *The Modern Researcher.* New York: Harcourt, Brace & World, 1970.

Gibaldi, Joseph, and Walter S. Achtert. *MLA Handbook for Writers of Research Papers.* 3rd ed. New York: The Modern Language Association of America, 1988.

Kraus, Keith. *Murder, Mischief, and Mayhem: A Process for Creative Research Papers.* Urbana, IL: National Council of Teachers of English, 1978.

Newman, Robert P., and Dale R. Newman. *Evidence.* Boston: Houghton Mifflin, 1969.

Tryzna, Thomas. "Approaches to Research Writing: A Review of Handbooks with Some Suggestions." *College Composition and Communication* 34 (May 1983) 202–7.

van Leunen, Mary-Claire. *A Handbook for Scholars.* New York: Knopf, 1978.

CHAPTER 5

Brostoff, Anita. "Coherence: 'Next to' Is Not 'Connected to,'" *College Composition and Communication* 32 (October 1981): 278–94.

Gibson, Walker. *Persona: A Style Study for Readers and Writers*. New York: Random House, 1969.

_____. *Tough, Sweet, and Stuffy*. Bloomington, IN: Indiana UP, 1966. 28–54.

Winterowd, Ross, "The Grammar of Coherence," *College English* 31 (May 1970): 828–35.

Zinnser, William. *On Writing Well*. New York: Harper & Row, 1980.

CHAPTER 6

Altick, Richard D. *Preface to Critical Reading*, 5th ed. New York: Holt, Rinehart & Winston, 1969.

Corbett, Edward P. J. *Classical Rhetoric for the Modern Student*, 2nd ed. New York: Oxford UP, 1971.

Gibson, Walker. *Persona: A Style Study for Readers and Writers*. New York: Random House, 1969.

Lakoff, George, and Mark Johnson. *Metaphors We Live By*. Chicago: The University of Chicago Press, 1980.

Lucas, F. L. "Party of One" ("What Is Style?"), *Holiday*, March 1960. 11, 14–16, 18–21.

Strunk, William, and E. B. White. *The Elements of Style*, 3rd ed. New York: Macmillan, 1979.

Zinnser, William. *On Writing Well*. New York: Harper & Row, 1980.

CHAPTER 7

Ayers, Alfred Jules. *Language, Truth, and Logic*. New York: Dover Publications, Inc., 1952. 35–41.

Beardsley, Monroe C. *Thinking Straight: Principles of Reasoning for Readers and Writers*, 4th ed. Englewood Cliffs, NJ: Prentice-Hall, 1976.

_____. *Writing With Reason: Logic for Composition*. Englewood Cliffs, NJ: Prentice-Hall, 1975.

Cohen, Morris R. *A Preface to Logic*. New York: Holt, Rinehart & Winston, Inc., 1965.

Harris, Sydney J. *For the Time Being*. Boston: Houghton Mifflin Co., 1972.

Watson, James. *The Double Helix*. New York: Atheneum, 1968.

Winterowd, W. Ross. *Rhetoric: A Synthesis*. New York: Holt, Rinehart & Winston, Inc., 1968.

CHAPTER 8

Beardsley, Monroe C. *Thinking Straight: Principles of Reasoning for Readers and Writers*, 4th ed. Englewood Cliffs, NJ: Prentice-Hall, 1976.

_____. *Writing With Reason: Logic for Composition*. Englewood Cliffs, NJ: Prentice-Hall, 1975.

Castaneda, Hector Neri. "On a Proposed Revolution in Logic." *Philosophy of Science* 27 (1960): 279–92.

Cooley, J. C. "On Mr. Toulmin's Revolution in Logic." *Journal of Philosophy* 56 (1959): 297–319.

Copi, Irving R. *An Introduction to Logic*, 6th ed. New York: Macmillan, 1982.

Corbett, Edward P. J. *Classical Rhetoric for the Modern Student*. 2nd ed. New York: Oxford UP, 1971.

Emmet, E. R. *Handbook of Logic: The Use of Reason*. Totowa, NJ: Littlefield, Adams & Co., 1979.

Fulkerson, Richard. "Logic and Teachers of English?" *Rhetoric Review* 4.2 (January 1986): 198–207.

Johnson, Ralph H. "Toulmin's Bold Experiment." *Informal Logic Newsletter.* 3.2 (1981): 16–27 and 3.3 (1981): 13–20.

Plato. *Plato: Five Dialogues*. Trans. G. M. A. Grube. Indianapolis: Hackett Publishing Co., 1982.

Salmon, Wesley C. *Logic*. 2nd ed. Englewood Cliffs, NJ: Prentice-Hall, 1973.

Toulmin, Stephen C. *The Uses of Argument*. Cambridge: Cambridge University Press, 1964.

Weaver, Richard M. *Composition*. New York: Henry Holt, 1957.

CHAPTER 9

Kahane, Howard. *Logic and Contemporary Rhetoric: The Use of Reason in Everyday Life*, 4th ed. Belmont, CA: Wadsworth Publishing Co. Chapters 2–4.

Kilgore, William. *An Introductory Logic*, 2nd ed. New York: Holt, Rinehart & Winston, 1979. 11–29.

Munson, Ronald. *The Way of Words: An Informal Logic*. Boston: Houghton Mifflin Co., 1976. 260–314.

Rank, Hugh. "Teaching about Public Persuasion: Rationale and a Schema." Ed. Daniel Dieterich. *Teaching about Doublespeak*. Urbana, IL: National Council of Teachers of English, 1976.

Roll, Charles W., and Albert H. Cantril. *Polls: Their Use and Misuse in Politics*. Cabin John, MD: Seven Locks Press, 1972.

Index

A

Abstracts, locating, 91–95
Ad hominem fallacy (*See* Attack, personal; Threat)
Ad misericordiam fallacy (*See* Pity, appeal to)
Ad populum fallacy (*See* Popular sentiments, appeal to)
Advertising
  claims in, 323–29
  examples of, 330–34
Affirmative statements, distribution in, 249–52
Almanacs, locating, 91–95
Alternative, fallacy of affirming, 269–70
Alternative arguments, 269–70
Analogy
  arguing from, 214–16
  evaluating, 216
  fallacious, 216, 341
  literal, 214–15
  metaphorical, 215 (*See also* Metaphor)
Anaphora, 187
Anastrophe, 187–88
Antecedent
  fallacy of denying, 268
  in hypothetical arguments, 267–68
Antithesis, 187
Appeals, fallacious, 301
  to authority, 304
  bandwagon, 302–3
  to pity, 303–4
  to popular sentiments, 301–2
  snob appeal, 302

A priori premises, 4–5
Argument
  creating, 30–52
  distinguished from persuasion, 2–3
  emotion in, 13–14
  ethos in, 14–15
  finding conclusions, 8–9
  formal, 245, 254–56, 258–61
  limiting with qualifiers, 11–12
  logic in, 12–13
  premises of, 6, 8–9
  relationships in, 6–8, 245–47
  rhetorical context of, 31–36
  role of definition in, 64–68
  sound, 247–48
  verbal signals of, 8–9
Aristotle, 2, 14, 255
Assertion, 6
  arguable, 7
Assumption, 10–11, 299–300 (*See also* Inferences)
Assumptions, fallacious, 299
  circular reasoning, 299–300
  complex questions, 300
  loaded phrases, 300
Attack, personal, 304–5 (*See also* Threat)
Audience, 32–36, 38, 45, 46 (*See also* Reader)
Authority, appeal to
  fallacious, 304
  legitimate, 85–86

B

Backing, 262–63
Baker, Sheridan, 40

Bandwagon fallacy, 302–3
Begging the question, 259, 261, 265, 299
Bennett, William J., 375–77
Benvenisti, Meron, 420–22
Bias, 124–32 (*See also* Slanting)
Bibliographies, locating, 90
Bird, Caroline, 393–97
Black or white fallacy, 270
Bruner, Jerome Seymour, 211
Buckley, William F., Jr., 22–26
Burnam, Tom, 213
Byron, William J., 398–403

C

Carr, Albert Z., 230–33
Categorical arguments, 254–56, 257
Causal reasoning, 219–23
    evaluating, 222–23
    fallacious (*See* Post hoc fallacy)
    necessary and sufficient causes, 220
    necessary causes, 221
    sufficient causes, 221
Charged language, 13
Circular reasoning, 259, 299–300
Citation of sources
    in the humanities, 111–14
    in the natural sciences, 115–16
    in the social sciences, 114–15
Claiborne, Robert, 152
Claim, 262–63
Clarity, achieving, 162–69
Clarke, Arthur C., 279–84
Class terms, 8, 249
Cliché, 191
Climax, 188
Coherence, achieving, 136, 153–59
Common knowledge, body of, 110
Complaint, 22–26
Complex questions (fallacy), 300
Composition, fallacy of, 260
Conclusion
    of argument, finding, 8–9
    of essay, 144–46
Confirmation of argument, 143
Connotation of words, 164
Consequent
    fallacy of affirming, 268
    in hypothetical arguments, 267

Contradictions
    apparent, 42–43
    real, 42–43
Contradictory premises, 340
Contrary evidence, lack of, 307–8
Copi, Irving, 67–68
Copula, 250
Coulson, Robert E., 352–55
Creativity
    in argument, 31–32
    in research, 82–84

D

Darrow, Clarence, 266–67, 383–88
Data, 262–63
Deane, Nancy Hilts, 109–10
Deductive reasoning, 244–72
    alternative, 269–70
    categorical, 254–55
        rules for, 255
    disjunctive (*See* Alternative)
    distinguished from inductive, 245, 246–47
    distribution in, 248–53
    enthymemes, 263–65
    formal fallacies, 258–61
    form of, 255, 267, 269
    hypothetical, 267–69
    syllogism, 254–56
    terms in, 248–49
    truth of premises, 247–48
    validity of, 247, 255, 267, 269
Definition, 59–68
    to clarify argument, 65–66
    to control argument, 66–67
    in developing thesis, 40
    how to define, 60–61
    judging, 61–62
    of key terms, 151–52
    persuasive, 67–68
    power of, 66–67
    reportive, 60–61
    stipulative, 61
Development
    of essay, 44–45, 50, 52, 138
    of paragraph, 151–52
Diction, 163–66, 172, 182, 195–96
Dicto simpliciter (*See* Overgeneralization)
Didion, Joan, 76–79

Disjunctive arguments (*See* Alternative arguments)
Distortion of arguments, 305–7
Distribution of terms, 248–53
Dodges
    lack of contrary evidence, 307–8
    shifting burden of proof, 308
    shifting ground, 308–9
Doyle, Arthur Conan, 286–90

E

Ellipsis, 157, 187
Ellipsis dots, 107–8
Emotional appeal, 13–14, 59, 137
    stronger than reason, 201
Encyclopedias, locating, 89
Enthymeme, 46–48, 50, 254, 263–65
Epstein, Joseph, 160
Equivocation, 259
Ethical appeal, 14–16, 33, 36, 179
Ethics committee of American
    Fertility Society, 358–63
Ethics in persuasion, 2–4, 230–33,
    296–97, 346
Ethos (*See* Ethical appeal; Persona)
Evidence (*See also* Research)
    citation of sources, 111–15
    computer databases, as source of,
        93–95
    evaluating, 95–100
    examples, 84–85
    locating background, 88–90
    locating current, 90–95
    primary, 97–98
    recent, 96–97
    representative, 99–100
    secondary, 97–98
    sufficient, 100
    unbiased, 98–99
    using, 103–16
Exaggeration, 306
Examples
    arguing from, 224–27
    as evidence, 84–85
Exposition, 143

F

Fact, 6, 40, 42, 121
    hypothesis contrary to, 342

Fallacies, 258–61, 296–310 (*See also*
    Individual fallacies)
    appeals, 301–4
    assumptions, 299–300
    attacks, 304–5
    detecting, 309–10
    distortions, 305–7
    dodges, 307–9
    formal, 258–61, 297–98
        (*chart*), 298
    material, 298–309
Fallacy of the shared characteristic,
    259
False dilemma, 298
Figures of speech, 184–88 (*See also*
    Schemes; Tropes)
Flaubert, Gustave, 244

G

Gambler's fallacy, 226
Generalizations, 224–28 (*See also*
    Stereotypes)
    hasty, 225–26, 228, 340
    unqualified, 339 (*See also*
        Overgeneralization)
Grammar and mechanics, 166–69
Guilt by association, 259

H

Halberstam, David, 98–99
Harris, Sydney J., 217
Hayakawa, S. I., 117–22
Hyperbole (*See* Exaggeration)
Hypothesis, 268–69
    contrary to fact, 342
Hypothetical arguments, 267–69

I

Illicit process, 260
Indexes, locating, 91–95
Inductive reasoning, 211–28
    from analogy, 214–16
    from cause or effect, 219–23
    distinguished from deductive, 245,
        246–47
    from examples, 224–28
    inductive leaps, 211–13
Inferences, 117, 118–20

..fluence, questions of
    as thesis, 44–46, 48
Introduction of essay, 138–42
Invented reader, the, 35–36
Invention of arguments,
    through examining influences and
        consequences, 44–48
    through finding and resolving
        contradictions, 41–43
    through topical checklists, 37–40
Ionesco, Eugene, 291–93
Irony, 185
Issues, 34, 36, 38–39, 60

J

James, William, 201–3
Jargon, 165–66
Judgment, 117, 120–22

K

Khouri, Rami, 417–19
King, Martin Luther, Jr., 406–416
Kristol, Irving, 369–72
Kushner, Harold, 18

L

Language, charged, 13–14
Lapham, Lewis, 205–8
Lebowitz, Fran, 348–50
Leonard, Arthur S., 378–82
Lewis, C. S., 389–92
Lippmann, Walter, 158
Litotes (See Understatement)
Loaded phrases, 300
Logic in argument, 11, 12–13, 245,
    246–48, 253, 254, 291–93
    limitations of, 262–63
Lucas, F. L., 35, 193

M

MacLeish, Archibald, 74
Mannes, Marya, 28
Marks, Albert, Jr., 314–15
May, William E., 364–68
Metaphor, 62, 140, 184–85, 190–93,
    196, 215
    clichéd, 191–92
    mixed, 192
Middle term, undistributed, 259–60

Misericordiam, ad, appeal (See Pity)
Morgan, Robin, 313–14

N

Negative statements, distribution in,
    248–52
Nichter, Rhoda, 351
Nixon, Richard, 316–20
Non sequiturs, 297

O

Oboler, Eli M., 373–74
Ong, Walter, 35
Organization
    classical divisions, 138–46, 276–77
Overgeneralization, 260, 339
Oversimplification, 306–7
Overstatement, 186

P

Paradox, 42, 185
Paragraph completeness, 151–52
Parallelism, 154–58, 186–87, 197
Particular affirmative statements, 251,
    252
Particular negative statements, 251,
    253
Particulars, arguing from (See
    Evidence; Examples)
Pathos (See Emotional appeal)
Pavlov, Ivan Petrovich, 82
Persona, 2, 15–16, 32–33, 38, 159,
    166, 172, 179 (See also Purpose;
    Reader)
Persuasion
    through definition, 65, 66–68
    distinguished from argument, 2
    fallacious, 296–310
    style as element of, 179–82, 190–
        93, 194–95, 200
Pity, appeal to, 3, 303–4, 341
Plagiarism, avoiding, 109–11
Plato, 2, 309
Poisoning the well, 342 (See also
    Attack, personal)
Policy, questions of
    as thesis, 44–45
Popular sentiments, appeal to, 301,
    302
Post hoc fallacy, 221–22, 340

Predication, illogical, 167–69
Premises of arguments, 6–7, 40, 211–13, 216, 245–47
contradictory, 340
explicit, 4, 40, 46–47
implicit, 10–11, 47
major, 47, 255–56
minor, 47, 255–56
Prewriting, 31–46
Proposition, 6
affirmative, 249–52
negative, 249–53
Purpose, 32–33

Q

Qualifiers, 11–12, 263, 265
Quarrel, 1
Quota, problem of defining, 65–66
Quotations
incorporating, 104–9
using in argument, 103–4

R

Raphael, *The School of Athens*, 2–3
Reader
attempts to manipulate, 13–14
consideration of, in invention, 33–36
effect on content of argument, 35–36, 45
invented, 35–36
Reason, role of, 30, 201–3
Reasons, "good" vs. "real," 28, 29
Red herring, 298
Refutation of opposing views, 143–44
Relationships in argument, 6–8, 245–47
Repetition
of grammatical patterns (*See* Parallelism)
of key terms, 154–55
of pronouns, 155
Repetitiousness, avoiding, 155–58, 197–98
Report, 117–18 (*See also* Fact)
Research
creativity in, 82–83
example of essay, 124–32
finding evidence, 84–88 (*See also* Evidence)

Revision
to achieve unity, 138
aims of, 136–37
to complete argument, 138–46
macro- (large-scale), 137–50
micro- (small-scale), 151–69
Rhetoric, 1
Rhetorica ad Herennium, 38
Rhetorical context, 50, 195 (*See also* Audience; Purpose; Persona)
Rhetorical question, 186
as advertising device, 328–29
as conclusion, 144
Robinson, Edwin Arlington, 241
Robinson, James Harvey, 28, 29
Runkle, Gerald, 60

S

Salmon, Wesley, 247
Schemes, 186–88
Schrank, Jeffrey, 297, 323–29
"Scientific method," 211–12
Sentence openers, 196–97
Shared characteristic, fallacy of, 259–60
Shaw, George Bernard, 179
Shifting burden of proof, 308
Shifting ground, 308–9
Shulman, Max, 336–44
Sindler, Allan P., 65–66
Slanting, 13–14
Snob appeal, 302
Socrates, 2
Sorites, 255, 266
Sources, citation of, 109–116 (*See also* Evidence)
Statistics, 42, 87–88, 328
Stereotypes
in audience analysis, 34–36
Stock issues (*See* Topics)
Straw man fallacy (*See* Exaggeration)
Strunk, William, 194
Student essays, 19–20, 53–54, 126–32, 173–74, 175–76, 321–22
Style, 179–200
clarity, 162–66
coherence, 153–59
diction, 163–66, 172, 182, 195–96
elements of, 182
figures of speech, 184–93
schemes, 186–88
tropes, 184–86
grammatical elements of, 182

.bordination
 of grammatical elements, 195, 196
 of ideas, 154
Summarizing, 103
Syfers, Judy, 234–35
Syllogism, 254–57, 264–65, 291–93
 alternative, 269–70
 categorical, 254–61
 hypothetical, 267–69
Szasz, Thomas, 66–67

T

Tautology, 259
Teacher, Stuart and Lawrence, 159–60
Television news, distortion in, 126–32
Term, 46, 248, 255–56
Testimony, authoritative, 85
Thesis
 defined, 8, 37
 enthymeme as, 46–48
 evaluating enthymeme for, 50–51
 invention strategies for, 37–48
Threat, 305
Topics, 37–40
Toulmin, Stephen, 262–263
Transitions, 158–59
Trivial objections, 307
Tropes, 184–86
Truth
 as aim of argument, 1–4, 206
 distinguished from validity, 247–48
Tuchman, Barbara, 273–75
Tu quoque fallacy (See Attack,
 personal)

U

Understatement, 185–86
Unity in essay, 136, 138

Universal affirmative statement, 250–
 51
Universal negative statement, 251–52

V

Validity in deductive reasoning, 247,
 253, 254–56, 258–61
Value, questions of
 as thesis, 44–45
Van Doren, Mark, 30
Verbal signals of argument, 8–9, 264
Verifiability, 117–18

W

Wainwright, Loudon, 152
Ward, Andrew, 237–39
Warrant, 262–63
Watson, James, 212
Weasal claims, 324–25
Weaver, Richard, 259
Wertheimer, Alan, 356–57
Whately, Richard, 139
Whitehead, Alfred North, 155
Wolfe, Tom, 69–72
Wordiness, eliminating, 162–66
"Works Cited" page, 113–14, 132
Writer-reader relationship
 attempts to manipulate, 66–68, 297
 effect on content of argument, 33–
  36, 38
 effects of grammar and diction
  upon, 166–69
 effect on persuasiveness, 14–16
 in invention of arguments, 32–37
Writing as discovery, 30, 43